Professional Assembly Language

Professional Assembly Language

Richard Blum

Wiley Publishing, Inc.

Professional Assembly Language

Published by
Wiley Publishing, Inc.
10475 Crosspoint Boulevard
Indianapolis, IN 46256
www.wiley.com

Published simultaneously in Canada

ISBN: 978-0-7645-7901-1

10 9 8 7 6

1MA/SW/QR/QV/IN

For general information on our other products and services or to obtain technical support, please contact our Customer Care Department within the U.S. at (800) 762-2974, outside the U.S. at (317) 572-3993 or fax (317) 572-4002.

Wiley also publishes its books in a variety of electronic formats. Some content that appears in print may not be available in electronic books.

Blum, Richard. 1962-
 Professional assembly language / Richard Blum.
   p. cm.
 Includes index.
 ISBN 978-0-7645-7901-1 (paper/website)
1. Assembly language (Computer program language) 1. Title.
QA76.73.A8B58 2005
005.13'6—dc22

2004029116

About the Author

Richard Blum has worked for a large U.S. government organization for more than 15 years. During that time, he has had the opportunity to program utilities in various programming languages: C, C++, Java, and Microsoft VB.NET and C#. With this experience, Rich has often found the benefit of reviewing assembly language code generated by compilers and utilizing assembly language routines to speed up higher-level language programs.

Rich has a bachelor of science degree in electrical engineering from Purdue University, where he worked on many assembly language projects. (Of course, this was back in the eight-bit processor days.) He also has a master of science degree in management from Purdue University, specializing in Management Information Systems.

When Rich is not being a computer nerd, he is either playing electric bass for the church worship band or spending time with his wife, Barbara, and two daughters, Katie Jane and Jessica.

Credits

Executive Editor
Chris Webb

Development Editor
Adaobi Obi Tulton

Production Editor
William A. Barton

Technical Editor
Paul Carter

Copy Editor
Luann Rouff

Editorial Manager
Kathryn Malm Bourgoine

Vice President & Executive Group Publisher
Richard Swadley

Vice President and Publisher
Joseph B. Wikert

Project Coordinator
Erin Smith

Graphics and Production Specialists
Jonelle Burns
Amanda Carter
Carrie A. Foster
Lauren Goddard
Denny Hager
Joyce Haughey

Quality Control Technicians
David Faust
Susan Moritz
Carl William Pierce

Media Development Specialist
Angie Denny

Proofreading
TECHBOOKS Production Services

Indexing
Richard T. Evans

This book is dedicated to my wife, Barbara, and my daughters, Katie Jane and Jessica. "Trust in the Lord with all your heart and lean not on your own understanding; in all ways acknowledge him, and he will make your paths straight." Pr 3:5-6 (NIV)

Acknowledgments

First, all honor, glory, and praise go to God, who through His Son makes all things possible and gives us the gift of eternal life.

Many thanks go to the great team of people at John Wiley & Sons Publishing. Thanks to Chris Webb, the acquisitions editor, for offering me the opportunity to write this book. I am forever indebted to Adaobi Obi Tulton, the development editor, for her work in making this book presentable and her overall guidance through the book writing process. Also, many thanks go to Paul Carter, the technical editor of the book. Paul's comments throughout the book were invaluable in presenting the topic in the best way and for pointing out my goofs and blunders. I would also like to thank Carole McClendon at Waterside Productions, Inc., for arranging this opportunity for me, and for helping out in my writing career.

Finally, I would like to thank my parents, Mike and Joyce Blum, for their dedication and support while raising me, and to my wife, Barbara, and daughters, Katie Jane and Jessica, for their love, patience, and understanding, especially while I was writing this book.

Contents

Contents

Contents

Contents

Contents

Contents

Contents

Contents

Introduction

Assembly language is one of the most misunderstood programming languages in use. When the term assembly language is used, it often invokes the idea of low-level bit shuffling and poring over thousand-page instruction manuals looking for the proper instruction format. With the proliferation of fancy high-level language development tools, it is not uncommon to see the phrase "assembly language programming is dead" pop up among various programming newsgroups.

However, assembly language programming is far from dead. Every high-level language program must be compiled into assembly language before it can be linked into an executable program. For the high-level language programmer, understanding how the compiler generates the assembly language code can be a great benefit, both for directly writing routines in assembly language and for understanding how the high-level language routines are converted to assembly language by the compiler.

Who This Book Is For

The primary purpose of this book is to teach high-level language programmers how their programs are converted to assembly language, and how the generated assembly language code can be tweaked. That said, the main audience for this book is programmers already familiar with a high-level language, such as C, C++, or even Java. This book does not spend much time teaching basic programming principles. It assumes that you are already familiar with the basics of computer programming, and are interested in learning assembly language to understand what is happening underneath the hood.

However, if you are new to programming and are looking at assembly language programming as a place to start, this book does not totally ignore you. It is possible to follow along in the chapters from the start to the finish and obtain a basic knowledge of how assembly language programming (and programming in general) works. Each of the topics presented includes example code that demonstrates how the assembly language instructions work. If you are completely new to programming, I recommend that you also obtain a good introductory text to programming to round out your education on the topic.

What This Book Covers

The main purpose of this book is to familiarize C and C++ programmers with assembly language, show how compilers create assembly language routines from C and C++ programs, and show how the generated assembly language routines can be spruced up to increase the performance of an application.

All high-level language programs (such as C and C++) are converted to assembly language by the compiler before being linked into an executable program. The compiler uses specific rules defined by the creator of the compiler to determine exactly how the high-level language statements are converted. Many programmers just write their high-level language programs and assume the compiler is creating the proper executable code to implement the program.

However, this is not always the case. When the compiler converts the high-level language code statements into assembly language code, quirks and oddities often pop up. In addition, the compiler is often written to follow the conversion rules so specifically that it does not recognize time-saving shortcuts that can be made in the final assembly language code, or it is unable to compensate for poorly written high-level routines. This is where knowledge of assembly language code can come in handy.

This book shows that by examining the assembly language code generated by the compiler before linking it into an executable program, you can often find places where the code can be modified to increase performance or provide additional functionality. The book also helps you understand how your high-level language routines are affected by the compiler's conversion process.

How This Book Is Structured

The book is divided into three sections. The first section covers the basics of the assembly language programming environment. Because assembly language programming differs among processors and assemblers, a common platform had to be chosen. This book uses the popular Linux operating system, running on the Intel family of processors. The Linux environment provides a wealth of program developer tools, such as an optimizing compiler, an assembler, a linker, and a debugger, all at little or no charge. This wealth of development tools in the Linux environment makes it the perfect setting for dissecting C programs into assembly language code.

The chapters in the first section are as follows:

Chapter 1, "What Is Assembly Language?" starts the section off by ensuring that you understand exactly what assembly language is and how it fits into the programming model. It debunks some of the myths of assembly language, and provides a basis for understanding how to use assembly language with high-level languages.

Chapter 2, "The IA-32 Platform," provides a brief introduction to the Intel Pentium family of processors. When working with assembly language, it is important that you understand the underlying processor and how it handles programs. While this chapter is not intended to be an in-depth analysis of the operation of the IA-32 platform, it does present the hardware and operations involved with programming for that platform.

Chapter 3, "The Tools of the Trade," presents the Linux open-source development tools that are used throughout the book. The GNU compiler, assembler, linker, and debugger are used in the book for compiling, assembling, linking, and debugging the programs.

Chapter 4, "A Sample Assembly Language Program," demonstrates how to use the GNU tools on a Linux system to create, assemble, link, and debug a simple assembly language program. It also shows how to use C library functions within assembly language programs on Linux systems to add extra features to your assembly language applications.

The second section of the book dives into the basics of assembly language programming. Before you can start to analyze the assembly language code generated by the compiler, you must understand the assembly language instructions. The chapters in this section are as follows:

Chapter 5, "Moving Data," shows how data elements are moved in assembly language programs. The concepts of registers, memory locations, and the stack are presented, and examples are shown for moving data between them.

Chapter 6, "Controlling Execution Flow," describes the branching instructions used in assembly language programs. Possibly one of the most important features of programs, the ability to recognize branches and optimize branches is crucial to increasing the performance of an application.

Chapter 7, "Using Numbers," discusses how different number data types are used in assembly language. Being able to properly handle integers and floating-point values is important within the assembly language program.

Chapter 8, "Basic Math Functions," shows how assembly language instructions are used to perform the basic math functions such as addition, subtraction, multiplication, and division. While these are generally straightforward functions, subtle tricks can often be used to increase performance in this area.

Chapter 9, "Advanced Math Functions," discusses the IA-32 Floating Point Unit (FPU), and how it is used to handle complex floating-point arithmetic. Floating-point arithmetic is often a crucial element to data processing programs, and knowing how it works greatly benefits high-level language programmers.

Chapter 10, "Working with Strings," presents the various assembly language string-handling instructions. Character data is another important facet of high-level language programming. Understanding how the assembly language level handles strings can provide insights when working with strings in high-level languages.

Chapter 11, "Using Functions," begins the journey into the depths of assembly language programming. Creating assembly language functions to perform routines is at the core of assembly language optimization. It is good to know the basics of assembly language functions, as they are often used by the compiler when generating the assembly language code from high-level language code.

Chapter 12, "Using Linux System Calls," completes this section by showing how many high-level functions can be performed in assembly language using already created functions. The Linux system provides many high-level functions, such as writing to the display. Often, you can utilize these functions within your assembly language program.

The last section of the book presents more advanced assembly language topics. Because the main topic of this book is how to incorporate assembly language routines in your C or C++ code, the first few chapters show just how this is done. The remaining chapters present some more advanced topics to round out your education on assembly language programming. The chapters in this section include the following:

Chapter 13, "Using Inline Assembly," shows how to incorporate assembly language routines directly in your C or C++ language programs. Inline assembly language is often used for "hard-coding" quick routines in the C program to ensure that the compiler generates the appropriate assembly language code for the routine.

Chapter 14, "Calling Assembly Libraries," demonstrates how assembly language functions can be combined into libraries that can be used in multiple applications (both assembly language and high-level language). It is a great time-saving feature to be able to combine frequently used functions into a single library that can be called by C or C++ programs.

Chapter 15, "Optimizing Routines," discusses the heart of this book: modifying compiler-generated assembly language code to your taste. This chapter shows exactly how different types of C routines (such as if-then statements and for-next loops) are produced in assembly language code. Once you understand what the assembly language code is doing, you can add your own touches to it to customize the code for your specific environment.

Chapter 16, "Using Files," covers one of the most overlooked functions of assembly language programming. Almost every application requires some type of file access on the system. Assembly language programs are no different. This chapter shows how to use the Linux file-handling system calls to read, write, and modify data in files on the system.

Chapter 17, "Using Advanced IA-32 Features," completes the book with a look at the advanced Intel Single Instruction Multiple Data (SIMD) technology. This technology provides a platform for programmers to perform multiple arithmetic operations in a single instruction. This technology has become crucial in the world of audio and video data processing.

What You Need to Use This Book

All of the examples in this book are coded to be assembled and run on the Linux operating system, running on an Intel processor platform. The Open Source GNU compiler (gcc), assembler (gas), linker (ld), and debugger (gdb) are used extensively throughout the book to demonstrate the assembly language features. Chapter 4, "A Sample Assembly Language Program," discusses specifically how to use these tools on a Linux platform to create, assemble, link, and debug an assembly language program. If you do not have an installed Linux platform available, Chapter 4 demonstrates how to use a Linux distribution that can be booted directly from CD, without modifying the workstation hard drive. All of the GNU development tools used in this book are available without installing Linux on the workstation.

Conventions

To help you get the most from the text and keep track of what's happening, we've used a number of conventions throughout the book.

Tips, hints, tricks, and asides to the current discussion are offset and placed in italics like this.

As for styles in the text:

❏   We *highlight* important words when we introduce them.

❏   We show filenames, URLs, and code within the text like so: `persistence.properties`.

❏   We present code in two different ways:

```
In code examples we highlight new and important code with a gray background.
```

```
The gray highlighting is not used for code that's less important in the present
context, or has been shown before.
```

Source Code

As you work through the examples in this book, you may choose either to type in all the code manually or to use the source code files that accompany the book. All of the source code used in this book is available for download at www.wrox.com. Once at the site, simply locate the book's title (either by using the Search box or by using one of the title lists) and click the Download Code link on the book's detail page to obtain all the source code for the book.

> *Because many books have similar titles, you may find it easiest to search by ISBN; this book's ISBN is 0-764-57901-0.*

Once you download the code, just decompress it with your favorite compression tool. Alternately, you can go to the main Wrox code download page at www.wrox.com/dynamic/books/download.aspx to see the code available for this book and all other Wrox books.

Errata

We make every effort to ensure that there are no errors in the text or in the code. However, no one is perfect, and mistakes do occur. If you find an error in one of our books, such as a spelling mistake or faulty piece of code, we would be very grateful for your feedback. By sending in errata, you may save another reader hours of frustration, and at the same time you will be helping us provide even higher quality information.

To find the errata page for this book, go to www.wrox.com and locate the title using the Search box or one of the title lists. Then, on the book details page, click the Book Errata link. On this page, you can view all errata that has been submitted for this book and posted by Wrox editors. A complete book list, including links to each book's errata, is also available at www.wrox.com/misc-pages/booklist.shtml.

If you don't spot "your" error on the Book Errata page, go to www.wrox.com/contact/techsupport.shtml and complete the form there to send us the error you have found. We'll check the information, and, if appropriate, post a message to the book's errata page and fix the problem in subsequent editions of the book.

p2p.wrox.com

For author and peer discussion, join the P2P forums at p2p.wrox.com. The forums are a Web-based system for you to post messages relating to Wrox books and related technologies and interact with other readers and technology users. The forums offer a subscription feature to e-mail you topics of interest of your choosing when new posts are made to the forums. Wrox authors, editors, other industry experts, and your fellow readers are present on these forums.

Introduction

At http://p2p.wrox.com you will find a number of different forums that will help you not only as you read this book, but also as you develop your own applications. To join the forums, just follow these steps:

1.   Go to p2p.wrox.com and click the Register link.

2.   Read the terms of use and click Agree.

3.   Complete the required information to join as well as any optional information you wish to provide and click Submit.

4.   You will receive an e-mail with information describing how to verify your account and complete the joining process.

You can read messages in the forums without joining P2P, but in order to post your own messages you must join.

Once you join, you can post new messages and respond to messages other users post. You can read messages at any time on the Web. If you would like to have new messages from a particular forum e-mailed to you, click the Subscribe to this Forum icon by the forum name in the forum listing.

For more information about how to use the Wrox P2P, be sure to read the P2P FAQs for answers to questions about how the forum software works as well as many common questions specific to P2P and Wrox books. To read the FAQs, click the FAQ link on any P2P page.

1

What Is Assembly Language?

One of the first hurdles to learning assembly language programming is understanding just what assembly language is. Unlike other programming languages, there is no one standard format that all assemblers use. Different assemblers use different syntax for writing program statements. Many beginning assembly language programmers get caught up in trying to figure out the myriad of different possibilities in assembly language programming.

The first step in learning assembly language programming is defining just what type of assembly language programming you want to (or need to) use in your environment. Once you define your flavor of assembly language, it is easy to get started learning and using assembly language in both standalone and high-level language programs.

This chapter begins the journey by showing where assembly language comes from, and defining why assembly language programming is used. To understand assembly language programming, you must first understand the basics of its underlying purpose — programming in processor instruction code. Next, the chapter shows how high-level languages are converted to raw instruction code by compilers and linkers. After having that information, it will be easier for you to understand how assembly language programs and high-level language programs differ, and how they can both be used to complement one another.

Processor Instructions

At the lowest layer of operation, all computer processors (microcomputers, minicomputers, and mainframe computers) manipulate data based on binary codes defined internally in the processor chip by the manufacturer. These codes define what functions the processor should perform, utilizing the data provided by the programmer. These preset codes are referred to as *instruction codes*. Different types of processors contain different types of instruction codes. Processor chips are often categorized by the quantity and type of instruction codes they support.

While the different types of processors can contain different types of instruction codes, they all handle instruction code programs similarly. This section describes how processors handle instructions and what the instruction codes look like for a sample processor chip.

Instruction code handling

As a computer processor chip runs, it reads instruction codes that are stored in memory. Each instruction code set can contain one or more bytes of information that instruct the processor to perform a specific task. As each instruction code is read from memory, any data required for the instruction code is also stored and read in memory. The memory bytes that contain the instruction codes are no different than the bytes that contain the data used by the processor.

To differentiate between data and instruction codes, special *pointers* are used to help the processor keep track of where in memory the data and instruction codes are stored. This is shown in Figure 1-1.

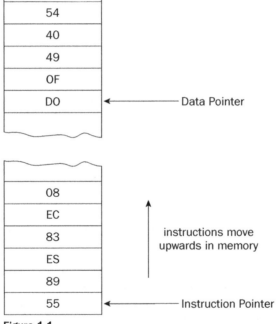

Figure 1-1

The *instruction pointer* is used to help the processor keep track of which instruction codes have already been processed and what code is next in line to be processed. Of course, there are special instruction codes that can change the location of the instruction pointer, such as jumping to a specific location in the program.

Similarly, a *data pointer* is used to help the processor keep track of where the data area in memory starts. This area is called the *stack*. As new data elements are placed in the stack, the pointer moves "down" in memory. As data is read from the stack, the pointer moves "up" in memory.

Each instruction code can contain one or more bytes of information for the processor to handle. For example, the instruction code bytes (in hexadecimal format)

```
C7 45 FC 01 00 00 00
```

tell an Intel IA-32 series processor to load the decimal value 1 into a memory offset location defined by a processor register. The instruction code contains several pieces of information (defined later in the "Opcode" section) that clearly define what function is to be performed by the processor. After the processor completes processing one instruction code set, it reads the next one in memory (as pointed to by the instruction pointer). The instructions must be placed in memory in the proper format and order for the processor to properly step through the program code.

Every instruction must contain at least 1 byte called the *operation code* (or *opcode* for short). The opcode defines what function the processor should perform. Each processor family has its own predefined opcodes that define all of the functions available. The next section shows how the opcodes used in the Intel IA-32 family of microprocessors are structured. These are the types of processor opcodes that are used in all of the examples in this book.

Instruction code format

The Intel IA-32 family of microprocessors includes all of the current types of microprocessors used in modern IBM-platform microcomputers (see Chapter 2, "The IA-32 Platform"), including the popular Pentium line of microprocessors. A specific format for instruction codes is used in the IA-32 family of microprocessors, and understanding the format of these instructions will help you in your assembly language programming. The IA-32 instruction code format consists of four main parts:

❏　Optional instruction prefix

❏　Operational code (opcode)

❏　Optional modifier

❏　Optional data element

Figure 1-2 shows the layout of the IA-32 instruction code format.

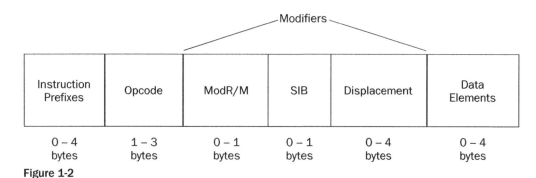

Instruction Prefixes	Opcode	ModR/M	SIB	Displacement	Data Elements
0 – 4 bytes	1 – 3 bytes	0 – 1 bytes	0 – 1 bytes	0 – 4 bytes	0 – 4 bytes

Figure 1-2

Each of the parts is used to completely define a specific instruction for the processor to perform. The following sections describe each of the four parts of the instruction code and how they define the instruction performed by the processor.

The Intel Pentium processor family is not the only set of processor chips to utilize the IA-32 instruction code format. The AMD corporation also produces a line of chips that are fully compatible with the Intel IA-32 instruction code format.

Opcode

As shown in Figure 1-2, the only required part of the IA-32 instruction code format is the opcode. Each instruction code must include an opcode that defines the basic function or task to be performed by the processor.

The opcode is between 1 and 3 bytes in length, and uniquely defines the function that is performed. For example, the 2-byte opcode OF A2 defines the IA-32 CPUID instruction. When the processor executes this instruction code, it returns specific information about the microprocessor in different registers. The programmer can then use additional instruction codes to extract the information from the processor registers to determine the type and model of microprocessor on which the program is running.

Registers are components within the processor chip that are used to temporarily store data while being handled by the processor. They are covered in more detail in Chapter 2, "The IA-32 Platform."

Instruction prefix

The instruction prefix can contain between one and four 1-byte prefixes that modify the opcode behavior. These prefixes are categorized into four different groups, based on the prefix function. Only one prefix from each group can be used at one time to modify the opcode (thus the maximum of four prefix bytes). The four prefix groups are as follows:

- ❏ Lock and repeat prefixes
- ❏ Segment override and branch hint prefixes
- ❏ Operand size override prefix
- ❏ Address size override prefix

The lock prefix indicates that any shared memory areas will be used exclusively by the instruction. This is important for multiprocessor and hyperthreaded systems. The repeat prefixes are used to indicate a repeating function (usually used when handling strings).

The segment override prefixes define instructions that can override the defined segment register value (described in more detail in Chapter 2). The branch hint prefixes attempt to give the processor a clue as to the most likely path the program will take in a conditional jump statement (this is used with predictive branching hardware).

The operand size override prefix informs the processor that the program will switch between 16-bit and 32-bit operand sizes within the instruction code. This enables the program to warn the processor when it uses larger-sized operands, helping to speed up the assignment of data to registers.

The address size override prefix informs the processor that the program will switch between 16-bit and 32-bit memory addresses. Either size can be declared as the default size for the program, and this prefix informs the processor that the program is switching to the other.

Modifiers

Some opcodes require additional modifiers to define what registers or memory locations are involved in the function. The modifiers are contained in three separate values:

❑ addressing-form specifier (ModR/M) byte

❑ Scale-Index-Base (SIB) byte

❑ One, two, or four address displacement bytes

The ModR/M byte

The ModR/M byte consists of three fields of information, as shown in Figure 1-3.

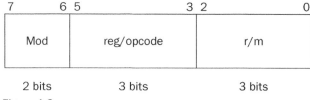

Figure 1-3

The mod field is used with the r/m field to define the register or addressing mode used in the instruction. There are 24 possible addressing modes, along with eight possible general-purpose registers that can be used in the instruction, making 32 possible values.

The reg/opcode field is used to enable three more bits to further define the opcode function (such as opcode subfunctions), or it can be used to define a register value.

The r/m field is used to define another register to use as the operand of the function, or it can be combined with the mod field to define the addressing mode for the instruction.

The SIB byte

The SIB byte also consists of three fields of information, as shown in Figure 1-4.

Figure 1-4

The scale field specifies the scale factor for the operation. The index field specifies the register that is used as the index register for memory access. The base field specifies the register that is used as the base register for memory access.

The combination of the ModR/M and SIB bytes creates a table that can define many possible combinations of registers and memory modes for accessing data. The Intel specification sheets for the Pentium processor define all of the possible combinations that are used with the ModR/M and SIB bytes.

The address displacement byte

The address displacement byte is used to indicate an offset to the memory location defined in the ModR/M and SIB bytes. This can be used as an index to a base memory location to either store or access data within memory.

Data element

The final part of the instruction code is the data element that is used by the function. While some instruction codes read data from memory locations or processor registers, some include data within the instruction code itself. Often this value is used to represent a static numeric value, such as a number to be added, or a memory location. This value can contain 1, 2, or 4 bytes of information, depending on the data size.

For example, the following sample instruction code shown earlier:

```
C7 45 FC 01 00 00 00
```

defines the opcode C7, which is the instruction to move a value to a memory location. The memory location is defined by the 45 FC modifier (which defines –4 bytes (the FC value) from the memory location pointed to by the value in the EBP register (the 45 value). The final 4 bytes define the integer value that is placed in that memory location (in this case, the value 1).

> *As you can see from this example, the value 1 was written as the 4-byte hexadecimal value 01 00 00 00. The order of the bytes in the data stream depends on the type of processor used. The IA-32 platform processors use "little-endian" notation, whereby the lower-value bytes appear first in order (when reading left to right). Other processors use "big-endian" order, whereby the higher-value bytes appear first in order. This concept is extremely important when specifying data and memory location values in your assembly language programs.*

High-Level Languages

If it looks like programming in pure processor instruction code is difficult, it is. Even the simplest of programs require the programmer to specify a lot of opcodes and data bytes. Trying to manage a huge program full of just instruction codes would be a daunting task. To help save the sanity of programmers, high-level languages (HLLs) were created.

HLLs enable programmers to create functions using simpler terms, rather than raw processor instruction codes. Special reserved keywords are used to define variables (memory locations for data), create loops (jump over instruction codes), and handle input and output from the program. However, the processor does not have any knowledge about how to handle the HLL code. The code must be converted by some mechanism to simple instruction code format for the processor to handle. This section defines the different types of HLLs and then shows how the HLL code is converted to the instruction code for the processor to execute.

Types of high-level languages

While programmers can choose from many different HLLs available, they all can be classified into two different categories, based on how they are run on the computer:

❏ Compiled languages

❏ Interpreted languages

While it is possible for different implementations of the same programming language to be either compiled or interpreted, these categories are used to show how a particular HLL implementation defines how the programs are run on the processor. The following sections describe the methods used to run programs and show how they affect how the processor operates with them.

Compiled languages

Most production applications are created using compiled HLLs. The programmer creates a program using common statements for the language which carry out the logic of the application. The text program statements are then converted into a set of instruction codes that can be run on the processor. Usually, what is commonly called *compiling* a program is actually a two-step process:

❏ Compiling the HLL statements into raw instruction codes

❏ Linking the raw instruction codes to produce an executable program

Figure 1-5 demonstrates this process.

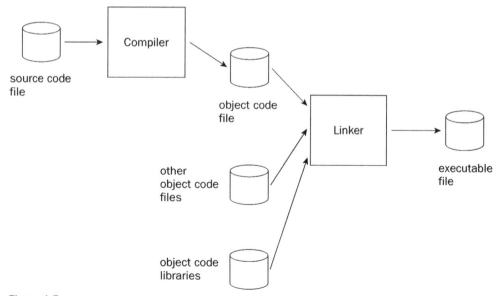

Figure 1-5

The compiling step converts the text programming language statements into the instruction codes required to carry out the application function. Each of the HLL lines of code are matched up with one or more instruction codes pertaining to the specific processor on which the application will run. For example, the simple HLL code

```
int main()
{
    int i = 1;
    exit(0);
}
```

is compiled into the following IA-32 instruction codes:

```
55
89 E5
83 EC 08
C7 45 FC 01 00 00 00
83 EC 0C
6A 00
E8 D1 FE FF FF
```

This step produces an intermediate file, called an *object code file*. The object code file contains the instruction codes that represent the core of the application functions, as shown above. The object code file itself cannot be run by the operating system. Often the host operating system requires special file formats for executable files (program files that can be run on the system), and the HLL program may require program functions from other object files. Another step is required to add these components.

After the code is compiled into an object file, a *linker* is used to link the application object code file with any additional object files required by the application and to create the final executable output file. The output of the linker is an executable file that can only be run on the operating system for which the program is written. Unfortunately, each operating system uses a different format for executable files, so an application compiled on a Microsoft Windows workstation will not work as is on a Linux workstation, and vice versa.

> *Object files that contain commonly used functions can be combined into a single file, called a library file. The library file can then be linked into multiple applications either at compile time (called static libraries), or at the time the application is run on the system (called dynamic libraries).*

Interpreted languages

As opposed to compiled programs, which run by themselves on a processor, an interpreted language program is read and run by a separate program. The separate program is a host for the application program, reading and interpreting the program as it is processed. It is the job of the host program to convert the interpreted program code into the proper instruction codes for the processor as the program is running.

Obviously, the downside to using interpreted languages is speed. Instead of the program being compiled directly to instruction codes that are run on the processor, an intermediary program reads each line of program code and processes the required functions. The amount of time the host program takes to read the code and execute it adds additional delays to the execution of the application.

With the resulting reduction in speed when using interpreted languages, you may be wondering why anyone still uses them. One answer is convenience. With compiled programs, every time a change is made to the program, the program must be recompiled and relinked with the proper code libraries. With interpreted programs, changes can be quickly made to the source code file and the program rerun to check for errors. In addition, with interpreted languages, the interpreter application automatically determines what functions need to be included with the core code to support functions.

> *Today's programming language environment muddies the waters between compiled and interpreted languages. No one specific language can be classified in either category. Instead, individual implementations of different HLLs are categorized. For example, while many BASIC programming implementations require interpreters to interpret the BASIC code into an executable program, there are many BASIC implementations that enable the programmer to compile the BASIC programs into executable instruction code.*

Hybrid languages

Hybrid languages are a recent trend in programming that combine the features of a compiled program with the versatility and ease of an interpreted program. A perfect example is the popular Java programming language.

The Java programming language is compiled into what is called *byte code*. The byte code is similar to the instruction code you would see on a processor, but is itself not compatible with any current processor family (although there have been plans to create a processor that can run Java byte code as instruction sets).

Instead, the Java byte code must be interpreted by a Java Virtual Machine (JVM), running separately on the host computer. The Java byte code is portable, in that it can be run by any JVM on any type of host computer. The advantage is that different platforms can have their own specific JVMs, which are used to interpret the same Java byte code without it having to be recompiled from the original source code.

High-level language features

If you are a professional programmer, most likely you do most (if not all) of your coding using a high-level language. You may or may not have had the luxury of choosing which HLL you use for your projects, but either way, there is no doubt that it makes your job easier. This section describes two of the most useful features of HLLs, portability and standardization, which help set HLLs apart from assembly language programming.

Portability

As described earlier in the "Processor Instructions" section, instruction code programming is highly dependent on the processor used in the computer. Each of the different families of processors utilize different instruction code formats, as well as different methods for storing data (big endian vs. little endian). Instruction codes written for an IA-32 platform will not work on a MIPS processor platform.

Imagine writing a 10,000-line instruction code program for your new application, which runs on a Sun Sparc workstation, and then being asked to port it to a Linux workstation running on a Pentium computer. Because the microprocessor used for the Sun Sparc workstation does not use the same instruction codes as the Pentium, all of your code would need to be redone for the new instruction codes—ouch.

HLLs have the capability to be ported to other operating systems and other processor platforms by simply recompiling the program on the new platform. When the program is recompiled, it is automatically rewritten using the instruction codes for the destination processor.

However, in practice, nontrivial programs use operating system APIs that make it difficult to simply recompile the source code for another platform. For example, a program directly using the MS Windows API will not compile under Linux.

Standardization

Another useful feature of HLLs is the abundance of standards available for the languages. Both the Institute of Electrical and Electronics Engineers (IEEE) and the American National Standards Institute (ANSI) have created standard specifications for many different HLLs.

This means that you are guaranteed to obtain the same results from source code compiled with a standard compiler on one type of operating system and processor as you would compiling on a different type of operating system and processor. Each compiler is created to interpret the standard language constructs into instruction code for the destination processor to produce the same functionality across the processor platforms.

Assembly Language

While creating large applications using an HLL is often simpler than using raw instruction codes, it doesn't necessarily mean that the resulting program will be efficient. Unfortunately, in order to increase portability and comply with standards, many compilers code to the "least common denominator." This means that compilers creating instruction codes for advanced processor chips may not utilize special instruction codes unique to those processors to help create faster applications.

One feature that many of the new processors on the market offer is advanced mathematics handling instruction codes. These instruction codes help speed up complex mathematical expression processing by using larger-than-normal byte sizes to represent numbers (either 64 or 128 bits). Unfortunately, many compilers don't take advantage of these advanced instruction codes. Fortunately, there is a simple solution for the programmer. In environments where execution speed is critical, assembly language programming can come to the rescue. Of course, the first step to improving execution speed is to ensure that the best algorithm is used in the first place. Optimizing a poor algorithm does not compensate for using a fast algorithm in the first place.

Assembly language enables programmers to directly create instruction code programs without having to worry about the many different instruction code set combinations on the processor. Instead, an assembly language program uses *mnemonics* to represent instruction codes. The mnemonics enables the programmer to use English-style words to represent individual instruction codes. The assembly language mnemonics are easily converted to the raw instruction codes by an assembler.

This section describes the assembly language mnemonic system, and how it is used to create raw instruction code programs that can be run on the processor.

An assembly language program consists of three components that are used to define the program operations:

- ❏ Opcode mnemonics
- ❏ Data sections
- ❏ Directives

The following sections describe each of these components and show how they are used within the assembly language program to create the resulting instruction code program.

Opcode mnemonics

The core of an assembly language program is the instruction codes used to create the program. To help facilitate writing the instruction codes, assemblers equate mnemonic words with instruction code functions, such as moving or adding data elements. For example, the instruction code sample

```
55
89 E5
83 EC 08
C7 45 FC 01 00 00 00
83 EC 0C
6A 00
E8 D1 FE FF FF
```

can be written in assembly language as follows:

```
push %ebp
mov  %esp, %ebp
sub  $0x8, %esp
movl $0x1, -4(%ebp)
sub  $0xc, %esp
push $0x0
call 8048348
```

Instead of having to know what each byte of instruction code represents, the assembly language programmer can use easier-to-remember mnemonic codes, such as push, mov, sub, and call, to represent the instruction codes.

Different assemblers use different mnemonics to represent instruction codes. While trends have emerged to standardize assembler mnemonics, there is still quite a vast variety of mnemonic codes, not only between processor families but even between assemblers used for the same processor instruction code sets.

Each processor manufacturer publishes developer manuals detailing all of the instruction codes implemented by a specific chip set. The Intel IA-32 developer manuals are freely available at the Intel Web site (www.intel.com). These developer manuals take over 1,000 pages just to enumerate and describe all of the instruction codes for the Pentium family of processors.

Defining data

Besides the instruction codes, most programs also require data elements to be used to hold variable and constant data values that are used throughout the program. HLLs use variables to define sections of memory to hold data. For example, it is not uncommon to see the following in an HLL program:

```
long testvalue = 150;
char message[22] = {"This is a test message"};
float pi = 3.14159;
```

Each of these statements is interpreted by the HLL compiler to reserve memory locations of a specific number of bytes to store values that may or may not change during the course of the program. Each time the program references the variable name (such as testvalue), the compiler knows to access the specified location in memory to read or change the byte values.

Assembly language also enables the programmer to define data items that will be stored in memory. One of the advantages of programming in assembly language is that it provides you with greater control over where and how your data is stored in memory. The following sections describe two methods used to store and retrieve data in assembly language.

Using memory locations

Similar to the HLL method of defining data, assembly language enables you to declare a variable that points to a specific location in memory. Defining variables in assembly language consists of two parts:

1. A label that points to a memory location

2. A data type and default value for the memory bytes

The data type determines how many bytes are reserved for the variable. In an assembly language program, this would look like the following:

```
testvalue:
    .long 150
message:
    .ascii "This is a test message"
pi:
    .float 3.14159
```

As you can see from the data types, assembly language allows you to declare the type of data stored in the memory location, along with the default values placed in the memory location, similar to most HLL methods. Each data type occupies a specific number of bytes, starting at the memory location reserved for the label. This is shown in Figure 1-6.

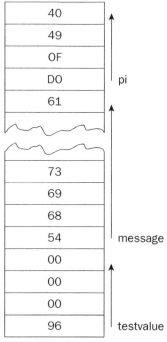

Figure 1-6

The first data element declared, testvalue, is placed in memory as a 4-byte hexadecimal value in little-endian order (96 00 00 00). The next data element, message, is placed immediately after the last byte of the testvalue data element. Because the message data element is a text value, it is placed in memory in the order the text characters appear in the string. Finally, the last data element, pi, is placed in memory immediately after the last byte of the message data element (the floating point is discussed in great detail in Chapter 7, "Using Numbers."

The memory locations are referenced within the assembly language program based on the label used to define the starting location. A sample assembly language program would look like the following:

```
movl testvalue, %ebx
addl $10, %ebx
movl %ebx, testvalue
```

The first instruction loads the EBX register with the 4-byte value located at the memory location pointed to by the testvalue label (which was defined with a value of 150). The next instruction adds 10 (in decimal) to the value stored in the EBX register and puts the result back in the EBX register. Finally, the register value is stored in the memory location referenced by the testvalue label. This new value can then be referenced again in the program using the testvalue label, and it will have the value of 160 (this process is explained in detail in Chapter 5, "Moving Data," and Chapter 8, "Basic Math Functions").

Using the stack

Another method used to store and retrieve data in assembly language is called the *stack*. The stack is a special memory area usually reserved for passing data elements between functions in the program. It can also be used for temporarily storing and retrieving data elements.

The stack is a region of memory reserved at the end of the memory range that the computer reserves for the application. A pointer (called the *stack pointer*) is used to point to the next memory location in the stack to put or take data. Much like a stack of papers, when a data element is placed in the stack, it becomes the first item that can be removed from the stack (assuming you can only take papers off of the top of the paper stack).

When calling functions in an assembly language program, you usually place any data elements that you want passed to the function on the top of the stack. When the function is called, it can retrieve the data elements from the stack.

> *The different methods of storing and retrieving data are discussed in greater detail in Chapter 5, "Moving Data."*

Directives

Instructions and data are not the only elements that make up an assembly language program. Assemblers reserve special keywords for instructing the assembler how to perform special functions as the mnemonics are converted to instruction codes.

You saw an example of directives in the previous section when the data elements were defined. The data types were declared using assembler directives used in the GNU assembler. The `.long`, `.ascii`, and `.float` directives are used to alert the assembler that a specific type of data is being declared. As shown in the example, directives are preceded by a period to set them apart from labels.

Directives are another area in which the different assemblers vary. Many different directives are used to help make the programmer's job of creating instruction codes easier. Some modern assemblers have lists of directives that can rival many HLL features, such as while loops, and if-then statements! The older, more traditional assemblers, however, keep the directives to a minimum, forcing the assembly language programmer to use the mnemonic codes to create the program logic.

One of the most important directives used in the assembly language program is the `.section` directive. This directive defines the section of memory in which the assembly language program is defining elements. All assembly language programs have at least three sections that must be declared:

❑   A data section

❑   A bss section

❑   A text section

The data section is used to declare the memory region where data elements are stored for the program. This section cannot be expanded after the data elements are declared, and it remains static throughout the program.

The bss section is also a static memory section. It contains buffers for data to be declared later in the program. What makes this section special is that the buffer memory area is zero-filled.

The text section is the area in memory where the instruction code is stored. Again, this area is fixed, in that it contains only the instruction codes that are declared in the assembly language program.

These directives used in an assembly language program are demonstrated in Chapter 4, "A Sample Assembly Language Program."

Summary

While assembly language programming is often referred to as a single programming language category, in reality there are a wide variety of different types of assembly language assemblers. Each assembler uses slightly different formats to represent instruction codes, data, and special directives for assembling the final program. The first step to programming in assembly language is deciding which assembler you need to use, and what format it uses.

The purpose of using assembly language is to code as closely to raw processor code as possible. The code recognized by the processor is called instruction code. Each processor family has its own set of instruction codes that define the functions the processor can perform. Each processor family also uses specific formats for the instruction code. The Intel IA-32 family of processors uses a format that consists of four parts. An opcode is used to define which processor instruction should be used. An optional prefix may be used to modify the behavior of the instruction. An optional modifier may also be used to define what registers or memory locations are used in the instruction. Finally, an optional data element may be included, which defines specific data values used in the instruction.

Trying to create large-scale programs using raw instruction codes is not an easy task. Each instruction code must be programmed byte by byte in the proper order for the application to run. Instead of forcing programmers to learn all of the instruction codes, developers have created high-level languages, which enable programmers to create programs in a shorthand method, which is then converted into the proper instruction codes by a compiler. High-level languages use simple keywords and terms to define one or more instruction codes. This enables programmers to concentrate on the logic of the application program, rather than worry about the details of the underlying processor instruction codes.

The downside of using high-level languages is that the programmer is dependant on the compiler creator to convert programming logic to the instruction code run by the processor. There is no guarantee that the created instruction codes will be the most efficient method of programming the logic. For programmers who want maximum efficiency, or the capability to have greater control over how the program is handled by the processor, assembly language programming offers an alternative.

Assembly language programming enables the programmer to program with instruction codes, but by using simple mnemonic terms to refer to those instruction codes. This provides programmers with both the ease of a high-level language and the control offered by using instruction codes.

Unfortunately, assembly language assemblers are not standardized, and there are many different forms of assembly language. All assemblers contain three elements: opcode mnemonics, data elements, and directives. The opcode mnemonics are used to code the programming logic, and data elements are used to define memory locations to hold both constant and variable data elements. Directives are one of the most controversial elements of assemblers. Directives help the programmer define specific functions, such as declaring data types, and define memory regions within the program. Some assemblers take directives to a higher level, providing directives that support many high-level language functions, such as advanced data management and logic programming.

The next chapter discusses the specific layout of the Intel IA-32 processor family. Before you can start programming for the Pentium family of processors, it is important to understand how the hardware is laid out. Knowing how the processor handles data will enable you to program more efficiently, increasing the speed of your applications.

2

The IA-32 Platform

One key to successful assembly language programming is knowing the environment you are programming for. The biggest part of that environment is the processor. Knowing the hardware platform your program will run on is crucial to being able to exploit both basic and advanced functions of the processor. Often, the whole point of using assembly language is to exploit low-level features of the processor within your application program. Knowing what elements can be used to assist your programs in gaining the most speed possible can mean the difference between a fast application and a slow application.

At the time of this writing, the most popular processor platform by far used in workstations and servers is the Intel Pentium family of processors. The hardware and instruction code set designed for the Pentium processors is commonly referred to as the IA-32 platform.

This chapter describes the hardware elements that make up the Intel IA-32 platform. The first part of the chapter describes the basic components found in the IA-32 processor platforms. Then the chapter describes the advanced features found in the newer Pentium 4 processor chips in the IA-32 family. Finally, the different processors that are contained within the IA-32 platform are discussed, showing what features to watch out for with the different types of processors, both from Intel and from other manufacturers.

Core Parts of an IA-32 Processor

While different processor families incorporate different instruction sets and capabilities, there is a core set of components that can be found on most processors. Most introductory computer science classes teach four basic components of a computer. Figure 2-1 shows a basic block diagram of these core components.

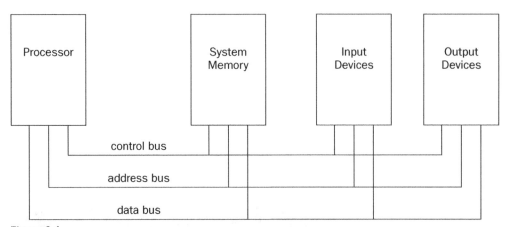

Figure 2-1

The processor contains the hardware and instruction codes that control the operation of the computer. It is connected to the other elements of the computer (the memory storage unit, input devices, and output devices) using three separate buses: a control bus, an address bus, and a data bus.

The control bus is used to synchronize the functions between the processor and the individual system elements. The data bus is used to move data between the processor and the external system elements. An example of this would be reading data from a memory location. The processor places the memory address to read on the address bus, and the memory storage unit responds by placing the value stored in that memory location on the data bus for the processor to access.

The processor itself consists of many components. Each component has a separate function in the processor's ability to process data. Assembly language programs have the ability to access and control each of these elements, so it is important to know what they are. The main components in the processor are as follows:

- ❑ Control unit
- ❑ Execution unit
- ❑ Registers
- ❑ Flags

Figure 2-2 shows these components and how they interact within the processor.

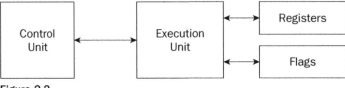

Figure 2-2

The following sections describe each of the core components, and how they are implemented in the IA-32 platform.

Control unit

At the heart of the processor is the control unit. The main purpose of the control unit is to control what is happening at any time within the processor. While the processor is running, instructions must be retrieved from memory and loaded for the processor to handle. The job of the control unit is to perform four basic functions:

1. Retrieve instructions from memory.

2. Decode instructions for operation.

3. Retrieve data from memory as needed.

4. Store the results as necessary.

The instruction counter retrieves the next instruction code from memory and prepares it to be processed. The instruction decoder is used to decode the retrieved instruction code into a micro-operation. The micro-operation is the code that controls the specific signals within the processor chip to perform the function of the instruction code.

When the prepared micro-operation is ready, the control unit passes it along to the execution unit for processing, and retrieves any results to store in an appropriate location.

The control unit is the most hotly researched part of the processor. Many advances in microprocessor technology fall within the control unit section. Intel has made numerous advancements in speeding up the operations within the control unit. One of the most beneficial advancements is the manner in which instructions are retrieved and processed by the control unit.

At the time of this writing, the latest Intel processor (the Pentium 4) uses a control unit technology called NetBurst. The NetBurst technology incorporates four separate techniques to help speed up processing in the control unit. Knowing how these techniques operate can help you optimize your assembly language programs. The NetBurst features are as follows:

❑ Instruction prefetch and decoding

❑ Branch prediction

❑ Out-of-order execution

❑ Retirement

These techniques work together to make the control unit of the Pentium 4 processor. Figure 2-3 shows how these elements interact.

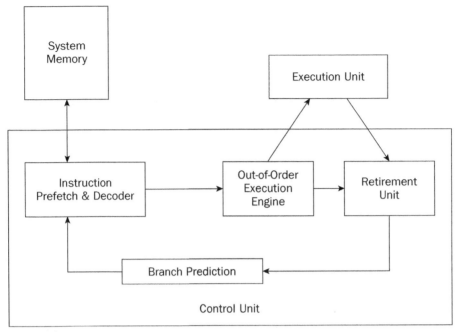

Figure 2-3

The following sections describe each of these techniques as implemented in the Pentium 4 processor.

Instruction prefetch and decoding pipeline

Older processors in the IA-32 family fetched instructions and data directly from system memory as they were needed by the execution unit. Because it takes considerably longer to retrieve data from memory than to process it, a backlog occurs, whereby the processor is continually waiting for instructions and data to be retrieved from memory. To solve this problem, the concept of *prefetching* was created.

Although the name sounds odd, prefetching involves attempting to retrieve (fetch) instructions and/or data before they are actually needed by the execution unit. To incorporate prefetching, a special storage area is needed on the processor chip itself—one that can be easily accessed by the processor, quicker than normal memory access. This was solved using *pipelining*.

Pipelining involves creating a memory cache on the processor chip from which both instructions and data elements can be retrieved and stored ahead of the time that they are required for processing. When the execution unit is ready for the next instruction, that instruction is already available in the cache and can be quickly processed. This is demonstrated in Figure 2-4.

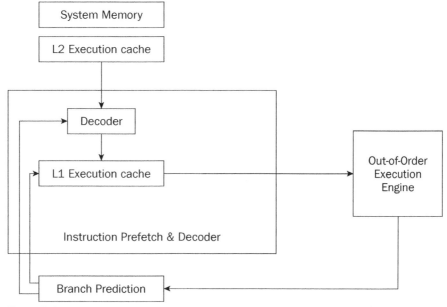

Figure 2-4

The IA-32 platform implements pipelining by utilizing two (or more) layers of cache. The first cache layer (called L1) attempts to prefetch both instruction code and data from memory as it thinks it will be needed by the processor. As the instruction pointer moves along in memory, the prefetch algorithm determines which instruction codes should be read and placed in the cache. In a similar manner, if data is being processed from memory, the prefetch algorithm attempts to determine what data elements may be accessed next and also reads them from memory and places them in cache.

Of course, one pitfall to caching instructions and data is that there is no guarantee that the program will execute instructions in a sequential order. If the program takes a logic branch that moves the instruction pointer to a completely different location in memory, the entire cache is useless and must be cleared and repopulated with instructions from the new location.

To help alleviate this problem, a second cache layer was created. The second cache layer (called L2) can also hold instruction code and data elements, separate from the first cache layer. When the program logic jumps to a completely different area in memory to execute instructions, the second layer cache can still hold instructions from the previous instruction location. If the program logic jumps back to the area, those instructions are still being cached and can be processed almost as quickly as instructions stored in the first layer cache.

While assembly language programs cannot access the instruction and data caches, it is good to know how these elements work. By minimizing branches in programs, you can help speed up the execution of the instruction codes in your program.

Branch prediction unit

While implementing multiple layers of cache is one way to help speed up processing of program logic, it still does not solve the problem of "jumpy" programs. If a program takes many different logic branches, it may well be impossible for the different layers of cache to keep up, resulting in more last-minute memory access for both instruction code and data elements.

To help solve this problem, the IA-32 platform processors also incorporate *branch prediction*. Branch prediction uses specialized algorithms to attempt to predict which instruction codes will be needed next within a program branch.

Special statistical algorithms and analysis are incorporated to determine the most likely path traveled through the instruction code. Instruction codes along that path are prefetched and loaded into the cache layers.

The Pentium 4 processor utilizes three techniques to implement branch prediction:

❑ Deep branch prediction

❑ Dynamic data flow analysis

❑ Speculative execution

Deep branch prediction enables the processor to attempt to decode instructions beyond multiple branches in the program. Again, statistical algorithms are implemented to predict the most likely path the program will take throughout the branches. While this technique is helpful, it is not totally foolproof.

Dynamic data flow analysis performs statistical real-time analysis of the data flow throughout the processor. Instructions that are predicted to be necessary for the flow of the program but not reached yet by the instruction pointer are passed to the out-of-order execution core (described next). In addition, any instructions that can be executed while the processor is waiting for data related to another instruction are processed.

Speculative execution enables the processor to determine what distant instruction codes not immediately in the instruction code branch are likely to be required, and attempt to process those instructions, again using the out-of-order execution engine.

Out-of-order execution engine

The out-of-order execution engine is one of the greatest improvements to the Pentium 4 processor in terms of speed. This is where instructions are prepared for processing by the execution unit. It contains several buffers to change the order of instructions within the pipeline to increase the performance of the control unit. This is demonstrated in Figure 2-5.

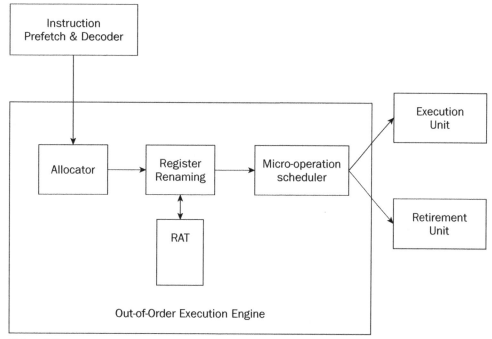

Figure 2-5

Instructions retrieved from the prefetch and decoding pipeline are analyzed and reordered, enabling them to be executed as quickly as possible. By analyzing a large number of instructions, the out-of-order execution engine can find independent instructions that can be executed (and their results saved) until required by the rest of the program. The Pentium 4 processor can have up to 126 instructions in the out-of-order execution engine at any one time.

There are three sections within the out-of-order execution engine:

❏ The allocator

❏ Register renaming

❏ The micro-operation scheduler

The allocator is the traffic cop for the out-of-order execution engine. Its job is to ensure that buffer space is allocated properly for each instruction that the out-of-order execution engine is processing. If a needed resource is not available, the allocator will stall the processing of the instruction and allocate resources for another instruction that can complete its processing.

The register renaming section allocates logical registers to process instructions that require register access. Instead of the eight general-purpose registers available on the IA-32 processor (described later in the "Registers" section), the register renaming section contains 128 logical registers. It maps register requests made by instructions into one of the logical registers, to allow simultaneous access to the same register by multiple instructions. The register mapping is done using the register allocation table (RAT). This helps speed up processing instructions that require access to the same register sets.

The micro-operation scheduler determines when a micro-operation is ready for processing by examining the input elements that it requires. Its job is to send micro-operations that are ready to be processed to the retirement unit, while still maintaining program dependencies. The micro-operation scheduler uses two queues to place micro-operations in — one for micro-operations that require memory access and one for micro-operations that do not. The queues are tied to dispatch ports. Different types of Pentium processors may contain a different number of dispatch ports. The dispatch ports send the micro-operations to the retirement unit.

Retirement unit

The retirement unit receives all of the micro-operations from the pipeline decoders and the out-of-order execution engine and attempts to reassemble the micro-operations into the proper order for the program to properly execute.

The retirement unit passes micro-operations to the execution unit for processing in the order that the out-of-order execution engine sends them, but then monitors the results, reassembling the results into the proper order for the program to execute.

This is accomplished using a large buffer area to hold micro-operation results and place them in the proper order as they are required.

When a micro-operation is completed and the results placed in the proper order, the micro-operation is considered retired and is removed from the retirement unit. The retirement unit also updates information in the branch prediction unit to ensure that it knows which branches have been taken, and which instruction codes have been processed.

Execution unit

The main function of the processor is to execute instructions. This function is performed in the execution unit. A single processor can actually contain multiple execution units, capable of processing multiple instruction codes simultaneously.

The execution unit consists of one or more Arithmetic Logic Units (ALUs) The ALUs are specifically designed to handle mathematical operations on different types of data. The Pentium 4 execution unit includes separate ALUs for the following functions:

❑   Simple-integer operations

❑   Complex-integer operations

❑   Floating-point operations

Low-latency integer execution unit

The low-latency integer execution unit is designed to quickly perform simple integer mathematical operations, such as additions, subtractions, and Boolean operations. Pentium 4 processors are capable of performing two low-latency integer operations per clock cycle, effectively doubling the processing speed.

Complex-integer execution unit

The complex-integer execution unit handles more involved integer mathematical operations. The complex-integer execution unit handles most shift and rotate instructions in four clock cycles. Multiplication and division operations involve long calculation times, and often take 14 to 60 clock cycles.

Floating-point execution unit

The floating-point execution unit differs between the different processors in the IA-32 family. All Pentium processors can process floating-point mathematical operations using the standard floating-point execution unit. Pentium processors that contain MMX and SSE support also perform these calculations in the floating-point execution unit.

The floating-point execution unit contains registers to handle data elements that contain 64-bit to 128-bit lengths. This enables larger floating-point values to be used in calculations, which can speed up complex floating-point calculations, such as digital signal processing and video compression.

Registers

Most of the operations of the processor require processing data. Unfortunately, the slowest operations a processor can undertake are trying to read or store data in memory. As shown in Figure 2-1, when the processor accesses a data element, the request must travel outside of the processor, across the control bus, and into the memory storage unit. This process is not only complicated, but also forces the processor to wait while the memory access is being performed. This downtime could be spent processing other instructions.

To help solve this problem, the processor includes internal memory locations, called *registers*. The registers are capable of storing data elements for processing without having to access the memory storage unit. The downside to registers is that a limited number of them are built into the processor chip.

The IA-32 platform processors have multiple groups of registers of different sizes. Different processors within the IA-32 platform include specialized registers. The core groups of registers available to all processors in the IA-32 family are shown in the following table.

Register	Description
General purpose	Eight 32-bit registers used for storing working data
Segment	Six 16-bit registers used for handling memory access
Instruction pointer	A single 32-bit register pointing to the next instruction code to execute

Table continued on following page

Register	Description
Floating-point data	Eight 80-bit registers used for floating-point arithmetic data
Control	Five 32-bit registers used to determine the operating mode of the processor
Debug	Eight 32-bit registers used to contain information when debugging the processor

The following sections describe the more common registers in greater detail.

General-purpose registers

The general-purpose registers are used to temporarily store data as it is processed on the processor. The general-purpose registers have evolved from the old 8-bit 8080 processor days to 32-bit registers available in the Pentium processors. Each new version of general-purpose registers is created to be completely backwardly compatible with previous processors. Thus, code that uses 8-bit registers on the 8080 chips is still valid on 32-bit Pentium chips.

While most general-purpose registers can be used for holding any type of data, some have acquired special uses, which are consistently used in assembly language programs. The following table shows the general-purpose registers available on the Pentium platform, and what they are most often used for.

Register	Description
EAX	Accumulator for operands and results data
EBX	Pointer to data in the data memory segment
ECX	Counter for string and loop operations
EDX	I/O pointer
EDI	Data pointer for destination of string operations
ESI	Data pointer for source of string operations
ESP	Stack pointer
EBP	Stack data pointer

The 32-bit EAX, EBX, ECX, and EDX registers can also be referenced by 16-bit and 8-bit names to represent the older versions of the registers. Figure 2-6 shows how the registers can be referenced.

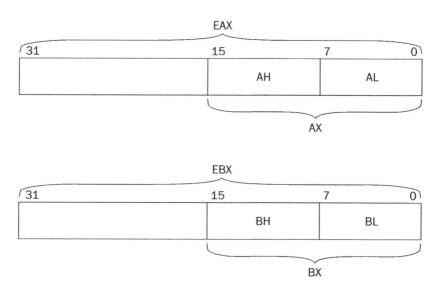

Figure 2-6

By using the reference AX, the lower 16 bits of the EAX register are used. By using the reference AL, the lower 8 bits of the EAX register are used. AH references the next 8 higher bits after AL.

Segment registers

The segment registers are used specifically for referencing memory locations. The IA-32 processor platform allows three different methods of accessing system memory:

❏ Flat memory model

❏ Segmented memory model

❏ Real-address mode

The flat memory model presents all system memory as a contiguous address space. All instructions, data, and the stack are contained in the same address space. Each memory location is accessed by a specific address, called a *linear address*.

The segmented memory model divides the system memory into groups of independent segments, referenced by pointers located in the segment registers. Each segment is used to contain a specific type of data. One segment is used to contain instruction codes, another data elements, and a third the program stack.

Memory locations in segments are defined by logical addresses. A logical address consists of a segment address and an offset address. The processor translates a logical address to a corresponding linear address location to access the byte of memory.

The segment registers are used to contain the segment address for specific data access. The following table describes the available segment addresses.

Segment Register	Description
CS	Code segment
DS	Data segment
SS	Stack segment
ES	Extra segment pointer
FS	Extra segment pointer
GS	Extra segment pointer

Each segment register is 16 bits and contains the pointer to the start of the memory-specific segment. The CS register contains the pointer to the code segment in memory. The code segment is where the instruction codes are stored in memory. The processor retrieves instruction codes from memory based on the CS register value, and an offset value contained in the EIP instruction pointer register. A program cannot explicitly load or change the CS register. The processor assigns its value as the program is assigned a memory space.

The DS, ES, FS, and GS segment registers are all used to point to data segments. By having four separate data segments, the program can help separate data elements, ensuring that they do not overlap. The program must load the data segment registers with the appropriate pointer value for the segments, and reference individual memory locations using an offset value.

The SS segment register is used to point to the stack segment. The stack contains data values passed to functions and procedures within the program.

If a program is using the real address mode, all of the segment registers point to the zero linear address, and are not changed by the program. All instruction codes, data elements, and stack elements are accessed directly by their linear address.

Instruction pointer register

The instruction pointer register (or EIP register), sometimes called the *program counter,* keeps track of the next instruction code to execute. While this sounds like a simple process, with the implementation of the instruction prefetch cache it is not. The instruction pointer points to the next instruction to execute.

An application program cannot directly modify the instruction pointer per se. You cannot specify a memory address and place it in the EIP register. Instead, you must use normal program control instructions, such as jumps, to alter the next instruction to be read into the prefetch cache.

In a flat memory model, the instruction pointer contains the linear address of the memory location for the next instruction code. If the application is using a segmented memory model, the instruction pointer points to a logical memory address, referenced by the contents of the CS register.

Control registers

The five control registers are used to determine the operating mode of the processor, and the characteristics of the currently executing task. The individual control registers are described in the following table.

Control Register	Description
CR0	System flags that control the operating mode and states of the processor
CR1	Not currently used
CR2	Memory page fault information
CR3	Memory page directory information
CR4	Flags that enable processor features and indicate feature capabilities of the processor

The values in the control registers cannot be directly accessed, but the data contained in the control register can be moved to a general-purpose register. Once the data is in a general-purpose register, an application program can examine the bit flags in the register to determine the operating status of the processor and/or currently running task.

If a change is required to a control register flag value, the change can be made to the data in the general-purpose register, and the register moved to the control register. Systems programmers usually modify the values in the control registers. Normal user application programs do not usually modify control registers entries, although they might query flag values to determine the capabilities of the host processor chip on which the application is running.

Flags

For each operation that is performed in the processor, there must be a mechanism to determine whether the operation was successful or not. The processor flags are used to perform this function.

Flags are important to assembly language programs, as they are the only means available to determine whether a program's function succeeded or not. For example, if an application performed a subtraction operation that resulted in a negative value, a special flag within the processor would be set. Without checking the flag, the assembly language program would not have any way to know that something went wrong.

The IA-32 platform uses a single 32-bit register to contain a group of status, control, and system flags. The EFLAGS register contains 32 bits of information that are mapped to represent specific flags of information. Some bits are reserved for future use, to allow additional flags to be defined in future processors. At the time of this writing, 17 bits are used for flags.

The flags are divided into three groups based on function:

❑ Status flags

❑ Control flags

❑ System flags

The following sections describe the flags found in each group.

Status flags

The status flags are used to indicate the results of a mathematical operation by the processor. The current status flags are shown in the following table.

Flag	Bit	Name
CF	0	Carry flag
PF	2	Parity flag
AF	4	Adjust flag
ZF	6	Zero flag
SF	7	Sign flag
OF	11	Overflow flag

The carry flag is set if a mathematical operation on an unsigned integer value generates a carry or a borrow for the most significant bit. This represents an overflow condition for the register involved in the mathematical operation. When an overflow occurs, the data remaining in the register is not the correct answer to the mathematical operation.

The parity flag is used to indicate whether the result register in a mathematical operation contains corrupt data. As a simple check for validity, the parity flag is set if the total number of 1 bits in the result is even, and is cleared if the total number of 1 bits in the result is odd. By checking the parity flag, an application can determine whether the register has been corrupted since the operation.

The adjust flag is used in Binary Coded Decimal (BCD) mathematical operations (see Chapter 7, "Using Numbers"). The adjust flag is set if a carry or borrow operation occurs from bit 3 of the register used for the calculation.

The zero flag is set if the result of an operation is zero. This is most often used as an easy way to determine whether a mathematical operation results in a zero value.

The sign flag is set to the most significant bit of the result, which is the sign bit. This indicates whether the result is positive or negative.

The overflow flag is used in signed integer arithmetic when a positive value is too large, or a negative value is too small, to be properly represented in the register.

Control flags

Control flags are used to control specific behavior in the processor. Currently, only one control flag is defined, the DF flag, or direction flag. It is used to control the way strings are handled by the processor.

When the DF flag is set (set to one), string instructions automatically decrement memory addresses to get the next byte in the string. When the DF flag is cleared (set to zero), string instructions automatically increment memory addresses to get the next byte in the string.

System flags

The system flags are used to control operating system–level operations. Application programs should never attempt to modify the system flags. The system flags are listed in the following table.

Flag	Bit	Name
TF	8	Trap flag
IF	9	Interrupt enable flag
IOPL	12 and 13	I/O privilege level flag
NT	14	Nested task flag
RF	16	Resume flag
VM	17	Virtual-8086 mode flag
AC	18	Alignment check flag
VIF	19	Virtual interrupt flag
VIP	20	Virtual interrupt pending flag
ID	21	Identification flag

The trap flag is set to enable single-step mode. In single-step mode, the processor performs only one instruction code at a time, waiting for a signal to perform the next instruction. This feature is extremely useful when debugging assembly language applications.

The interrupt enable flag controls how the processor responds to signals received from external sources.

The I/O privilege field indicates the I/O privilege level of the currently running task. This defines access levels for the I/O address space. The privilege field value must be less than or equal to the access level required to access the I/O address space; otherwise, any request to access the address space will be denied.

The nested task flag controls whether the currently running task is linked to the previously executed task. This is used for chaining interrupted and called tasks.

The resume flag controls how the processor responds to exceptions when in debugging mode.

The virtual-8086 flag indicates that the processor is operating in virtual-8086 mode instead of protected or real mode.

The alignment check flag is used (along with the AM bit in the CR0 control register) to enable alignment checking of memory references.

The virtual interrupt flag replicates the IF flag when the processor is operating in virtual mode.

The virtual interrupt pending flag is used when the processor is operating in virtual mode to indicate that an interrupt is pending.

The ID flag is interesting in that it indicates whether the processor supports the CPUID instruction. If the processor is able to set or clear this flag, it supports the CPUID instruction. If not, then the CPUID instruction is not available.

Advanced IA-32 Features

The core features of the IA-32 platform mentioned so far are available on all of the processors in the family, starting with the 80386 processor. This section describes some advanced features that the assembly language programmer can utilize when creating programs specifically designed for the Pentium processors.

The x87 floating-point unit

Early processors in the IA-32 family required a separate processor chip to perform floating-point mathematical operations. The 80287 and 80387 processors specialized in providing floating-point arithmetic operations for the computer chips. Programmers who needed fast processing of floating-point operations were forced to turn to additional hardware to support their needs.

Starting with the 80486 processor, the advanced arithmetic functions found in the 80287 and 80387 chips were incorporated into the main processor. To support these functions, additional instruction codes as well as additional registers and execution units were required. Together these elements are referred to as the x87 floating-point unit (FPU).

The x87 FPU incorporates the following additional registers:

FPU Register	Description
Data registers	Eight 80-bit registers for floating-point data
Status register	16-bit register to report the status of the FPU
Control register	16-bit register to control the precision of the FPU
Tag register	16-bit register to describe the contents of the eight data registers

FPU Register	Description
FIP register	48-bit FPU instruction pointer (FIP) points to the next FPU instruction
FDP register	48-bit FPU data pointer (FDP) points to the data in memory
Opcode register	11-bit register to hold the last instruction processed by the FPU

The FPU registers and instruction codes enable assembly language programs to quickly process complex floating-point mathematical functions, such as those required for graphics processing, digital signal processing, and complex business applications. The FPU can process floating-point arithmetic considerably faster than the software simulation used in the standard processor without the FPU. Whenever possible, the assembly language programmer should utilize the FPU for floating-point arithmetic.

Multimedia extensions (MMX)

The Pentium II processor introduced another method for programmers to perform complex integer arithmetic operations. MMX was the first technology to support the Intel Single Instruction, Multiple Data (SIMD) execution model.

The SIMD model was developed to process larger numbers, commonly found in multimedia applications. The SIMD model uses expanded register sizes and new number formats to speed up the complex number crunching required for real-time multimedia presentations.

The MMX environment includes three new floating-point data types that can be handled by the processor:

- ❏ 64-bit packed byte integers
- ❏ 64-bit packed word integers
- ❏ 64-bit packed doubleword integers

These data types are described in detail in Chapter 7, "Using Numbers." To handle the new data formats, MMX technology incorporates the eight FPU registers as special-purpose registers. The MMX registers are named MM0 through MM7, and are used to perform integer arithmetic on the 64-bit packed integers.

While the MMX technology improved processing speeds for complex integer arithmetic, it did nothing for programs that require complex floating-point arithmetic. That problem was solved with the SSE environment.

Streaming SIMD extensions (SSE)

The next generation of SIMD technology was implemented starting with the Pentium III processor. SSE enhances performance for complex floating-point arithmetic, often used in 3-D graphics, motion video, and video conferencing.

The first implementation of SSE in the Pentium III processor incorporated eight new 128-bit registers (called XMM0 through XMM7) and a new data type — a 128-bit packed single-precision floating point. The SSE technology also incorporated additional new instruction codes for processing up to four 128-bit packed single-precision floating-point numbers in a single instruction.

The second implementation of SSE (SSE2) in the Pentium 4 processors incorporates the same XMM registers that SSE uses, and also introduces five new data types:

- ❑ 128-bit packed double-precision floating point
- ❑ 128-bit packed byte integers
- ❑ 128-bit packed word integers
- ❑ 128-bit packed doubleword integers
- ❑ 128-bit packed quadword integers

These data types are also described in detail in Chapter 7. The new data types and the corresponding instruction codes enable programmers to utilize even more complex mathematical operations within their programs. The 128-bit double-precision floating-point data types allow for advanced 3-D geometry techniques, such as ray tracing, to be performed with minimal processor time.

A third implementation of SSE (SSE3) does not create any new data types, but provides several new instructions for processing both integer and floating-point values in the XMM registers.

Hyperthreading

One of the most exciting features added to the Pentium 4 processor line is *hyperthreading*. Hyperthreading enables a single IA-32 processor to handle multiple program execution threads simultaneously.

The hyperthreading technology consists of two or more logical processors located on a single physical processor. Each logical processor contains a complete set of general-purpose, segment, control, and debug registers. All of the logical processors share the same execution unit. The out-of-order execution core is responsible for handling the separate threads of instruction codes provided by the different logical processors.

Most of the advantages of hyperthreading appear at the operating system level. Multitasking operating systems, such as Microsoft Windows and the various UNIX implementations, can assign application threads to the individual logical processors. To the application programmer, hyperthreading may not appear to be that much of a benefit.

The IA-32 Processor Family

At the time of this writing, the IA-32 family of processors is the most popular computing platform used in desktop workstations and many server environments. The most popular operating system that utilizes the IA-32 platform is Microsoft Windows, although other popular operating systems run on the IA-32 platform, such as Novell file servers, and UNIX-based OSs such as Linux and the BSD derivatives.

While many advances in the IA-32 processor platform have been made throughout the years, many features are common to all IA-32 processors. The features mentioned in this chapter form the core of all assembly language programs written for the IA-32 platform. However, knowing the special features available on a particular processor can help speed your assembly language program along very nicely. This section describes the different processors available in the IA-32 family, and how their features must be taken into consideration when programming for the platform.

Intel processors

Of course, Intel is the main supplier of processors in the IA-32 platform. In today's computing environment, the most commonly used processor platform is the Pentium processor. It is extremely unusual to encounter hardware from the earlier IA-32 processors, such as the 80486 processor.

Unfortunately, several different types of Pentium processors are still active in businesses, schools, and homes. Creating assembly language programs that utilize advanced IA-32 features found only on the latest processors may limit your application's marketability. Conversely, if you know that your programming environment consists of a specific type of processor, utilizing available features may help give your application the performance boost needed to smoke the competition.

This section describes the different types of Pentium processors commonly available in workstations and servers, highlighting the features that are available with each processor.

The Pentium processor family

The core of the Pentium processor line is, of course, the base Pentium processor. The Pentium processor was introduced in 1993 as a replacement for the 80486 processor. The Pentium processor was the first processor to incorporate the dual execution pipeline, and was the first processor to use a full 32-bit address bus and 64-bit internal data path.

While the performance benefits of the Pentium processor were obvious, from a programming point of view, the Pentium processor did not provide any new features beyond the 80486 architecture. All of the core registers and instruction codes from the 80486 processor were supported, including the internal FPU support.

The P6 processor family

The P6 processor family was introduced in 1995 with the Pentium Pro processor. The Pentium Pro processor incorporated a completely new architecture from the original Pentium processor. The P6 family of processors were the first to utilize a superscalar microarchitecture, which greatly increased performance by enabling multiple execution units and instruction prefetch pipelines.

The Pentium MMX and Pentium II processors, part of the P6 family, were the first processors to incorporate MMX technology, and also introduced new low-power states that enabled the processor to be put in sleep mode when idling. This feature helped conserve power, and became the ideal platform for laptop computing devices.

The Pentium III processor was the first processor to incorporate SSE technology, enabling programmers to perform complex floating-point arithmetic operations both quickly and easily.

The Pentium 4 processor family

The Pentium 4 processor was introduced in 2000, and again started a new trend in microprocessor design. The Pentium 4 utilizes the Intel NetBurst architecture, which provides extremely fast processing speeds by incorporating the instruction pipelines, the out-of-order execution core, and execution units.

The Pentium 4 processor supports SSE3, a more advanced SSE technology that implements additional floating-point operations to support high-speed multimedia computations.

The Pentium Xeon processor family

In 2001, Intel introduced the Pentium Xeon processor. It is primarily intended for multi-processor server operations. It supports the MMX, SSE, SSE2, and SSE3 technologies.

Non-Intel processors

While the IA-32 platform is often considered to be an Intel thing, there are many other non-Intel processors available on the market that also implement the IA-32 features. It is possible that your assembly language application may be run on a non-Intel platform, so it is important that you understand some differences between the platforms.

AMD processors

Today, Intel's biggest competitor is AMD. AMD has released a competing processor chip for every release of Intel's Pentium processor. It is not uncommon to run across Microsoft Windows workstations using AMD processors. The following table shows the AMD processor's history.

AMD Processor	Equivalent to	Notes
K5	Pentium	100% software compatible
K6	Pentium MMX	Pentium with full MMX support
K6-2	Pentium II	Uses 3D Now technology
K6-III	Pentium III	
Athlon	Pentium 4	
Athlon XP	Pentium 4 w/SSE	

For the assembly language programmer, the most important difference between AMD and Intel processors is apparent when using SIMD technology. While AMD has duplicated the MMX technology, it has not fully duplicated the newer SSE technology. When Intel introduced SSE in the Pentium II processor, AMD took a different route. The AMD K6-2 processor uses a different SIMD technology called 3D Now. The 3D Now technology uses similar registers and data types as SSE, but it is not software compatible. This has caused high-speed programmers considerable difficulty when programming for SSE functions.

With the release of the Athlon XP processor in 2001, AMD supported SSE integer arithmetic. At the time of this writing, the newest AMD processor chips now fully support SSE technology.

Cyrix processors

While the Cyrix corporation has not been in business for a few years, their IA-32 platform processors still live on in many workstations and low-end servers. It is still possible to run across a Cyrix processor in various environments.

The evolution of the Cyrix processor family mirrored the Intel processors for many versions. The first Pentium-grade processor produced by Cyrix was originally called the 6x86 processor. It is 100 percent software compatible with the Pentium processor. When Intel introduced MMX technology, Cyrix produced the 6x86MX processor (they didn't have a license to call it MMX, but MX was close enough).

When Cyrix was sold to the VIA chipset company, the original Cyrix processor line was renamed. The 6x86 processor was called the M1, and the 6x86MX processor was called M2. Again, these processors retained their compatibility with their Pentium counterparts.

Before the demise of the Cyrix processor, one final version made it to market. Dubbed the Cyrix III, it was also compatible with the Pentium III processor. Unfortunately, similar to AMD, it too had to support SSE using the 3D Now technology, which made it incompatible with assembly language programs written for SSE.

Summary

Before writing an assembly language program, you must know the target processor used when the program is executed. The most popular processor platform in use today is the Intel IA-32 platform. This platform includes the Pentium family of processors from Intel, as well as the Athlon processors from AMD.

The flagship of the IA-32 platform is the Intel Pentium 4 processor. It incorporates the NetBurst architecture to quickly and easily process instructions and data. The core of the NetBurst architecture includes a control unit, an execution unit, registers, and flags.

The control unit controls how the execution unit processes instructions and data. Speed is accomplished by prefetching and decoding instructions from memory long before the execution unit processes them. Instructions can also be processed out of order and the results stored until they are needed in the application.

The execution unit in a Pentium 4 processor has the capability of processing multiple instructions concurrently. Simple integer processes are performed quickly and stored in the out-of-order area in the control unit until needed. Complex integer and floating-point processes are also streamlined to increase performance.

Registers are used as local data storage within the processor to prevent costly memory access for data. The IA-32 platform processors provide several general-purpose registers for holding data and pointers as the program is executed. Instructions are retrieved from memory based on the value of the instruction pointer register. The control register controls the processor's behavior.

A special register containing several flags determines the status and operation of the processor. Each flag represents a different operation within the processor. Status flags indicate the result of operations performed by the processor. Control flags control how the processor behaves for specific operations. System flags determine operating system behavior, and should not be touched by application programmers.

Innovation in the IA-32 platform is alive and well. Many new features have been introduced in recent processor releases. The floating-point unit (FPU) has been incorporated into Pentium processors to assist in floating-point mathematical operations.

To further support complex mathematical processing, the Single Instruction, Multiple Data (SIMD) technology enables the processing of large numerical values in both integer and floating-point form. The Multimedia Extensions (MMX) enable programmers to use 64-bit integers in high-precision integer calculations. Following that, the Streaming SIMD Extensions (SSE) technology enables programmers to use 128-bit single-precision floating-point values, and subsequently, the SSE2 technology enables the use of 128-bit double-precision floating-point data values. These new data types greatly speed up the processing of mathematically intensive programs, such as those used for multimedia processing and digital signal processing.

When programming for the IA-32 platform, you should be aware of the different processors available, and know what functions each processor type supports. The core of the IA-32 platform is the original Pentium processor. It supports the core IA-32 registers and instruction sets, along with simple built-in FPU support. Similar to the Pentium processor, AMD produced the K5 processor, and Cyrix produced the 6x86 processor. Each of these processors is 100 percent software compatible with the IA-32 instruction code set.

Intel introduced MMX functionality in the Pentium II processor line. Following suit, AMD incorporated MMX features in the K6 processor, and Cyrix with the 6x86MX processor. All of these processors include the MMX registers, and the additional MMX instruction codes.

The SSE technology is where things get complicated in the IA-32 world. The Pentium II processor introduced SSE registers and instruction sets, but unfortunately, other processor manufacturers were not able to directly incorporate these features. Instead, AMD and Cyrix implemented the 3D Now technology in their K6-2 (AMD) and Cyrix III (Cyrix) processors. The 3D Now technology provided the same 64-bit integer data types as SSE, but the instruction codes were different.

At the time of this writing, the Pentium 4 processor is the flagship processor for Intel. It supports SSE3 technology, as well as the NetBurst architecture. The AMD rival is the Athlon XP, which now incorporates SSE registers and instruction sets, making it software compatible with the Pentium 4 processor.

Now that you have an understanding of the hardware platform used in this book, it's time to examine the software development environment. The next chapter discusses the assembly language tools that are available in the Linux operating system environment. By using Linux, you can leverage the GNU development tools to create a professional software development environment with minimal cost.

3

The Tools of the Trade

Now that you are familiar with the IA-32 hardware platform, it's time to dig into the tools necessary to create assembly language programs for it. To create assembly language programs, you must have some type of development environment. Many different assembly language development tools are available, both commercially and for free. You must decide which development environment works best for you.

This chapter first examines what development tools you should have to create assembly language programs. Next, the programming development tools produced by the GNU project are discussed. Each tool is described, including downloading and installation.

The Development Tools

Just like any other profession, programming requires the proper tools to perform the job. To create a good assembly language development environment, you must have the proper tools at your disposal. Unlike a high-level language environment in which you can purchase a complete development environment, you often have to piece together an assembly language development environment. At a minimum you should have the following:

- ❏ An assembler
- ❏ A linker
- ❏ A debugger

Additionally, to create assembly language routines for other high-level language programs, you should also have these tools:

❏ A compiler for the high-level language

❏ An object code disassembler

❏ A profiling tool for optimization

The following sections describe each of these tools, and how they are used in the assembly language development environment.

The assembler

To create assembly language programs, obviously you need some tool to convert the assembly language source code to instruction code for the processor. This is where the assembler comes in.

As mentioned in Chapter 1, "What Is Assembly Language?," assemblers are specific to the underlying hardware platform for which you are programming. Each processor family has its own instruction code set. The assembler you select must be capable of producing instruction codes for the processor family on your system (or the system you are developing for).

The assembler produces the instruction codes from source code created by the programmer. If you remember from Chapter 1, there are three components to an assembly language source code program:

❏ Opcode mnemonics

❏ Data sections

❏ Directives

Unfortunately, each assembler uses different formats for each of these components. Programming using one assembler may be totally different from programming using another assembler. While the basics are the same, the way they are implemented can be vastly different.

The biggest difference between assemblers is the assembler directives. While opcode mnemonics are closely related to processor instruction codes, the assembler directives are unique to the individual assembler. The directives instruct the assembler how to construct the instruction code program. While some assemblers have a limited number of directives, some have an extensive number of directives. Directives do everything from defining program sections to implementing if-then statements or while loops.

You may also have to take into consideration how you will write your assembly language programs. Some assemblers come complete with built-in editors that help recognize improper syntax while you are typing the code, while others are simply command-line programs that can only assemble an existing code text file. If the assembler you choose does not contain an editor, you must select a good editor for your environment. While using the UNIX vi editor can work for simple programs, you probably wouldn't want to code a 10,000-line assembly program using it.

The bottom line for choosing an assembler is its ability to make creating an instruction code program for your target environment as simple as possible. The next sections describe some common assemblers that are available for the Intel IA-32 platform.

MASM

The granddaddy of all assemblers for the Intel platform, the Microsoft Assembler (MASM) is the product of the Microsoft Corporation. It has been available since the beginning of the IBM-compatible PC, enabling programmers to produce assembly language programs in both the DOS and Windows environments.

Because MASM has been around for so long, numerous tutorials, books, and example programs are floating around, many of which are free or low-cost. While Microsoft no longer sells MASM as a stand-alone product, it is still bundled with the Microsoft's Visual Studio product line of compilers. The benefit of using Visual Studio is its all-encompassing Integrated Development Environment (IDE). Microsoft has also allowed various companies and organizations to distribute just the MASM 6.0 files free of charge, enabling you to assemble your programs from a command prompt. Doing a Web search for MASM 6.0 will produce a list of sites where it can be downloaded free of charge.

Besides MASM, an independent developer, Steve Hutchessen, has created the MASM32 development environment. MASM32 incorporates the original MASM assembler and the popular Windows Win32 Application Programming Interface (API), used mainly in C and C++ applications. This enables assembly language programmers to create full-blown Windows programs entirely in assembly language programs. The MASM32 Web site is located at www.masm32.com.

NASM

The Netwide Assembler (NASM) was developed originally as a commercial assembler package for the UNIX environment. Recently, the developers have released NASM as open-source software for both the UNIX and Microsoft environments. It is fully compatible with all of the Intel instruction code set and can produce executable files in UNIX, 16-bit MS-DOS, and 32-bit Microsoft Windows formats.

Similar to MASM, quite a few books and tutorials are available for NASM. The NASM download page is located at http://nasm.sourceforge.net.

GAS

The Free Software Foundation's GNU project has produced many freely available software packages that run in the UNIX operating system environment. The GNU assembler, called **gas,** is the most popular cross-platform assembler available for UNIX.

That is correct, I did say cross-platform. While earlier I mentioned that assemblers are specific to individual processor families, gas is an exception. It was developed to operate on many different processor platforms. Obviously, it must know which platform it is being used on, and creates instruction code programs depending on the underlying platform. Usually gas is capable of automatically detecting the underlying hardware platform and creates appropriate instruction codes for the platform with no operator intervention.

One unique feature of gas is its ability to create instruction codes for a platform other than the one you are programming on. This enables a programmer working on an Intel-based computer to create assembly language programs for a system that is MIPS-based. Of course, the downside is that the programmer can't test the produced program code on the host system.

This book uses the GNU assembler to assemble all of the examples. Not only is it a good standalone assembler, it is also what the GNU C compiler uses to convert the compiled C and C++ programs to instruction codes. By knowing how to program assembly language with gas, you can also easily incorporate assembly language functions in your existing C and C++ applications, which is one of the main points of this book.

HLA

The High Level Assembler (HLA) is the creation of Professor Randall Hyde. It creates Intel instruction code applications on DOS, Windows, and Linux operating systems.

The primary purpose of HLA was to teach assembly language to beginning programmers. It incorporates many advanced directives to help programmers make the leap from a high-level language to assembly language (thus its name). It also has the ability to use normal assembly code statements, providing programmers with a robust platform for easily migrating from high-level languages such as C or C++ to assembly language.

The HLA Web site is located at `http://webster.cs.ucr.edu`. Professor Hyde uses this Web site as a clearinghouse for various assembler information. Not only is a lot of information for HLA located there, it also includes links to many other assembler packages.

The linker

If you are familiar with a high-level language environment, it is possible that you have never had to directly use a **linker.** Many high-level languages such as C and C++ perform both the compile and link steps with a single command.

The process of linking objects involves resolving all defined functions and memory address labels declared in the program code. To do this, any external functions, such as the C language `printf` function, must be included with the object code (or a reference made to an external dynamic library). For this to work automatically, the linker must know where the common object code libraries are located on the computer, or the locations must be manually specified with compiler command-line parameters.

However, most assemblers do not automatically link the object code to produce the executable program file. Instead, a second manual step is required to link the assembly language object code with other libraries and produce an executable program file that can be run on the host operating system. This is the job of the linker.

When the linker is invoked manually, the developer must know which libraries are required to completely resolve any functions used by the application. The linker must be told where to find function libraries and which object code files to link together to produce the resulting file.

Every assembler package includes its own linker. You should always use the appropriate linker for the assembler package you are developing with. This helps ensure that the library files used to link functions together are compatible with each other, and that the format of the output file is correct for the target platform.

The debugger

If you are a perfect programmer, you will never need to use a debugger. However, it is more likely that somewhere in your assembly language programming future you will make a mistake—either a small typo in your 10,000-line program, or a logic mistake in your mathematical algorithm functions. When this happens, it is handy to have a good debugger available in your toolkit.

Similar to assemblers, debuggers are specific to the operating system and hardware platform for which the program was written. The debugger must know the instruction code set of the hardware platform, and understand the registers and memory handling methods of the operating system.

Most debuggers provide four basic functions to the programmer:

❏   Running the program in a controlled environment, specifying any runtime parameters required

❏   Stopping the program at any point within the program

❏   Examining data elements, such as memory locations and registers

❏   Changing elements in the program while it is running, to facilitate bug removal

The debugger runs the program within its own controlled "sandbox." The sandbox enables the program to access memory areas, registers, and I/O devices, but all under the control of the debugger. The debugger is able to control how the program accesses items and can display information about how and when the program accesses the items.

At any point during the execution of the program, the debugger is able to stop the program and indicate where in the source code the execution was stopped. To accomplish this, the debugger must know the original source code and what instruction codes were generated from which lines of source code. The debugger requires additional information to be compiled into the executable file to identify these elements. Using a specific command-line parameter when the program is compiled or assembled usually accomplishes this task.

When the program is stopped during execution, the debugger is able to display any memory area or register value associated with the program. Again, this is accomplished by running the program within the debugger's sandbox, enabling the debugger to peek inside the program as it is executing. By being able to see how individual source code statements affect the values of memory locations and registers, the programmer can often see where an error in the program occurs. This feature is invaluable to the programmer.

Finally, the debugger provides a means for the programmer to change data values within the program as it is executing. This enables the programmer to make changes to the program as it is running and see how the changes affect the outcome of the program. This is another invaluable feature, saving the time of having to change values in source code, recompiling the source code, and rerunning the executable program file.

The compiler

If all you plan to do is program in assembly language, a high-level language compiler is not necessary. However, as a professional programmer, you probably realize that creating full-blown applications using only assembly language, although possible, would be a massive undertaking.

Instead, most professional programmers attempt to write as much of the application as possible in a high-level language, such as C or C++, and concentrate on optimizing the trouble spots using assembly language programming. To do this, you must have the proper compiler for your high-level language.

The compiler's job is to convert the high-level language into instruction code for the processor to execute. Most compilers, though, produce an intermediate step. Instead of directly converting the source code to instruction code, the compiler converts the source code to assembly language code. The assembly language code is then converted to instruction code, using an assembler. Many compilers include the assembler process within the compiler, although not all do.

After converting the C or C++ source code to assembly language, the GNU compiler uses the GNU assembler to produce the instruction codes for the linker. You can stop the process between these steps and examine the assembly language code that is generated from the C or C++ source code. If you think something can be optimized, the generated assembly language code can be modified, and the code assembled into new instruction codes.

The object code disassembler

When trying to optimize a high-level language, it usually helps to see how that code is being run on the processor. To do that you need a tool to view the instruction code that is generated by the compiler from the high-level language source code. The GNU compiler enables you to view the generated assembly language code before it is assembled, but what about after the object file is already created?

A **disassembler program** takes either a full executable program or an object code file and displays the instruction codes that will be run by the processor. Some disassemblers even take the process one step further by converting the instruction codes into easily readable assembly language syntax.

After viewing the instruction codes generated by the compiler, you can determine if the compiler produced sufficiently optimized instruction codes or not. If not, you might be able to create your own instruction code functions to replace the compiler-generated functions to improve the performance of your application.

The profiler

If you are working in a C or C++ programming environment, you often need to determine which functions your program is spending most of its time performing. By finding the process-intensive functions, you can narrow down which functions are worth your time trying to optimize. Spending days optimizing a function that only takes 5 percent of the program's processing time would be a waste of your time.

To determine how much processing time each function is taking, you must have a **profiler** in your toolkit. The profiler is able to track how much processor time is spent in each function as it is used during the course of the program execution.

In order to optimize a program, once you narrow down which functions are causing the most time drain, you can use the disassembler to see what instruction codes are being generated. After analyzing the algorithms used to ensure they are optimized, it is possible that you can manually generate the instruction codes using advanced processor instructions that the compiler did not use to optimize the function.

The GNU Assembler

The GNU assembler program (called gas) is the most popular assembler for the UNIX environment. It has the ability to assemble instruction codes from several different hardware platforms, including the following:

- ❏ VAX
- ❏ AMD 29K
- ❏ Hitachi H8/300
- ❏ Intel 80960
- ❏ M680x0
- ❏ SPARC
- ❏ Intel 80x86
- ❏ Z8000
- ❏ MIPS

All of the assembly language examples in this book are written for gas. Many UNIX systems include gas in the installed operating system programs. Most Linux distributions include it by default in the development kit implementations.

This section describes how you can download and install gas, as well as how to create and assemble assembly language programs using it.

Installing the assembler

Unlike most other development packages, the GNU assembler is not distributed in a package by itself. Instead, it is bundled together with other development software in the GNU `binutils` package.

You may or may not need all of the subpackages included with the `binutils` package, but it is not a bad idea to have them installed on your system. The following table shows all of the programs installed by the current `binutils` package (version 2.15):

Package	Description
addr2line	Converts addresses into filenames and line numbers
ar	Creates, modifies, and extracts file archives
as	Assembles assembly language code into object code
c++filt	Filter to demangle C++ symbols
gprof	Program to display program profiling information
ld	Linker to convert object code files into executable files
nlmconv	Converts object code into Netware Loadable Module format
nm	Lists symbols from object files
objcopy	Copies and translates object files
objdump	Displays information from object files
ranlib	Generates an index to the contents of an archive file
readelf	Displays information from an object file in ELF format
size	Lists the section sizes of an object or archive file
strings	Displays printable strings found in object files
strip	Discards symbols
windres	Compiles Microsoft Windows resource files

Most Linux distributions that support software development already include the binutils package (especially when the distribution includes the GNU C compiler). You can check for the binutils package using your particular Linux distribution package manager. On my Mandrake Linux system, which uses RedHat Package Management (RPM) to install packages, I checked for binutils using the following command:

```
$ rpm -qa | grep binutils
libbinutils2-2.10.1.0.2-4mdk
binutils-2.10.1.0.2-4mdk
$
```

The output from the rpm query command shows that two RPM packages are installed for binutils. The first package, libbinutils2, installs the low-level libraries required by the binutils packages. The second package, binutils, installs the actual packages. The package available on this system is version 2.10.

If you have a Linux distribution based on the Debian package installer, you can query the installed packages using the dpkg command:

```
$ dpkg -1 | grep binutil
ii  binutils       2.14.90.0.7-3  The GNU assembler, linker and binary utilities
ii  binutils-doc   2.14.90.0.7-3  Documentation for the GNU assembler, linker
$
```

The output shows that the `binutils` version 2.14 package is installed on this Linux system.

*It is often recommended not to change the **binutils** package on your Linux distribution if one is already installed and being used. The **binutils** package contains many low-level library files that are used to compile operating system components. If those library files change or are moved, bad things can happen to your system, very bad things.*

If your system does not include the `binutils` package, you can download the package from the `binutils` Web site, located at `http://sources.redhat.com/binutils`. This Web page contains a link to the `binutils` download page, `ftp://ftp.gnu.org/gnu/binutils/`. From there you can download the source code for the current version of `binutils`. At the time of this writing, the current version is 2.15, and the download file is called `binutils-2.15.tar.gz`.

After the installation package is downloaded, it can be extracted into a working directory with the following command:

```
tar -zxvf binutils-2.15.tar.gz
```

This command creates a working directory called `binutils-2.15` under the current directory. To compile the `binutils` packages, change to the working directory, and use the following commands:

```
./configure
make
```

The configure command examines the host system to ensure that all of the packages and utilities required to compile the packages are available on the system. Once the software packages have been compiled, you can use the `make install` command to install the software into common areas for others to use.

Using the assembler

The GNU assembler is a command-line-oriented program. It should be run from a command-line prompt, with the appropriate command-line parameters. One oddity about the assembler is that although it is called gas, the command-line executable program is called `as`.

The command-line parameters available for `as` vary depending on what hardware platform is used for the operating system. The command-line parameters common to all hardware platforms are as follows:

```
as [-a[cdhlns][=file]] [-D] [--defsym sym=val]
   [-f] [--gstabs] [--gstabs+] [--gdwarf2] [--help]
   [-I dir] [-J] [-K] [-L]
   [--listing-lhs-width=NUM] [--listing-lhs-width2=NUM]
   [--listing-rhs-width=NUM] [--listing-cont-lines=NUM]
   [--keep-locals] [-o objfile] [-R] [--statistics] [-v]
   [-version] [--version] [-W] [--warn] [--fatal-warnings]
   [-w] [-x] [-Z] [--target-help] [target-options]
   [--|files ...]
```

These command-line parameters are explained in the following table:

Parameter	Description
-a	Specifies which listings to include in the output
-D	Included for backward compatibility, but ignored
--defsym	Define symbol and value before assembling source code
-f	Fast assemble, skips comments and white space
--gstabs	Includes debugging information for each source code line
--gstabs+	Includes special gdb debugging information
-I	Specify directories to search for include files
-J	Do not warn about signed overflows
-K	Included for backward compatibility, but ignored
-L	Keep local symbols in the symbol table
--listing-lhs-width	Set the maximum width of the output data column
--listing-lhs-width2	Set the maximum width of the output data column for continual lines
--listing-rhs-width	Set the maximum width of input source lines
--listing-cont-lines	Set the maximum number of lines printed in a listing for a single line of input
-o	Specify name of the output object file
-R	Fold the data section into the text section
--statistics	Display the maximum space and total time used by the assembly
-v	Display the version number of as
-W	Do not display warning messages
--	Use standard input for source files

An example of converting the assembly language program test.s to the object file test.o would be as follows:

```
as -o test.o test.s
```

This creates an object file test.o containing the instruction codes for the assembly language program. If anything is wrong in the program, the assembler will let you know and indicates where the problem is in the source code:

```
$ as -o test.o test.s
test.s: Assembler messages:
test.s:16: Error: no such instruction: `mpvl $4,%eax'
$
```

The preceding error message specifically points out that the error occurred in line 16 and displays the text for that line. Oops, looks like a typo in line 16.

A word about opcode syntax

One of the more confusing parts of the GNU assembler is the syntax it uses for representing assembly language code in the source code file. The original developers of gas chose to implement AT&T opcode syntax for the assembler.

The AT&T opcode syntax originated from AT&T Bell Labs, where the UNIX operating system was created. It was formed based on the opcode syntax of the more popular processor chips used to implement UNIX operating systems at the time. While many processor manufacturers used this format, unfortunately Intel chose to use a different opcode syntax.

Because of this, using gas to create assembly language programs for the Intel platform can be tricky. Most documentation for Intel assembly language programming uses the Intel syntax, while most documentation written for older UNIX systems uses AT&T syntax. This can cause confusion and extra work for the gas programmer.

Most of the differences appear in specific instruction formats, which will be covered as the instructions are discussed in the chapters. The main differences between Intel and AT&T syntax are as follows:

❑   AT&T immediate operands use a $ to denote them, whereas Intel immediate operands are undelimited. Thus, when referencing the decimal value 4 in AT&T syntax, you would use $4, and in Intel syntax you would just use 4.

❑   AT&T prefaces register names with a %, while Intel does not. Thus, referencing the EAX register in AT&T syntax, you would use %eax.

❑   AT&T syntax uses the opposite order for source and destination operands. To move the decimal value 4 to the EAX register, AT&T syntax would be movl $4, %eax, whereas for Intel it would be mov eax, 4.

❑   AT&T syntax uses a separate character at the end of mnemonics to reference the data size used in the operation, whereas in Intel syntax the size is declared as a separate operand. The AT&T instruction movl $test, %eax is equivalent to mov eax, dword ptr test in Intel syntax.

❑   Long calls and jumps use a different syntax to define the segment and offset values. AT&T syntax uses ljmp $section, $offset, whereas Intel syntax uses jmp section:offset.

While the differences can make it difficult to switch between the two formats, if you stick to one or the other you should be OK. If you learn assembly language coding using the AT&T syntax, you will be comfortable creating assembly language programs on most any UNIX system available, on most any hardware platform. If you plan on doing cross-platform work between UNIX and Microsoft Windows systems, you may want to consider using Intel syntax for your applications.

The GNU assembler does provide a method for using Intel syntax instead of AT&T syntax, but at the time of this writing it is somewhat clunky and mostly undocumented. The .intel_syntax directive in an assembly language program tells as to assemble the instruction code mnemonics using Intel syntax instead of AT&T syntax. Unfortunately, there are still numerous limitations to this method. For example, even though the source and destination orders switch to Intel syntax, you must still prefix register names with the percent sign (as in AT&T syntax). It is hoped that some future version of as will support full Intel syntax assembly code.

All of the assembly language programs presented in this book use the AT&T syntax.

The GNU Linker

The GNU linker, ld, is used to link object code files into either executable program files or library files. The ld program is also part of the GNU binutils package, so if you already have the GNU assembler installed, the linker is likely to be installed.

The format of the ld command is as follows:

```
ld [-o output] objfile...
    [-Aarchitecture] [-b input-format] [-Bstatic]
    [-Bdynamic] [-Bsymbolic] [-c commandfile] [--cref]
    [-d|-dc|-dp]
    [-defsym symbol=expression] [--demangle]
    [--no-demangle] [-e entry] [-embedded-relocs] [-E]
    [-export-dynamic] [-f name] [--auxiliary name]
    [-F name] [--filter name] [-format input-format]
    [-g] [-G size] [-h name] [-soname name] [--help]
    [-i] [-lar] [-Lsearchdir] [-M] [-Map mapfile]
    [-m emulation] [-n|-N] [-noinhibit-exec]
    [-no-keep-memory] [-no-warn-mismatch] [-Olevel]
    [-oformat output-format] [-R filename] [-relax]
    [-r|-Ur] [-rpath directory] [-rpath-link directory]
    [-S] [-s] [-shared] [-sort-common]
    [-split-by-reloc count] [-split-by-file]
    [-T commandfile]
    [--section-start sectionname=sectionorg]
    [-Ttext textorg] [-Tdata dataorg] [-Tbss bssorg]
    [-t] [-u sym] [-V] [-v] [--verbose] [--version]
    [-warn-common] [-warn-constructors]
    [-warn-multiple-gp] [-warn-once]
    [-warn-section-align] [--whole-archive]
    [--no-whole-archive] [--wrap symbol] [-X] [-x]
```

While that looks like a lot of command-line parameters, in reality you should not have to use very many of them at any one time. This just shows that the GNU linker is an extremely versatile program and has many different capabilities. The following table describes the command-line parameters that are used for the Intel platform.

Parameter	Description
-b	Specifies the format of the object code input files.
-Bstatic	Use only static libraries.
-Bdynamic	Use only dynamic libraries.
-Bsymbolic	Bind references to global symbols in shared libraries.
-c	Read commands from the specified command file.
--cref	Create a cross-reference table.
-d	Assign space to common symbols even if relocatable output is specified.
-defsym	Create the specified global symbol in the output file.
--demangle	Demangle symbol names in error messages.
-e	Use the specified symbol as the beginning execution point of the program.
-E	For ELF format files, add all symbols to the dynamic symbol table.
-f	For ELF format shared objects, set the DT_AUXILIARY name.
-F	For ELF format shared objects, set the DT_FILTER name.
-format	Specify the format of the object code input files (same as -b).
-g	Ignored. Used for compatibility with other tools.
-h	For ELF format shared objects, set the DT_SONAME name.
-i	Perform an incremental link.
-l	Add the specified archive file to the list of files to link.
-L	Add the specified path to the list of directories to search for libraries.
-M	Display a link map for diagnostic purposes.
-Map	Create the specified file to contain the link map.
-m	Emulate the specified linker.
-N	Specifies read/write text and data sections.
-n	Sets the text section to be read only.
-noinhibit-exec	Produce an output file even if non-fatal link errors appear.
-no-keep-memory	Optimize link for memory usage.
-no-warn-mismatch	Allow linking mismatched object files.

Table continued on following page

Parameter	Description
-O	Generate optimized output files.
-o	Specify the name of the output file.
-oformat	Specify the binary format of the output file.
-R	Read symbol names and addresses from the specified filename.
-r	Generates relocatable output (called partial linking).
-rpath	Add the specified directory to the runtime library search path.
-rpath-link	Specify a directory to search for runtime shared libraries.
-S	Omits debugger symbol information from the output file.
-s	Omits all symbol information from the output file.
-shared	Create a shared library.
-sort-common	Do not sort symbols by size in output file.
-split-by-reloc	Creates extra sections in the output file based on the specified size.
-split-by-file	Creates extra sections in the output file for each object file.
--section-start	Locates the specified section in the output file at the specified address.
-T	Specifies a command file (same as -c).
-Ttext	Use the specified address as the starting point for the text section.
-Tdata	Use the specified address as the starting point for the data section.
-Tbss	Use the specified address as the starting point for the bss section.
-t	Displays the names of the input files as they are being processed.
-u	Forces the specified symbol to be in the output file as an undefined symbol.
-warn-common	Warn when a common symbol is combined with another common symbol.
-warn-constructors	Warn if any global constructors are not used.
-warn-once	Warn only once for each undefined symbol.
-warn-section-align	Warn if the output section address is changed due to alignment.
--whole-archive	For the specified archive files, include all of the files in the archive.
-X	Delete all local temporary symbols.
-x	Delete all local symbols.

For the simplest case, to create an executable file from an object file generated from the assembler, you would use the following command:

```
ld -o mytest mytest.o
```

This command creates the executable file test from the object code file test.o. The executable file is created with the proper permissions so it can be run from the command line in a UNIX console. Here's an example of the process:

```
$ld -o test test.o
$ ls -al test
-rwxr-xr-x    1 rich       rich             787 Jul  6 11:53 test
$ ./test
Hello world!
$
```

The linker automatically created the executable file with UNIX 755 mode access, allowing anyone on the system to execute it but only the owner to modify it.

The GNU Compiler

The GNU Compiler Collection (gcc) is the most popular development system for UNIX systems. Not only is it the default compiler for Linux and most open-source BSD-based systems (such as FreeBSD and NetBSD), it is also popular on many commercial UNIX distributions as well.

gcc is capable of compiling many different high-level languages. At the time of this writing, gcc could compile the following high-level languages:

- ❏ C
- ❏ C++
- ❏ Objective-C
- ❏ Fortran
- ❏ Java
- ❏ Ada

Not only does gcc provide a means for compiling C and C++ applications, it also provides the libraries necessary to run C and C++ applications on the system. The following sections describe how to install gcc on your system and how to use it to compile high-level language programs.

Downloading and installing gcc

Many UNIX systems already include the C development environment, installed by default. The gcc package is required to compile C and C++ programs. For systems using RPM, you can check for gcc using the following:

```
$ rpm -qa | grep gcc
gcc-cpp-2.96-0.48mdk
gcc-2.96-0.48mdk
gcc-c++-2.96-0.48mdk
$
```

This shows that the gcc C and C++ compilers version 2.96 are installed. If your system does not have the gcc package installed, the first place to look should be your Linux distribution CDs. If a version of gcc came bundled with your Linux distribution, the easiest thing to do is to install it from there. As with the binutils package, the gcc package includes many libraries that must be compatible with the programs running on the system, or problems will occur.

If you are using a UNIX system that does not have a gcc package, you can download the gcc binaries (remember, you can't compile source code if you don't have a compiler) from the gcc Web site. The gcc home page is located at http://gcc.gnu.org.

At the time of this writing, the current version of gcc available is version 3.4.0. If the current gcc package is not available as a binary distribution for your platform, you can download an older version to get started, and then download the complete source code distribution for the latest version.

Using gcc

The GNU compiler can be invoked using several different command-line formats, depending on the source code to compile and the underlying hardware of the operating system. The generic command line format is as follows:

```
gcc [-c|-S|-E] [-std=standard]
    [-g] [-pg] [-Olevel]
    [-Wwarn...] [-pedantic]
    [-Idir...] [-Ldir...]
    [-Dmacro[=defn]...] [-Umacro]
    [-foption...] [-mmachine-option...]
    [-o outfile] infile...
```

The generic parameters are described in the following table.

Parameter	Description
-c	Compile or assemble code, but do not link
-S	Stop after compiling, but do not assemble
-E	Stop after preprocessing, but do not compile
-o	Specifies the output filename to use
-v	Display the commands used at each stage of compilation
-std	Specifies the language standard to use
-g	Produce debugging information

Parameter	Description
-pg	Produce extra code used by gprof for profiling
-O	Optimize executable code
-W	Sets compiler warning message level
-pedantic	Issue mandatory diagnostics listing in the C standard
-I	Specify directories for include files
-L	Specify directories for library files
-D	Predefine macros used in the source code
-U	Cancel any defined macros
-f	Specify options used to control the behavior of the compiler
-m	Specify hardware-dependant options

Again, many command-line parameters can be used to control the behavior of gcc. In most cases, you will only need to use a couple of parameters. If you plan on using the debugger to watch the program, the -g parameter must be used. For Linux systems, the -gstabs parameter provides additional debugging information in the program for the GNU debugger (discussed later in the "Using GDB" section).

To test the compiler, you can create a simple C language program to compile:

```
#include <stdio.h>
int main()
{
   printf("Hello, world!\n");
   exit(0);
}
```

This simple C program can be compiled and run using the following commands:

```
$ gcc -o ctest ctest.c
$ ls -al ctest
-rwxr-xr-x    1 rich     rich          13769 Jul  6 12:02 ctest*
$ ./ctest
Hello, world!
$
```

As expected, the gcc compiler creates an executable program file, called ctest, and assigns it the proper permissions to be executed (note that this format does not create the intermediate object file). When the program is run, it produces the expected output on the console.

One extremely useful command-line parameter in gcc is the -S parameter. This creates the intermediate assembly language file created by the compiler, before the assembler assembles it. Here's a sample output using the -S parameter:

```
$ gcc -S ctest.c
$ cat ctest.s
        .file   "ctest.c"
        .version        "01.01"
gcc2_compiled.:
                .section        .rodata
.LC0:
        .string "Hello, world!\n"
.text
        .align 16
.globl main
        .type   main,@function
main:
        pushl   %ebp
        movl    %esp, %ebp
        subl    $8, %esp
        subl    $12, %esp
        pushl   $.LC0
        call    printf
        addl    $16, %esp
        subl    $12, %esp
        pushl   $0
        call    exit
.Lfe1:
        .size   main,.Lfe1-main
        .ident  "GCC: (GNU) 2.96 20000731 (Linux-Mandrake 8.0 2.96-0.48mdk)"
$
```

The ctest.s file shows how the compiler created the assembly language instructions to implement the C source code program. This is useful when trying to optimize C applications to determine how the compiler is implementing various C language functions in instruction code. You may also notice that the generated assembly language program uses two C functions—printf and exit. In Chapter 4, "A Sample Assembly Language Program," you will see how assembly language programs can easily use the C library functions already installed on your system.

The GNU Debugger Program

Many professional programmers use the GNU debugger program (gdb) to debug and troubleshoot C and C++ applications. What you may not know is that it can also be used to debug assembly language programs as well. This section describes the gdb package, including how to download, install, and use its basic features. It is used throughout the book as the debugger tool for assembly language applications.

Downloading and installing gdb

The gdb package is often a standard part of Linux and BSD development systems. You can use the appropriate package manager to determine whether it is installed on your system:

```
$ rpm -qa | grep gdb
libgdbm1-1.8.0-14mdk
libgdbm1-devel-1.8.0-14mdk
gdb-5.0-11mdk
$
```

This Mandrake Linux system has version 5.0 of the gdb package installed, along with two library packages used by gdb.

If your system does not have gdb installed, you can download it from its Web site at www.gnu.org/software/gdb/gdb.html. At the time of this writing, the current version of gdb is 6.1.1 and is available for download from ftp://sources.redhat.com/pub/gdb/releases in file gdb-6.1.tar.gz.

After downloading the distribution file, it can be unpacked into a working directory using the following command:

```
tar -zxvf gdb-6.1.tar.gz
```

This creates the directory gdb-6.1, with all of the source code files. To compile the package, go to the working directory, and use the following commands:

```
./configure
make
```

This compiles the source code files into the necessary library files and the gdb executable file. These can be installed using the command **make install**.

Using gdb

The GNU debugger command-line program is called gdb. It can be run with several different parameters to modify its behavior. The command-line format for gdb is as follows:

```
gdb [-nx] [-q] [-batch] [-cd=dir] [-f] [-b bps] [-tty=dev]
    [-s symfile] [-e prog] [-se prog] [-c core] [-x cmds] [-d dir]
    [prog[core|procID]]
```

The command-line parameters are described in the following table.

Parameter	Description
-b	Set the line speed of the serial interface for remote debugging
-batch	Run in batch mode
-c	Specify the core dump file to analyze
-cd	Specify the working directory
-d	Specify a directory to search for source files

Table continued on following page

Parameter	Description
-e	Specify the file to execute
-f	Output filename and line numbers in standard format when debugging
-nx	Do not execute commands from .gdbinit file
-q	Quiet mode — don't print introduction
-s	Specify the filename for symbols
-se	Specify the filename for both symbols and to execute
-tty	Set device for standard input and output
-x	Execute gdb commands from the specified file

To use the debugger, the executable file must have been compiled or assembled with the -gstabs option, which includes the necessary information in the executable file for the debugger to know where in the source code file the instruction codes relate. Once gdb starts, it uses a command-line interface to accept debugging commands:

```
$ gcc -gstabs -o ctest ctest.c
$ gdb ctest
GNU gdb 5.0mdk-11mdk Linux-Mandrake 8.0
Copyright 2001 Free Software Foundation, Inc.
GDB is free software, covered by the GNU General Public License, and you are
welcome to change it and/or distribute copies of it under certain conditions.
Type "show copying" to see the conditions.
There is absolutely no warranty for GDB.  Type "show warranty" for details.
This GDB was configured as "i386-mandrake-linux"...
(gdb)
```

At the gdb command prompt, you can enter debugging commands. A huge list of commands can be used. Some of the more useful ones are described in the following table.

Command	Description
break	Set a breakpoint in the source code to stop execution
watch	Set a watchpoint to stop execution when a variable reaches a specific value
info	Observe system elements, such as registers, the stack, and memory
x	Examine memory location
print	Display variable values

Command	Description
run	Start execution of the program within the debugger
list	List specified functions or lines
next	Step to the next instruction in the program
step	Step to the next instruction in the program
cont	Continue executing the program from the stopped point
until	Run the program until it reaches the specified source code line (or greater)

Here's a short example of a gdb session:

```
(gdb) list
1        #include <stdio.h>
2
3        int main()
4        {
5                printf("Hello, world!\n");
6                exit(0);
7        }
(gdb) break main
Breakpoint 1 at 0x8048496: file ctest.c, line 5.
(gdb) run
Starting program: /home/rich/palp/ctest

Breakpoint 1, main () at ctest.c:5
5                printf("Hello, world!\n");
(gdb) next
Hello, world!
6                exit(0);
(gdb) next

Program exited normally.
(gdb)quit
$
```

First, the list command is used to show the source code line numbers. Next, a breakpoint is created at the main label using the break command, and the program is started with the run command. Because the breakpoint was set to main, the program immediately stops running before the first source code statement after main. The next command is used to step to the next line of source code, which executes the printf statement. Another next command is used to execute the exit statement, which terminates the application. Although the application terminated, you are still in the debugger, and can choose to run the program again.

The KDE Debugger

The GNU debugger is an extremely versatile tool, but its user interface leaves quite a bit to be desired. Often, trying to debug large applications with gdb can be difficult. To fix this, several different graphical front-end programs have been created for gdb. One of the more popular ones is the KDE debugger (kdbg), created by Johannes Sixt.

The kdbg package uses the K Desktop Environment (KDE) platform, an X-windows graphical environment used mainly on open-source UNIX systems such as Linux, but also available on other UNIX platforms. It was developed using the Qt graphical libraries, so the Qt runtime libraries must also be installed on the system.

Downloading and installing kdbg

Many Linux distributions include the kdbg package as an extra package that is not installed by default. You can check the distribution package manager on your Linux system to see if it is already installed, or if it can be installed from the Linux distribution disks. On my Mandrake system, it is included in the supplemental programs disk:

```
$ ls kdbg*
kdbg-1.2.0-0.6mdk.i586.rpm
$
```

If the package is not included with your Linux system, you can download the source code for the kdbg package from the kdbg Web site, http://members.nextra.at/johsixt/kdbg.html. At the time of this writing, the current stable release of kdbg is version 1.2.10. The current beta release is 1.9.5.

*The **kdbg** source code installation requires that the KDE development header files be available. These are usually included in the KDE development package with the Linux distribution and may already be installed.*

Using kdbg

After installing kdbg, you can use it by opening a command prompt window from the KDE desktop and typing the **kdbg** command. After kdbg starts, you must select both the executable file to debug, as well as the original source code file using either the File menu items or the toolbar icons.

Once the executable and source code files are loaded, you can begin the debugging session. Because kdbg is a graphical interface for gdb, the same commands are available, but in a graphical form. You can set breakpoints within the application by highlighting the appropriate line of source code and clicking the stop sign icon on the toolbar (see Figure 3-1).

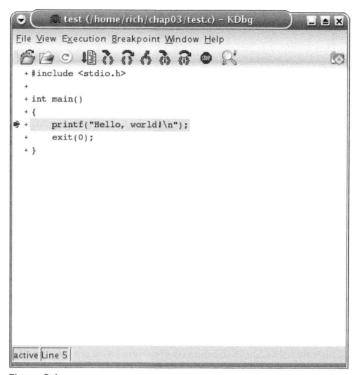

Figure 3-1

If you want to watch memory or register values during the execution of the program, you can select them by clicking the View menu item, and selecting which windows you want to view. You can also open an output window to view the program output as it executes. Figure 3-2 shows an example of the Registers window.

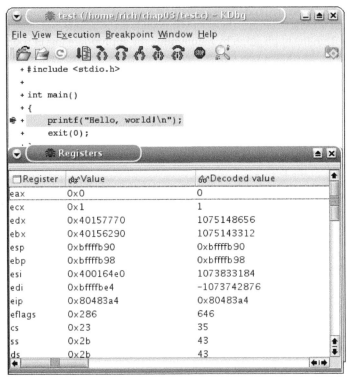

Figure 3-2

After the program files are loaded, and the desired view windows are set, you can start the program execution by clicking the run icon button. Just as in gdb, the program will execute until it reaches the first breakpoint. When it reaches the breakpoint, you can step through the program using the step icon button until the program finishes.

The GNU Objdump Program

The GNU objdump program is another utility found in the binutils package that can be of great use to programmers. Often it is necessary to view the instruction codes generated by the compiler in the object code files. The objdump program will display not only the assembly language code, but the raw instruction codes generated as well.

This section describes the objdump program, and how you can use it to view the underlying instruction codes contained within a high-level language program.

Using objdump

The objdump command-line parameters specify what functions the program will perform on the object code files, and how it will display the information it retrieves. The command-line format of objdump is as follows:

```
objdump [-a|--archive-headers] [-b bfdname|--target=bfdname]
        [-C|--demangle[=style] ] [-d|--disassemble]
        [-D|--disassemble-all] [-z|--disassemble-zeroes]
        [-EB|-EL|--endian={big | little }] [-f|--file-headers]
        [--file-start-context] [-g|--debugging]
        [-e|--debugging-tags] [-h|--section-headers|--headers]
        [-i|--info] [-j section|--section=section]
        [-l|--line-numbers] [-S|--source]
        [-m machine|--architecture=machine]
        [-M options|--disassembler-options=options]
        [-p|--private-headers] [-r|--reloc]
        [-R|--dynamic-reloc] [-s|--full-contents]
        [-G|--stabs] [-t|--syms] [-T|--dynamic-syms]
        [-x|--all-headers] [-w|--wide]
        [--start-address=address] [--stop-address=address]
        [--prefix-addresses] [--[no-]show-raw-insn]
        [--adjust-vma=offset] [-V|--version] [-H|--help]
        objfile...
```

The command-line parameters are described in the following table.

Parameter	Description
-a	If any files are archives, display the archive header information
-b	Specify the object code format of the object code files
-C	Demangle low-level symbols into user-level names
-d	Disassemble the object code into instruction code
-D	Disassemble all sections into instruction code, including data
-EB	Specify big-endian object files
-EL	Specify little-endian object files
-f	Display summary information from the header of each file
-G	Display the contents of the debug sections
-h	Display summary information from the section headers of each file
-i	Display lists showing all architectures and object formats
-j	Display information only for the specified section

Parameter	Description
-l	Label the output with source code line numbers
-m	Specify the architecture to use when disassembling
-p	Display information specific to the object file format
-r	Display the relocation entries in the file
-R	Display the dynamic relocation entries in the file
-s	Display the full contents of the specified sections
-S	Display source code intermixes with disassembled code
-t	Display the symbol table entries of the files
-T	Display the dynamic symbol table entries of the files
-x	Display all available header information of the files
--start-address	Start displaying data at the specified address
--stop-address	Stop displaying data at the specified address

The objdump program is an extremely versatile tool to have available. It can decode many different types of binary files besides just object code files. For the assembly language programmer, the -d parameter is the most interesting, as it displays the disassembled object code file.

An objdump example

Using the sample C program, you can create an object file to dump by compiling the program with the -c option:

```
$ gcc -c ctest.c
$ objdump -d ctest.o

ctest.o:     file format elf32-i386

Disassembly of section .text:

00000000 <main>:
   0:   55                      push   %ebp
   1:   89 e5                   mov    %esp,%ebp
   3:   83 ec 08                sub    $0x8,%esp
   6:   83 ec 0c                sub    $0xc,%esp
   9:   68 00 00 00 00          push   $0x0
   e:   e8 fc ff ff ff          call   f <main+0xf>
  13:   83 c4 10                add    $0x10,%esp
  16:   83 ec 0c                sub    $0xc,%esp
  19:   6a 00                   push   $0x0
  1b:   e8 fc ff ff ff          call   1c <main+0x1c>
$
```

The disassembled object code file created by your system may differ from this example depending on the specific compiler and compiler version used. This example shows both the assembly language mnemonics created by the compiler and the corresponding instruction codes. You may notice, however, that the memory addresses referenced in the program are zeroed out. These values will not be determined until the linker links the application and prepares it for execution on the system. In this step of the process, however, you can easily see what instructions are used to perform the functions.

The GNU Profiler Program

The GNU profiler (gprof) is another program included in the binutils package. This program is used to analyze program execution and determine where "hot spots" are in the application.

The application hot spots are functions that require the most amount of processing time as the program runs. Often, they are the most mathematically intensive functions, but that is not always the case. Functions that are I/O intensive can also increase processing time.

This section describes the GNU profiler, and provides a simple demonstration that illustrates how it is used in a C program to view how much time different functions consume in an application.

Using the profiler

As with all the other tools, gprof is a command-line program that uses multiple parameters to control its behavior. The command-line format for gprof is as follows:

```
gprof [ -[abcDhilLsTvwxyz] ] [ -[ACeEfFJnNOpPqQZ][name] ]
      [ -I dirs ] [ -d[num] ] [ -k from/to ]
      [ -m min-count ] [ -t table-length ]
      [ --[no-]annotated-source[=name] ]
      [ --[no-]exec-counts[=name] ]
      [ --[no-]flat-profile[=name] ] [ --[no-]graph[=name] ]
      [ --[no-]time=name] [ --all-lines ] [ --brief ]
      [ --debug[=level] ] [ --function-ordering ]
      [ --file-ordering ] [ --directory-path=dirs ]
      [ --display-unused-functions ] [ --file-format=name ]
      [ --file-info ] [ --help ] [ --line ] [ --min-count=n ]
      [ --no-static ] [ --print-path ] [ --separate-files ]
      [ --static-call-graph ] [ --sum ] [ --table-length=len ]
      [ --traditional ] [ --version ] [ --width=n ]
      [ --ignore-non-functions ] [ --demangle[=STYLE] ]
      [ --no-demangle ] [ image-file ] [ profile-file ... ]
```

This alphabet soup of parameters is split into three groups:

❑   Output format parameters

❑   Analysis parameters

❑   Miscellaneous parameters

The output format options, described in the following table, enable you to modify the output produced by gprof.

Parameter	Description
-A	Display source code for all functions, or just the functions specified
-b	Don't display verbose output explaining the analysis fields
-C	Display a total tally of all functions, or only the functions specified
-i	Display summary information about the profile data file
-I	Specifies a list of search directories to find source files
-J	Do not display annotated source code
-L	Display full pathnames of source filenames
-p	Display a flat profile for all functions, or only the functions specified
-P	Do not print a flat profile for all functions, or only the functions specified
-q	Display the call graph analysis
-Q	Do not display the call graph analysis
-y	Generate annotated source code in separate output files
-Z	Do not display a total tally of functions and number of times called
--function-reordering	Display suggested reordering of functions based on analysis
--file-ordering	Display suggested object file reordering based on analysis
-T	Display output in traditional BSD style
-w	Set the width of output lines
-x	Every line in annotated source code is displayed within a function
--demangle	C++ symbols are demangled when displaying output

The analysis parameters, described in the following table, modify the way gprof analyzes the data contained in the analysis file.

Parameter	Description
-a	Does not analyze information about statically declared (private) functions
-c	Analyze information on child functions that were never called in the program

Parameter	Description
-D	Ignore symbols that are not known to be functions (only on Solaris and HP OSs)
-k	Don't analyze functions matching a beginning and ending symspec
-l	Analyze the program by line instead of function
-m	Analyze only functions called more than a specified number of times
-n	Analyze only times for specified functions
-N	Don't analyze times for the specified functions
-z	Analyze all functions, even those that were never called

Finally, the miscellaneous parameters, described in the following table, are parameters that modify the behavior of gprof, but don't fit into either the output or analysis groups.

Parameter	Description
-d	Put gprof in debug mode, specifying a numerical debug level
-O	Specify the format of the profile data file
-s	Force gprof to just summarize the data in the profile data file
-v	Print the version of gprof

In order to use gprof on an application, you must ensure that the functions you want to monitor are compiled using the -pg parameter. This parameter compiles the source code, inserting a call to the mcount subroutine for each function in the program. When the application is run, the mcount subroutine creates a call graph profile file, called gmon.out, which contains timing information for each function in the application.

> *Be careful when running the application, as each run will overwrite the **gmon.out** file. If you want to take multiple samples, you must include the name of the output file on the **gprof** command line and use different filenames for each sample.*

After the program to test finishes, the gprof program is used to examine the call graph profile file to analyze the time spent in each function. The gprof output contains three reports:

❑ A flat profile report, which lists total execution times and call counts for all functions

❑ A listing of functions sorted by the time spent in each function and its children

❑ A listing of cycles, showing the members of the cycles and their call counts

By default, the gprof output is directed to the standard output of the console. You must redirect it to a file if you want to save it.

A profile example

To demonstrate the gprof program, you must have a high-level language program that uses functions to perform actions. I created the following simple demonstration program in C, called demo.c, to demonstrate the basics of gprof:

```
#include <stdio.h>

void function1()
{
        int i, j;
        for(i=0; i <100000; i++)
                j += i;
}
void function2()
{
        int i, j;
        function1();
        for(i=0; i < 200000; i++)
                j = i;
}

int main()
{
        int i, j;
        for (i = 0; i <100; i++)
                function1();

        for(i = 0; i<50000; i++)
                function2();
        return 0;
}
```

This is about as simple as it gets. The main program has two loops: one that calls function1() 100 times, and one that calls function2() 50,000 times. Each of the functions just performs simple loops, although function2() also calls function1() every time it is called.

The next step is to compile the program using the -pg parameter for gprof. After that the program can be run:

```
$ gcc -o demo demo.c -pg
$ ./demo
$
```

When the program finishes, the gmon.out call graph profile file is created in the same directory. You can then run the gprof program against the demo program, and save the output to a file:

```
$ ls -al gmon.out
-rw-r--r--    1 rich     rich           426 Jul  7 12:39 gmon.out
$ gprof demo > gprof.txt
$
```

Notice that the gmon.out file was not referenced in the command line, just the name of the executable program. gprof automatically uses the gmon.out file located in the same directory. This example redirected the gprof output to a file named gprof.txt. The resulting file contains the complete gprof report for the program. Here's what the flat profile section looked like on my system:

```
  %   cumulative   self              self     total
 time   seconds    seconds    calls  us/call  us/call  name
 67.17   168.81    168.81     50000  3376.20  5023.11  function2
 32.83   251.32     82.51     50100  1646.91  1646.91  function1
```

This report shows the total processor time and times called for each individual function that was called by main. As expected, function2 took the majority of the processing time.

The next report is the call graph, which shows the breakdown of time by individual functions, and how the functions were called:

```
index % time    self  children    called     name
                                               <spontaneous>
[1]    100.0    0.00   251.32                 main [1]
                168.81  82.35   50000/50000       function2 [2]
                  0.16   0.00     100/50100       function1 [3]
-----------------------------------------------
                168.81  82.35   50000/50000       main [1]
[2]     99.9  168.81  82.35   50000         function2 [2]
                 82.35   0.00   50000/50100       function1 [3]
-----------------------------------------------
                  0.16   0.00     100/50100       main [1]
                 82.35   0.00   50000/50100       function2 [2]
[3]     32.8   82.51   0.00   50100         function1 [3]
-----------------------------------------------
```

Each section of the call graph shows the function analyzed (the one on the line with the index number), the functions that called it, and its child functions. This output is used to track the flow of time throughout the program.

A Complete Assembly Development System

Now that you know all the pieces needed for an assembly language development environment, it's time to put them all together. One of the best environments for using GNU utilities is the Linux operating system. Many freely available Linux distributions contain all of the GNU utilities presented in this chapter already installed. This section describes some of the basics of the Linux system, along with the GNU utilities necessary for creating an assembly language development environment.

The basics of Linux

If you are new to the Linux environment, you may need some background information before trying out a Linux distribution. When people talk about the Linux operating system, they are really talking about an entire suite of programs, not all of them necessarily related to Linux. The key to building a Linux system is understanding the components that comprise the system, and knowing where and how to get them.

Linus Torvalds is credited with creating and guiding the development of the Linux operating system kernel. The operating system kernel is the software that interacts with the hardware and handles the low-level functions of an operating system, such as file access control, and handling memory and hardware interfaces. Just loading a Linux kernel on a computer would be a pretty boring experience. You need additional programs to interact with the devices to really do anything.

This is where the GNU project comes in. The GNU project has developed many applications over the years that help system administrators and programmers with any UNIX-type operating system, with Linux being one of the more popular.

When you download a Linux distribution, what you are downloading is the Linux kernel, bundled with a set of utilities to perform the desired functions for the type of system you want to build. Most of the standard UNIX functions have been implemented by the GNU project. Depending on what you want your particular Linux system do to, you may or may not want to install all of the available GNU programs.

After you build your base Linux system, you will want to create your specific development environment. When you decide which tools you want to include on your system, first check to see if they are available on the distribution disks included with the Linux distribution. This is by far the easiest way to install packages, especially if you are using a distribution that includes an automated package manager, such as Red Hat `rpm` or Debian `dpkg`.

If you do not (or cannot) install a complete Linux system, the next best thing is to use a bootable CD distribution. With a bootable CD distribution, the entire Linux system is stored on a bootable CD. To run Linux, just place the CD in your computer and reboot. The Linux system will load in memory, and create a virtual disk in memory. The operating system on the hard drive is never touched. When you are finished, just take the CD out and reboot from the hard drive. Most bootable Linux CD distributions do an excellent job of auto-detecting workstation hardware, such as network cards, sound cards, and various graphics cards.

One of my favorite bootable Linux CD distributions for development is MEPIS Linux. The MEPIS Linux distribution is based on the Debian Linux, but comes as a bootable CD that can also be easily installed on your hard drive if you choose to do so. It is one of the easiest ways to install Linux on an existing workstation system.

Another reason MEPIS is one of my favorites is that, at the time of this writing, the MEPIS bootable CD contains a complete development environment, including `gas`, `ld`, `gcc`, `gdb`, `gprof`, and even `kdbg`. By just booting from the MEPIS CD, you have an automatic Linux assembly language development system!

The following sections describe how to download and use the MEPIS Linux distribution.

Downloading and running MEPIS

The MEPIS Web site is located at `www.mepis.org`. From that page, you can purchase a CD, buy a premium download subscription, or go to a free download mirror site. At the time of this writing, the current full release version of MEPIS is 2003-10, patch 2, and the current beta version is 2004-b05.

*At the time of this writing, there is also a separate version of MEPIS called Simply-MEPIS. This version includes the compiler, assembler, and linker software but does not include the **gdb** debugger. This must be downloaded and installed separately.*

The full version MEPIS CD is downloaded as two separate `.iso` format files:

❑   `mepis-2003-10.02.cd1.iso` contains the main MEPIS software.

❑   `mepis-2003-10.02.cd2.iso` contains additional packages in Debian package format.

If you plan on downloading the distribution files, you might want to find a high-speed Internet connection, as the file is 694MB in size. After downloading the `.iso` files, you must have a workstation with a CD burner, and software that allows burning CDs from `.iso` files. After burning the `.iso` files to CDs, you are ready to start MEPIS Linux.

The first `.iso` file contains the complete operating system that can be run from the CD. First ensure that your workstation allows booting from CDs (an option that is set in the system BIOS). When you boot from the MEPIS Linux CD, a boot screen appears, asking for any special boot parameters. In most cases, you can simply press Enter to continue the boot process. If you have a video card that is not supported by MEPIS, you can enter boot prompt parameters. See the MEPIS Web site for specific details.

After the system boots, the KDE desktop login screen appears, with two preconfigured user IDs, `demo` and `root`. You can log in as either account, but it is safest to use the demo account. The password for `demo` is **demo**, and the password for `root` is **root**.

Your new development system

When you log into the MEPIS system, you will see the KDE desktop environment displayed. This is similar to a Microsoft Windows desktop environment, with desktop icons, a taskbar, and a Start button (although it is not called Start on the KDE desktop). You can open a command prompt session by clicking the shell icon on the taskbar. You can also open an editor session using any one of several different editors from the Editors menu item.

When creating the program file, be careful to save the file as plain text. MEPIS includes some fancy word processing editors, such as OpenOffice Writer, which can save documents in a special binary format. The GNU assembler is not able to read these formats.

After creating your assembly language program text file, you can use the `as` and `ld` commands from a command prompt session to assemble and link the program. If you are creating high-level language programs, MEPIS also includes the `gcc` compiler for C and C++ applications.

When it is time for debugging, MEPIS includes the `gdb` and `kdbg` programs. The `gdb` program can be accessed from a command prompt session, while the `kdbg` program is available on the menu under the Development section.

The only drawback to running a development system from a bootable CD is when it is time to save your work. By default, the system uses RAM memory as a virtual disk. Any program stored under the default file system is only stored in memory. The next time you boot from the CD, the files will be gone.

To solve this problem, you should have some type of media available that MEPIS can access. Unfortunately, at the time of this writing, MEPIS is unable to write data to hard drives using the NTFS format (commonly used in Windows 2000 and XP workstations). If you have a hard drive formatted using the FAT32 format, MEPIS will be able to write to there. Also, MEPIS can write files to a floppy disk, and to most USB flash drives. As a last resort, if your workstation is on a local area network (LAN), you can always copy the files over by either using the FTP protocol or mounting a Windows shared drive to the system. My favorite method is to use a Windows share on a separate computer. It's just as simple as mapping in the Windows world.

Summary

Every programmer needs a development environment in which to create application programs. Unfortunately, assembly language programmers must often create their own development environment. There are many different pieces to bring together to create the perfect development environment.

At a minimum, you will need a text editor, an assembler package, and a linker package (usually the assembler and linker packages come bundled together). The assembler is used to convert the assembly language code into instruction code for the specific processor used to run the application. The linker is then used to convert the raw instruction code into an executable program by combining any necessary libraries, and resolving any memory references necessary for memory storage.

Besides the assembler and linker, it is often useful to have a debugger and an object code disassembler available. The debugger enables you to step through your program, watching how each instruction modifies registers and memory locations. The disassembler enables you to view the instruction codes in an object code file generated by either an assembly language program or a high-level language program.

If you plan on using high-level languages with your assembly code, you will also need a compiler to build the executable code from the high-level language source code. Many compilers also have the capability to show the instruction codes that are generated from the source code, enabling you to see what is really happening from the source code instructions. This is where assembly language programming can really come in handy. By examining the generated instruction codes, you can sometimes determine that there is a better way to implement a function than the way the compiler did, and then do it yourself.

Another final tool that is useful for programmers is a profiler. The profiler is used to analyze the performance of an application. By examining which functions consume the most processing time, you can determine which ones are worth trying to optimize to increase the performance of the application.

Although many versions of these tools are available, this book uses the tools developed by the GNU project. These tools are all freely available and run on most any UNIX system. Most of the core tools are available in the GNU `binutils` package. The assembler, `as`, the linker, `ld`, the object code disassembler, `objdump`, and the profiler, `gprof`, are all contained in the `binutils` package. The GNU debugger is called `gdb`, and the GNU compiler is called `gcc`.

Now that your development environment is complete, it's time to start doing some assembly language programming. The next chapter describes how to use the tools to create a sample assembly language program.

A Sample Assembly Language Program

With all of your development tools in order, it's time to start learning about assembly language programming. Assembly language programs use a common template and format (specific to the assembler used), which you can develop and use for all of your applications.

This chapter walks you through a basic assembly language program template for the GNU assembler. The first section of the chapter describes the common items found in assembly language programs, and how they can be used to define a common template. The next section shows a sample program, and how to assemble and run it. Next you will learn how to debug the sample program using the GNU debugger. The last section of this chapter demonstrates how to incorporate C library functions into your assembly language programs.

The Parts of a Program

As shown in Chapter 1, "What Is Assembly Language?," the assembly language program consists of defined sections, each of which has a different purpose. The three most commonly used sections are as follows:

- ❑ The data section
- ❑ The bss section
- ❑ The text section

The text section is required in all assembly language programs. It is where the instruction codes are declared within the executable program. The data and bss sections are optional, but often used within a program. The data section declares data elements that are declared with an initial value. These data elements are used as variables within the assembly language program. The bss section declares data elements that are instantiated with a zero (or null) value. These data elements are most often used as buffer areas within the assembly language program.

The following sections describe how to declare the different sections in an assembly language program written for the GNU assembler, which is the assembler used throughout this book.

Defining sections

The GNU assembler declares sections using the .section declarative statement. The .section statement takes a single argument, the type of section it is declaring. Figure 4-1 shows the layout of an assembly language program.

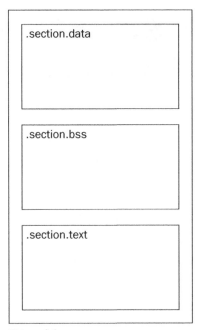

Figure 4-1

Figure 4-1 demonstrates the normal way the sections are placed in the program. The bss section should always be placed before the text section, but the data section can be moved to follow the text section, although that is not the standard. Besides being functional, your assembly language programs should also be easily readable. Keeping all of the data definitions together at the beginning of the source code makes it easier for other programmers to pick up your work and understand it.

Defining the starting point

When the assembly language program is converted to an executable file, the linker must know what the starting point is in your instruction code. For simple programs with only a single instruction path, finding the starting point is not usually a problem. However, in more complex programs that use several functions scattered throughout the source code, finding where the program starts can be an issue.

To solve this problem, the GNU assembler declares a default label, or identifier, that should be used for the entry point of the application. The _start label is used to indicate the instruction from which the program should start running. If the linker cannot find this label, it will produce an error message:

```
$ ld -o badtest badtest.o
ld: warning: cannot find entry symbol _start; defaulting to 08048074
$
```

As you can see from the linker output, if the linker cannot find the _start label, it will attempt to find the starting point of the program, but for complex programs there is no guarantee that it will guess correctly.

> *You can use a different label besides **_start** as the starting point. You can use the -e parameter of the linker to define what the new starting point is called.*

Besides declaring the starting label in the application, you also need to make the entry point available for external applications. This is done with the .globl directive.

The .globl directive declares program labels that are accessible from external programs. If you are writing a bunch of utilities that are being used by external assembly or C language programs, each function section label should be declared with a .globl directive.

Armed with this information, you can create a basic template for all your assembly language programs. The template should look something like this:

```
.section.data

        <  initialized data here>

.section .bss

        < uninitialized data here>

.section .text
.globl _start
_start:

    <instruction code goes here>
```

With this template in hand, you are ready to start coding assembly language programs. The next section walks through a simple application that shows how to build an application from the assembly language program source code.

Creating a Simple Program

Now it is time to create a simple assembly language application to demonstrate how all of the pieces fit together. To start off, a simple application that centers on a single instruction code is created. The CPUID instruction code is used to gather information about the processor on which the program is running. You can extract vendor and model information from the processor and display it for your customers to see.

The following sections describe the CPUID instruction and show how to implement an assembly language program to utilize it.

The CPUID instruction

The CPUID instruction is one assembly language instruction that is not easily performed from a high-level language application. It is a low-level instruction that queries the processor for specific information, and returns the information in specific registers.

The CPUID instruction uses a single register value as input. The EAX register is used to determine what information is produced by the CPUID instruction. Depending on the value of the EAX register, the CPUID instruction will produce different information about the processor in the EBX, ECX, and EDX registers. The information is returned as a series of bit values and flags, which must be interpreted to their proper meaning.

The following table shows the different output options available for the CPUID instruction.

EAX Value	CPUID Output
0	Vendor ID string, and the maximum CPUID option value supported
1	Processor type, family, model, and stepping information
2	Processor cache configuration
3	Processor serial number
4	Cache configuration (number of threads, number of cores, and physical properties)
5	Monitor information
80000000h	Extended vendor ID string and supported levels
80000001h	Extended processor type, family, model, and stepping information
80000002h - 80000004h	Extended processor name string

The sample program created in this chapter utilizes the zero option to retrieve the simple Vendor ID string from the processor. When the value of zero is placed in the EAX register, and the CPUID instruction is executed, the processor returns the Vendor ID string in the EBX, EDX , and ECX registers as follows:

❑   EBX contains the low 4 bytes of the string.

❑   EDX contains the middle 4 bytes of the string.

❑   ECX contains the last 4 bytes of the string.

The string values are placed in the registers in little-endian format; thus, the first part of the string is placed in the lower bits of the register. Figure 4-2 shows how this works.

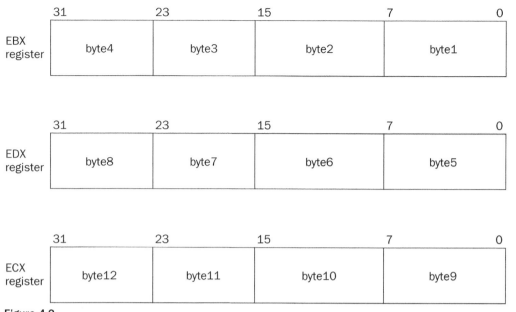

Figure 4-2

The sample program takes the register values and displays the information to the customer in a human-readable format. The next section presents the sample program.

*Not all processors in the IA-32 platform utilize the **CPUID** instruction the same way. In a real application, you should perform a few tests to ensure that the processor supports the **CPUID** instruction. To keep things simple, the example program presented in this chapter does not perform any of these tests. It's possible that you may be using a processor that does not support the **CPUID** instruction, although most modern processors do support it (including Intel Pentium processors, Cyrix processors, and AMD processors).*

The sample program

Armed with your knowledge about how the CPUID instruction works, it's time to start writing a simple program to utilize that information. This program is a simple application to check the Vendor ID string that is produced by the CPUID instruction. Here's the sample program, cpuid.s:

```
#cpuid.s Sample program to extract the processor Vendor ID
.section .data
output:
    .ascii "The processor Vendor ID is 'xxxxxxxxxxxx'\n"
.section .text
.globl _start
_start:
    movl $0, %eax
    cpuid
```

```
movl $output, %edi
movl %ebx, 28(%edi)
movl %edx, 32(%edi)
movl %ecx, 36(%edi)
movl $4, %eax
movl $1, %ebx
movl $output, %ecx
movl $42, %edx
int $0x80
movl $1, %eax
movl $0, %ebx
int $0x80
```

This program uses quite a few different assembly language instructions. For now, don't worry too much about what they are; that will be described in detail in subsequent chapters. For now, concentrate on how the instructions are placed in the program, the flow of how they operate, and how the source code file is converted into an executable program file. So that you're not totally lost, here's a brief explanation of what's going on in the source code.

First, in the data section, a string value is declared:

```
output:
    .ascii "The processor Vendor ID is 'xxxxxxxxxxxx'\n"
```

The .ascii declarative is used to declare a text string using ASCII characters. The string elements are predefined and placed in memory, with the starting memory location denoted by the label output. The x's are used as placeholders in the memory area reserved for the data variable. When the vendor ID string is extracted from the processor, it will be placed in the data at those memory locations.

You should recognize the next section of the program from the template. It declares the instruction code section, and the normal starting label of the application:

```
.section .text
.globl _start
_start:
```

The first thing the program does is load the EAX register with a value of zero, and then run the CPUID instruction:

```
movl $0, %eax
cpuid
```

The zero value in EAX defines the CPUID output option (the Vendor ID string in this case). After the CPUID instruction is run, you must collect the response that is divided up between the three output registers:

```
movl $output, %edi
movl %ebx, 28(%edi)
movl %edx, 32(%edi)
movl %ecx, 36(%edi)
```

The first instruction creates a pointer to use when working with the output variable declared in memory. The memory location of the output label is loaded into the EDI register. Next, the contents of the three registers containing the Vendor ID string pieces are placed in the appropriate locations in the data memory, based on the EDI pointer. The numbers outside the parentheses represent the location relative to the output label where the data is placed. This number is added to the address in the EDI register to determine what address the register's value is written to. This process replaces the x's that were used as placeholders with the actual Vendor ID string pieces (note that the Vendor ID string was divided into the registers in the strange order EBX, EDX, and ECX).

When all of the Vendor ID string pieces are placed in memory, it's time to display the information:

```
movl $4, %eax
movl $1, %ebx
movl $output, %ecx
movl $42, %edx
int $0x80
```

This program uses a Linux system call (int $0x80) to access the console display from the Linux kernel. The Linux kernel provides many preset functions that can be easily accessed from assembly applications. To access these kernel functions, you must use the int instruction code, which generates a software interrupt, with a value of 0x80. The specific function that is performed is determined by the value of the EAX register. Without this kernel function, you would have to send each output character yourself to the proper I/O address of the display. The Linux system calls are a great time-saver for assembly language programmers.

The complete list of Linux system calls, and how to use them, is discussed in Chapter 12, "Using Linux System Calls."

The Linux write system call is used to write bytes to a file. Following are the parameters for the write system call:

❑   EAX contains the system call value.

❑   EBX contains the file descriptor to write to.

❑   ECX contains the start of the string.

❑   EDX contains the length of the string.

If you are familiar with UNIX, you know that just about everything is handled as a file. The standard output (STDOUT) represents the display terminal of the current session, and has a file descriptor of 1. Writing to this file descriptor displays the information on the console screen.

The bytes to display are defined as a memory location to read the information from, and the number of bytes to display. The ECX register is loaded with the memory location of the output label, which defines the start of the string. Because the size of the output string is always the same, we can hard-code the size value in the EDX register.

After the Vendor ID information is displayed, it's time to cleanly exit the program. Again, a Linux system call can help. By using system call 1 (the exit function), the program is properly terminated, and returns to the command prompt. The EBX register contains the exit code value returned by the program to the shell. This can be used to produce different results in a shell script program, depending on situations within the assembly language program. A value of zero indicates the program executed successfully.

Building the executable

With the assembly language source code program saved as `cpuid.s`, you can build the executable program using the GNU assembler and GNU linker as follows:

```
$ as -o cpuid.o cpuid.s
$ ld -o cpuid cpuid.o
$
```

The output from these commands is not too exciting (unless of course you had some typos in your code). The first step uses the `as` command to assemble the assembly language source code into the object code file `cpuid.o`. The second step uses `ld` to link that object code file into the executable file `cpuid`.

If you did have a typo in the source code, the assembler will indicate the line in which the typo is located:

```
$ as -o cpuid.o cpuid.s
cpuid.s: Assembler messages:
cpuid.s:15: Error: no such instruction: `mavl %edx,32(%edi)'
$
```

Running the executable

After the linker generates the executable program file, it is ready to be run. Here's a sample output from my MEPIS system running on a Pentium 4 processor:

```
$ ./cpuid
The processor Vendor ID is 'GenuineIntel'
$
```

Excellent! The program ran as expected! One of the benefits of Linux is that some distributions will run on most any old piece of junk you might have sitting around. Here's the output from an old 200MHz PC with a Cyrix 6x86MX processor on which I ran Mandrake Linux 6.0:

```
$ ./cpuid
The processor Vendor ID is 'CyrixInstead'
$
```

You gotta love the humor of system engineers.

Assembling using a compiler

Because the GNU Common Compiler (`gcc`) uses the GNU assembler to compile C code, you can also use it to assemble and link your assembly language program in a single step. While this is not a common method to use, it is available when necessary.

There is one problem when using `gcc` to assemble your programs. While the GNU linker looks for the `_start` label to determine the beginning of the program, `gcc` looks for the `main` label (you might recognize that from C or C++ programming). You must change both the `_start` label and the `.globl` directive defining the label in your program to look like the following:

```
.section .text
.globl main
main:
```

After doing that, it is a snap to assemble and link programs:

```
$ gcc -o cpuid cpuid.s
$ ./cpuid
The processor Vendor ID is 'GenuineIntel'
$
```

Debugging the Program

In this simple example, unless you introduced some typing errors in the source code, the program should have run with the expected results. Unfortunately, that is not always the case in assembly language programming.

In more complicated programs, it is easy to make a mistake when assigning registers and memory locations, or trying special instruction codes to handle complex data issues. When this happens, it is good to have a debugger handy to step through the program and watch how the data is handled.

This section shows how to use the GNU debugger to walk through the sample program, watching how the registers and memory location are changed throughout the process.

Using gdb

In order to debug the assembly language program, you must first reassemble the source code using the `-gstabs` parameter:

```
$ as -gstabs -o cpuid.o cpuid.s
$ ld -o cpuid cpuid.o
$
```

As with the first time it was assembled, the source code assembles with no error or warning messages. By specifying the `-gstabs` parameter, extra information is assembled into the executable program file to help `gdb` walk through the source code. While the executable program file created with the `-gstabs` parameter still runs and behaves just like the original program, it is not a wise idea to use the `-gstabs` parameter unless you are specifically debugging an application.

Because the `-gstabs` parameter adds additional information to the executable program file, the resulting file becomes larger than it needs to be just to run the application. For this example program, assembling without the `-gstabs` parameter produces the following file:

```
-rwxr-xr-x   1 rich     rich           771 2004-07-13 07:32 cpuid
```

When assembling with the -gstabs parameter, the program file becomes the following:

```
-rwxr-xr-x    1 rich    rich        1099 2004-07-13 07:20 cpuid
```

Notice that the file size went from 771 bytes to 1,099 bytes. Although the difference is trivial for this example, imagine what happens with a 10,000-line assembly language program! Again, it is best to not use the debugging information if it is not necessary.

Stepping through the program

Now that the executable program file contains the necessary debugging information, you can run the program within gdb:

```
$ gdb cpuid
GNU gdb 6.0-debian
Copyright 2003 Free Software Foundation, Inc.
GDB is free software, covered by the GNU General Public License, and you are
welcome to change it and/or distribute copies of it under certain conditions.
Type "show copying" to see the conditions.
There is absolutely no warranty for GDB.  Type "show warranty" for details.
This GDB was configured as "i386-linux"...
(gdb)
```

The GNU debugger starts, with the program loaded into memory. You can run the program from within gdb using the run command:

```
(gdb) run
Starting program: /home/rich/palp/chap04/cpuid
The processor Vendor ID is 'GenuineIntel'

Program exited normally.
(gdb)
```

As you can see from the output, the program ran within the debugger just as it did from the command line. That's not especially exciting. Now it's time to freeze the program as it starts, and step through each line of source code individually.

To do that, you must set a **breakpoint**. Breakpoints are places in the program code where you want the debugger to stop running the program and let you look at things. There are several different options you can use when setting a breakpoint. You can choose to stop execution at any of the following:

❑ A label

❑ A line number in the source code

❑ A data value when it reaches a specific value

❑ A function after it is performed a specific number of times

For this simple example, we will set a breakpoint at the beginning of the instruction codes, and watch the program as it progresses through the source code.

When specifying breakpoints in assembly language programs, you must specify the location relative to the nearest label. Because this sample program has only one label in the instruction code section, every breakpoint must be specified from _start. The format of the break command is

```
break *label+offset
```

where label is the label in the source code to reference, and offset is the number of lines from the label where execution should stop.

To set a breakpoint at the first instruction, and then start the program, you would use the following commands:

```
(gdb) break *_start
Breakpoint 1 at 0x8048075: file cpuid.s, line 11.
(gdb) run
Starting program: /home/rich/palp/chap04/cpuid
The processor Vendor ID is 'GenuineIntel'

Program exited normally.
(gdb)
```

The breakpoint was specified using the *_start parameter, which specifies the first instruction code after the _start label. Unfortunately, when the program is run, it ignores the breakpoint, and runs through the entire program. This is a well-known bug in the current version of gdb. It has been around for a while, but hopefully it will be fixed soon.

To work around this problem, you have to include a dummy instruction as the first instruction code element after the _start label. In assembly, the dummy instruction is called NOP, for no operation.

If you modify the cpuid.s source code by adding a NOP instruction immediately after the _start label, it should look like this:

```
_start:
    nop
    movl $0, %eax
    cpuid
```

After adding the NOP instruction, you can create a breakpoint at that location, signified as _start+1. Now, after assembling with the -gstabs parameter (and don't forget to link the new object code file), you can try out the debugger again:

```
(gdb) break *_start+1
Breakpoint 1 at 0x8048075: file cpuid.s, line 12.
(gdb) run
Starting program: /home/rich/palp/chap04/cpuid

Breakpoint 1, _start () at cpuid.s:12
12          movl $0, %eax
Current language:  auto; currently asm
(gdb)
```

Perfect! The program started and then paused at (what use to be) the first instruction code. Now you can step your way through the program using either the next or step commands:

```
(gdb) next
_start () at cpuid.s:13
13          cpuid
(gdb) next
_start () at cpuid.s:14
14          movl $output, %edi
(gdb) step
_start () at cpuid.s:15
15          movl %ebx, 28(%edi)
(gdb) step
_start () at cpuid.s:16
16 @code last w/screen:movl %edx, 32(%edi)
```

Each next or step command executes the next line of source code (and tells you what line number that is). Once you have walked through the section you were interested in seeing, you can continue to run the program as normal using the cont command:

```
 (gdb) cont
Continuing.
The processor Vendor ID is 'GenuineIntel'

Program exited normally.
 (gdb)
```

The debugger picks up from where it was stopped and finishes running the program as normal.

While it is good to walk through the program slowly, it is even better to be able to examine data elements as you are walking. The debugger provides a method for you to do that, as described in the next section.

Viewing the data

Now that you know how to stop the program at specific locations, it's time to examine the data elements at each stop. Several different gdb commands are used to examine the different types of data elements.

The two most common data elements to examine are registers and memory locations used for variables. The commands used for displaying this information are shown in the following table.

Data Command	Description
info registers	Display the values of all registers
print	Display the value of a specific register or variable from the program
x	Display the contents of a specific memory location

The `info registers` command is great for seeing how all of the registers are affected by an instruction:

```
(gdb) s
_start () at cpuid.s:13
13          cpuid
(gdb) info registers
eax            0x0         0
ecx            0x0         0
edx            0x0         0
ebx            0x0         0
esp            0xbffffd70        0xbffffd70
ebp            0x0         0x0
esi            0x0         0
edi            0x0         0
eip            0x804807a        0x804807a
eflags         0x346       838
cs             0x23        35
ss             0x2b        43
ds             0x2b        43
es             0x2b        43
fs             0x0         0
gs             0x0         0
(gdb) s
_start () at cpuid.s:14
14          movl $output, %edi
(gdb) info registers
eax            0x2         2
ecx            0x6c65746e        1818588270
edx            0x49656e69        1231384169
ebx            0x756e6547        1970169159
esp            0xbffffd70        0xbffffd70
ebp            0x0         0x0
esi            0x0         0
edi            0x0         0
eip            0x804807c        0x804807c
eflags         0x346       838
cs             0x23        35
ss             0x2b        43
ds             0x2b        43
es             0x2b        43
fs             0x0         0
gs             0x0         0
(gdb)
```

This output shows that before the CPUID instruction is executed, the EBX, ECX, and EDX registers all contain zero. After the CPUID instruction, they contain the values from the Vendor ID string.

The print command can also be used to display individual register values. Including a modifier can modify the output format of the print command:

❑   print/d to display the value in decimal

❑   print/t to display the value in binary

❑   print/x to display the value in hexadecimal

An example of the print command would be the following:

```
(gdb) print/x $ebx
$9 = 0x756e6547
(gdb) print/x $edx
$10 = 0x49656e69
(gdb) print/x $ecx
$11 = 0x6c65746e
(gdb)
```

The x command is used to display the values of specific memory locations. Similar to the print command, the x command output can be modified by a modifier. The format of the x command is

```
x/nyz
```

where n is the number of fields to display, y is the format of the output, and can be

❑   c for character

❑   d for decimal

❑   x for hexadecimal

and z is the size of the field to be displayed:

❑   b for byte

❑   h for 16-bit word (half-word)

❑   w for 32-bit word

The following example uses the x command to display the memory locations at the output label:

```
(gdb) x/42cb &output
0x80490ac <output>:84 'T'   104 'h' 101 'e' 32 ' '   112 'p' 114 'r' 111 'o'99 'c'
0x80490b4 <output+8>:101 'e' 115 's' 115 's' 111 'o' 114 'r' 32 ' '   86 'V' 101 'e'
0x80490bc <output+16>:110 'n' 100 'd' 111 'o' 114 'r' 32 ' '   73 'I'   68 'D' 32 ' '
0x80490c4 <output+24>:105 'i' 115 's' 32 ' ' 39 '\''  71 'G'   101 'e' 110 'n'117 'u'
0x80490cc <output+32>:105 'i' 110 'n' 101 'e' 73 'I' 110 'n' 116 't' 101 'e'108 'l'
0x80490d4 <output+40>:39 '\''  10 '\n'
(gdb)
```

This command displays the first 42 bytes of the output variable (the ampersand sign is used to indicate that it is a memory location) in character mode (which also shows the decimal values as well). This feature is invaluable when tracking instructions that manipulate memory locations.

Using C Library Functions in Assembly

The cpuid.s program used the Linux system calls to display the Vendor ID string information on the console. There are other ways to perform this function without using the system calls.

One method is to use the standard C library functions that are well known to C programmers. It is easy to tap into that resource to utilize many common C functions.

This section describes how to utilize C library functions within your assembly language programs. First, the common printf C function is described, and a new version of the cpuid.s program is shown using the printf function. Then, the next section shows how to assemble and link programs that use C library functions.

Using printf

The original cpuid.s program used Linux system calls to display the results. If you have the GNU C compiler installed on your system, you can just as easily use the common C functions that you are probably already familiar with.

The C libraries contain many of the functions that are common to C programs, such as printf and exit. For this version of the program, the Linux system calls are replaced with equivalent C library calls. Here's the cpuid2.s program:

```
#cpuid2.s View the CPUID Vendor ID string using C library calls
.section .data
output:
    .asciz "The processor Vendor ID is '%s'\n"
.section .bss
    .lcomm buffer, 12
.section .text
.globl _start
_start:
    movl $0, %eax
    cpuid
    movl $buffer, %edi
    movl %ebx, (%edi)
    movl %edx, 4(%edi)
    movl %ecx, 8(%edi)
    pushl $buffer
    pushl $output
    call printf
    addl $8, %esp
    pushl $0
    call exit
```

The printf function uses multiple input parameters, depending on the variables to be displayed. The first parameter is the output string, with the proper codes used to display the variables:

```
output:
    .asciz "The processor Vendor ID is '%s'\n"
```

Notice that this uses the .asciz directive instead of .ascii. The printf function expects a null-terminated string as the output string. The .asciz directive adds the null character to the end of the defined string.

The next parameter used is the buffer that will contain the Vendor ID string. Because the value of the buffer does not need to be defined, it is declared in the bss section as a 12-byte buffer area using the `.lcomm` directive:

```
.section .bss
    .lcomm buffer, 12
```

After the CPUID instruction is run, the registers containing the Vendor ID string pieces are placed in the `buffer` variable in the same way that they were in the original `cpuid.s` program.

To pass the parameters to the `printf` C function, you must push them onto the stack. This is done using the PUSHL instruction. The parameters are placed on the stack in reverse order from how the `printf` function retrieves them, so the buffer value is placed first, followed by the output string value. After that, the `printf` function is called using the CALL instruction:

```
pushl $buffer
pushl $output
call printf
addl $8, %esp
```

The ADDL instruction is used to clear the parameters placed on the stack for the `printf` function. The same technique is used to place a zero return value on the stack for the C `exit` function to use.

Linking with C library functions

When you use C library functions in your assembly language program, you must link the C library files with the program object code. If the C library functions are not available, the linker will fail:

```
$ as -o cpuid2.o cpuid2.s
$ ld -o cpuid2 cpuid2.o
cpuid2.o: In function `_start':
cpuid2.o(.text+0x3f): undefined reference to `printf'
cpuid2.o(.text+0x46): undefined reference to `exit'
$
```

In order to link the C function libraries, they must be available on your system. On Linux systems, there are two ways to link C functions to your assembly language program. The first method is called **static linking**. Static linking links function object code directly into your application executable program file. This creates huge executable programs, and wastes memory if multiple instances of the program are run at the same time (each instance has its own copy of the same functions).

The second method is called **dynamic linking**. Dynamic linking uses libraries that enable programmers to reference the functions in their applications, but not link the function codes in the executable program file. Instead, dynamic libraries are called at the program's runtime by the operating system, and can be shared by multiple programs.

On Linux systems, the standard C dynamic library is located in the file `libc.so.x`, where x is a value representing the version of the library. On my MEPIS system, this is the file `libc.so.5`. This library file contains the standard C functions, including `printf` and `exit`.

This file is automatically linked to C programs when using gcc. You must manually link it to your program object code for the C functions to operate. To link the libc.so file, you must use the -l parameter of the GNU linker. When using the -l parameter, you do not need to specify the complete library name. The linker assumes that the library will be in a file:

```
/lib/libx.so
```

where the x is the library name specified on the command-line parameter — in this case, the letter c. Thus, the command to link the program would be as follows:

```
$ ld -o cpuid2 -lc cpuid2.o
$ ./cpuid2
bash: ./cpuid2: No such file or directory
$
```

Well, that's interesting. The program object code linked with the standard C functions library file just fine, but when I tried to run the resulting executable file, the preceding error message was generated.

The problem is that the linker was able to resolve the C functions, but the functions themselves were not included in the final executable program (remember that we used a dynamically linked library). The linker assumed that the necessary library files would be found at runtime. Obviously, that was not the case in this instance.

To solve this problem, you must also specify the program that will load the dynamic library at runtime. For Linux systems, this program is ld-linux.so.2, normally found in the /lib directory. To specify this program, you must use the -dynamic-linker parameter of the GNU linker:

```
$ ld -dynamic-linker /lib/ld-linux.so.2 -o cpuid2 -lc cpuid2.o
$ ./cpuid2
The processor Vendor ID is 'GenuineIntel'
$
```

There, that's much better. Now when the executable program is run, it uses the ld-linux.so.2 dynamic loader program to find the libc.so library, and the program runs just fine.

It is also possible to use the gcc compiler to assemble and link the assembly language program and C library functions. In fact, in this case it's a lot easier. The gcc compiler automatically links in the necessary C libraries without you having to do anything special.

First, remember that to compile assembly language programs with gcc, you must change the _start label to main. After that, all you need to do is compile the source code with a single command:

```
$ gcc -o cpuid2 cpuid2.s
$ ./cpuid2
The processor Vendor ID is 'GenuineIntel'
$
```

The GNU compiler automatically linked the proper C library functions for you.

Summary

When creating your assembly language programs, it is a good idea to have a common program template for the assembler you are using. The template can be used as a starting point for all programs that are created with the assembler.

The template used with the GNU assembler requires specific sections to be defined. The GNU assembler uses sections to divide the different data areas within the program. The data section contains data that is placed in specific memory locations, referenced by labels. The program can refer to the data memory area by the label, and modify the memory locations as necessary. The bss section is used to contain uninitialized data elements, such as working buffers. This is ideal for creating large buffer areas. The text section is used to hold the actual instruction codes for the program. Once this area is created, it cannot be changed by the program.

The final piece of the template should define the starting point in your programs. The GNU assembler uses the _start label to declare the location of the first instruction to process. You can use a different label, but the label must then be specified with the -e parameter in the linker command. To make the _start label accessible to run, you must also define it as a global label. This is done using the .globl directive in the source code.

With a template ready, you can start creating programs. This chapter created a simple test program using the CPUID instruction to extract the Vendor ID string from the processor. The program was assembled using the GNU assembler, and linked using the GNU linker.

After the program was tested, the GNU debugger was used to show how to debug assembly language programs. The programs must be assembled using the -gstabs parameter, so the debugger can match instruction codes with source code lines. Also remember to include a NOP instruction immediately after the _start label if you need to stop the program execution before the first instruction code.

The GNU debugger enables you to walk through the program code line by line, watching the values of registers and memory locations along the way. This is an invaluable tool when trying to hunt down logic problems in algorithms, or even typos where the wrong register is used in an instruction.

Finally, the sample program was modified to show how to utilize C functions within assembly language programs. The printf and exit functions were used to display data and cleanly exit the program. To use C functions, the assembly language program must be linked with the C libraries on the host system. The best way to do that is to use the C dynamic libraries. Linking using dynamic libraries requires another command-line parameter for the linker, the -dynamic-linker parameter. This specifies the program used by the operating system to dynamically find and load the library files.

This ends the introduction to the assembly language section. It is hoped that you now have a good idea of what assembly language is, and how it will be beneficial to your high-level language applications. The next section of the book shows the basics of assembly language programming. The next chapter tackles the sometimes difficult task of manipulating data within assembly language programs.

5

Moving Data

One of the biggest jobs of an assembly language program is handling data objects. In every assembly language program, you will have to manage some type of data elements. This chapter discusses how assembly language programs handle data and the optimal ways to do that.

The first section shows how to define data elements for use in the assembly language program. The next section shows how to move data between registers and memory. Next, conditional move instructions are discussed, showing how to move data dependent on specific actions. After that, data exchange instructions are described, showing how to swap data between registers, and between registers and memory. Finally, the stack is discussed, including the instructions used for manipulating data on the stack.

Defining Data Elements

The GNU assembler provides many different ways to define and handle data elements in your assembly language program. It's up to you to choose the best way to deal with the data your application requires. The data and bss sections both provide methods for defining data elements. The following sections describe the methods available to define data in assembly language applications

The data section

The data section of the program is the most common place to define data elements. The data section defines specific memory locations where items are stored. These items can be referenced from the instruction codes in the program, and read and modified at will.

The data section is declared using the .data directive. Any data elements declared in this section are reserved in memory and can be read or written to by instructions in the assembly language program.

There is another type of data section called **.rodata**. *Any data elements defined in this section can only be accessed in read-only mode (thus the **ro** prefix).*

Two statements are required to define a data element in the data section: a label and a directive.

The label is used as a tag to reference the data element, much like a variable name in a C program. The label has no meaning to the processor; it is just a place for the assembler to use as a reference point when trying to access the memory location.

Besides the label, you must define how many bytes will be reserved for the data element. This is done using an assembler directive. The directive instructs the assembler to reserve a specified amount of memory for the data element to be referenced by the label.

The amount of memory reserved depends on the type of data that is defined, and the number of items of that type that will be declared. The following table shows the different directives that can be used to reserve memory for specific types of data elements.

Directive	Data Type
.ascii	Text string
.asciz	Null-terminated text string
.byte	Byte value
.double	Double-precision floating-point number
.float	Single-precision floating-point number
.int	32-bit integer number
.long	32-bit integer number (same as .int)
.octa	16-byte integer number
.quad	8-byte integer number
.short	16-bit integer number
.single	Single-precision floating-point number (same as .float)

After the directive is declared, a default value (or values) must be defined. This sets the data in the reserved memory location to the specific values.

An example of declaring a data element in the data section is as follows:

```
output:
.ascii "The processor Vendor ID is 'xxxxxxxxxxxx'\n"
```

This code snippet sets aside 42 bytes of memory, places the defined string sequentially in the memory bytes, and assigns the label `output` to the first byte. When the memory location `output` is referenced later in the program, the assembler knows to go to the memory location at the start of the text string.

The same applies to numbers. The code

```
pi:
.float 3.14159
```

assigns the floating-point representation of 3.14159 to the memory locations referenced by the `pi` label.

Chapter 7, "Using Numbers," describes in greater detail how floating-point numbers are stored in memory.

You are not limited to defining just one value on the directive statement line. You can define multiple values on the line, with each value being placed in memory in the order it appears in the directive. For example, the code

```
sizes:
.long 100,150,200,250,300
```

places the long integer (4 bytes) value of 100 in the memory location starting at reference `sizes`, then places the 4 bytes for the value 150 after that in memory, and so on. This acts as an array of values. Each individual value can be referenced by its relative location in the list. Knowing that each long integer value is 4 bytes, you can reference the 200 value by accessing the memory location `sizes+8` (and reading 4 bytes).

You can define as many data elements as you need in the data section. Just remember that the label must precede the directive defining the data:

```
.section .data
msg:
    .ascii "This is a test message"
factors:
    .double 37.45, 45.33, 12.30
height:
    .int 54
length:
    .int 62, 35, 47
```

Each data element is placed in memory in the order it is defined in the data section. Elements with multiple values are placed in the order listed in the directive. Figure 5-1 demonstrates how this looks.

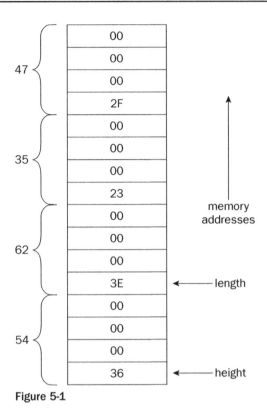

Figure 5-1

The lowest memory value contains the first data element. The bytes are placed sequentially in memory. The next data element immediately follows the previous element.

Be careful when defining data elements and then using them in the program. The program will not know if you are handling the data properly. For example, if you define two 16-bit integer data values, but then reference one as a 32-bit integer value, the assembler will still read the 4 bytes of memory required, even though it will be the wrong value.

Defining static symbols

Although the data section is intended primarily for defining variable data, you can also declare static data symbols here as well. The .equ directive is used to set a constant value to a symbol that can be used in the text section, as shown in the following examples:

```
.equ factor, 3
.equ LINUX_SYS_CALL, 0x80
```

Once set, the data symbol value cannot be changed within the program. The .equ directive can appear anywhere in the data section, although to make life easier for anyone else who may need to read your program, it's best to define them all at once either before or after the other data that is defined.

To reference the static data element, you must use a dollar sign before the label name. For example, the instruction

```
movl $LINUX_SYS_CALL, %eax
```

moves the value assigned to the LINUX_SYS_CALL symbol to the EAX register.

The bss section

Defining data elements in the bss section is somewhat different from defining them in the data section. Instead of declaring specific data types, you just declare raw segments of memory that are reserved for whatever purpose you need them for.

The GNU assembler uses two directives to declare buffers, as shown in the following table.

Directive	Description
.comm	Declares a common memory area for data that is not initialized
.lcomm	Declares a local common memory area for data that is not initialized

While the two sections work similarly, the local common memory area is reserved for data that will not be accessed outside of the local assembly code. The format for both of these directives is

```
.comm symbol, length
```

where symbol is a label assigned to the memory area, and length is the number of bytes contained in the memory area, as shown in the following example:

```
.section .bss
.lcomm buffer, 10000
```

These statements assign a 10,000-byte memory area to the buffer label. Local common memory areas cannot be accessed by functions outside of where they were declared (they can't be used in .globl directives).

One benefit to declaring data in the bss section is that the data is not included in the executable program. When data is defined in the data section, it must be included in the executable program, since it must be initialized with a specific value. Because the data areas declared in the bss section are not initialized with program data, the memory areas are reserved at runtime, and do not have to be included in the final program.

You can see this by creating a test assembly language program and watching the size of the executable program as data elements are declared. First, let's look at a sample program with no data elements:

```
# sizetest1.s - A sample program to view the executable size
.section .text
.globl _start
_start:
```

```
    movl $1, %eax
    movl $0, %ebx
    int $0x80
```

Now, assemble and link the program, and then view the size of it:

```
$ as -o sizetest1.o sizetest1.s
$ ld -o sizetest1 sizetest1.o
$ ls -al sizetest1
-rwxr-xr-x   1 rich     rich          724 Jul 16 13:54 sizetest1*
$
```

The total size of the executable program file is 724 bytes. Now, let's create another test program, this time adding a 10,000-byte buffer declared in the bss section:

```
# sizetest2.s - A sample program to view the executable size
.section .bss
    .lcomm buffer, 10000
.section .text
.globl _start
_start:
    movl $1, %eax
    movl $0, %ebx
    int $0x80
```

Again, assemble and link the program, and then view the size of it:

```
$ as -o sizetest2.o sizetest2.s
$ ld -o sizetest2 sizetest2.o
$ ls -al sizetest2
-rwxr-xr-x   1 rich     rich          747 Jul 16 13:57 sizetest2*
$
```

Not bad. We added a 10,000-byte buffer, but the size of the executable program file only increased by 23 bytes. Now, let's create a third test program, this time using the .fill directive to create a 10,000-byte buffer in the data section:

```
# sizetest3.s - A sample program to view the executable size
.section .data
buffer:
    .fill 10000
.section .text
.globl _start
_start:
    movl $1, %eax
    movl $0, %ebx
    int $0x80
```

The .fill directive enables the assembler to automatically create the 10,000 data elements for you. The default is to create one byte per field, and fill it with zeros. You could have declared a .byte data value, and listed 10,000 bytes yourself. After assembling and linking the application, you can see the total size of the executable program:

```
$ as -o sizetest3.o sizetest3.s
$ ld -o sizetest3 sizetest3.o
$ ls -al sizetest3
-rwxr-xr-x   1 rich     rich          10747 Jul 16 14:00 sizetest3
$
```

Wow, look at the size of the executable program. The 10,000 bytes of buffer space is added to the executable program, making it considerably larger than necessary.

Moving Data Elements

After data elements have been defined, you must know how to handle them. Because the data elements are located in memory, and many of the processor instructions utilize registers, the first step to handling data elements is to be able to move them around between memory and registers.

The MOV instruction is used as a general-purpose data mover. It is one of the most often used instructions in assembly language programs. The following sections describe the different ways you can use the MOV instruction to move data around in your program.

The MOV instruction formats

The basic format of the MOV instruction is as follows:

```
movx source, destination
```

The source and destination values can be memory addresses, data values stored in memory, data values defined in the instruction statement, or registers.

Remember that the GNU assembler uses AT&T style syntax, so the source and destination operands are in the opposite order from what is shown in the Intel documentation.

The GNU assembler adds another dimension to the MOV instruction, in that the size of the data element moved must be declared. The size is declared by adding an additional character to the MOV mnemonic. Thus, the instruction becomes

```
movx
```

where x can be the following:

- ❑   l for a 32-bit long word value
- ❑   w for a 16-bit word value
- ❑   b for an 8-bit byte value

Thus, to move the 32-bit EAX register to the 32-bit EBX register, you would use the instruction

```
movl %eax, %ebx
```

whereas for the 16-bit registers, the instruction would be

```
movw %ax, %bx
```

and for the 8-bit registers:

```
movb %al, %bl
```

There are very specific rules for using the MOV instruction. Only certain things can be moved to other things, as shown in the following combinations for a MOV instruction:

❑ An immediate data element to a general-purpose register

❑ An immediate data element to a memory location

❑ A general-purpose register to another general-purpose register

❑ A general-purpose register to a segment register

❑ A segment register to a general-purpose register

❑ A general-purpose register to a control register

❑ A control register to a general-purpose register

❑ A general-purpose register to a debug register

❑ A debug register to a general-purpose register

❑ A memory location to a general-purpose register

❑ A memory location to a segment register

❑ A general-purpose register to a memory location

❑ A segment register to a memory location

The following sections describe these scenarios in more detail, and show examples for each one.

> *Note a caveat to these rules. As you will see in Chapter 10, "Working with Strings," the* **MOVS** *instructions are special-use instructions for moving string values from one memory location to another memory location. These instructions are not covered in this chapter.*

Moving immediate data to registers and memory

The easiest task of moving data into registers and memory locations is moving immediate data. Immediate data is directly specified in the instruction code statement, and cannot be changed during runtime.

Following are some examples of moving immediate data:

```
movl $0, %eax       # moves the value 0 to the EAX register
movl $0x80, %ebx    # moves the hexadecimal value 80 to the EBX register
movl $100, height   # moves the value 100 to the height memory location
```

Each of these instructions specifies the value of the data element within the instruction code. Note that each value must be preceded by a dollar sign to indicate that it is an immediate value. The values can also be expressed in several different formats, decimal (such as 10, 100, or 230) or hexadecimal (such as 0x40, 0x3f, or 0xff). These values cannot be changed after the program is assembled and linked into the executable program file.

Moving data between registers

The next basic task of the MOV instruction is moving data from one processor register to another. This is the quickest way to move data with the processor. It is often advisable to keep data in processor registers as much as possible to decrease the amount of time spent trying to access memory locations.

The eight general-purpose registers (EAX, EBX, ECX, EDX, EDI, ESI, EBP, and ESP) are the most common registers used for holding data. These registers can be moved to any other type of register available. Unlike the general-purpose registers, the special-purpose registers (the control, debug, and segment registers) can only be moved to or from a general-purpose register.

Some examples of moving data between registers are as follows:

```
movl %eax, %ecx   # move 32-bits of data from the EAX register to the ECX register
movw %ax, %cx     # move 16-bits of data from the AX register to the CX register
```

Moving data between similarly sized registers is easy. What gets tricky is moving data between dissimilarly sized registers. You must be careful when specifying larger-sized registers to receive smaller-sized data. The instruction

```
movb %al, %bx
```

will produce an error by the assembler. This instruction attempts to move the 8 bits in the AL register to the lower 8 bits in the BX register. Instead, you should move the entire %ax register to the %bx register using the MOVW instruction.

Moving data between memory and registers

Moving data between registers is a simple task; unfortunately, moving data between registers and memory is not so easy. You must consider several things when moving data to and from memory locations. This section shows the different scenarios you will encounter when dealing with moving things between memory and registers.

Moving data values from memory to a register

The first thing you must decide is how the memory address will be represented in the instruction code. The simplest case is to use the label used to define the memory location:

```
movl value, %eax
```

This instruction moves the data value located at the memory location specified by the value label to the EAX register. This is actually a little trickier than it sounds. Remember that the MOVL instruction moves 32 bits of information; thus, it is moving 4 bytes of data starting at the memory location referenced by the `value` label. If you have less than 4 bytes of data, you must use one of the other MOV instructions, such as MOVB for 1 byte, or MOVW for 2 bytes.

Here's an example to show what happens:

```
# movtest1.s - An example of moving data from memory to a register
.section .data
    value:
        .int 1
.section .text
.globl _start
    _start:
        nop
        movl value, %ecx
        movl $1, %eax
        movl $0, %ebx
        int $0x80
```

Now, assemble the `movtest1.s` program with the `-gstabs` parameter, link it, and run the program in the debugger:

```
$ as -gstabs -o movtest1.o movtest1.s
$ ld -o movtest1 movtest1.o
$ gdb -q movtest1
(gdb) break *_start+1
Breakpoint 1 at 0x8048075: file movtest1.s, line 10.
(gdb) run
Starting program: /home/rich/palp/chap05/movtest1

Breakpoint 1, _start () at movtest1.s:10
10          movl (value), %ecx
Current language:  auto; currently asm
(gdb) print/x $ecx
$1 = 0x0
(gdb) next
11          movl $1, %eax
(gdb) print/x $ecx
$2 = 0x1
(gdb)
```

As expected, the value stored in the memory location was moved to the ECX register.

Moving data values from a register to memory

Placing the data back in a memory location uses a similar approach:

```
movl %ecx, value
```

This instruction moves the 4 bytes of data stored in the ECX register to the memory location specified by the `value` label. As before, this instruction moves 4 bytes of data, so it will use four memory locations to store the data. Here's a code example of this instruction in action:

```
# movtest2.s - An example of moving register data to memory
.section .data
   value:
       .int 1
.section .text
.globl _start
   _start:
       nop
       movl $100, %eax
       movl %eax, value
       movl $1, %eax
       movl $0, %ebx
       int $0x80
```

Again, assemble the movtest2.s program with the -gstabs parameter, link it, and then run it in the debugger:

```
$ as -o movtest2.o -gstabs movtest2.s
$ ld -o movtest2 movtest2.o
$ gdb -q movtest2
(gdb) break *_start+1
Breakpoint 1 at 0x8048075: file movtest2.s, line 11.
(gdb) run
Starting program: /home/rich/palp/chap05/movtest2

Breakpoint 1, _start () at movtest2.s:11
11          movl $100, %eax
Current language:  auto; currently asm
(gdb) x/d &value
0x804908c <value>:        1
(gdb) s
12          movl %eax, value
(gdb) s
13          movl $1, %eax
(gdb) x/d &value
0x804908c <value>:        100
(gdb)
```

By examining the memory location referenced by the value label (using the x gdb command), you can see the initial value of 1 is stored. After stepping through the program until the value of the EAX register is moved to the memory location, you can check it again. This time the value is 100, so the register value was indeed stored in the memory location.

This technique works fine when accessing a single data element referenced by a label, but becomes complicated if you need to reference multiple values, such as in a data array. The next section describes how to handle these situations.

Using indexed memory locations

As shown previously in the "Defining Data Elements" section, you can specify more than one value on a directive to place in memory:

```
values:
    .int 10, 15, 20, 25, 30, 35, 40, 45, 50, 55, 60
```

This creates a sequential series of data values placed in memory. Each data value occupies one unit of memory (which in this case is a long integer, or 4 bytes). When referencing data in the array, you must use an index system to determine which value you are accessing.

The way this is done is called **indexed memory mode.** The memory location is determined by the following:

❑ A base address

❑ An offset address to add to the base address

❑ The size of the data element

❑ An index to determine which data element to select

The format of the expression is

```
base_address(offset_address, index, size)
```

The data value retrieved is located at

```
base_address + offset_address + index * size
```

If any of the values are zero, they can be omitted (but the commas are still required as placeholders). The offset_address and index value must be registers, but the size value can be a numerical value. For example, to reference the value 20 from the values array shown, you would use the following instructions:

```
movl $2, %edi
movl values(, %edi, 4), %eax
```

This instruction loads the third index value of 4 bytes from the values label to the EAX register (remember, the array starts with index 0). Most often, you will use a register counter as the index value, and change that value to match the array element you need to work with. This is shown in the movtest3.s sample program:

```
# movtest3.s - Another example of using indexed memory locations
.section .data
output:
    .asciz "The value is %d\n"
values:
    .int 10, 15, 20, 25, 30, 35, 40, 45, 50, 55, 60
.section .text
.globl _start
_start:
    nop
    movl $0, %edi
loop:
```

```
movl values(, %edi, 4), %eax
pushl %eax
pushl $output
call printf
addl $8, %esp
inc %edi
cmpl $11, %edi
jne loop
movl $0, %ebx
movl $1, %eax
int $0x80
```

Because this example uses the C printf function, remember to link it with the C library dynamic linker on your system:

```
$ as -o movtest3.o movtest3.s
$ ld -dynamic-linker /lib/ld-linux.so.2 -lc -o movtest3 movtest3.o
$ ./movtest3
The value is 10
The value is 15
The value is 20
The value is 25
The value is 30
The value is 35
The value is 40
The value is 45
The value is 50
The value is 55
The value is 60
$
```

The movtest3.s program walks through the data array specified by the values label, displaying each value on the console. It uses the EDI register as an index to walk through the array:

```
movl values(, %edi, 4), %eax
```

After each value is displayed, the EDI register value is incremented (using the INC instruction, which adds one to the register). The program checks the value of the EDI register, and loops back to retrieve the next array value if the maximum value has not been met. Don't worry too much about the auxiliary code used in this example. All of these instructions are covered in later chapters. Concentrate on how the program manipulates the data array defined.

*Because this is just an example and not a real application, a hard-coded value is used to check when the **EDI** register has reached the end of the array. In a real-life situation, you would want to dynamically determine the number of items in the array, and loop until they have all been read.*

Using indirect addressing with registers

Besides holding data, registers can also be used to hold memory addresses. When a register holds a memory address, it is referred to as a **pointer**. Accessing the data stored in the memory location using the pointer is called **indirect addressing.**

This technique can be the most confusing part of accessing data. If you are already accustomed to using pointers in C or C++, you should have no problem with indirect addressing. If not, this might take a while to sink in.

While using a label references the data value contained in the memory location, you can get the memory location address of the data value by placing a dollar sign ($) in front of the label in the instruction. Thus the instruction

```
movl $values, %edi
```

is used to move the memory address the `values` label references to the `EDI` register.

Remember that in a flat memory model, all memory addresses are represented by 32-bit numbers.

If you have read Chapter 4, "A Sample Assembly Language Program," you already saw indirect addressing in action. The `cpuid.s` program used the following instruction:

```
movl $output, %edi
```

This instruction moves the memory address of the `output` label to the `EDI` register. The dollar sign ($) before the label name instructs the assembler to use the memory address, and not the data value located at the address.

The next instruction in the `cpuid.s` program:

```
movl %ebx, (%edi)
```

is the other half of the indirect addressing mode. Without the parentheses around the `EDI` register, the instruction would just load the value in the `EBX` register to the `EDI` register. With the parentheses around the `EDI` register, the instruction instead moves the value in the `EBX` register to the memory location contained in the `EDI` register.

This is a very powerful tool. Similar to pointers in C and C++, it enables you to control memory address locations with a register. The real power is realized by incrementing the indirect addressing value contained in the register. Unfortunately, the GNU assembler has a somewhat odd way of doing that.

Instead of just allowing you to add a value to the register, you must place the value outside of the parentheses, like so:

```
movl %edx, 4(%edi)
```

This instruction places the value contained in the `EDX` register in the memory location 4 bytes after the location pointed to by the `EDI` register. You can also go in the opposite direction:

```
movl %edx, -4(%edi)
```

This instruction places the value in the memory location 4 bytes before the location pointed to by the `EDI` register.

Here's an example program, `movtest4.s`, that demonstrates indirect addressing mode:

```
# movtest4.s - An example of indirect addressing
.section .data
values:
    .int 10, 15, 20, 25, 30, 35, 40, 45, 50, 55, 60
.section .text
.globl _start
_start:
    nop
    movl values, %eax
    movl $values, %edi
    movl $100, 4(%edi)
    movl $1, %edi
    movl values(, %edi, 4), %ebx
    movl $1, %eax
    int $0x80
```

To get the full benefit from this example, assemble it with the `-gstabs` parameter and watch it run in the debugger:

```
$ gdb -q movtest4
(gdb) break *_start+1
Breakpoint 1 at 0x8048075: file movtest4.s, line 10.
(gdb) run
Starting program: /home/rich/palp/chap05/movtest4

Breakpoint 1, _start () at movtest4.s:10
10          movl values, %eax
Current language:  auto; currently asm
(gdb)
```

First, look at the values stored in the memory locations referenced by the `value` label:

```
(gdb) x/4d &values
0x804909c <values>:      10      15      20      25
```

It was loaded with the data specified in the `.int` directive (the `4d` parameter of the `x` command displays the first four elements, and in decimal mode). Next, step through the program to load the first data element from the `values` array to the EAX register:

```
(gdb) s
11          movl $values, %edi
(gdb) print $eax
$1 = 10
(gdb)
```

As expected, the EAX register now contains the value `10`, the first element in the array. Continue to step through the program and watch the `values` memory address get loaded into the EDI register:

```
(gdb) s
12          movl $100, 4(%edi)
(gdb) print/x $edi
$2 = 0x804909c
(gdb)
```

The EDI register now holds the hexadecimal value of 0x804909c. This is the memory address the value label references. The next instruction moves the immediate data value of 100 to the memory address 4 bytes after the address to which the EDI register points. This should be the second data element in the values array. You can see that from displaying the values array using the x command:

```
(gdb) s
13          movl $1, %edi
(gdb) x/4d &values
0x804909c <values>:     10     100     20     25
(gdb)
```

Sure enough, the 100 value has replaced the 15 value as the second data element in the values array. The next instructions load the second data element of the array into the EBX register:

```
movl $1, %edi
movl values(, %edi, 4), %ebx
```

The remainder of the program uses the exit Linux system call to terminate the program. The exit code from the program should be the newly created second data array element (100) that was placed in the EBX register. This value can be checked by examining the exit code in the shell. This is done using the special environment variable $?:

```
$ ./movtest4
$ echo $?
100
$
```

Conditional Move Instructions

The MOV instruction is a very powerful instruction to have at your disposal. It is the backbone of most assembly language programs. However, there are ways it can be improved. Over the years, Intel has tweaked the IA-32 platform to provide additional functionality, making assembly language programmers' jobs easier. The **conditional move** instructions are one of those tweaks, available starting in the P6 family of Pentium processors (the Pentium Pro, Pentium II, and newer).

A conditional move instruction is just what its name implies, a MOV instruction that takes place under specific conditions. In older assembly language programs, you will see code that looks like the following:

```
    inc %ecx
    jnc continue
    movl $0, %ecx
continue:
```

This code snippet first increments the value in the ECX register by one. If the ECX register does not over-flow (the Carry flag is not set), the JNC instruction jumps to the continue label. If the register overflows, it is caught by the JNC instruction, and the ECX register is set back to zero (this concept is covered in Chapter 6, "Controlling Execution Flow").

The value of the ECX register depends on its condition, which must be checked with a jump instruction. Instead of having to utilize a jump instruction to check the Carry flag, you can use a conditional move instruction, which will do that for you.

While this is a trivial example, in more complicated production applications the conditional move instruction can prevent the processor from implementing JMP instructions, which helps out the prefetch cache condition of the processor, usually speeding up the application.

The following sections describe the conditional move instructions, and demonstrate how to use them in your assembly language programs.

The CMOV instructions

A whole host of instructions are included in the conditional move instruction set. All of the instructions have the format

```
cmovx source, destination
```

where x is a one- or two-letter code denoting the condition that will trigger the move action. The condi-tions are based on the current values in the EFLAGS register. The specific bits that are used by the condi-tional move instructions are shown in the following table.

EFLAGS Bit	Name	Description
CF	Carry flag	A mathematical expression has created a carry or borrow
OF	Overflow flag	An integer value is either too large or too small
PF	Parity flag	The register contains corrupt data from a mathematical operation
SF	Sign flag	Indicates whether the result is negative or positive
ZF	Zero flag	The result of the mathematical operation is zero

The conditional move instructions are grouped together in pairs, with two instructions having the same meaning. For example, a value can be above another value, but it can also be not below or equal to the value. Both conditions are equivalent, but both have separate conditional move instructions.

The conditional move instructions are divided into instructions used for signed operations and for unsigned operations. The signed operations involve comparisons that utilize the Sign flag, while the unsigned operations involve comparisons that disregard the Sign flag (for a complete description of signed an unsigned operations, see Chapter 7, "Using Numbers").

The following table shows the unsigned conditional move instructions.

Instruction Pair	Description	EFLAGS Condition
CMOVA/CMOVNBE	Above/not below or equal	(CF or ZF) = 0
CMOVAE/CMOVNB	Above or equal/not below	CF=0
CMOVNC	Not carry	CF=0
CMOVB/CMOVNAE	Below/not above or equal	CF=1
CMOVC	Carry	CF=1
CMOVBE/CMOVNA	Below or equal/not above	(CF or ZF) = 1
CMOVE/CMOVZ	Equal/zero	ZF=1
CMOVNE/CMOVNZ	Not equal/not zero	ZF=0
CMOVP/CMOVPE	Parity/parity even	PF=1
CMOVNP/CMOVPO	Not parity/parity odd	PF=0

As you can see from the table, the unsigned conditional move instructions rely on the Carry, Zero, and Parity flags to determine the difference between two operands. If the operands are signed values, a different set of conditional move instructions must be used, as shown in the following table.

Instruction Pair	Description	EFLAGS Condition
CMOVGE/CMOVNL	Greater or equal/not less	(SF xor OF)=0
CMOVL/CMOVNGE	Less/not greater or equal	(SF xor OF)=1
CMOVLE/CMOVNG	Less or equal/not greater	((SF xor OF) or ZF)=1
CMOVO	Overflow	OF=1
CMOVNO	Not overflow	OF=0
CMOVS	Sign (negative)	SF=1
CMOVNS	Not sign (non-negative)	SF=0

The difference between signed and unsigned numbers is discussed in more detail in Chapter 7.

The signed conditional move instructions utilize the Sign and Overflow flags to indicate the condition of the comparison between the operands.

The conditional move instructions need some type of mathematical instruction that sets the EFLAGS register to operate. Here's an example of the CMOV instruction in action:

```
movl value, %ecx
cmp %ebx, %ecx
cmova %ecx, %ebx
```

This code snippet loads the ECX register with a data value referenced by the value label, and then uses the CMP instruction to compare that value with the value held in the EBX register. The CMP instruction subtracts the first operand from the second and sets the EFLAGS registers appropriately. The CMOVA instruction is then used to replace the value in EBX with the value in ECX if the value is larger than what was originally in the EBX register.

> *Remember that in AT&T syntax, the order of the operands in the* **CMP** *and* **CMOVA** *instructions are reversed from the Intel documentation. This can be confusing.*

The conditional move instruction saves the assembly language programmer from having to code jump statements after the compare statement. This concept is expanded in the example program shown in the next section.

Using CMOV instructions

The cmovtest.s program demonstrates using the conditional move instructions. Here's what the program looks like:

```
# cmovtest.s - An example of the CMOV instructions
.section .data
output:
    .asciz "The largest value is %d\n"
values:
    .int 105, 235, 61, 315, 134, 221, 53, 145, 117, 5
.section .text
.globl _start
_start:
    nop
    movl values, %ebx
    movl $1, %edi
loop:
    movl values(, %edi, 4), %eax
    cmp %ebx, %eax
    cmova %eax, %ebx
    inc %edi
    cmp $10, %edi
    jne loop
    pushl %ebx
    pushl $output
    call printf
    addl $8, %esp
    pushl $0
    call exit
```

The cmovtest.s program finds the largest integer in a series defined in the values array. It uses some instructions that are covered in later chapters, but for now, just watch how the conditional move statements work.

The EBX register is used to hold the current largest integer found. To start off, the first value in the array is loaded into the EBX register.

The array elements are then loaded one by one into the EAX register, and compared with the value in the EBX register. If the value in the EAX register is larger, it is moved to the EBX register, and becomes the new largest value. By stepping through the program section in the debugger, you can see the process in action:

```
(gdb) s
14          movl values(, %edi, 4), %eax
(gdb) s
15          cmp %ebx, %eax
(gdb) print $eax
$1 = 235
(gdb) print $ebx
$2 = 105
(gdb)
```

At this point, the first value in the array (105) is loaded in the EBX register, and the second value (235) is loaded in the EAX register. Next, the CMP and CMOVA instructions are run, and the EBX register is checked again:

```
(gdb) s
16          cmova %eax, %ebx
(gdb) s
17          inc %edi
(gdb) print $ebx
$3 = 235
(gdb)
```

As expected, the larger value (235) was moved into the EBX register. This process continues until all of the values in the array have been tested. At the end, the value remaining in the EBX register is the largest value in the array. The output of the program should come up with the largest value in the array:

```
$ ./cmovtest
The largest value is 315
$
```

Exchanging Data

Sometimes in programs it becomes necessary to switch the location of data elements. One drawback to the MOV instructions is that it is difficult to switch the values of two registers without using a temporary intermediate register. For example, to exchange the values in the EAX and EBX register, you would have to do something like what is demonstrated in Figure 5-2.

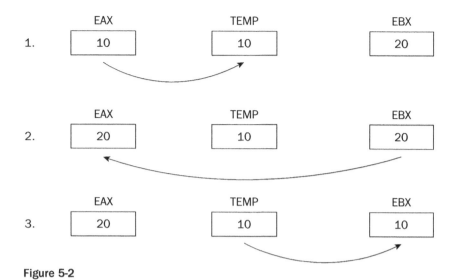

Figure 5-2

Figure 5-2 illustrates the use of an intermediate register to exchange the data in two registers. The instruction codes would look like this:

```
movl %eax, %ecx
movl %ebx, %eax
movl %ecx, %ebx
```

Three instructions are required, as well as a spare register to hold the intermediate value. The data exchange instructions solve this problem. Data can be exchanged between registers with no intermediate registers required. This section describes the data exchange instructions, and demonstrates how they are used in a program.

The data exchange instructions

Several instructions are included in the data exchange instruction set. Each one has a specific purpose, and can come in handy when handling data in programs. The instructions are described in the following table.

Instruction	Description
XCHG	Exchanges the values of two registers, or a register and a memory location
BSWAP	Reverses the byte order in a 32-bit register
XADD	Exchanges two values and stores the sum in the destination operand
CMPXCHG	Compares a value with an external value and exchanges it with another
CMPXCHG8B	Compares two 64-bit values and exchanges it with another

The following sections describe each of these instructions in more detail.

XCHG

The XCHG instruction is the simplest in the group. It can exchange data values between two general-purpose registers, or between a register and a memory location.

The format of the instruction is as follows:

```
xchg operand1, operand2
```

Either operand1 or operand2 can be a general-purpose register or a memory location (but both cannot be a memory location). The command can be used with any general-purpose 8-, 16-, or 32-bit register, although the two operands must be the same size.

When one of the operands is a memory location, the processor's LOCK signal is automatically asserted, preventing any other processor from accessing the memory location during the exchange.

*Be careful when using the **XCHG** instruction with memory locations. The **LOCK** process is very time-consuming, and can be detrimental to your program's performance.*

BSWAP

The BSWAP instruction is a powerful tool to have handy when working with systems that have different byte orientations. The BSWAP instruction reverses the order of the bytes in a register. Bits 0 through 7 are swapped with bits 24 through 31, while bits 8 through 15 are swapped with bits 16 through 23. This is demonstrated in Figure 5-3.

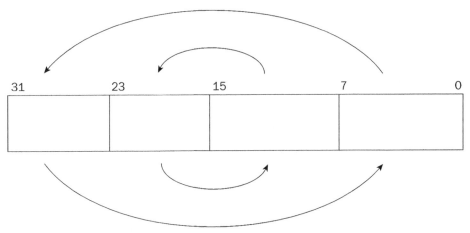

Figure 5-3

It is important to remember that the bits are not reversed; but rather, the individual bytes contained within the register are reversed. This produces a big-endian value from a little-endian value, and visa versa.

Here's a quick test of the BSWAP instruction, the swaptest.s program:

```
# swaptest.s - An example of using the BSWAP instruction
.section .text
.globl _start
_start:
    nop
    movl $0x12345678, %ebx
    bswap %ebx
    movl $1, %eax
    int $0x80
```

This program simply loads the hexadecimal value 12345678 into the EBX register and then swaps the bytes using the BSWAP instruction. You can see what happens in the debugger:

```
$ gdb -q swaptest
(gdb) break *_start+1
Breakpoint 1 at 0x8048075: file swaptest.s, line 5.
(gdb) run
Starting program: /home/rich/palp/chap05/swaptest

Breakpoint 1, _start () at swaptest.s:5
5           movl $0x12345678, %ebx
Current language:  auto; currently asm
(gdb) step
_start () at swaptest.s:6
6           bswap %ebx
(gdb) print/x $ebx
$1 = 0x12345678
(gdb) step
_start () at swaptest.s:7
7           movl $1, %eax
(gdb) print/x $ebx
$2 = 0x78563412
(gdb)
```

With the program stopped after the first MOVL instruction, you can check the hexadecimal value of the EBX register, and sure enough it's 12345678. Now, after stepping through the BSWAP instruction and displaying the EBX register, it is 78563412, the reverse endian order of the original value.

XADD

The XADD instruction is used to exchange the values between two registers, or a memory location and a register, add the values, and then store them in the destination location (either a register or a memory location). The format of the XADD instruction is

```
xadd source, destination
```

where source must be a register, and destination can be either a register or a memory location, and contains the results of the addition. The registers can be 8-, 16-, or 32-bit register values. The XADD instruction is available starting with the 80486 processors.

CMPXCHG

The CMPXCHG instruction compares the destination operand with the value in the EAX, AX, or AL registers. If the values are equal, the value of the source operand value is loaded into the destination operand. If the values are not equal, the destination operand value is loaded into the EAX, AX, or AL registers. The CMPXCHG instruction is not available on processors earlier than the 80486.

In the GNU assembler, the format of the CMPXCHG instruction is

```
cmpxchg source, destination
```

which is the reverse of the Intel documents. The destination operand can be an 8-, 16-, or 32-bit register, or a memory location. The source operand must be a register whose size matches the destination operand.

The cmpxchgtest.s program demonstrates the CMPXCHG instruction:

```
# cmpxchgtest.s - An example of the cmpxchg instruction
.section .data
data:
    .int 10
.section .text
.globl _start
_start:
    nop
    movl $10, %eax
    movl $5, %ebx
    cmpxchg %ebx, data
    movl $1, %eax
    int $0x80
```

The memory location referenced by the data label is compared with the value in the EAX register using the CMPXCHG instruction. Because they are equal, the value in the source operand (EBX) is loaded in the data memory location, and the value in the EBX register remains the same. You can check this behavior using the debugger:

```
(gdb) run
Starting program: /home/rich/palp/chap05/cmpxchgtest

Breakpoint 1, _start () at cmpxchgtest.s:9
9           movl $10, %eax
Current language:  auto; currently asm
(gdb) step
10          movl $5, %ebx
(gdb) step
11          cmpxchg %ebx, data
(gdb) x/d &data
0x8049090 <data>:        10
(gdb) s
12          movl $1, %eax
(gdb) print $eax
$3 = 10
```

```
(gdb) print $ebx
$4 = 5
(gdb) x/d &data
0x8049090 <data>:        5
(gdb)
```

Before the CMPXCHG instruction, the value of the data memory location is 10, which matches the value set in the EAX register. After the CMPXCHG instruction, the value in EBX (which is 5) is moved to the data memory location.

You can also test the other option by changing the value assigned to the data label to something other than 10. Because that value does not match the value in EAX, you will notice that the data value is not changed, but the EAX value now contains the value you set in the data label.

CMPXCHG8B

As you can tell from the instruction name, the CMPXCHG8B instruction is similar to the CMPXCHG instruction, but with a twist — it works with 8-byte values (thus the 8B on the end). This instruction is not supported on IA_32 processors earlier than the Pentium processor. The format of the CMPXCHG8B instruction takes only a single operand:

```
cmpxchg8b destination
```

The destination operand references a memory location, where 8 bytes will be compared with the 8-byte value contained in the EDX and EAX registers (with EDX being the high-order register and EAX being the low-order register). If the destination value matches the value contained in the EDX:EAX pair, the 64-bit value located in the ECX:EBX register pair is moved to the destination memory location. If not, the value in the destination memory address is loaded in the EDX:EAX register pair.

To demonstrate this, here's the cmpxchg8btest.s program:

```
# cmpxchg8btest.s - An example of the cmpxchg8b instruction
.section .data
data:
    .byte 0x11, 0x22, 0x33, 0x44, 0x55, 0x66, 0x77, 0x88

.section .text
.globl _start
_start:
    nop
    movl $0x44332211, %eax
    movl $0x88776655, %edx
    movl $0x11111111, %ebx
    movl $0x22222222, %ecx
    cmpxchg8b data
    movl $0, %ebx
    movl $1, %eax
    int $0x80
```

The data label defines 8 bytes of memory with a specific pattern defined. The EAX and EDX registers contain the same pattern (with EDX being the high-order bytes and EAX being the low-order bytes).

115

Notice how the bytes are arranged in the registers as compared to the memory locations. Next, the EBX and ECX registers are loaded with a completely different data pattern to set them apart. The CMPXCHG8B instruction is used to compare the data referenced by the data label with the EDX:EAX register pair.

To see the CMPXCHG8B instruction in action, you need to run this program in the debugger. First, look at the data values referenced by the data label before the CMPXCHG8B instruction:

```
$ gdb -q cmpxchg8btest
(gdb) break *_start+1
Breakpoint 1 at 0x8048075: file cmpxchg8btest.s, line 10.
(gdb) run
Starting program: /home/rich/palp/chap05/cmpxchg8btest

Breakpoint 1, _start () at cmpxchg8btest.s:10
10          movl $0x44332211, %eax
Current language:  auto; currently asm
(gdb) x/8b &data
0x804909c <data>:   0x11    0x22    0x33    0x44    0x55    0x66    0x77    0x88
(gdb) s
11          movl $0x88776655, %edx
(gdb) s
12          movl $0x11111111, %ebx
(gdb) s
13          movl $0x22222222, %ecx
(gdb) s
14          cmpxchg8b data
(gdb) s
15          movl $0, %ebx
(gdb) x/8b &data
0x804909c <data>:   0x11    0x11    0x11    0x11    0x22    0x22    0x22    0x22
(gdb)
```

The 8b option is used with the x command to display all 8 bytes located at the data label. As you can see from the output, indeed the values in the ECX:EBX registers were placed in the data memory location.

Using the data exchange instruction

Classic examples of the data exchange instructions in action are sort routines. Many different algorithms are used to sort an array of data. Some of them are more efficient than others, but almost all of them search through the data array and swap elements to get them in the proper order.

The bubble.s example uses the classic bubble sort algorithm to sort an array of integers. While not the most efficient sort method, the bubble sort is the easiest to understand and demonstrate. First, here's the source code for the program:

```
# bubble.s - An example of the XCHG instruction
.section .data
values:
    .int 105, 235, 61, 315, 134, 221, 53, 145, 117, 5
.section .text
.globl _start
```

```
_start:
    movl $values, %esi
    movl $9, %ecx
    movl $9, %ebx
loop:
    movl (%esi), %eax
    cmp %eax, 4(%esi)
    jge skip
    xchg %eax, 4(%esi)
    movl %eax, (%esi)
skip:
    add $4, %esi
    dec %ebx
    jnz loop
    dec %ecx
    jz end
movl $values, %esi
    movl %ecx, %ebx
    jmp loop
end:
    movl $1, %eax
    movl $0, %ebx
    int $0x80
```

This is the longest example program presented so far in the book, but it is the most useful. Again, don't worry too much about instructions not covered yet. The program uses a lot of jumps, which are discussed in greater detail in Chapter 6, "Controlling Execution Flow."

The basic algorithm for a bubble sort from a high-level language perspective looks like this:

```
for(out = array_size-1; out>0, out--)
{
    for(in = 0; in < out; in++)
    {
        if (array[in] > array[in+1])
            swap(array[in], array[in+1]);
    }
}
```

There are two loops. The inner loop runs through the array, checking the adjacent array value to see which is larger. If a larger value is found in front of a smaller value, the two values are swapped in the array. This continues through to the end of the array.

When the first pass has completed, the largest value in the array should be at the end of the array, but the remaining values are not in any particular order. You must take N-1 passes through an array of N elements before all of the elements are in sorted order. The outer loop controls how many total passes of the inner loop are performed. For each new pass of the inner loop, there is one less element to check, as the last element of the previous pass should be in the proper order.

This algorithm is implemented in the assembly language program using a data array and two counters, EBX and ECX. The EBX counter is used for the inner loop, decreasing each time an array element is tested. When it reaches zero, the ECX counter is decreased, and the EBX counter is reset. This process continues until the ECX counter reaches zero. This indicates that all of the required passes have been completed.

117

The actual comparing and swapping of array values is done using indirect addressing. The ESI register is loaded with the memory address of the start of the data array. The ESI register is then used as a pointer to each array element during the comparison section:

```
movl (%esi), %eax
    cmp %eax, 4(%esi)
    jge skip
    xchg %eax, 4(%esi)
    movl %eax, (%esi)
skip:
```

First, the value in the first array element is loaded into the EAX register, and compared with the second array element (located 4 bytes from the first). If the second element is already larger than or equal to the first element, nothing happens and the program moves on to the next pair.

If the second element is less than the first element, the XCHG instruction is used to swap the first element (loaded into the EAX register) with the second element in memory. Next, the second element (now loaded into the EAX register) is then placed in the first element location in memory.

After this, the ESI register is incremented by 4 bytes, now pointing to the second element in the array. The process is then repeated, now using the second and third array elements. This continues until the end of the array is reached.

This simple sample program does not produce any output. Instead, to see if it really works, you can use the debugger and view the values array before and after the program is run. Here's a sample output of the program in action:

```
$ as -gstabs -o bubble.o bubble.s
$ ld -o bubble bubble.o
$ gdb -q bubble
(gdb) break *end
Breakpoint 1 at 0x80480a5: file bubble.s, line 28.
(gdb) x/10d &values
0x80490b4 <values>:        105     235     61      315
0x80490c4 <values+16>:     134     221     53      145
0x80490d4 <values+32>:     117     5
(gdb) run
Starting program: /home/rich/palp/chap05/bubble

Breakpoint 1, end () at bubble.s:28
28          movl $1, %eax
Current language:  auto; currently asm
(gdb) x/10d &values
0x80490b4 <values>:        5       53      61      105
0x80490c4 <values+16>:     117     134     145     221
0x80490d4 <values+32>:     235     315
(gdb)
```

To capture the data array values at the end of the program, a breakpoint is created at the end label. The values at the start of the program reflect the order the values were placed in the .int directive definition. After the program runs, the values are checked. Sure enough, they have been reordered in the proper order.

The Stack

As described in Chapter 1, "What Is Assembly Language Programming?," the stack is another memory element used by the program. The stack is one of the most misunderstood items in assembly language programs, and causes considerable grief for some rookie programmers.

This section explains the stack and the instructions used to access it.

How the stack works

The stack is a special reserved area in memory for placing data. What makes it special is the way in which data is inserted and removed from the stack area. As demonstrated earlier in Figure 5-1, data elements are placed in the data section in a sequential manner, starting at the lowest memory location in the data section, and working toward higher memory locations.

The stack behaves just the opposite. The stack is reserved at the end of the memory area, and as data is placed on the stack, it grows downward. This is demonstrated in Figure 5-4.

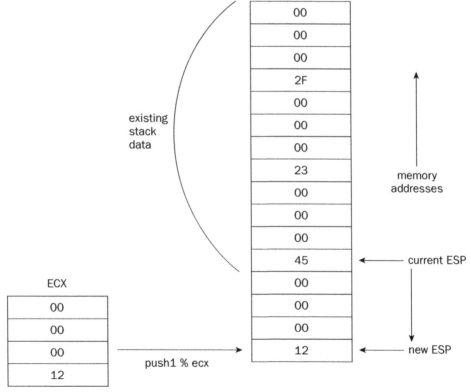

Figure 5-4

The bottom of the stack (or top of memory) contains data elements placed there by the operating system when the program is run. Any command-line parameters used when running the program are entered onto the stack, and the stack pointer is set to the bottom of the data elements. Following that is the area where you can place your program data.

The analogy typically used to describe the stack is to think of a stack of plates. As each plate is placed on the top of the plate stack, it becomes the next in line to be taken off from the top. As each data element is placed at the top of the memory stack, it becomes the next in line to be retrieved from the stack. It is not possible to remove a data value from the middle of the stack (although you can cheat and peek at the value).

As each data element is added to the stack area, a pointer is used to keep track of where the start of the stack is. The ESP register contains the memory address of the start of the stack. While not prohibited, it is not advisable to use the ESP register for any other purpose in your program. If the program loses track of the start of the stack, odd things can happen.

It is your responsibility as the assembly language programmer to keep track of what data is in the stack, and to retrieve it appropriately. As you will see in Chapter 11, "Using Functions," the stack is an important element in passing data between functions. If you place extraneous data onto the stack without setting the stack pointer appropriately, your functions may pick up the wrong values as the passed arguments.

Instead of manually setting and worrying about the stack pointer, the IA-32 instruction set includes some instructions to help you along. The next section describes the two instructions used for accessing data in the stack.

PUSHing and POPing data

Placing new data items in the stack is called **pushing.** The instruction used to perform this task is the PUSH instruction.

The simple format of the PUSH instruction is

```
pushx source
```

where x is a one-character code for the size of the data, and source is the data element to place on the stack. The data elements that you can PUSH are as follows:

- ❏ 16-bit register values
- ❏ 32-bit register values
- ❏ 16-bit memory values
- ❏ 32-bit memory values
- ❏ 16-bit segment registers
- ❏ 8-bit immediate data values

❑   16-bit immediate data values

❑   32-bit immediate data values

The character used to represent the data size is the same format as for the MOV instructions, although only the 16- and 32-bit data values are allowed to be PUSH'd:

❑   l for a long word (32 bits)

❑   w for a word (16 bits)

The size code must match the data element declared in the instruction or an error will occur. Some examples of using the PUSH instruction are as follows:

```
pushl %ecx  # puts the 32-bit value of the ECX register on the stack
pushw %cx   # puts the 16-bit value of the CX register on the stack
pushl $100  # puts the value of 100 on the stack as a 32-bit integer value
pushl data  # puts the 32-bit data value referenced by the data label
pushl $data # puts the 32-bit memory address referenced by the data label
```

*Note the difference between using the label **data** versus the memory location **$data**. The first format (without the dollar sign) places the data value contained in the memory location in the stack, whereas the second format places the memory address referenced by the label in the stack.*

Now that you have all the data on the stack, it's time to retrieve the data from the stack. The POP instruction is used for doing that part.

Similar to the PUSH instruction, the POP instruction uses the following format:

```
popx destination
```

where x is the one-character code for the size of the data element, and destination is the location to receive the data. The following data elements can be used to receive data using the POP instruction:

❑   16-bit registers

❑   16-bit segment registers

❑   32-bit registers

❑   16-bit memory locations

❑   32-bit memory locations

Obviously, you cannot place data from the stack into an immediate data value. Some examples of using the POP instruction are as follows:

```
popl %ecx    # place the next 32-bits in the stack in the ECX register
popw %cx     # place the next 16-bits in the stack in the CX register
popl value   # place the next 32-bits in the stack in the value memory location
```

The pushpop.s program is an example of pushing and popping various data types on the stack:

```
# pushpop.s - An example of using the PUSH and POP instructions
.section .data
data:
    .int 125

.section .text
.globl _start
_start:
    nop
    movl $24420, %ecx
    movw $350, %bx
    movb $100, %eax
    pushl %ecx
    pushw %bx
    pushl %eax
    pushl data
    pushl $data

    popl %eax
    popl %eax
    popl %eax
    popw %ax
    popl %eax
    movl $0, %ebx
    movl $1, %eax
    int $0x80
```

Although this is a somewhat trivial example, it will give you a good idea of how the stack works. Run the program in the debugger, and watch the values of the ESP register as the PUSH instructions are executed. You should see the ESP register decrease with each data element added to the stack, pointing to the new start of the stack. This shows that the stack is indeed moving downward in memory.

When I started the program, the ESP register contained the following value:

```
(gdb) print/x $esp
$1 = 0xbffffd70
```

After completing all of the PUSH instructions, it contained the following:

```
(gdb) print/x $esp
$2 = 0xbffffd5e
```

By subtracting the two memory locations, you can see that the ESP pointer has moved 18 bytes. Adding up the total data PUSH'd, it indeed totals 18 bytes.

Likewise, as each data element is removed from the stack using the POP instruction, the ESP register increases, showing that the stack is shrinking back upwards in memory. After the last POP, it should equal its original value.

PUSHing and POPing all the registers

The following table describes a few additional PUSH and POP instructions that can come in handy.

Instruction	Description
PUSHA/POPA	Push or pop all of the 16-bit general-purpose registers
PUSHAD/POPAD	Push or pop all of the 32-bit general-purpose registers
PUSHF/POPF	Push or pop the lower 16 bits of the EFLAGS register
PUSHFD/POPFD	Push or pop the entire 32 bits of the EFLAGS register

The PUSHA and POPA instructions are great for quickly setting aside and retrieving the current state of all the general-purpose registers at once. The PUSHA instruction pushes the 16-bit registers so they appear on the stack in the following order: DI, SI, BP, BX, DX, CX, and finally, AX. The PUSHAD instruction pushes the 32-bit counterparts of these registers in the same order. The POPA and POPAD instructions retrieve the registers in the reverse order they were pushed.

The behavior of the POPF and POPFD instructions varies depending on the processor mode of operation. When the processor is running in protected mode in ring 0 (the privileged mode), all of the nonreserved flags in the EFLAGS register can be modified, with the exception of the VIP, VIF, and VM flags. The VIP and VIF flags are cleared, and the VM flag is not modified.

When the processor is running in protected mode in a higher level ring (an unprivileged mode), the same results as the ring 0 mode are obtained, and the IOFL field is not allowed to be modified.

Manually using the ESP and EBP registers

The PUSH and POP instructions are not the only way to get data onto and off of the stack. You can also manually place data on the stack by utilizing the ESP register as a memory pointer.

Often, instead of using the ESP register itself, you will see many programs copy the ESP register value to the EBP register. It is common in assembly language functions to use the EBP pointer to point to the base of the working stack space for the function. Instructions that access parameters stored on the stack reference them relative to the EBP value (this is discussed in detail in Chapter 11, "Using Functions").

Optimizing Memory Access

Memory access is one of the slowest functions the processor performs. When writing assembly language programs that require high performance, it is best to avoid memory access as much as possible. Whenever possible, it is best to keep variables in registers on the processor. Register access is highly optimized for the processor, and is the quickest way to handle data.

When it is not possible to keep all of the application data in registers, you should try to optimize the memory access for the application. For processors that use data caching, accessing memory in a sequential order in memory helps increase cache hits, as blocks of memory will be read into cache at one time.

One other item to think about when using memory is how the processor handles memory reads and writes. Most processors (including those in the IA-32 family) are optimized to read and write memory locations in specific cache blocks, beginning at the start of the data section. On a Pentium 4 processor, the size of the cache block is 64 bits. If you define a data element that crosses a 64-bit block boundary, it will require two cache operations to retrieve or store the data element in memory.

To solve this problem, Intel suggests following these rules when defining data:

❏   Align 16-bit data on a 16-byte boundary.

❏   Align 32-bit data so that its base address is a multiple of four.

❏   Align 64-bit data so that its base address is a multiple of eight.

❏   Avoid many small data transfers. Instead, use a single large data transfer.

❏   Avoid using larger data sizes (such as 80- and 128-bit floating-point values) in the stack.

Aligning data within the data section can be tricky. The order in which data elements are defined can be crucial to the performance of your application. If you have a lot of similarly sized data elements, such as integer and floating-point values, place them together at the beginning of the data section. This ensures that they will maintain the proper alignment. If you have a lot of odd-sized data elements, such as strings and buffers, place those at the end of the data section so they won't throw off the alignment of the other data elements.

The gas assembler supports the .align directive, which is used to align defined data elements on specific memory boundaries. The .align directive is placed immediately before the data definition in the data section, instructing the assembler to position the data element on a memory boundary (this is shown in Chapter 17, "Using Advanced IA-32 Features").

Summary

This chapter discussed the crucial topic of moving data within your program. Almost every program must move data elements between memory and registers. Doing this requires knowing only a handful of instruction codes.

Before you can move data, you must be able to define it in your programs. The data and bss sections in the program provide areas where data can be defined. The data section enables you to define default values for data elements, such as strings, integers, and floating-point numbers. The bss section enables you to reserve large quantities of space for buffers without having to assign default values. By default, the bss section assigns zeros to all data bytes.

The MOV instruction is essential for moving data. It can move data from one register to another register, from a memory location to a register, or from a register to a memory location. It cannot, however, move data from one memory location to another memory location.

The MOV instruction must also include an ending character to denote the size of the data: l for 32 bits, w for 16 bits, and b for 8 bits. The two operands are the source location and the destination location (and remember, these are in opposite order from the Intel format).

Besides the standard MOV instructions, there are also conditional move instructions. These instructions move data between locations under specific conditions. The CMOV instructions observe the carry, parity, overflow, sign, and zero flags to determine whether a move should be made or not.

Another class of instructions is the data exchange instructions. These instructions can swap the values of two separate registers, or a register and a memory location, in a single instruction. The XCHG instruction is used to exchange values automatically. The CMPXCHG and CMPXCHG8B instructions first compare the destination value with a specific external value. If they match, the exchange with the source register is made. If not, the destination value is placed in the external location. The BSWAP instruction is used for swapping the high-order and low-order bytes in a register. It comes in handy if you need to communicate between big-endian and little-endian machines.

Finally, the memory stack was discussed. The stack is a place in memory where data can be placed by one function or operation, and retrieved by a separate function or operation. This is the place where data can be easily passed between functions. It is also used for local variables to functions.

The next chapter tackles the subject of altering the execution flow of a program. Almost all assembly language programs utilize some type of execution flow statements to alter the behavior of the program depending on the variable values during runtime. Being able to control the execution flow of the program, as well as being able to program the execution flow as smoothly as possible, are two topics that all assembly language programmers need to understand.

6

Controlling
Execution Flow

When the processor runs your programs, it is unlikely that it will start with the first instruction and proceed sequentially through all the instructions in the program until the last instruction. Instead, your program will most likely use branches and loops to perform the necessary logic to implement the functions it needs.

Similar to high-level languages, assembly language provides instructions to help the programmer code logic into applications. By jumping to different sections of the program, or looping through sections multiple times, you can alter the way the program handles data.

This chapter describes the different assembly language instructions used to do jumps and loops. Because both of these functions manipulate the instruction pointer, the first section provides a brief refresher on how the instruction pointer is used to keep track of the next instruction to process, and what instructions can alter the instruction pointer. The next section discusses unconditional branches and demonstrates how they are used in assembly language programs. After that, conditional branches are presented, showing how they can be used to implement logic functions in the application. The next two sections describe loops, special instructions that enable the program to loop through data for a predetermined number of times. Finally, you will learn some tips for optimizing programs that utilize jumps and loops.

The Instruction Pointer

Before diving into the details of changing the course of the program, it is a good idea to first understand how the program is executed on the processor. The instruction pointer is the traffic cop for the processor. It determines which instruction in the program is the next in line to be executed. It proceeds in a sequential manner through the instruction codes programmed in the application.

However, as described in Chapter 2, "The IA-32 Platform," it is not always an easy task to determine when and where the next instruction is. With the invention of the instruction prefetch cache, many instructions are preloaded into the processor cache before they are actually ready to be executed. With the invention of the out-of-order engine, many instructions are even executed ahead of time in the application, and the results are placed in order as required by the application by the retirement unit.

With all of this confusion, it can be difficult to determine what exactly is the "next instruction." While there is a lot of work going on behind the scenes to speed up execution of the program, the processor still needs to sequentially step through the program logic to produce the proper results. Within that framework, the instruction pointer is crucial to determining where things are in the program. This is shown in Figure 6-1.

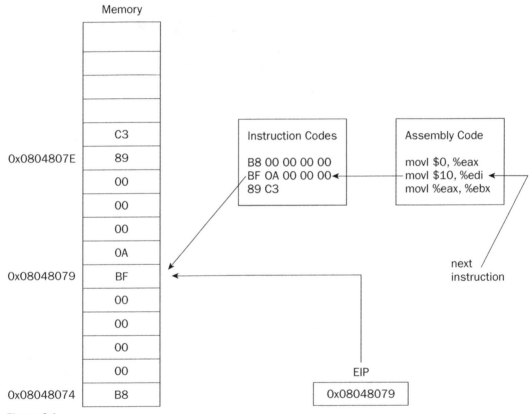

Figure 6-1

An instruction is considered executed when the processor retirement unit executes the result from the out-of-order engine from the instruction. After that instruction is executed, the instruction pointer is incremented to the next instruction in the program code. That instruction may or may not have already been performed by the out-of-order engine, but either way, the retirement unit does not process its results until it is time to do so in the program logic.

As the instruction pointer moves through the program instructions, the EIP register is incremented. Remember, instructions can be multiple bytes in length, so pointing to the next instruction is more than just incrementing the instruction pointer by one each time.

Your program cannot directly modify the instruction pointer. You do not have the capability to directly change the value of the EIP register to point to a different location in memory with a MOV instruction. You can, however, utilize instructions that alter the value of the instruction pointer. These instructions are called **branches.**

A branch instruction can alter the value of the EIP register either unconditionally (unconditional branches), or based on a value of a condition (conditional branches). The following sections describe unconditional and conditional branches and show how they affect the instruction pointer and the course of the program logic.

Unconditional Branches

When an unconditional branch is encountered in the program, the instruction pointer is automatically routed to a different location. You can use three types of unconditional branches:

❑ Jumps

❑ Calls

❑ Interrupts

Each of these unconditional branches behaves differently within the program, and it is up to you to decide which one to use within the program logic. The following sections describe the differences between each of these types of unconditional branches and how to implement them in your assembly language programs.

Jumps

The jump is the most basic type of branch used in assembly language programming. If you are familiar with the BASIC programming language, you have most likely seen GOTO statements. Jump statements are the assembly language equivalent of the BASIC GOTO statement.

In structured programming, GOTO statements are considered to be a sign of bad coding. Programs are supposed to be compartmentalized and flow in a sequential manner, calling functions instead of jumping around the program code. In assembly language programs, jump instructions are not considered bad programming, and in fact are required to implement many functions. However, they can have a detrimental impact on your program's performance (see "Optimizing Branch Instructions" later in this chapter).

The jump instruction uses a single instruction code:

```
jmp location
```

where location is the memory address to jump to. In assembly language, the location value is declared as a label within the program code. When the jump occurs, the instruction pointer is changed to the memory address of the instruction code located immediately after the label. This is shown in Figure 6-2.

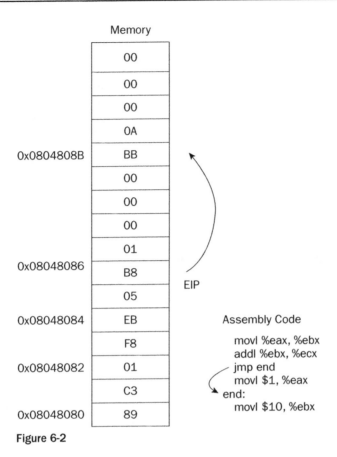

Figure 6-2

The JMP instruction changes the instruction pointer value to the memory location specified in the JMP instruction.

Behind the scenes, the single assembly jump instruction is assembled into one of three different types of jump opcodes:

❑   Short jump

❑   Near jump

❑   Far jump

The three jump types are determined by the distance between the current instruction's memory location and the memory location of the destination point (the "jump to" location). Depending on the number of bytes jumped, the different jump types are used. A short jump is used when the jump offset is less than 128 bytes. A far jump is used in segmented memory models when the jump goes to an instruction in another segment. The near jump is used for all other jumps.

When using the assembly language mnemonic instruction, you do not need to worry about the length of the jump. A single jump instruction is used to jump anywhere in the program code (although there may be a performance difference, as described later in the "Optimizing Branch Instructions" section).

The following `jumptest.s` program demonstrates the operation of an unconditional jump instruction:

```
# jumptest.s - An example of the jmp instruction
.section .text
.globl _start
_start:
    nop
    movl $1, %eax
    jmp overhere
    movl $10, %ebx
    int $0x80
overhere:
    movl $20, %ebx
    int $0x80
```

The `jumptest.s` program simply assigns the value 1 to the EAX register for the exit Linux system call. Then, a jump instruction is used to jump over the part where the value 10 is assigned to the EBX register, and the Linux system call is made. Instead, the program jumps to where the value 20 is assigned to the EBX register, and the Linux system call is made. You can ensure that the jump occurred by running the program and checking the result code generated in Linux:

```
$ as -o jumptest.o jumptest.s
$ ld -o jumptest jumptest.o
$ ./jumptest
$ echo $?
20
$
```

Indeed, the expected result code was produced due to the jump. That in itself might not be too exciting. Instead, you can watch the actual memory locations used in the program with the debugger and the `objdump` programs.

First, you can see how the instruction codes are arranged in memory by using the `objdump` program to disassemble the assembled code:

```
$ objdump -D jumptest

jumptest:       file format elf32-i386

Disassembly of section .text:

08048074 <_start>:
 8048074:       90                      nop
 8048075:       b8 01 00 00 00          mov    $0x1,%eax
 804807a:       eb 07                   jmp    8048083 <overhere>
 804807c:       bb 0a 00 00 00          mov    $0xa,%ebx
 8048081:       cd 80                   int    $0x80

08048083 <overhere>:
 8048083:       bb 14 00 00 00          mov    $0x14,%ebx
 8048088:       cd 80                   int    $0x80
$
```

The disassembler output shows the memory locations that will be used by each instruction (the value shown in the first column). Now, you can run the jumptest program in the debugger and watch what happens:

```
$ as -gstabs -o jumptest.o jumptest.s
$ ld -o jumptest jumptest.o
$ gdb -q jumptest
(gdb) break *_start+1
Breakpoint 1 at 0x8048075: file jumptest.s, line 5.
(gdb) run
Starting program: /home/rich/palp/chap06/jumptest

Breakpoint 1, _start () at jumptest.s:5
5           movl $1, %eax
Current language:  auto; currently asm
(gdb) print/x $eip
$1 = 0x8048075
(gdb)
```

After assembling the code for the debugger (using the -gstabs parameter), and setting the breakpoint at the start of the program, run the program and view the first memory location used (shown in the EIP register). The value is 0x8048075, which corresponds to the same memory location shown in the obj-dump output. Next, step through the debugger until the jump instruction has been executed, and then display the EIP register value again:

```
(gdb) step
_start () at jumptest.s:6
6           jmp overhere
(gdb) step
overhere () at jumptest.s:10
10          movl $20, %ebx
(gdb) print $eip
$2 = (void *) 0x8048083
(gdb)
```

As expected, the program jumped to the 0x8048083 location, which is exactly where the overhere label pointed to, as shown in the objdump output.

Calls

The next type of unconditional branch is the call. A call is similar to the jump instruction, but it remembers where it jumped from and has the capability to return there if needed. This is used when implementing functions in assembly language programs.

Functions enable you to write compartmentalized code; that is, you can separate different functions into different sections of the text. If multiple areas of the program use the same functions, the same code does not need to be written multiple times. The single function can be referenced using call statements.

The call instruction has two parts. The first part is the actual CALL instruction, which requires a single operand, the address of the location to jump to:

```
call address
```

The `address` operand refers to a label in the program, which is converted to the memory address of the first instruction in the function.

The second part of the call instruction is the return instruction. This enables the function to return to the original part of the code, immediately after the `CALL` instruction. The return instruction has no operands, just the mnemonic `RET`. It knows where to return to by looking at the stack. This is demonstrated in Figure 6-3.

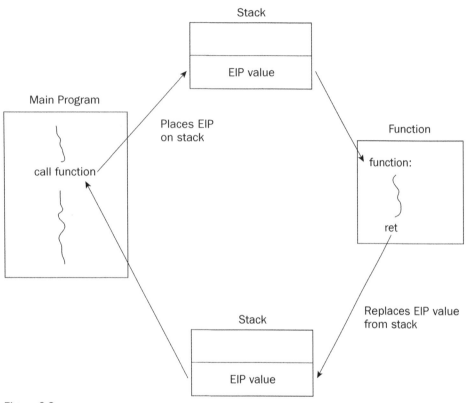

Figure 6-3

When the `CALL` instruction is executed, it places the `EIP` register onto the stack and then modifies the `EIP` register to point to the called function address. When the called function is completed, it retrieves the old `EIP` register value from the stack and returns control back to the original program.

How functions return to the main program is possibly the most confusing part of using functions in assembly language. It is not as simple as just using the `RET` instruction at the end of a function. Instead, it relates to how information is passed to functions and how functions read and store that information.

This is all done using the stack. As mentioned in Chapter 5, "Moving Data," not only can the data on the stack be referenced using `PUSH` and `POP` instructions, it can also be directly referenced using the `ESP` register, which points to the last entry in the stack. Functions normally copy the `ESP` register to the `EBP` register, and then use the EBP register value to retrieve information passed on the stack before the CALL instruction, and to place variables on the stack for local data storage (see Chapter 11, "Using Functions"). This complicates how the stack pointer is manipulated within the function.

This is a somewhat simplified explanation of how functions use the stack. Chapter 11, "Using Functions," describes this in great detail, explaining and demonstrating how functions use the stack for data storage.

The return address is added to the stack when the CALL instruction is executed. When the called function begins, it must store the ESP register somewhere it can be restored to its original form before the RET instruction attempts to return to the calling location. Because the stack may also be manipulated within the function, the EBP register is often used as a base pointer to the stack. Thus, the ESP register is usually copied to the EBP register at the beginning of the function as well.

While this seems confusing, it is not too difficult if you create a standard template to use for all of your function calls. The form to remember for functions is as follows:

```
function_label:
    pushl %ebp
    movl %esp, %ebp
    < normal function code goes here>
    movl %ebp, %esp
    popl %ebp
    ret
```

Once the EBP register has been saved, it can be used as the base pointer to the stack for all access to the stack within the function. Before returning to the calling program, the ESP register must be restored to the location pointing to the calling memory location.

A simple call example is demonstrated in the calltest.s program:

```
# calltest.s - An example of using the CALL instruction
.section .data
output:
    .asciz "This is section %d\n"
.section .text
.globl _start
_start:
    pushl $1
    pushl $output
    call printf
    add  $8, %esp          # should clear up stack
    call overhere
    pushl $3
    pushl $output
    call printf
    add  $8, %esp          # should clear up stack
    pushl $0
    call exit
overhere:
    pushl %ebp
```

```
movl %esp, %ebp
pushl $2
pushl $output
call printf
add  $8, %esp              # should clear up stack
movl %ebp, %esp
popl %ebp
ret
```

The `calltest.s` program begins by using the `printf` C function to display the first text line, showing where the program is. Next, the CALL instruction is used to transfer control to the `overhere` label. At the `overhere` label, the ESP register is copied to the EBP pointer so it can be restored at the end of the function. The `printf` function is used again to display a second line of text, and then the ESP and EBP registers are restored.

Control of the program returns to the instruction immediately after the CALL instruction, and the third text line is displayed, again using the `printf` function. The output should look like this:

```
$ ./calltest
This is section 1
This is section 2
This is section 3
$
```

Be careful when calling external functions from your application. There is no guarantee that the function will return your registers in the same way that you left them before the call. This is discussed in more detail in Chapter 11.

Interrupts

The third type of unconditional branch is the interrupt. An interrupt is a way for the processor to "interrupt" the current instruction code path and switch to a different path. Interrupts come in two varieties:

❑   Software interrupts

❑   Hardware interrupts

Hardware devices generate hardware interrupts. They are used to signal events happening at the hardware level (such as when an I/O port receives an incoming signal). Programs generate software interrupts. They are a signal to hand off control to another program.

When a program is called by an interrupt, the calling program is put on hold, and the called program takes over. The instruction pointer is transferred to the called program, and execution continues from within the called program. When the called program is complete, it can return control back to the calling program (using an interrupt return instruction).

Software interrupts are provided by the operating system to enable applications to tap into functions within the operating system, and in some cases even the underlying BIOS system. In the Microsoft DOS operating system, many functions are provided with the 0x21 software interrupt. In the Linux world, the 0x80 interrupt is used to provide low-level kernel functions.

You have already seen several examples of using the software interrupt in many of the example programs presented so far. Simply using the INT instruction with the 0x80 value transfers control to the Linux system call program. The Linux system call program has many subfunctions that can be used. The subfunctions are performed based on the value of the EAX register at the time of the interrupt. For example, placing the value of 1 in the EAX register before the interrupt calls the exit Linux system call function.

Chapter 12, "Using Linux System Calls," describes all of the functions available with the 0x80 interrupt.

When debugging an application that contains software interrupts, it is difficult to see what is happening within the interrupt section, as the debugging information is not compiled into the functions. You may have noticed when running the debugger that it performs the interrupt instruction but then immediately returns back to the normal program.

Conditional Branches

Unlike unconditional branches, conditional branches are not always taken. The result of the conditional branch depends on the state of the EFLAGS register at the time the branch is executed.

There are many bits in the EFLAGS register, but the conditional branches are only concerned with five of them:

- ❏ Carry flag (CF) - bit 0 (lease significant bit)
- ❏ Overflow flag (OF) - bit 11
- ❏ Parity flag (PF) - bit 2
- ❏ Sign flag (SF) - bit 7
- ❏ Zero flag (ZF) - bit 6

Each conditional jump instruction examines specific flag bits to determine whether the condition is proper for the jump to occur. With five different flag bits, several jump combinations can be performed. The following sections describe the individual jump instructions.

Conditional jump instructions

The conditional jumps determine whether or not to jump based on the current value of the EFLAGS register. Several different conditional jump instructions use different bits of the EFLAGS register. The format of the conditional jump instruction is

```
jxx address
```

where xx is a one- to three-character code for the condition, and address is the location within the program to jump to (usually denoted by a label). The following table describes all of the conditional jump instructions available.

Instruction	Description	EFLAGS
JA	Jump if above	CF=0 and ZF=0
JAE	Jump if above or equal	CF=0
JB	Jump if below	CF=1
JBE	Jump if below or equal	CF=1 or ZF=1
JC	Jump if carry	CF=1
JCXZ	Jump if CX register is 0	
JECXZ	Jump if ECX register is 0	
JE	Jump if equal	ZF=1
JG	Jump if greater	ZF=0 and SF=OF
JGE	Jump if greater or equal	SF=OF
JL	Jump if less	SF<>OF
JLE	Jump if less or equal	ZF=1 or SF<>OF
JNA	Jump if not above	CF=1 or ZF=1
JNAE	Jump if not above or equal	CF=1
JNB	Jump if not below	CF=0
JNBE	Jump if not below or equal	CF=0 and ZF=0
JNC	Jump if not carry	CF=0
JNE	Jump if not equal	ZF=0
JNG	Jump if not greater	ZF=1 or SF<>OF
JNGE	Jump if not greater or equal	SF<>OF
JNL	Jump if not less	SF=OF
JNLE	Jump if not less or equal	ZF=0 and SF=OF
JNO	Jump if not overflow	OF=0
JNP	Jump if not parity	PF=0
JNS	Jump if not sign	SF=0
JNZ	Jump if not zero	ZF=0
JO	Jump if overflow	OF=1
JP	Jump if parity	PF=1
JPE	Jump if parity even	PF=1
JPO	Jump if parity odd	PF=0
JS	Jump if sign	SF=1
JZ	Jump if zero	ZF=1

You may notice that many of the conditional jump instructions seem redundant (such as JA for jump if above and JG jump if greater). The difference is when working with signed and unsigned values. The jump instructions using the above and lower keywords are used for evaluating unsigned integer values. You will learn more about the different types of integers in Chapter 7, "Using Numbers."

The conditional jump instructions take a single operand in the instruction code — the address to jump to. While usually a label in an assembly language program, the operand is converted into an offset address in the instruction code. Two types of jumps are allowed for conditional jumps:

❑ Short jumps

❑ Near jumps

A short jump uses an 8-bit signed address offset, whereas a near jump uses either a 16-bit or 32-bit signed address offset. The offset value is added to the instruction pointer.

Conditional jump instructions do not support far jumps in the segmented memory model. If you are programming in the segmented memory model, you must use programming logic to determine whether the condition exists, and then implement an unconditional jump to the instructions in the separate segment.

To be able to use a conditional jump, you must have an operation that sets the EFLAGS register before the conditional jump. The next section shows some examples of using conditional jumps in assembly language programs.

The compare instruction

The compare instruction is the most common way to evaluate two values for a conditional jump. The compare instruction does just what its name says, it compares two values and sets the EFLAGS registers accordingly.

The format of the CMP instruction is as follows:

```
cmp operand1, operand2
```

The CMP instruction compares the second operand with the first operand. It performs a subtraction operation on the two operands behind the scenes (operand2 – operand1). Neither of the operands is modified, but the EFLAGS register is set as if the subtraction took place.

*When using the GNU assembler, remember that **operand1** and **operand2** are the reverse from what is described in the Intel documentation for the **CMP** instruction. This little feature has caused many hours of debugging nightmares for many an assembly language programmer.*

The following `cmptest.s` program is shown as a quick demonstration of how the compare and conditional jump instructions work together:

```
# cmptest.s - An example of using the CMP and JGE instructions
.section .text
.globl _start
_start:
    nop
    movl $15, %eax
    movl $10, %ebx
    cmp %eax, %ebx
    jge greater
    movl $1, %eax
    int $0x80
greater:
    movl $20, %ebx
    movl $1, %eax
    int $0x80
```

The `cmptest.s` program first assigns to immediate data values: the value 15 to the EAX register, and the value 10 to the EBX register. Next, the CMP instruction is used to compare the two registers, and the JGE instruction is used to branch, depending on the values:

```
cmp %eax, %ebx
jge greater
```

Because the value of the EBX register is less than the value of EAX, the conditional branch is not taken. The instruction pointer moves on to the next instruction, which moves the immediate value of 1 to the EAX register, and then calls the Linux exit system call. You can test this by running the program and displaying the result code:

```
$ ./cmptest
$ echo $?
10
$
```

Indeed, the branch was not taken, and the value in the EBX register remained at 10.

The preceding example compared the values of two registers. Following are some other examples of the CMP instruction:

```
cmp $20, %ebx    ; compare EBX with the immediate value 20
cmp data, %ebx   ; compare EBX with the value in the data memory location
cmp (%edi), %ebx ; compare EBX with the value referenced by the EDI pointer
```

Examples of using the flag bits

Trying to code conditional jump instructions can be tricky. It helps to have an understanding of each of the flag bits that must be present in order for the different conditions to be met. The following sections demonstrate how each of the flag bits affect the conditional jumps, so you can get a feeling for what to look for when coding your programming logic.

Using the Zero flag

The Zero flag is the easiest thing to check when doing conditional jumps. The JE and JZ instructions both branch if the Zero flag is set (the two operands are equal). The Zero flag can be set by either a CMP instruction or a mathematical instruction that evaluates to Zero, as shown in the following example:

```
movl $30, %eax
subl $30, %eax
jz overthere
```

The JZ instruction would be performed, as the result of the SUB instruction would be Zero (the SUB instruction is covered in Chapter 8, "Basic Math Functions").

You can also use the Zero flag when decreasing the value of a register to determine whether it has reached Zero:

```
movl $10, %edi
loop1:
    < other code instructions>
    dec %edi
    jz out
    jmp loop1
out:
```

This code snippet uses the EDI register as an indexed counter that counts back from 10 to 1 (when it reaches zero, the JZ instruction will exit the loop).

Using the overflow flag

The overflow flag is used specifically when working with signed numbers (see Chapter 7). It is set when a signed value is too large for the data element containing it. This usually happens during arithmetic operations that overflow the size of the register holding the data, as shown in the following example:

```
    movl $1, %eax       ; move 1 to the EAX register
    movb $0x7f, %bl     ; move the signed value 127 to the 8-bit BL register
    addb $10, %bl       ; Add 10 to the BL register
    jo overhere
    int $0x80           ; call the Linux system call
overhere:
    movl $0, %ebx       ; move 0 to the EBX register
    int $0x80           ; call the Linux system call
```

This code snippet adds 10 to a signed byte value of 127. The result would be 137, which is a valid value in the byte, but not within a signed byte number (which can only use –127 to 127). Because the signed value is not valid, the overflow flag is set, and the JO instruction is implemented.

Using the parity flag

The parity flag indicates the number of bits that should be one in a mathematical answer. This can be used as a crude error-checking system to ensure that the mathematical operation was successful.

If the number of bits set to one in the resultant is even, the parity bit is set (one). If the number of bits set to one in the resultant is odd, the parity bit is not set (zero).

To test this concept, you can create the `paritytest.s` program:

```
# paritytest.s - An example of testing the parity flag
.section .text
.globl _start
_start:
    movl $1, %eax
    movl $4, %ebx
    subl $3,  %ebx
    jp overhere
    int $0x80
overhere:
    movl $100, %ebx
    int $0x80
```

In this snippet, the result from the subtraction is 1, which in binary is 00000001. Because the number of one bits is odd, the parity flag is not set, so the JP instruction should not branch; instead, the program should exit with a result code of the result of the subtraction, 1:

```
$ ./paritytest
$ echo $?
1
$
```

To test the opposite, change the SUB instruction line to create a result with an even number of one bits:

```
subl $1, %ebx
```

The result of this subtraction will be 3, which in binary is 00000011. Because this is an even number of one bits, the parity flag will be set, and the JP instruction should branch to the `overhere` label, setting the result code to `100`:

```
$ ./paritytest
$ echo $?
100
$
```

Yes, it worked as expected!

Using the sign flag

The sign flag is used in signed numbers to indicate a sign change in the value contained in the register. In a signed number, the last (highest order) bit is used as the sign bit. It indicates whether the numeric representation is negative (set to 1) or positive (set to 0).

This is handy when counting within a loop and watching for zero. You saw with the Zero flag that the flag was set when the value that was being decreased reached zero. However, if you are dealing with arrays, most likely you also need to stop after the zero value, not at the zero value (because the first offset is 0).

Using the sign flag, you can tell when a value has passed from 0 to –1, as shown in the following signtest.s program:

```
# signtest.s - An example of using the sign flag
.section .data
value:
    .int 21, 15, 34, 11, 6, 50, 32, 80, 10, 2
output:
    .asciz "The value is: %d\n"
.section .text
.globl _start
_start:
    movl $9, %edi
loop:
    pushl value(, %edi, 4)
    pushl $output
    call printf
    add $8, $esp
    dec %edi
    jns loop
    movl $1, %eax
    movl $0, %ebx
    int $0x80
```

The signtest.s program walks backward through a data array using the EDI register as an index, decreasing it for each array element. The JNS instruction is used to detect when the value of the EDI register becomes negative, and loops back to the beginning if not.

Because the signtest.s program uses the printf C function, remember to link it with the dynamic loader (as described in Chapter 4, "A Sample Assembly Language Program"). The output from the program should look like this:

```
$ ./signtest
The value is: 2
The value is: 10
The value is: 80
The value is: 32
The value is: 50
The value is: 6
The value is: 11
The value is: 34
The value is: 15
The value is: 21
$
```

Using the carry flag

The carry flag is used in mathematical expressions to indicate when an overflow has occurred in an unsigned number (remember that signed numbers use the overflow flag). The carry flag is set when an instruction causes a register to go beyond its data size limit.

Unlike the overflow flag, the DEC and INC instructions do not affect the carry flag. For example, this code snippet will not set the carry flag:

```
movl $0xffffffff, %ebx
inc %ebx
jc overflow
```

However, this code snippet will set the carry flag, and the JC instruction will jump to the overflow location:

```
movl $0xffffffff, %ebx
addl $1,  %ebx
jc overflow
```

The carry flag will also be set when an unsigned value is less than zero. For example, this code snippet will also set the carry flag:

```
movl $2, %eax
subl $4, %eax
jc overflow
```

The resulting value in the EAX register is 254, which represents –2 as a signed number, the correct answer. This means that the overflow flag would not be set. However, because the answer is below zero for an unsigned number, the carry flag is set.

Unlike the other flags, there are instructions that can specifically modify the carry flag. These are described in the following table.

Instruction	Description
CLC	Clear the carry flag (set it to zero)
CMC	Complement the carry flag (change it to the opposite of what is set)
STC	Set the carry flag (set it to one)

Each of these instructions directly modifies the carry flag bit in the EFLAGS register.

Loops

Loops are another way of altering the instruction path within the program. Loops enable you to code repetitive tasks with a single loop function. The loop operations are performed repeatedly until a specific condition is met.

The following sections describe the different loop instructions available for you to use and show an example of using loops within an assembly language program.

The loop instructions

In the `signtest.s` example program shown in the section "Using the sign flag," you created a loop by using a jump instruction and decreasing a register value. The IA-32 platform provides a simpler mechanism for performing loops in assembly language programs: the loop instruction family.

The loop instructions use the ECX register as a counter and automatically decrease its value as the loop instruction is executed. The following table describes the instructions in the loop family.

Instruction	Description
LOOP	Loop until the ECX register is zero
LOOPE/LOOPZ	Loop until either the ECX register is zero, or the ZF flag is not set
LOOPNE/LOOPNZ	Loop until either the ECX register is zero, or the ZF flag is set

The LOOPE/LOOPZ and LOOPNE/LOOPNZ instructions provide the additional benefit of monitoring the Zero flag.

The format for each of these instructions is

```
loop address
```

where `address` is a label name for a location in the program code to jump to. Unfortunately, the loop instructions support only an 8-bit offset, so only short jumps can be performed.

Before the loop starts, you must set the value for the number of iterations to perform in the ECX register. This usually looks something like the following:

```
    < code before the loop >
    movl $100, %ecx
loop1:
    < code to loop through >
    loop loop1
    < code after the loop >
```

Be careful with the code inside the loop. If the ECX register is modified, it will affect the operation of the loop. Use extra caution when implementing function calls within the loop, as functions can easily trash the value of the ECX register without you knowing it.

An added benefit of the loop instructions is that they decrease the value of the ECX register without affecting the EFLAGS register flag bits. When the ECX register reaches zero, the Zero flag is not set.

A loop example

As a simple example to demonstrate how the LOOP instruction works, here's the loop.s program:

```
# loop.s - An example of the loop instruction
.section .data
output:
    .asciz "The value is: %d\n"
.section .text
.globl _start
_start:
    movl $100, %ecx
    movl $0, %eax
loop1:
    addl %ecx, %eax
    loop loop1
    pushl %eax
    pushl $output
    call printf
    add $8, %esp
    movl $1, %eax
    movl $0, %ebx
    int $0x80
```

The loop.s program computes the arithmetic series of the number stored in the ECX register and then displays it on the console (using the printf function, so remember to link with the C library and the dynamic linker). The LOOP instruction is used to continually loop through the ADD function until the value of ECX is zero.

Preventing LOOP catastrophes

There is one common problem with the LOOP instruction that sometimes bites assembly language programmers. What if you used the loop.s example program and set the ECX register to zero? Try it and see what happens. Here's the output when I tried it:

```
$ ./loop
The value is: -2147483648
$
```

That is obviously not the correct answer. So what happened? The answer lies in the way the LOOP instruction behaves. When the LOOP instruction is executed, it first decreases the value in ECX by one, and then it checks to see whether it is zero. Using this logic, if the value of ECX is already zero before the LOOP instruction, it will be decreased by one, making it -1. Because this value is not zero, the LOOP instruction continues on its way, looping back to the defined label. The loop will eventually exit when the register overflows, and the incorrect value is displayed.

To correct this problem, you need to check for the special condition when the ECX register contains a zero value. Fortunately, Intel has provided a special instruction just for that purpose. If you remember from the "Conditional Branches" section earlier, the JCXZ instruction is used to perform a conditional branch if the ECX register is zero. This is exactly what we need to solve this problem.

The betterloop.s program uses the JCXZ instruction to provide some rudimentary error-checking for the application:

```
# betterloop.s - An example of the loop and jcxz instructions
.section .data
output:
    .asciz "The value is: %d\n"
.section .text
.globl _start
_start:
    movl $0, %ecx
movl $0, %eax
    jcxz done
loop1:
    addl %ecx, %eax
    loop loop1
done:
    pushl %eax
    pushl $output
    call printf
    movl $1, %eax
    movl $0, %ebx
    int $0x80
```

The betterloop.s program adds a single instruction, the JCXZ instruction, before the loop starts, and a single label to reference the ending instruction codes. Now if the ECX register contains a zero value, the JCXZ instruction catches it, and immediately goes to the output section. Running the program demonstrates that indeed it solves the problem:

```
$ ./betterloop
The value is: 0
$
```

Duplicating High-Level Conditional Branches

If you program in C, C++, Java, or any other high-level language, you probably use a lot of conditional statements that look completely different from the assembly language ones. You can mimic the high-level language functions using the assembly language code you learned in this chapter.

The easiest way to learn how to code high-level functions in assembly language is to see how the assembler does it. The following sections walk through disassembling C language functions to show how they are performed using assembly language.

if statements

The most common conditional statement used in high-level languages is the if statement. The following program, ifthen.c, demonstrates how this is commonly used in C programs:

```
/* ifthen.c - A sample C if-then program */
#include <stdio.h>

int main()
{
   int a = 100;
   int b = 25;
   if (a > b)
   {
      printf("The higher value is %d\n", a);
   } else
      printf("The higher value is %d\n", b);
return 0;
}
```

Because the purpose of this exercise is to see how the code will be converted to assembly language, the actual C program is pretty trivial—just a simple comparison of two known values. You can view the generated assembly language code by using the -S parameter of the GNU compiler:

```
$ gcc -S ifthen.c
$ cat ifthen.s
        .file   "ifthen.c"
        .section        .rodata
.LC0:
        .string "The higher value is %d\n"
        .text
.globl main
        .type   main, @function
main:
        pushl   %ebp
        movl    %esp, %ebp
        subl    $24, %esp
        andl    $-16, %esp
        movl    $0, %eax
        subl    %eax, %esp
        movl    $100, -4(%ebp)
        movl    $25, -8(%ebp)
        movl    -4(%ebp), %eax
        cmpl    -8(%ebp), %eax
        jle     .L2
        movl    -4(%ebp), %eax
        movl    %eax, 4(%esp)
        movl    $.LC0, (%esp)
        call    printf
        jmp     .L3
.L2:
```

```
        movl    -8(%ebp), %eax
        movl    %eax, 4(%esp)
        movl    $.LC0, (%esp)
        call    printf
.L3:
        movl    $0, (%esp)
        call    exit
        .size   main, .-main
        .section    .note.GNU-stack,"",@progbits
        .ident  "GCC: (GNU) 3.3.2 (Debian)"
$
```

That's a lot of assembly code for a simple C function! Now you can see why I wanted to keep the C code simple. Now we can walk through the code step by step to see what it is doing.

The first section of the code:

```
pushl   %ebp
movl    %esp, %ebp
subl    $24, %esp
andl    $-16, %esp
movl    $0, %eax
subl    %eax, %esp
```

stores the EBP register so it can be used as a pointer to the local stack area in the program. The stack pointer, ESP, is then manually manipulated to make room for putting local variables on the stack.

The next section of the code creates the two variables used in the If statement:

```
movl    $100, -4(%ebp)
movl    $25, -8(%ebp)
```

The first instruction manually moves the value for the a variable into a location on the stack (4 bytes in front of the location pointed to by the EBP register). The second instruction manually moves the value for the b variable into the next location on the stack (8 bytes in front of the location pointed to by the EBP register). This technique, commonly used in functions, is discussed in Chapter 11. Now that both variables are stored on the stack, it's time to execute the if statement:

```
movl    -4(%ebp), %eax
cmpl    -8(%ebp), %eax
jle     .L2
```

First, the value for the a variable is moved to the EAX register, and then that value is compared to the value for the b variable, still in the local stack. Instead of looking for the if condition a > b, the assembly language code is looking for the opposite, a <= b. If the statement evaluates to "true," the jump to the .L2 label is made, which is the "else" part of the If statement:

```
.L2:
        movl    -8(%ebp), %eax
        movl    %eax, 4(%esp)
        movl    $.LC0, (%esp)
        call    printf
```

This is the code to print the answer for the b variable, which was contained in the else part of the If statement. First the b variable value is retrieved and manually placed on the stack, and then the location of the output text (located at the .LC0 label) is placed on the stack. With both elements on the stack, the printf C function is called to display the answer. The code then proceeds to the ending instructions.

If the JLE instruction was false, then a is not less than or equal to b, and the jump is not performed. Instead, the "then" part of the If statement is performed:

```
movl    -4(%ebp), %eax
movl    %eax, 4(%esp)
movl    $.LC0, (%esp)
call    printf
jmp     .L3
```

Here, the a variable is loaded onto the stack, along with the output text. Then the printf C function is called to display the answer, and execution jumps to the .L3 label. Finally, all roads load to the exit C function:

```
.L3:
    movl    $0, (%esp)
    call    exit
    .size   main, .-main
    .section        .note.GNU-stack,"",@progbits
    .ident  "GCC: (GNU) 3.3.2 (Debian)"
```

It is pretty easy to see the if-then logic contained in the assembly language code. You can apply the same logic to any if-then situation you need in your assembly language programs.

At first it may appear that the implementation of the if-then logic in assembly language is backwards. It might seem to be easier for the jump instruction to evaluate for the "true" condition to jump to the "then" section. There is a reason why the opposite situation is used, which is shown in the "Optimizing Branch Instructions" section later in this chapter.

The assembly language code used to implement an if statement looks like the following:

```
if:
    <condition to evaluate>
    jxx  else        ; jump to the else part if the condition is false
<code to implement the "then" statements>
jmp end             ;jump to the end
else:
    < code to implement the "else" statements>
end:
```

Of course, this was a trivial example of an If statement. In a real production program, the condition to evaluate becomes much more complicated. In these situations, evaluating the condition for the if statement becomes just as crucial as the If statement code itself.

Instead of a single conditional jump instruction, there may be several, with each one evaluating a separate part of the if condition. For example, the C language if statement

```
if (eax < ebx) || (eax == ecx) then
```

creates the following assembly language code:

```
if:
    cmpl %eax, %ebx
    jle else
    cmpl %eax, %ecx
    jne else
then:
    < then logic code>
    jmp end
else:
    < else logic code >
end:
```

This If statement condition required two separate CMP instructions. Because the logical operator is an OR, if either CMP instruction evaluates to true, the program jumps to the else label. If the logical operator is an AND, you would need to use an intermediate label to ensure that both CMP instructions evaluate to true.

for loops

The next statement to tackle is for loops. Here's the sample C program used to start us off, the for.c program:

```
/* for.c - A sample C for program */
#include <stdio.h>

int main()
{
    int i = 0;
    int j;
    for (i = 0; i < 1000; i++)
    {
        j = i * 5;
        printf("The answer is %d\n", j);
    }
    return 0;
}
```

Again, this uses a pretty simplistic C program to demonstrate how for-next loops are implemented in assembly language code. Here's the assembly code generated by the GNU compiler:

```
$ gcc -S for.c
$ cat for.s
        .file   "for.c"
        .section        .rodata
.LC0:
        .string "The answer is %d\n"
        .text
.globl main
        .type   main, @function
```

```
        main:
        pushl   %ebp
        movl    %esp, %ebp
        subl    $24, %esp
        andl    $-16, %esp
        movl    $0, %eax
        subl    %eax, %esp
        movl    $0, -4(%ebp)
        movl    $0, -4(%ebp)
.L2:
        cmpl    $999, -4(%ebp)
        jle     .L5
        jmp     .L3
.L5:
        movl    -4(%ebp), %edx
        movl    %edx, %eax
        sall    $2, %eax
        addl    %edx, %eax
        movl    %eax, -8(%ebp)
        movl    -8(%ebp), %eax
        movl    %eax, 4(%esp)
        movl    $.LC0, (%esp)
        call    printf
        leal    -4(%ebp), %eax
        incl    (%eax)
        jmp     .L2
.L3:
        movl    $0, (%esp)
        call    exit
        .size   main, .-main
        .section        .note.GNU-stack,"",@progbits
        .ident  "GCC: (GNU) 3.3.2 (Debian)"
$
```

Similar to the if statement code, the for statement code first does some housekeeping with the ESP and EBP registers, manually setting the EBP register to the start of the stack, and making room for the variables used in the function. The for statement starts with the .L2 label:

```
.L2:
    cmpl    $999, -4(%ebp)
    jle     .L5
    jmp     .L3
```

The condition set in the for statement is set at the beginning of the loop. In this case, the condition is to determine whether the variable is less than 1,000. If the condition is true, execution jumps to the .L5 label, where the for loop code is. When the condition is false, execution jumps to the .L3 label, which is the ending code.

The For loop code is as follows:

```
.L5:
    movl    -4(%ebp), %edx
    movl    %edx, %eax
```

```
sall    $2, %eax
addl    %edx, %eax
movl    %eax, -8(%ebp)
movl    -8(%ebp), %eax
movl    %eax, 4(%esp)
movl    $.LC0, (%esp)
call    printf
```

The first variable location (the i variable in the C code) is moved to the EDX register, and then moved to the EAX register. The next two instructions are mathematical operations (which are covered in detail in Chapter 8). The CALL instruction performs a left shift of the EAX register two times. This is equivalent to multiplying the number in the EAX register by 4. The next instruction adds the EDX register value to the EAX register value. Now the EAX register contains the original value multiplied by 5 (tricky).

After the value has been multiplied by 5, it is stored in the location reserved for the second variable (the j variable in the C code). Finally, the value is placed on the stack, along with the location of the output text, and the printf C function is called.

The next part of the code gets back to the for statement function:

```
leal    -4(%ebp), %eax
incl    (%eax)
jmp     .L2
```

The LEA instruction has not been discussed yet. It loads the effective memory address of the declared variable into the register specified. Thus, the memory location of the first variable (i) is loaded into the EAX register. The next instruction uses the indirect addressing mode to increment the value pointed to by the EAX register by one. This in effect adds one to the i variable. After that, execution jumps back to the start of the for loop, where the I value will be tested to determine whether it is less than 1,000, and the whole process is performed again.

From this example you can see the framework for implementing for loops in assembly language. The pseudocode looks something like this:

```
for:
   <condition to evaluate for loop counter value>
   jxx forcode    ; jump to the code of the condition is true
   jmp end        ; jump to the end if the condition is false
forcode:
  < for loop code to execute>
  <increment for loop counter>
   jmp for        ; go back to the start of the For statement
end:
```

*The **while** loop code uses a format similar to the For loop code. Try creating a test **while** loop in a C program and viewing the generated assembly code. It will look similar to the **for** loop code shown here.*

Optimizing Branch Instructions

Branch instructions greatly impact the performance of applications. Most modern processors (including ones in the IA-32 family) utilize instruction prefetch caches to increase performance. As the program is run, the instruction prefetch cache is filled with sequential instructions.

As described in Chapter 2, the out-of-order engine attempts to execute instructions as soon as possible, even if earlier instructions in the program have not yet been executed. Branch instructions, however, create great havoc in the out-of-order engine. The following sections describe how modern Pentium processors handle branches, and what you can do to improve the performance of your assembly language programs.

Branch prediction

When a branch instruction is encountered, the processor out-of-order engine must determine the next instruction to be processed. The out-of-order unit utilizes a separate unit called the **branch prediction front end** to determine whether or not a branch should be followed. The branch prediction front end employs different techniques in its attempt to predict branch activity. When creating assembly language code that includes conditional branches, you should be aware of this processor feature.

Unconditional branches

With unconditional branches, the next instruction is not difficult to determine, but depending on how long of a jump there was, the next instruction may not be available in the instruction prefetch cache. This is demonstrated in Figure 6-4.

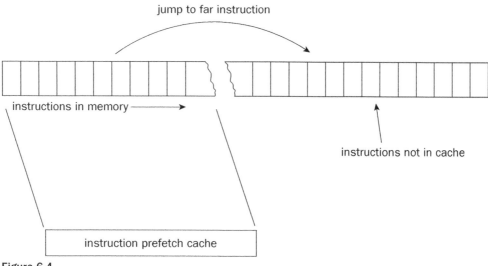

Figure 6-4

When the new instruction location is determined in memory, the out-of-order engine must first determine if the instruction is available in the prefetch cache. If not, the entire prefetch cache must be cleared, and reloaded with instructions from the new location. This can be costly to the performance of the application.

Conditional branches

Conditional branches present an even greater challenge to the processor. For each unconditional branch, the branch prediction unit must determine if the branch should be taken or not. Usually, when the out-of-order engine is ready to execute the conditional branch, not enough information is available to know for certain which direction the branch will take.

Instead, the branch prediction algorithms attempt to guess which path a particular conditional branch will take. This is done using rules and learned history. Three main rules are implemented by the branch prediction algorithms:

❑ Backward branches are assumed to be taken.

❑ Forward branches are assumed to be not taken.

❑ Branches that have been previously taken are taken again.

Using normal programming logic, the most often seen use of backward branches (branches that jump to previous instruction codes) is in loops. For example, the code snippet

```
      movl $100, $ecx
loop1:
      addl %cx, %eax
      decl %ecx
      jns loop1
```

will jump 100 times back to the loop1 label, but fall through to the next instruction only once. The first branching rule will always assume that the backwards branch will be taken. Out of the 101 times the branch is executed, it will only be wrong once.

Forward branches are a little trickier. The branch prediction algorithm assumes that most of the time conditional branches that go forward are not taken. In programming logic, this assumes that the code immediately following the jump instruction is most likely to be taken, rather than the jump that moves over the code. This situation is seen in the following code snippet:

```
        movl    -4(%ebp), %eax
        cmpl    -8(%ebp), %eax
        jle     .L2
        movl    -4(%ebp), %eax
        movl    %eax, 4(%esp)
        movl    $.LC0, (%esp)
        call    printf
        jmp     .L3
.L2:
        movl    -8(%ebp), %eax
        movl    %eax, 4(%esp)
        movl    $.LC0, (%esp)
```

```
        call    printf
.L3:
```

Does this look familiar? It is the code snippet from the analysis of the C program If statement. The code following the JLE instruction handles the "then" part of the If statement. From a branch prediction point of view, we can now see the reason why the JLE instruction was used instead of a JG instruction. When the compiler created the assembly language code, it attempted to maximize the code's performance by guessing that the "then" part of the If statement would be more likely to be taken than the "else" part. Because the processor branch prediction unit assumes forward jumps to not be taken, the "then" code would already be in the instruction prefetch cache, ready to be executed.

The final rule implies that branches that are performed multiple times are likely to follow the same path the majority of the time. The Branch Target Buffer (BTB) keeps track of each branch instruction performed by the processor, and the outcome of the branch is stored in the buffer area.

The BTB information overrides either of the two previous rules for branches. For example, if a backward branch is not taken the first time it is encountered, the branch prediction unit will assume it will not be taken any subsequent times, rather than assume that the backwards branch rule would apply.

The problem with the BTB is that it can become full. As the BTB becomes full, looking up branch results takes longer, and performance for executing the branch decreases.

Optimizing tips

While the processor tries its best to optimize how it handles branches, you can incorporate a few tricks into your assembly language programs to help it along. The following sections describe some of the branch optimization tricks recommended by Intel for use on the Pentium family of processors.

Eliminate branches

The most obvious way to solve branch performance problems is to eliminate the use of branches whenever possible. Intel has helped in this by providing some specific instructions.

In Chapter 5, "Moving Data," the CMOV instructions were discussed. These instructions were specifically designed to help the assembly language programmer avoid using branches to set data values. An example of using a CMOV instruction is as follows:

```
movl value, %ecx
cmpl %ebx, %ecx
cmova %ecx, %ebx
```

The CMOVA instruction checks the results from the CMP instruction. If the unsigned integer value in the ECX register is above the unsigned integer value in the EBX register, the value in the ECX register is placed in the EBX register. This functionality enabled us to create the cmovtest.s program, which determined the largest number in a series without a bunch of jump instructions.

Sometimes duplicating a few extra instructions can eliminate a jump. This small instruction overhead will easily fit into the instruction prefetch cache, and make up for the performance hit of the jump itself. A classic example of this is the situation in which a branch can occur within a loop:

```
loop:
    cmp data(, %edi, 4), %eax
    je part2
    call function1
    jmp looptest
part2:
    call function2
looptest:
    inc %edi
    cmpl $10, %edi
    jnz loop
```

The loop calls one of two functions, depending on the value read from the data array. After the function is called, a jump is made to the end of the loop to increase the index value of the array and loop back to the start of the loop. Each time the first function is called, the JMP instruction must be evaluated to jump forward to the looptest label. Because this is a forward branch, it will not be predicted to be taken, and a performance penalty will result.

To change this, you can modify the code snippet to look like the following:

```
loop:
    cmp data(, %edi, 4), %eax
    je part2
    call function1
    inc %edi
    cmp $10, %edi
    jnz loop
    jmp end
part2:
    call function2
    inc %edi
    cmp $10, %edi
    jnz loop
end:
```

Instead of using the forward branch within the loop, the looptest code was duplicated within the first function code section, eliminating one forward jump from the code.

Code predictable branches first

You can exploit the branch prediction unit rules to increase the performance of your application. As seen in the If statement code presented, placing code that is most likely to be taken as the fall-through of the jump forward statement increases the likelihood that it will be in the instruction prefetch cache when needed. Allow the jump instruction to jump to the less likely used code segments.

For code using backward branches, try to use the backward branch path as the most taken path. When implementing loops this is not usually a problem. However, in some cases you may have to alter the program logic to accomplish this.

Figure 6-5 sums up both of these scenarios.

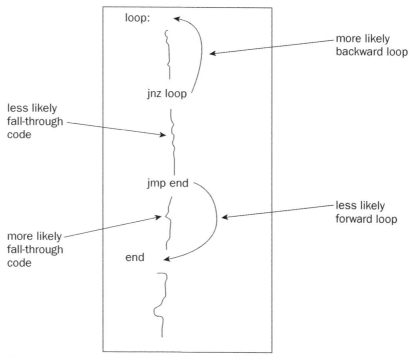

Figure 6-5

Unroll loops

While loops are generally covered by the backward branch rule, there is still a performance penalty even when they are predicted correctly. A better rule-of-thumb to use is to eliminate small loops whenever possible.

The problem appears in loop overhead. Even a simple loop requires a counter that must be checked for each iteration, and a jump instruction that must be evaluated. Depending on the number of program logic instructions within the loop, this can be a huge overhead.

For smaller loops, unrolling the loop can solve this problem. Unrolling the loop means to manually code each of the instructions multiple times instead of using the loop to go back over the same instruction. The following code is an example of a small loop that can be unrolled:

```
    movl values, %ebx
    movl $1, %edi
loop:
    movl values(, %edi, 4), %eax
    cmp %ebx, %eax
    cmova %eax, %ebx
    inc %edi
    cmp $4, %edi
    jne loop
```

This was the main loop from the `cmovtest.s` program in Chapter 5. Instead of looping through the instructions to look for the largest value four times, you can unroll the loop into a series of four moves:

```
movl values, %ebx
movl $values, %ecx
movl (%ecx), %eax
cmp %ebx, %eax
cmova %eax, %ebx
movl 4(%ecx), %eax
cmp %ebx, %eax
cmova %eax, %ebx
movl 8(%ecx), %eax
cmp %ebx, %eax
cmova %eax, %ebx
movl 12(%ecx), %eax
cmp %ebx, %eax
cmova %eax, %ebx
```

While the number of instructions has greatly increased, the processor will be able to feed all of them directly into the instruction prefetch cache, and zip through them in no time.

> *Be careful when unrolling loops though, as it is possible to unroll too many instructions, and fill the prefetch cache. This will force the processor to constantly fill and empty the prefetch cache.*

Summary

This chapter presented instructions to help you program logic into your assembly language programs. Just about every assembly language program needs the capability to branch to other parts of the instruction code depending on data values, or to loop through sections of code a specific number of times.

The IA-32 platform provides several instructions for coding branching and looping functions. There are two different types of branch functions: unconditional branches and conditional branches. Unconditional branches are performed regardless of external values or events, whereas conditional branches rely on an external value or event to branch.

There are three types of unconditional branches: jumps, calls, and interrupts. The unconditional jump is the most basic form of execution control. The JMP instruction forces the instruction pointer to change to the destination location, and the processor executes the next instruction at that spot. Calls are similar to jumps, but support the capability to return to the location after the call. The return location is stored in the stack area, and the called function must restore the stack back to its original condition before returning to the calling area. Software interrupts are used to provide access to low-level kernel functions in the operating system. Both Microsoft Windows and Linux provide system calls via software interrupts. The Linux system calls are available at software interrupt 0x80.

Conditional branches rely on the values of the EFLAGS register. Specifically, the carry, overflow, parity, sign, and Zero flags are used to affect the conditional branch. Specific branch instructions monitor specific flag bits, such as the JC instruction jumps when the carry flag is set, and the JZ instruction jumps when the Zero flag is set. The CMP instruction is helpful in comparing two values and setting EFLAGS bits for the conditional jump instruction.

Loops provide a method for you to easily replicate code functions without having to duplicate a lot of code. Just as in high-level languages, loops enable you to perform tasks a specific number of times by using a counter value that is decreased for each iteration. The LOOP instruction automatically uses the ECX register as the counter, and decreases and tests it during each iteration.

You can duplicate high-level language conditional functions such as If-then and For statements using common assembly language jumps and loops. To see how C functions are coded, you can use the -S parameter of the GNU compiler to view the generated assembly language code.

When working with Pentium processors, you can use some optimization techniques to increase the performance of your assembly language code. Pentium processors use the instruction prefetch cache, and attempt to load instructions as quickly as possible into the cache. Unfortunately, branch instructions can have a detrimental effect on the prefetch cache. As branches are detected in the cache, the out-of-order engine attempts to predict what path the branch is most likely to take. If it is wrong, the instruction prefetch cache is loaded with instructions that are not used, and processor time is wasted. To help solve this problem, you should be aware of how the processor predicts branches, and attempt to code your branches in the same manner. Also, eliminating branches whenever possible will greatly speed things up. Finally, examining loops and converting them into a sequential series of operations enables the processor to load all of the instructions into the prefetch cache, and not have to worry about branching for the loop.

The next chapter discusses how the processor deals with various types of numbers. Just as in high-level languages, there are multiple ways to represent numbers, and there are multiple ways that those numbers are handled in assembly language programs. Knowing all the different types of number formats can help you when working with mathematically intensive operations.

7

Using Numbers

Representing and working with numbers is a large part of any assembly language program. Almost every application uses some type of numerical data to process information. Just like high-level languages, assembly language can represent numbers in many different formats. If you are used to programming in C or C++, you are familiar with defining specific data type variables. Each time the variable is present, the compiler knows what type of data it represents. In assembly language programming, this is not always the case. Values stored in memory or registers can be interpreted as many different data types. It is your job as the assembly language programmer to ensure that the stored data is interpreted in the proper manner using the proper instructions. The purpose of this chapter is to describe the different number formats available, and demonstrate how they are used in assembly language programs.

The chapter starts off by describing the integer data types, unsigned and signed. After that, a discussion on the special Binary Coded Decimal data type is presented, along with examples of using it in programs. After that, floating-point numbers are tackled, including both the standard single and double-precision floating-point formats, and the Intel double-extended and packed single- and double-precision formats. Finally, some of the Intel instructions used to convert numeric data types from one format to another are presented.

Numeric Data Types

There are numerous ways to represent numerical values in assembly language programs. Often, you must utilize more than one data type to represent data elements within your assembly language program. The IA-32 platform contains several different numeric data types that can be used in assembly language programs. The core numeric data types are as follows:

- ❏ Unsigned integers
- ❏ Signed integers
- ❏ Binary-coded decimal
- ❏ Packed binary-coded decimal
- ❏ Single-precision floating-point
- ❏ Double-precision floating-point
- ❏ Double-extended floating-point

Besides these basic numeric data types, the SIMD extensions on Pentium processors add other advanced numeric data types:

- ❏ 64-bit packed integers
- ❏ 128-bit packed integers
- ❏ 128-bit packed single-precision floating-point
- ❏ 128-bit packed double-precision floating-point

While the list of available numeric data types is quite large, it is relatively easy to work with numbers in different data types within assembly language. The following sections describe each of these data types, and show examples of how they are used in assembly language programs.

Integers

The most basic form of numbers used in assembly language programs are integers. They can represent whole number quantities for a large range of values. This section describes the different types of integers available for use in your assembly language programs and shows how the processor handles each of the different types of integer values.

Standard integer sizes

Integers can be represented by a variety of sizes — that is, the number of bytes used to represent the integer quantity. The basic IA-32 platform supports four different integer sizes:

- ❏ **Byte:** 8 bits
- ❏ **Word:** 16 bits
- ❏ **Doubleword:** 32 bits
- ❏ **Quadword:** 64 bits

It is important to remember that integers stored in memory using more than 1 byte are stored in little-endian format. This means that the lowest-order byte is stored in the lowest memory location, and the remaining bytes are stored sequentially after that. However, when the integer values are moved to registers, the values are stored in big-endian format within the register (see Figure 7-1). Sometimes this is confusing to work with.

Memory

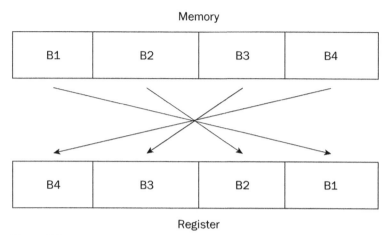

Register

Figure 7-1

The conversion happens behind the scenes within the processor, so you do not necessarily have to worry about this, but it is important when you are debugging an application and are watching data values. You might see something like this:

```
(gdb) x/x &data
0x80490bc <data>:       0x00000225
(gdb) x/4b &data
0x80490bc <data>:       0x25     0x02     0x00     0x00
(gdb) print/x $eax
$1 = 0x225
(gdb)
```

The decimal value 549 is stored in memory location data, and moved to the EAX register. The first gdb command uses the x command to display the value in memory located at the data label in hexadecimal format. The hexadecimal display shows what we would expect for the hex version of 549. The next command displays the 4 bytes that make up the integer value. Notice that the binary format version shows the 0x25 and 0x02 hex values reversed, which is what we would expect for little-endian format. The last command uses the print command to display the same value after it is loaded into the EAX register, again in hexadecimal format.

Unsigned integers

The unsigned integer is pretty much the "what you see is what you get" data type. The value of the bytes that compose the integer directly represents the integer value.

The four different sizes of unsigned integers can produce unsigned integers of different magnitudes, based on the number of bits used. These sizes are shown in the following table.

Bits	Integer Values
8	0 through 255
16	0 through 65,535
32	0 through 4,294,967,295
64	0 through 18,446,744,073,709,551,615

The 8-bit integer value is contained within a single byte (as expected). The binary value contained in the byte is the actual integer value. Thus, a byte with a binary value of 11101010 (which can be represented by the hexadecimal value 0xEA) has the unsigned integer value of 234.

The 16-bit unsigned integer value is contained in two consecutive bytes, which are combined to form a single word. An example of a word value as stored in a register is shown in Figure 7-2.

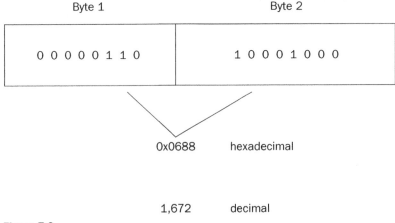

Figure 7-2

The 32-bit unsigned integer values are contained in four consecutive (big-endian) bytes, which are combined to form the doubleword. The doubleword is the most commonly used format for unsigned integers on the IA-32 platform. An example of a doubleword is shown in Figure 7-3.

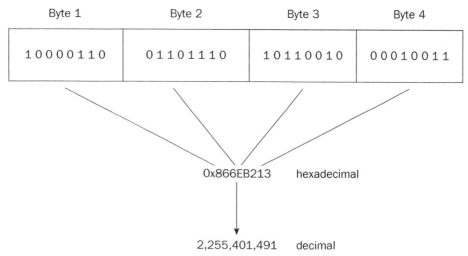

Figure 7-3

In Figure 7-3, each byte is represented by a hexadecimal pair (4 bits per hexadecimal value), which are combined to form the eight-character hexadecimal value. Again, this example uses big-endian format, as seen in the register.

The 64-bit unsigned integer values are contained in eight consecutive bytes, which together are the quadword. An example of a quadword is shown in Figure 7-4.

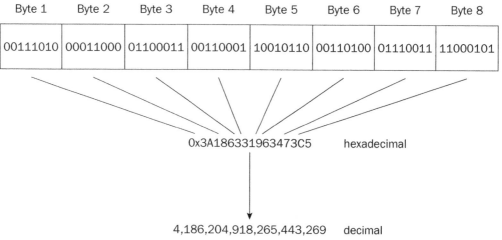

Figure 7-4

Signed integers

While using unsigned integers is easy, the downside is that there is no way to represent negative numbers. To solve this problem, a method of representing negative numbers on the processor needed to be adopted. There are three common methods used to depict negative numbers in computers:

- ❏ Signed magnitude
- ❏ One's complement
- ❏ Two's complement

All three methods use the same bit sizes as unsigned integers (byte, word, doubleword, and quadword), but represent the decimal values differently within the bits. The IA-32 platform uses the two's complement method to represent signed integers, but it's a good idea to understand how each of these methods work. The following sections describe each of them.

Signed magnitude

The signed magnitude method splits the bits that make up the signed integer into two parts: a sign bit and the magnitude bits. The most significant (leftmost) bit of the bytes is used to represent the sign of the value. Positive numbers contain a zero in the most significant bit, whereas negative numbers have a one there. The remaining bits in the value represent the magnitude of the number using their normal binary values, as shown in Figure 7-5.

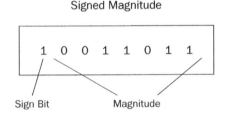

Signed Magnitude

1   0   0   1   1   0   1   1

Sign Bit   Magnitude

hexadecimal 0x9B

decimal -27

Figure 7-5

One problem with the signed magnitude method is that there are two different ways to express a zero value: 00000000 (decimal +0) and 10000000 (decimal -0). This can complicate some mathematical processes. Also, arithmetic using signed magnitude numbers is complicated, as adding and subtracting simple signed integers cannot be done in the same way as unsigned numbers. For example, doing a simple binary addition of the values 00000001 (decimal 1) and 10000001 (decimal –1) produces 10000010 (decimal –2), which is not the correct answer. Different arithmetic instructions for signed integers and unsigned numbers would be required on the processor.

One's complement

The one's complement method takes the inverse of the unsigned integer value to produce the similar negative value. The inverse changes any zero bits to ones, and any ones bits to zeroes. Thus, the one's complement of 00000001 would be 11111110. Again, as with signed magnitude numbers, one's complement numbers have some problems when performing mathematical operations. There are two ways of representing a zero value (00000000 and 11111111), and arithmetic with one's complement numbers is also complicated (it does not allow you to do standard binary math).

Two's complement

The two's compliment method solves the arithmetic problem of the signed magnitude and one's complement methods using a simple mathematical trick. For negative integer values, a one is added to the one's complement of the value.

For example, to find the two's complement value for decimal -1 you would do the following:

1. Take the one's complement of 00000001, which is 11111110.

2. Add one to the one's complement, which is 11111111.

Doing the same for the value -2 you would get 11111110, and for -3 it would be 11111101. You may notice a trend here. The two's complement value counts down from 11111111 (decimal –1) until it gets to 10000000, which represents -128. Of course, for multibyte integer sizes the same principle applies across the bytes.

While this seems like an odd thing to do, it solves all of the problems in adding and subtracting signed integers. For example, adding the values 00000001 (+1) and 11111111 (-1) produces the value 00000000, along with a carry value. The carry value is ignored in signed integer arithmetic, so the final value is indeed 0. The same hardware can be used to add and subtract both unsigned and signed values.

Given the same number of bits, the two's complement format represents the same number of values as its unsigned integer counterpart, but must divide the values between positive and negative numbers. Thus, the maximum value a signed integer value can have is half that of the unsigned value. The following table shows the minimum and maximum values for each type of signed integer.

Bits	Minimum and Maximum Signed Values
8	-128 to 127
16	-32,768 to 32,767
32	-2,147,483,648 to 2,147,483,647
64	-9,223,372,036,854,775,808 to 9,223,372,036,854,775,807

Using signed integers

The signed integer representation in memory and registers is often difficult to recognize unless you know what to expect. Sometimes the GNU debugger can help out, but sometimes even it is confused. The sample program inttest.s demonstrates this:

```
# inttest.s - An example of using signed integers
.section .data
data:
    .int -45
.section .text
.globl _start
_start:
    nop
    movl $-345, %ecx
    movw $0xffb1, %dx
    movl data, %ebx
    movl $1, %eax
    int $0x80
```

The inttest.s program demonstrates three different ways to store signed integer values in registers. The first two use immediate values to place negative signed integers in registers:

```
movl $-345, %ecx
movw $0xffb1, %dx
```

The MOVW instruction is used to place a 16-bit word signed integer value 0xFFB1 (-79) into the DX register. The third method uses the data label, which contains a signed integer value, and places it in the EBX register.

After assembling the program, you can run it in the debugger to watch what happens. Step through the instructions until all of the data is loaded into the registers. Next, use the info command to display the register values:

```
(gdb) info reg
eax            0x0        0
ecx            0xfffffea7       -345
edx            0xffb1     65457
ebx            0xffffffd3       -45
```

The debugger assumes that the EBX and ECX registers contain signed integer data and displays the answers using the data types we expected. Unfortunately, the EDX register had a problem. Because the debugger is trying to display the entire EDX register as a signed integer data value, it is assuming that the entire EDX register contains a single doubleword signed integer. Because it only contains a word integer, the interpreted value is wrong. Remember that the data within the register is still correct (0xFFB1), but what the debugger thinks that number represents is wrong.

Extending integers

The dilemma shown in the `inttest.s` program demonstrates how the processor handles signed integers in an environment of mixed integer sizes. Often, you will find yourself with one size of integer value and need to move the value to a larger size (such as moving a word to a doubleword). While this may seem like a trivial thing, sometimes it is not so trivial.

Extending unsigned integers

When converting unsigned integer values to a larger bit size (such as converting a word to a doubleword), you must ensure that all of the leading bits are set to zero. You should not simply copy one value to the other, as shown here:

```
movw %ax, %bx
```

There is no guarantee that the upper part of the EBX register contains zeroes. To accomplish this, you must use two instructions:

```
movl $0, %ebx
movw %ax, %ebx
```

The MOVL instruction is used to load a zero value in the EBX register. This guarantees that the EBX register is completely zero. Then you can safely move the unsigned integer value in the AX register to the EBX register.

To help you in these situations, Intel provides the MOVZX instruction. This instruction moves a smaller-sized unsigned integer value (in either a register or a memory location) to a larger-sized unsigned integer value (only in a register).

The format of the MOVZX instruction is

```
movzx source, destination
```

where `source` can be an 8-bit or 16-bit register or memory location, and `destination` can be a 16-bit or 32-bit register. The `movzxtest.s` program demonstrates this instruction:

```
# movzxtest.s - An example of the MOVZX instruction
.section .text
.globl _start
_start:
    nop
    movl $279, %ecx
    movzx %cl, %ebx
    movl $1, %eax
    int $0x80
```

The `movzxtest.s` program simply puts a large value in the ECX register, and then uses the MOVZX instruction to copy the lower 8 bits to the EBX register. Because the value placed in the ECX register used a word unsigned integer to represent it (it is larger than 255), the value in CL represents only part of the complete value. You can watch the program in the debugger and see what is happening to the registers:

```
$ gdb -q movzxtest
(gdb) break *_start+1
Breakpoint 1 at 0x8048075: file movzxtest.s, line 5.
(gdb) run
Starting program: /home/rich/palp/chap07/movzxtest

Breakpoint 1, _start () at movzxtest.s:5
5           movl $279, %ecx
Current language:  auto; currently asm
(gdb) s
6           movzx %cl, %ebx
(gdb) s
7           movl $1, %eax
(gdb) print $ecx
$1 = 279
(gdb) print $ebx
$2 = 23
(gdb) print/x $ecx
$3 = 0x117
(gdb) print/x $ebx
$4 = 0x17
(gdb)
```

By printing out the decimal values of the EBX and ECX registers, you can tell right away that the unsigned integer value was not copied correctly — the original value was 279 but the new value is only 23. By displaying the values in hexadecimal, you can see what happened. The original value in hex is 0x0117, which takes a doubleword to hold. The MOVZX instruction moved just the lower byte of the ECX register, but zeroed out the remaining bytes in the EBX register, producing the 0x17 value in the EBX register.

Extending signed integers

Extending signed integer values is different than extending unsigned integers. Padding the high bits with zeroes will change the value of the data for negative numbers. For example, the value -1 (11111111) moved to a doubleword would yield the value 0000000011111111, which in signed integer notation would be +127, not -1. For a signed extension to work, the new bits added must be set to a one value. Thus, the new doubleword would yield the value 1111111111111111, which is the signed integer notation for the value -1, which is what it should be.

Intel has provided the MOVSX instruction to allow extending signed integers and preserving the sign. It is similar to the MOVSZ instruction, but it assumes that the bytes to be moved are in signed integer format and attempts to preserve the signed integer value for the move. The movsxtest.s program is used to demonstrate this:

```
# movsxtest.s - An example of the MOVSX instruction
.section .text
.globl _start
_start:
    nop
    movw $-79, %cx
    movl $0, %ebx
```

```
movw %cx, %bx
movsx %cx, %eax
movl $1, %eax
movl $0, %ebx
int $0x80
```

The movsxtest.s program defines a negative value in the CX register (a doubleword size). It then attempts to copy the value to the EBX register by zeroing the EBX register, and using the MOV instruction. Next, the MOVSX instruction is used to move the CX value to the EAX register. To see what happens, you must run the program in the debugger, and display the register values:

```
(gdb) info reg
eax            0xffffffb1        -79
ecx            0xffb1    65457
edx            0x0       0
ebx            0xffb1    65457
```

After stepping through the program until after the MOVSX instruction, you can display the register values using the debugger info command. The ECX register contains the value 0x0000FFB1. The lower 16 bits contain the 0xFFB1 value, which is -79 in signed integer. When the CX register is moved to the EBX register, the EBX register contains the value 0x0000FFB1, which in signed integer is 65,457, not what we wanted.

After using the MOVSX instruction to move the CX register to the EAX register, the EAX register contains the value 0xFFFFFFB1, which in signed integer is -79. The MOVSX instruction properly added the leading ones to the value.

Just to make sure we are on the right track, the movsxtest2.s program does the same thing, but with a positive signed integer value:

```
# movsxtest2.s - Another example using the MOVSX instruction
.section .text
.globl _start
_start:
    nop
    movw $79, %cx
    xor %ebx, %ebx
    movw %cx, %bx
    movsx %cx, %eax
    movl $1, %eax
    movl $0, %ebx
    int $0x80
```

After assembling and linking the program, run it in the debugger and look at the register values:

```
(gdb) info reg
eax            0x4f      79
ecx            0x4f      79
edx            0x0       0
ebx            0x4f      79
```

This time when the CX register was moved to the empty EBX register, the value was in the proper format (because the leading zeroes are OK for positive numbers). Also, the MOVSX instruction correctly filled the EAX register with zeroes to produce the proper 32-bit signed integer value.

Defining integers in GAS

The example programs shown in the preceding section demonstrated how to use immediate data values in assembly language programs. You can also define signed integer values using directives in the data section.

Chapter 5, "Moving Data," shows how to use the .int, .short, and .long directives to define signed integer data values in the data section. These directives create doubleword signed integer values. It is also possible to create quadword signed integer values using the .quad directive.

The .quad directive enables you to define one or more signed integer values, but assigns 8 bytes for each value. To demonstrate this, the quadtest.s program is used:

```
# quadtest.s - An example of quad integers
.section .data
data1:
    .int 1, -1, 463345, -333252322, 0
data2:
    .quad 1, -1, 463345, -333252322, 0
.section .text
.globl _start
_start:
    nop
    movl $1, %eax
    movl $0, %ebx
    int $0x80
```

The quadtest.s program simply defines a five doubleword signed integer array at the data1 label, and a five quadword signed integer array (using the .quad directive) at the data2 label, and then exits the program. To see what is happening here, again assemble the program and run it in the debugger.

First, look at what the debugger thinks are the decimal values of the data1 and data2 arrays:

```
(gdb) x/5d &data1
0x8049084 <data1>:       1          -1        463345   -333252322
0x8049094 <data1+16>:    0
(gdb) x/5d &data2
0x8049098 <data2>:       1          0         -1       -1
0x80490a8 <data2+16>:    463345
(gdb)
```

The values for the data1 array are as expected, but look what happened to the values in the data2 array. This is not what was used in the program. The problem is that the debugger is assuming that these are doubleword signed integer values.

Next, look at how the array values are stored in memory at the data1 label location:

```
(gdb) x/20b &data1
0x8049084 <data1>:      0x01    0x00    0x00    0x00    0xff    0xff    0xff    0xff
0x804908c <data1+8>:    0xf1    0x11    0x07    0x00    0x1e    0xf9    0x22    0xec
0x8049094 <data1+16>:   0x00    0x00    0x00    0x00
(gdb)
```

This is as expected — each array element uses 4 bytes, and the values are placed in little-endian order. Now, look at the array values stored at the data2 label location:

```
(gdb) x/40b &data2
0x8049098 <data2>:      0x01    0x00    0x00    0x00    0x00    0x00    0x00    0x00
0x80490a0 <data2+8>:    0xff    0xff    0xff    0xff    0xff    0xff    0xff    0xff
0x80490a8 <data2+16>:   0xf1    0x11    0x07    0x00    0x00    0x00    0x00    0x00
0x80490b0 <data2+24>:   0x1e    0xf9    0x22    0xec    0xff    0xff    0xff    0xff
0x80490b8 <data2+32>:   0x00    0x00    0x00    0x00    0x00    0x00    0x00    0x00
(gdb)
```

As we told the assembler, the data values at the data2 label location were encoded using quadwords, so each value uses 8 bytes. Indeed, the assembler placed the values in the proper places, but the debugger didn't know how to handle displaying the values using just the x/d command.

If you want to display quadword signed integer values in the debugger, you must use the gd option:

```
(gdb) x/5gd &data2
0x8049098 <data2>:      1         -1
0x80490a8 <data2+16>:   463345    -333252322
0x80490b8 <data2+32>:   0
(gdb)
```

There, that's more like it.

SIMD Integers

The Intel Single Instruction Multiple Data (SIMD) technology provides additional ways to define integers (see Chapter 2, "The IA-32 Platform"). These new integer types enable the processor to perform arithmetic operations on a group of multiple integers simultaneously.

The SIMD architecture uses the packed integer data type. A packed integer is a series of bytes that can represent more than one integer value. Mathematical operations can be performed on the series of bytes as a whole, working on the individual integer values within the series in parallel (this concept is described in Chapter 17, "Using Advanced IA-32 Features"). The following sections describe the different SIMD packed integer types available on Pentium processors.

MMX integers

The Multimedia Extension (MMX) technology introduced in the Pentium MMX and Pentium II processors provided three new integer types:

❑   64-bit packed byte integers

❑   64-bit packed word integers

❑   64-bit packed doubleword integers

Each of these data types provides for multiple integer data elements to be contained (or packed) in a single 64-bit MMX register. Figure 7-6 demonstrates how each data type fits in the 64-bit register.

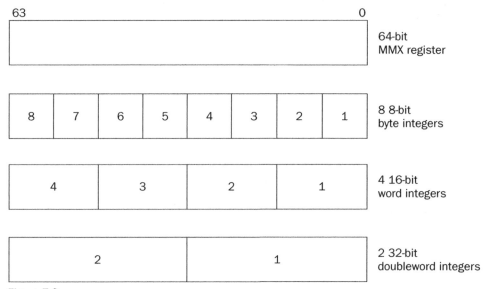

Figure 7-6

As shown in Figure 7-6, 8-byte integers, four-word integers, or two doubleword integers can be packed into a single 64-bit MMX register.

> *As discussed in Chapter 2, the **MMX** registers are mapped to the **FPU** registers, so be careful when using **MMX** registers. Remember to save any data stored in the **FPU** registers in memory before using any **MMX** register instructions. This is covered in the "Moving floating-point values" section later in the chapter.*

The MMX platform provides additional instructions for performing parallel mathematical operations on each of the integer values packed into the MMX register.

Moving MMX integers

You can use the MOVQ instruction to move data into an MMX register, but you must decide which of the three packed integer formats your application will use. The format of the MOVQ instruction is

```
movq source, destination
```

where source and destination can be an MMX register, an SSE register, or a 64-bit memory location (although you cannot move MMX integers between memory locations).

The `mmxtest.s` program demonstrates loading doubleword and byte integers into MMX registers:

```
# mmxtest.s - An example of using the MMX data types
.section .data
values1:
    .int 1, -1
values2:
    .byte 0x10, 0x05, 0xff, 0x32, 0x47, 0xe4, 0x00, 0x01
.section .text
.globl _start
_start:
    nop
    movq values1, %mm0
    movq values2, %mm1
    movl $1, %eax
    movl $0, %ebx
    int $0x80
```

The `mmxtest.s` program defines two data arrays. The first one (`values1`) defines two doubleword signed integers, while the second one (`values2`) defines 8-byte signed integer values. The MOVQ instruction is used to load the values into the first two MMX registers.

After assembling the source code, you can watch what happens in the debugger. After stepping through the MOVQ instructions, you can display the values in the MM0 and MM1 MMX registers:

```
(gdb) print $mm0
$1 = {uint64 = -4294967295, v2_int32 = {1, -1}, v4_int16 = {1, 0, -1, -1},
  v8_int8 = "\001\000\000\000ÿÿÿÿ"}
(gdb) print $mm1
$2 = {uint64 = 72308588487312656, v2_int32 = {855573776, 16835655},
  v4_int16 = {1296, 13055, -7097, 256}, v8_int8 = "\020\005ÿ2Gä\000\001"}
(gdb) print/x $mm1
$3 = {uint64 = 0x100e44732ff0510, v2_int32 = {0x32ff0510, 0x100e447},
  v4_int16 = {0x510, 0x32ff, 0xe447, 0x100}, v8_int8 = {0x10, 0x5, 0xff, 0x32,
    0x47, 0xe4, 0x0, 0x1}}
(gdb)
```

*On the Pentium processors, the **MMX** registers are mapped to the existing **FPU** registers, so depending on which version of **gdb** you are using, displaying the register information in the debugger might be a little tricky. In older versions of **gdb**, instead of being able to directly display the **MMX** registers, you must display their **FPU** register counterparts. The **mm0** register is mapped to the first **FPU** register, **st0r**, and the **mm1** register is mapped to the second **FPU** register, **st1** (this is described in detail in Chapter 9, "Advanced Math Functions"). Unfortunately, the debugger does not know how to interpret the data in the **FPU** registers, so you must display it as raw hexadecimal values and interpret it yourself.*

If you are using a newer version of the GNU debugger, you can directly display the MMX registers as shown in the preceding code. When displaying the registers, the debugger does not know what format the data is in, so it displays all of the possibilities. The first `print` command displays the contents of the MM0 register as doubleword integer values. Because the example uses doubleword integer values, the only display format that makes sense is the int32, which displays the correct information. You can produce just this format from the debugger by using the `print/f` command.

Unfortunately, because the MM1 register contains byte integer values, it cannot be displayed in decimal mode. Instead, you can use the x parameter of the print command to display the raw bytes in the register. With this command, you can see that the individual bytes were properly placed in the MM1 register.

SSE integers

The Streaming SIMD Extensions (SSE) technology (also described in Chapter 2) provides eight 128-bit XMM registers (named XMM0 through XMM7) for handling packed data. The SSE2 technology (introduced in the Pentium 4 processor) provides four additional packed signed integer data types:

❑   128-bit packed byte integers

❑   128-bit packed word integers

❑   128-bit packed doubleword integers

❑   128-bit packed quadword integers

These values are packed into the 128-bit XMM registers as shown in Figure 7-7.

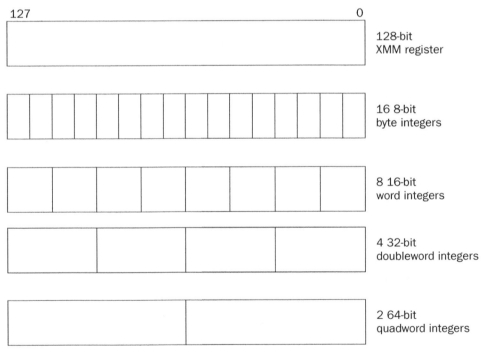

Figure 7-7

As shown in Figure 7-7, there can be 16-byte integers, eight-word integers, four doubleword integers, or two quadword integers packed into a single 128-bit SSE register. The SSE platform provides additional instructions for performing parallel mathematical operations on the packed data values in the SSE registers. This enables the processor to process significantly more information using the same clock cycles.

Moving SSE integers

The MOVDQA and MOVDQU instructions are used to move 128 bits of data into the XMM registers, or to move data between XMM registers. The A and U parts of the mnemonic stand for aligned and unaligned, referring to how the data is stored in memory. For data that is aligned on a 16-byte boundary, the A option is used; otherwise, the U option is used (Chapter 5, "Moving Data" describes aligned data).

The format of both the MOVDQA and MOVDQU instruction is

```
movdqa source, destination
```

where source and destination can be either an SSE 128-bit register, or a 128-bit memory location (but again, you cannot move data between two memory locations). The SSE instructions perform faster when using aligned data. Also, if a program uses the MOVDQA instruction on unaligned data, a hardware exception will result.

The ssetest.s program demonstrates moving 128-bit data values into SSE registers:

```
# ssetest.s - An example of using 128-bit SSE registers
.section .data
values1:
    .int 1, -1, 0, 135246
values2:
    .quad 1, -1
.section .text
.globl _start
_start:
    nop
    movdqu values1, %xmm0
    movdqu values2, %xmm1

    movl $1, %eax
    movl $0, %ebx
    int $0x80
```

The ssetest.s program defines two data arrays containing different types of integer data. The values1 array contains four doubleword signed integer values, while the values2 array contains two quadword signed integer values. The MOVDQU instruction is used to move both data arrays into SSE registers.

After assembling the program, you can watch the results in the debugger. The debugger is able to display the SSE registers (XMM0 through XMM7) using the print command:

```
(gdb) print $xmm0
$1 = {v4_float = {1.40129846e-45, -nan(0x7fffff), 0, 1.89520012e-40},
  v2_double = {-nan(0xfffff00000001), 2.8699144274488922e-309},
  v16_int8 = "\001\000\000\000ÿÿÿÿ\000\000\000\000N\020\002", v8_int16 = {1,
    0, -1, -1, 0, 4174, 2}, v4_int32 = {1, -1, 0, 135246}, v2_int64 = {
    -4294967295, 580877146914816},
  uint128 = 0x0002104e00000000ffffffff00000001}
(gdb) print $xmm1
$2 = {v4_float = {1.40129846e-45, 0, -nan(0x7fffff), -nan(0x7fffff)},
```

```
    v2_double = {4.9406564584124654e-324, -nan(0xffffffffffffff)},
    v16_int8 = "\001\000\000\000\000\000\000\000ÿÿÿÿÿÿÿÿ", v8_int16 = {1, 0, 0,
      0, -1, -1, -1, -1}, v4_int32 = {1, 0, -1, -1}, v2_int64 = {1, -1},
    uint128 = 0xffffffffffffffff0000000000000001}
(gdb)
```

After the MOVDQU instructions, the XMM0 and XMM1 registers contain the data values defined in the data section. The XMM0 register contains the four doubleword signed integer data values, and the XMM1 register contains the two quadword signed integer data values.

*Remember that the **ssetest.s** program will only run on Pentium III or later processors. Chapter 17, "Using Advanced IA-32 Features," describes the **MMX** and **SSE** instruction sets and demonstrates how they are used.*

Binary Coded Decimal

The Binary Coded Decimal (BCD) data type has been available for quite a long time in computer systems. The BCD format is often used to simplify working with devices that use decimal numbers (such as devices that must display numbers to humans, such as clocks and timers). Instead of converting decimal numbers to binary for mathematical operations, and then back to decimal again, the processor can keep the numbers in BCD format and perform the mathematical operations. Understanding how BCD works and how the processor uses it can come in handy in your assembly language programming. The following sections describe the BCD format and how the BCD data type is handled by the IA-32 platform.

What is BCD?

BCD does pretty much what is says, it codes decimal numbers in a binary format. Each BCD value is an unsigned 8-bit integer, with a value range of 0 to 9. The 8-bit values higher than 9 are considered invalid in BCD. Bytes containing BCD values are combined to represent decimal digits. In a multibyte BCD value, the lowest byte holds the decimal ones value, the next higher one holds the tens value, and so on. This is demonstrated in Figure 7-8.

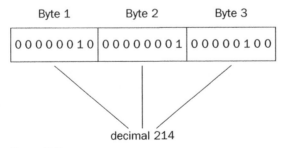

Figure 7-8

In Figure 7-8, the decimal value 214 is represented by the BCD value 00000010 00000001 00000100. The high-order byte holds the 100s value (2), the next order byte holds the tens value (1), and the low-order 4 bits holds the ones value (4).

As you can tell, BCD wastes space by using an entire byte for each decimal digit. Packed BCD was created to help compensate for that. Packed BCD enables a single byte to contain two BCD values. The low-order 4 bits of the byte contain the lower BCD value, and the high-order 4 bits of the byte contain the higher BCD value. This is demonstrated in Figure 7-9.

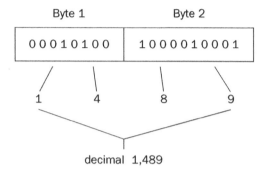

Figure 7-9

In Figure 7-9, the decimal value 1,489 is stored in a 2-byte BCD value. The first byte contains the first two decimal digits (1 and 4), while the second byte contains the last two decimal digits (8 and 9).

As you can see, even packed BCD is not efficient. Using 4 bytes, packed BCD can only represent numbers from 0 through 9,999. Using the same 4 bytes in an unsigned integer value can represent values up to 4,292,967,295.

As you can see from these examples, the general BCD format in the IA-32 platform only supports unsigned integer values. However, the IA-32 FPU provides a method for supporting signed BCD integers.

FPU BCD values

The FPU registers can be used for BCD arithmetic operations within the FPU. The FPU contains eight 80-bit registers (ST0 through ST7), which can also be used to hold 80-bit BCD values. The BCD values are stored using the lower 9 bytes, using packed BCD format, two BCD values per byte (producing 18 BCD digits). The last byte of the FPU register is mostly unused, with the exception of the highest-order bit. This bit is used as a sign indicator—a 1 indicates a negative BCD value, and a 0 indicates a positive value. This format is shown in Figure 7-10.

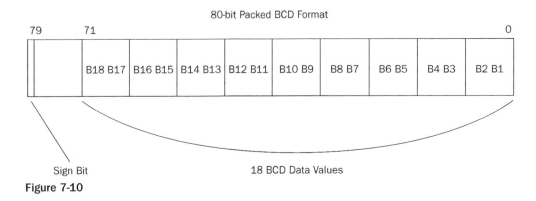

80-bit Packed BCD Format

79   71   0

| B18 B17 | B16 B15 | B14 B13 | B12 B11 | B10 B9 | B8 B7 | B6 B5 | B4 B3 | B2 B1 |

Sign Bit   18 BCD Data Values

Figure 7-10

This description is somewhat misleading. You must use the 80-bit packed BCD format to create values in memory for loading the BCD values into the FPU registers. Once the value is transferred to the FPU register, it is automatically converted to a double-extended-precision floating-point format (see the "Floating-Point Numbers" section later in this chapter). Any mathematical operations on the data within the FPU are performed in floating-point format. When you are ready to retrieve the results from the FPU, the floating-point value is automatically converted back to 80-bit packed BCD format.

Moving BCD values

The IA-32 instruction set includes instructions for working with 80-bit packed BCD values. The FBLD and FBSTP instructions can be used to load and retrieve 80-bit packed BCD values in the FPU registers.

Working with the FPU registers is a little different from working with the general-purpose registers. The eight FPU registers behave similarly to the stack area in memory. Values can be pushed and popped into and out of the FPU register pool. ST0 refers to the register at the top of the stack. When a value is pushed into the FPU register stack, it is placed in the ST0 register, and the previous value of ST0 is loaded into ST1.

*How the **FPU** registers work is described in more detail in Chapter 9, "Advanced Math Functions."*

The FBLD instruction is used to move a packed 80-bit BCD value into the FPU register stack. The format is simply

```
fbld source
```

where source is an 80-bit memory location.

The bcdtest.s program is designed to demonstrate the basics of loading and retrieving BCD values from the FPU registers:

```
# bcdtest.s - An example of using BCD integer values
.section .data
data1:
    .byte 0x34, 0x12, 0x00, 0x00, 0x00, 0x00, 0x00, 0x00, 0x00, 0x00
data2:
```

```
     .int 2
.section .text
.globl _start
_start:
    nop
    fbld data1
    fimul data2
    fbstp data1

    movl $1, %eax
    movl $0, %ebx
    int $0x80
```

The bcdtest.s program creates a simple BCD value representing the decimal value 1,234 at the memory location defined by the label data1 (remember that Intel uses little-endian notation). The FBLD instruction is used to load the value into the top of the FPU register stack (ST0). The FIMUL instruction (discussed in Chapter 9) is used to multiply the ST0 register by the integer value at the data2 memory location. Finally, the FBSTP instruction is used to move the new value on the stack back into the data1 memory location.

After assembling the program, you can run it in the debugger and watch what happens at different points in the program. First, before any instructions execute, look at the value at the data1 memory location:

```
(gdb) x/10b &data1
0x8049094 <data1>:    0x34    0x12    0x00    0x00    0x00    0x00    0x00    0x00
0x804909c <data1+8>: 0x00    0x00
(gdb)
```

Good. The BCD value for 1,234 is loaded at the data1 memory location. Next, step through the FBLD instruction, and check the value in the ST0 register using the info all command:

```
(gdb) s
12          fimul data2
(gdb) info all
 .
 .
 .
st0             1234      (raw 0x40099a40000000000000)
```

When you find the ST0 register value in the list of registers, it should show that it is loaded with the decimal value 1,234. You may notice, however, that the hexadecimal value of the register is not in 80-bit packed BCD format. Remember that the BCD value is converted to the floating-point representation while in the FPU.

Now step through the next instruction (FIMUL) and view the registers again:

```
(gdb) s
13          fbstp data1
(gdb) info all
 .
 .
 .
st0             2468      (raw 0x400a9a40000000000000)
```

Indeed, the value in the STO register was multiplied by 2. The last step should place the value in STO back into the data1 memory location. You can check that by displaying the memory location:

```
(gdb) x/10b &data1
0x8049094 <data1>:      0x68    0x24    0x00    0x00    0x00    0x00    0x00    0x00
0x804909c <data1+8>:    0x00    0x00
(gdb)
```

As expected, the new value was placed in the data1 memory location, back in BCD format.

Chapter 9 demonstrates how to use BCD values in arithmetic operations in more detail.

Floating-Point Numbers

Now that you know all about integers, it's time to move on to the more complicated numerical data type, floating-point numbers. In the past, integers were easier to work with, as the Intel processors have always contained built-in support for performing integer mathematical operations. In earlier Intel processors (such as the 80286 and 80386 chips) performing floating-point operations required either using software to simulate the floating-point values using integers, or purchasing a separate FPU chip that specialized in performing only floating-point arithmetic.

However, since the 80486 processor, the Intel IA-32 platform has directly supported floating-point operations. It is now just as easy for assembly language programmers to incorporate floating-point mathematical operations within their programs.

This section describes what the floating-point data type is, and demonstrates how it is used in assembly language programs.

What are floating-point numbers?

So far, all the number systems discussed in this chapter have revolved around whole numbers. Whole numbers represent numbers that are used for counting, such as one dog, two cats, and ten horses. Eventually, the concept of negative numbers was included along with whole numbers to incorporate the signed integer number system. Both the integer and BCD data types can only contain whole integer values.

As you know, not all numerical relationships can be described using integers. At some point, the concept of fractions was introduced. This meant that an infinite number of values could be contained between two integer values. Besides the infinite number of values between integers, there is also an infinite number of integer values in the number system. All of these numbers combined are referred to as *real numbers*. Real numbers can contain any numerical value from positive infinity to negative infinity, with any number of decimal places. An example of a real number would be 72,326.224576.

Working with real numbers on a computer can be a challenge, especially when there are many different magnitudes of numbers. The floating-point format was developed to produce a standard method for representing real numbers on computer systems.

Floating-point format

The floating-point format represents real numbers using a scientific notation. If you had any type of science class in school you are probably familiar with scientific notation. Scientific notation presents numbers as a *coefficient* (also called the *mantissa*) and an *exponent*, such as 3.6845×10^2. In the decimal world, the exponent is based on a value of 10, and represents the number of places the decimal point has been moved to produce the coefficient. Each time the decimal point is moved up, the exponent increases. Each time the decimal point is moved back, the exponent decreases.

For example, the real number 25.92 would be represented in scientific notation as 2.592×10^1. The value 2.592 is the coefficient, and the value 10^1 is the exponent. You must multiply the coefficient by the exponent to obtain the original real number. As another example, the value .00172 would be represented as 1.72×10^{-3}. The number 1.72 must be multiplied by 10^{-3} to obtain the original value.

Binary floating-point format

Computer systems use binary floating-point numbers, which express values in binary scientific notation format. Because the numbers are in binary format, the coefficient and exponent are based on a binary value, not a decimal value. An example of this would be 1.0101×2^2. Working with the fractional part of the coefficient (the part after the decimal place) can be confusing.

To decipher the binary floating-point value, you must first understand how fractional binary numbers work. In the decimal world, you are used to seeing values such as 0.159. What this value represents is $0 + \frac{1}{10} + \frac{5}{100} + \frac{9}{1000}$. The same principle applies to the binary world.

The coefficient value 1.0101 multiplied by the exponent 2^2 would yield the binary value 101.01, which represents the decimal whole number 5, plus the fraction $\frac{1}{2} + 1/4$. This yields the decimal value 5.25.

Fractional binary numbers are the most confusing part of dealing with floating-point values. The following table shows the first few binary fractions and their decimal equivalents.

Binary	Decimal Fraction	Decimal Value
0.1	$\frac{1}{2}$	0.5
.01	$\frac{1}{4}$	0.25
.001	$\frac{1}{8}$	0.125
.0001	$\frac{1}{16}$	.0625
.00001	$\frac{1}{32}$	.03125
.000001	$\frac{1}{64}$	0.015625

To help demonstrate binary fractions, the following table shows a few examples of using binary floating-point values:

Binary	Decimal Fraction	Decimal Value
10.101	2 + 1/2 + 1/8	2.625
10011.001	19 + 1/8	19.125
10110.1101	22 + 1/2 + 1/4 + 1/16	22.8125
1101.011	13 + 1/4 + 1/8	13.375

The examples in the table have a finite fractional part. However, just as decimal fractions can have a repeating value (such as the decimal value of 1/3), binary fractions can also have a repeating fraction value. These values must be truncated at some point and can only estimate the decimal fraction in binary.

> *Fortunately, the GNU assembler does this work for us, so don't get too worried if you are not completely comfortable with binary fractions and binary floating-point format.*

When writing binary floating-point values, the binary values are usually normalized. This process moves the decimal point to the leftmost digit and modifies the exponent to compensate. For example, the value 1101.011 becomes 1.101011×2^3.

Trying to properly represent binary floating-point numbers in a computer system was a challenge in the early days of computing. Fortunately, standards were developed to help programmers deal with floating-point numbers. A set of standard floating-point data types was created to simplify handling real numbers in computer programs. The next section describes the standard floating-point data types.

Standard floating-point data types

While there are an infinite number of possible real number values, processors have a finite number of bits available to handle the values. Because of this, a standard system was created for approximating real numbers in a computer environment. While the approximations are not perfect, they provide a system for working with a realistic subset of the real number system.

In 1985, the Institute of Electrical and Electronics Engineers (IEEE) created what is called the IEEE Standard 754 floating-point formats. These formats are used universally to represent real numbers in computer systems. Intel has adopted this standard in the IA-32 platform for representing floating-point values.

The IEEE Standard 754 floating-point standard defines real numbers as binary floating-point values using three components:

❑ A sign

❑ A significand

❑ An exponent

The sign bit denotes if the value is negative or positive. A one in the sign bit denotes a negative value, and a zero denotes a positive value.

The significand part represents the coefficient (or mantissa) of the floating-point number. The coefficient can be either *normalized* or *denormalized*. When a binary value is normalized, it is written with a one before the decimal point. The exponent is modified to accommodate how many bit positions have been shifted to accomplish this (similar to the scientific notation method). This means that in a normalized value, the significand is always comprised of a one and a binary fraction.

The exponent represents the exponent part of the floating-point number. Because the exponent value can be positive or negative, it is offset by a bias value. This ensures that the exponent field can only be a positive unsigned integer. It also limits the minimum and maximum exponent values available for use in the format. The general format of the binary floating-point number is shown in Figure 7-11.

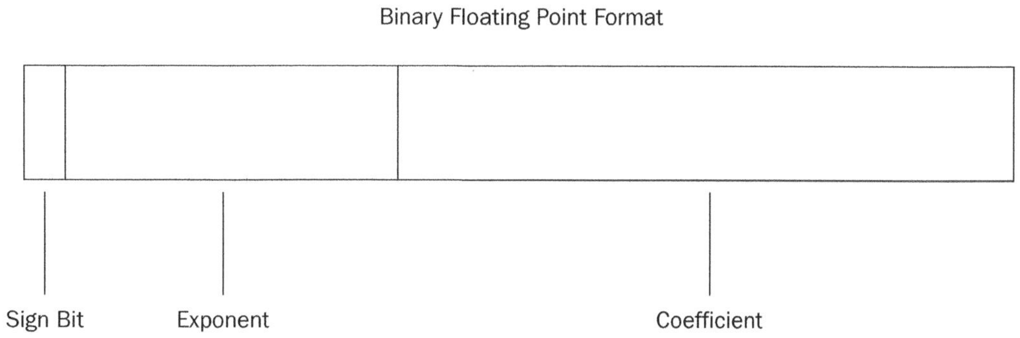

Binary Floating Point Format

Sign Bit   Exponent   Coefficient

Figure 7-11

These three parts of the floating-point number are contained within a fixed-size data format. The IEEE Standard 754 defines two sizes of floating-point numbers:

❑ 32-bits (called single-precision)

❑ 64-bits (called double-precision)

The number of bits available for representing the significand determines the precision. Figure 7-12 shows the bit layouts for the two different precision types.

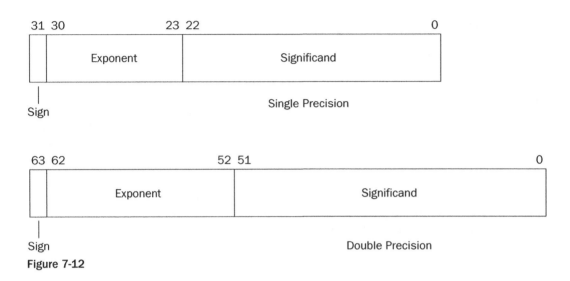

IEEE Standard 754 Floating Point Formats

Figure 7-12

The single-precision floating-point number uses a 23-bit significand value. However, the floating-point format assumes that the integer value of the significand will always be a one and does not use it in the significand value. This effectively makes 24 bits of precision for the significand. The exponent uses an 8-bit value, with a bias value of 127. This means that the exponent can have a value between -128 and +127 (binary exponent). This combination produces a decimal range for single-precision floating-point numbers of 1.18×10^{-38} to 3.40×10^{38}.

The double-precision floating-point number uses a 52-bit fraction value, which provides 53 bits of precision for the significand. The exponent uses an 11-bit value, with a bias value of 1023. This means that the exponent can have a value between -1022 and +1023 (binary exponent). This combination produces a decimal range for double-precision floating-point numbers of 2.23×10^{-308} to 1.79×10^{308}.

IA-32 floating-point values

The IA-32 platform uses both the IEEE Standard 754 single- and double-precision floating-point formats, along with its own 80-bit format called the double-extended-precision floating-point format. The three formats provide for different levels of precision when performing floating-point math. The double-extended-precision floating-point format is used within the FPU 80-bit registers during floating-point mathematical processes.

The Intel 80-bit double-extended-precision floating-point format uses 64 bits for the signficand and 15 bits for the exponent. The bias value used for the double-extended-precision floating-point format is 16,383, producing an exponent range of −16382 to +16383, for a decimal range of 3.37×10^{-4932} to 1.18×10^{4932}.

The following table sums up the three types of floating-point formats used on the standard IA-32 platform.

Data Type	Length	Significand Bits	Exponent Bits	Range
Single precision	32	24	8	1.18×10^{-38} to 3.40×10^{38}
Double precision	64	53	11	2.23×10^{-308} to 1.79×10^{308}
Double extended	80	64	15	3.37×10^{-4932} to 1.18×10^{4932}

Defining floating-point values in GAS

The GNU assembler provides directives for defining single-and double-precision floating-point values (see Chapter 5, "Moving Data"). At the time of this writing, gas does not have a directive for defining double-extended-precision floating-point values.

Floating-point values are stored in memory using the little-endian format. Arrays are stored in the order in which the values are defined in the directive. The .float directive is used to create 32-bit single-precision values, while the .double directive is used to create 64-bit double-precision values.

Moving floating-point values

The FLD instruction is used to move floating-point values into and out of the FPU registers. The format of the FLD instruction is

```
fld source
```

where source can be a 32-, 64-, or 80-bit memory location.

The floattest.s program demonstrates how floating-point data values are defined and used in assembly language programs:

```
# floattest.s - An example of using floating point numbers
.section .data

value1:
    .float 12.34
value2:
    .double 2353.631
.section .bss
    .lcomm data, 8
.section .text
.globl _start
_start:
    nop
    flds value1
```

```
        fldl  value2
        fstl  data

        movl  $1, %eax
        movl  $0, %ebx
        int   $0x80
```

The value1 label points to a single-precision floating-point value stored in 4 bytes of memory. The value2 label points to a double-precision floating-point value stored in 8 bytes of memory. The data label points to an empty buffer in memory that will be used to transfer a double-precision floating-point value.

The IA-32 FLD instruction is used for loading single- and double-precision floating-point numbers stored in memory onto the FPU register stack. To differentiate between the data sizes, the GNU assembler uses the FLDS instruction for loading single-precision floating-point numbers, and the FLDL instruction for loading double-precision floating-point numbers.

Similarly, the FST instruction is used for retrieving the top value on the FPU register stack and placing the value in a memory location. Again, for single-precision numbers, the instruction is FSTS, and for double-precision numbers, FSTL.

After assembling the floattest.s program, watch the memory locations and register values as the instructions execute. First, look at how the floating-point values are stored in the memory locations:

```
(gdb) x/4b &value1
0x8049094 <value1>: 0xa4    0x70    0x45    0x41
(gdb) x/8b &value2
0x8049098 <value2>: 0x8d    0x97    0x6e    0x12    0x43    0x63    0xa2    0x40
(gdb)
```

If you want to view the decimal values, you can use the f option of the x command:

```
(gdb) x/f &value1
0x8049094 <value1>: 12.3400002
(gdb) x/gf &value2
0x8049098 <value2>: 2353.6309999999999
(gdb)
```

Notice that when the debugger attempts to calculate the values for display, rounding errors are already present. The f option only displays single-precision numbers. To display the double-precision value, you need to use the gf option, which displays quadword values.

After stepping through the first FLDS instruction, look at the value of the ST0 register using either the info reg or print command:

```
(gdb) print $st0
$1 = 12.340000152587890625
(gdb)
```

The value in the `value1` memory location was correctly placed in the `ST0` register. Now step through the next instruction, and look at the value in the `ST0` register:

```
(gdb) print $st0
$2 = 2353.6309999999998581188265234231949
(gdb)
```

The value has been replaced with the newly loaded double-precision value (and the debugger correctly displayed the value as a double-precision floating-point number). To see what happened with the originally loaded value, look at the `ST1` register:

```
(gdb) print $st1
$3 = 12.340000152587890625
(gdb)
```

As expected, the value in ST0 was shifted down to the `ST1` register when the new value was loaded. Now look at the value of the `data` label, then step through the `FSTL` instruction, and look again:

```
(gdb) x/gf &data
0x80490a0 <data>:        0
(gdb) s
18          movl $1, %eax
(gdb) x/gf &data
0x80490a0 <data>:        2353.6309999999999
(gdb)
```

The `FSTL` instruction loaded the value in the `ST0` register to the memory location pointed to by the data label.

Using preset floating-point values

The IA-32 instruction set includes some preset floating-point values that can be loaded into the FPU register stack. These are shown in the following table.

Instruction	Description
FLD1	Push +1.0 into the FPU stack
FLDL2T	Push log(base 2) 10 onto the FPU stack
FLDL2E	Push log(base 2) e onto the FPU stack
FLDPI	Push the value of pi onto the FPU stack
FLDLG2	Push log(base 10) 2 onto the FPU stack
FLDLN2	Push log(base e) 2 onto the FPU stack
FLDZ	Push +0.0 onto the FPU stack

These instructions provide an easy way to push common mathematical values onto the FPU stack for operations with your data. You may notice something odd about the FLDZ instruction. In the floating-point data types, there is a difference between +0.0 and –0.0. For most operations they are considered the same value, but they produce different values when used in division (positive infinity and negative infinity).

The fpuvals.s program demonstrates how the preset floating-point values can be used:

```
# fpuvals.s - An example of pushing floating point constants
.section .text
.globl _start
_start:
    nop
    fld1
    fldl2t
    fldl2e
    fldpi
    fldlg2
    fldln2
    fldz

    movl $1, %eax
    movl $0, %ebx
    int $0x80
```

The fpuvals.s program simply pushes the various floating-point constants onto the FPU register stack. You can assemble the program and run it in the debugger to watch the FPU register stack as the instructions are executed. At the end of the list, the registers should look like this:

```
(gdb) info all
.
.
.
st0    0               (raw 0x00000000000000000000)
st1    0.6931471805599453094286904741849753    (raw 0x3ffeb17217f7d1cf79ac)
st2    0.3010299956639811952256464283594894    (raw 0x3ffd9a209a84fbcff799)
st3    3.1415926535897932385128089594061862    (raw 0x4000c90fdaa22168c235)
st4    1.4426950408889634073876517827983434    (raw 0x3fffb8aa3b295c17f0bc)
st5    3.3219280948873623478083405569094566    (raw 0x4000d49a784bcd1b8afe)
st6    1               (raw 0x3fff8000000000000000)
st7    0               (raw 0x00000000000000000000)
(gdb)
```

The values are in the reverse order from how they were placed into the stack.

SSE floating-point data types

Besides the three standard floating-point data types, Intel processors that implement the SSE technology include two advanced floating-point data types. The SSE technology incorporates eight 128-bit XMM registers (see Chapter 2 for more details) that can be used to hold packed floating-point numbers.

Similar to the packed BCD concept, packed floating-point numbers enable multiple floating-point values to be stored in a single register. Floating-point calculations can be performed in parallel using the multiple data elements, producing results quicker than sequentially processing the data.

The following two new 128-bit floating-point data types are available:

❏   128-bit packed single-precision floating-point (in SSE)

❏   128-bit packed double-precision floating-point (in SSE2)

Because a single-precision floating-point value requires 32 bits, the 128-bit register can hold four packed single-precision floating-point values. Similarly, it can hold two 64-bit packed double-precision floating-point values. This is shown in Figure 7-13.

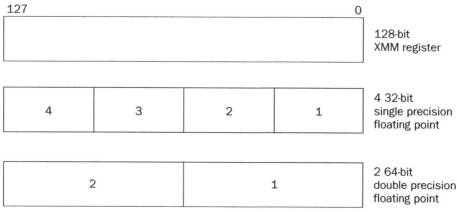

Figure 7-13

These new data types are not available in the FPU or MMX registers. They can only be used in the XMM registers and only on processors that support SSE or SSE2. Special instructions must be used to load and retrieve the data values, as well as special math instructions for performing mathematical operations on the packed floating-point data.

Moving SSE floating-point values

As expected, the IA-32 instruction set includes instructions for moving the new SSE floating-point data type values around the processor. The instructions are divided between the SSE instructions that operate on packed single-precision floating-point data, and the SSE2 instructions that operate on packed double-precision floating-point data.

SSE floating-point values

There is a complete set of instructions for moving 128-bit packed single-precision floating-point values between memory and the XMM registers on the processor. The instructions for moving SSE packed single-precision floating-point data are shown in the following table.

Instruction	Description
MOVAPS	Move four aligned, packed single-precision values to XMM registers or memory
MOVUPS	Move four unaligned, packed single-precision values to XMM registers or memory
MOVSS	Move a single-precision value to memory or the low doubleword of a register
MOVLPS	Move two single-precision values to memory or the low quadword of a register
MOVHPS	Move two single-precision values to memory or the high quadword of a register
MOVLHPS	Move two single-precision values from the low quadword to the high quadword
MOVHLPS	Move two single-precision values from the high quadword to the low quadword

Each of these instructions uses the 128-bit XMM registers to move packed 32-bit single-precision floating-point values between the XMM registers and memory. Not only can you move entire groups of packed single-precision floating-point values, you can also move a subset of two packed single-precision floating-point values between XMM registers.

An example of moving SSE packed single-precision floating-point values is shown in ssefloat.s:

```
# ssefloat.s - An example of moving SSE FP data types
.section .data
value1:
    .float 12.34, 2345.543, -3493.2, 0.44901
value2:
    .float -5439.234, 32121.4, 1.0094, 0.000003
.section .bss
    .lcomm data, 16
.section .text
.globl _start
_start:
    nop
    movups value1, %xmm0
    movups value2, %xmm1
    movups %xmm0, %xmm2
    movups %xmm0, data

    movl $1, %eax
    movl $0, %ebx
    int $0x80
```

The `ssefloat.s` program creates two data arrays of four single-precision floating-point values (`value1` and `value2`). These will become the packed data value to be stored in the XMM registers. Also, a data buffer is created with enough space to hold four single-precision floating-point values (a single packed value). The program then uses the MOVUPS instruction to move the packed single-precision floating-point values around between the XMM registers and memory.

After assembling the program, you can see what happens in the debugger. After stepping through the first three instructions, the XMM registers should look like this:

```
(gdb) print $xmm0
$1 = {v4_float = {5.84860315e+35, 2.63562489, 1.79352231e-36, 5.07264233},
   v2_double = {12.34, 2345.54300000000001},
   v16_int8 = "xxxx\024x(@u\223\030\004\026Sx@", v8_int16 = {18350, 31457,
      -20972, 16424, -27787, 1048, 21270, 16546}, v4_int32 = {2061584302,
      1076407828, 68719477, 1084379926}, v2_int64 = {4623136420479977390,
      4657376318677619573}, uint128 = 0x40a25316041893754028ae147ae147ae}
(gdb) print $xmm1
$2 = {v4_float = {-1.11704749e+24, -5.66396856, -1.58818684e-23, 6.98026705},
   v2_double = {-5439.2340000000004, 32121.400000000001},
   v16_int8 = "D\2131xxxx\232\231\231\231xxxx", v8_int16 = {-29884, -6292,
      16187, -16203, -26214, -26215, 24153, 16607}, v4_int32 = {-412316860,
      -1061863621, -1717986918, 1088380505}, v2_int64 = {-4560669521124488380,
      4674558677155944858}, uint128 = 0x40df5e599999999ac0b53f3be76c8b44}
(gdb) print $xmm2
$3 = {v4_float = {5.84860315e+35, 2.63562489, 1.79352231e-36, 5.07264233},
   v2_double = {12.34, 2345.54300000000001},
   v16_int8 = "xxxx\024x(@u\223\030\004\026Sx@", v8_int16 = {18350, 31457,
      -20972, 16424, -27787, 1048, 21270, 16546}, v4_int32 = {2061584302,
      1076407828, 68719477, 1084379926}, v2_int64 = {4623136420479977390,
      4657376318677619573}, uint128 = 0x40a25316041893754028ae147ae147ae}
(gdb)
```

As you can see from the output, all of the data was properly loaded into the XMM registers. The `v4_float` format shows the packed single-precision floating-point values that were used.

The final instruction step is to copy a value from the XMM register to the data location. You can display the results using the `x/4f` command:

```
(gdb) x/4f &data
0x80490c0 <data>:   12.3400002     2345.54297      -3493.19995     0.449010015
(gdb)
```

To display the bytes stored in the `data` memory location as four single-precision floating-point values, you can use the `4f` option of the `x` command. This interprets the 8 bytes into the proper format. The `data` memory location now contains the data loaded from the `value1` memory location into the XMM register, and copied to the `data` memory location. Just in case the rounding errors in the debugger fool you, you can double-check the answer in hexadecimal:

```
(gdb) x/16b &data
0x80490c0 <data>:      0xa4    0x70    0x45    0x41    0xb0    0x98    0x12    0x45
0x80490c8 <data+8>:    0x33    0x53    0x5a    0xc5    0xa4    0xe4    0xe5    0x3e
(gdb) x/16b &value1
0x804909c <value1>:    0xa4    0x70    0x45    0x41    0xb0    0x98    0x12    0x45
0x80490a4 <value1+8>:0x33      0x53    0x5a    0xc5    0xa4    0xe4    0xe5    0x3e
(gdb)
```

Yes, they do match!

SSE2 floating-point values

Similar to the SSE data types, the IA-32 platform includes instructions for moving the new SSE2 packed double-precision floating-point data types. The following table describes the new instructions that can be used.

Instruction	Description
MOVAPD	Move two aligned, double-precision values to XMM registers or memory
MOVUPD	Move two unaligned, double-precision values to XMM registers or memory
MOVSD	Move one double-precision value to memory or the low quadword of a register
MOVHPD	Move one double-precision value to memory or the high quadword of a register
MOVLPD	Move one double-precision value to memory or the low quadword of a register

Each of these instructions uses the 128-bit XMM register to move 64-bit double-precision floating-point values. The MOVAPD and MOVUPD instructions move the complete packed double-precision floating-point value into and out of the XMM registers.

The sse2float.s program demonstrates these instructions:

```
# sse2float.s - An example of moving SSE2 FP data types
.section .data
value1:
    .double 12.34, 2345.543
value2:
    .double -5439.234, 32121.4
.section .bss
    .lcomm data, 16
.section .text
.globl _start
```

```
_start:
    nop
    movupd value1, %xmm0
    movupd value2, %xmm1
    movupd %xmm0, %xmm2
    movupd %xmm0, data

    movl $1, %eax
    movl $0, %ebx
    int $0x80
```

This time the data values stored in memory are changed to double-precision floating-point values. Because the program will transfer packed values, an array of two values is created.

After assembling the program, you can again watch the operations in the debugger. After stepping through the MOVUPD instructions, look at the contents of the pertinent XMM registers:

```
(gdb) print $xmm0
$1 = {v4_float = {0.0587499999, 2.57562494, -7.46297859e-36, -2.33312488},
    v2_double = {10.42, -5.3300000000000001},
    v16_int8 = "xxp=\xx$@Rx\036\205xQ\025x", v8_int16 = {-23593, 15728, -10486,
        16420, -18350, -31458, 20971, -16363}, v4_int32 = {1030792151, 1076156170,
        -2061584302, -1072344597}, v2_int64 = {4622055556569408471,
        -4605684971923916718}, uint128 = 0xc01551eb851eb8524024d70a3d70a3d7}
(gdb) print $xmm1
$2 = {v4_float = {0, 2.265625, -107374184, 2.01249981}, v2_double = {4.25,
        2.1000000000000001},
    v16_int8 = "\000\000\000\000\000\000\021@xxxxxx\000@", v8_int16 = {0, 0, 0,
        16401, -13107, -13108, -13108, 16384}, v4_int32 = {0, 1074855936,
        -858993459, 1073794252}, v2_int64 = {4616471093031469056,
        4611911198408756429}, uint128 = 0x4000cccccccccccd4011000000000000}
(gdb) print $xmm2
$3 = {v4_float = {1.40129846e-44, 2.80259693e-44, 4.20389539e-44,
        5.60519386e-44}, v2_double = {4.2439915824246103e-313,
        8.4879831653432862e-313},
    v16_int8 = "\n\000\000\000\024\000\000\000\036\000\000\000(\000\000",
    v8_int16 = {10, 0, 20, 0, 30, 0, 40, 0}, v4_int32 = {10, 20, 30, 40},
    v2_int64 = {85899345930, 171798691870},
    uint128 = 0x000000280000001e000000140000000a}
(gdb) print $xmm3
$4 = {v4_float = {7.00649232e-45, 2.1019477e-44, 3.50324616e-44,
        4.90454463e-44}, v2_double = {3.1829936866949413e-313,
        7.4269852696136172e-313},
    v16_int8 = "\005\000\000\000\017\000\000\000\031\000\000\000#\000\000",
    v8_int16 = {5, 0, 15, 0, 25, 0, 35, 0}, v4_int32 = {5, 15, 25, 35},
    v2_int64 = {64424509445, 150323855385},
    uint128 = 0x000000230000001900000000f00000005}
(gdb)
```

Again you have to sift through the debugger output, but this time you are looking for the `v2_double` data types. The proper values have been moved to the registers.

Next, examine the data memory location to ensure that the proper values have been copied there as well:

```
(gdb) x/2gf &data
0x80490c0 <data>:        12.34    2345.5430000000001
(gdb)
```

Because the `data` memory location contains two double-precision floating-point values, you must use the `2gf` option of the `x` command to display both values stored at the memory location. Again, we got what we expected.

SSE3 instructions

On a final note, the SSE3 technology, available in Pentium 4 and later processors, adds three additional instructions to facilitate moving packed double-precision floating-point values around:

❑ **MOVSHDUP:** Moves a 128-bit value from memory or an XMM register, duplicating the second and fourth 32-bit data elements. Thus, moving the data element consisting of 32-bit single-precision floating-point values DCBA would create the 128-bit packed single-precision floating-point value consisting of DDBB.

❑ **MOVSLDUP:** Moves a 128-bit value from memory or an XMM register, duplicating the first and third 32-bit data elements. Thus, moving the data element consisting of 32-bit single-precision floating-point values DCBA would create the 128-bit packed single-precision floating-point value consisting of CCAA.

❑ **MOVDDUP:** Moves a 64-bit double-precision floating-point value from memory or an XMM register, duplicating it into a 128-bit XMM register. Thus, moving the data element consisting of 64-bit double-precision floating-point value A would create the 128-bit packed double-precision floating-point value AA.

*At the time of this writing, the only IA-32 processors that support **SSE3** instructions are the Pentium 4 Hyperthreading processors.*

Conversions

The IA-32 instruction set includes numerous instructions for converting data represented in one data type into another data type. It is not uncommon for a program to need to convert floating-point data to an integer value, or visa versa. These instructions provide an easy way to do it without having to code your own algorithms.

Conversion instructions

There are as many instructions for converting data types as there are different data types to convert from and to. The following table shows the conversion instructions.

Instruction	Converts
CVTDQ2PD	Packed doubleword integers to packed double-precision FP (XMM)
CVTDQ2PS	Packed doubleword integers to packed single-precision FP (XMM)
CVTPD2DQ	Packed double-precision FP to packed doubleword integers (XMM)
CVTPD2PI	Packed double-precision FP to packed doubleword integers (MMX)
CVTPD2PS	Packed double-precision FP to packed single-precision FP (XMM)
CVTPI2PD	Packed doubleword integers to packed double-precision FP (XMM)
CVTPI2PS	Packed doubleword integers to packed single-precision FP (XMM)
CVTPS2DQ	Packed single-precision FP to packed doubleword integers (XMM)
CVTPS2PD	Packed single-precision FP to packed double-precision FP (XMM)
CVTPS2PI	Packed single-precision FP to packed doubleword integers (MMX)
CVTTPD2PI	Packed double-precision FP to packed doubleword integers (MMX, truncated)
CVTTPD2DQ	Packed double-precision FP to packed doubleword integers (XMM, truncated)
CVTTPS2DQ	Packed single-precision FP to packed doubleword integers (XMM, truncated)
CVTTPS2PI	Packed single-precision FP to packed doubleword integers (MMX, truncated)

The descriptions in the table refer to the destination register in which the result can be placed, either an MMX register or an XMM register. Also, the last four instructions are truncated conversions. In the other instructions, if the conversion is inexact, the rounding is controlled by bits 13 and 14 in the XMM MXCSR register. These bits determine whether the values are rounded up or down. In a truncated conversion, rounding toward zero is automatically performed.

The source values can be obtained from either memory locations, MMX registers (for 64-bit values), or XMM registers (for 64- and 128-bit values).

A conversion example

The convtest.s program is presented as an example of converting data types:

```
# convtest.s - An example of data conversion
.section .data
value1:
    .float 1.25, 124.79, 200.0, -312.5
value2:
    .int 1, -435, 0, -25
.section .bss
data:
    .lcomm data, 16
.section .text
.globl _start
_start:
    nop
    cvtps2dq value1, %xmm0
    cvttps2dq value1, %xmm1
    cvtdq2ps value2, %xmm2
    movdqu %xmm0, data

    movl $1, %eax
    movl $0, %ebx
    int $0x80
```

The convtest.s program defines a packed single-precision floating-point value at memory location value1, and a packed doubleword integer value at memory location value2. The first pair of instructions enables you to compare the results of the CVTPS2DQ and CVTTPS2DQ instructions. The first instruction performs normal rounding, while the second truncates by rounding toward zero.

After the usual assembling and debugging, you can see how the conversion instructions operate by viewing the XMM registers and the data memory location. By viewing registers XMM0 and XMM1, you can see the difference in the truncation:

```
(gdb) print $xmm0
$1 = {v4_float = {1.40129846e-45, 1.75162308e-43, 2.80259693e-43,
    -nan(0x7ffec8)}, v2_double = {2.6524947387115311e-312,
    -nan(0xffec8000000c8)},
  v16_int8 = "\001\000\000\000}\000\000\000x\000\000\000xxxx", v8_int16 = {1,
    0, 125, 0, 200, 0, -312, -1}, v4_int32 = {1, 125, 200, -312}, v2_int64 = {
    536870912001, -1340029796152},
  uint128 = 0xfffffec8000000c80000007d00000001}
(gdb) print $xmm1
$2 = {v4_float = {1.40129846e-45, 1.7376101e-43, 2.80259693e-43,
    -nan(0x7ffec8)}, v2_double = {2.6312747808018783e-312,
    -nan(0xffec8000000c8)},
  v16_int8 = "\001\000\000\000|\000\000\000x\000\000\000xxxx", v8_int16 = {1,
    0, 124, 0, 200, 0, -312, -1}, v4_int32 = {1, 124, 200, -312}, v2_int64 = {
    532575944705, -1340029796152},
  uint128 = 0xfffffec8000000c80000007c00000001}
(gdb)
```

The values are displayed correctly in the v4_int32 format. As you can see, the normal conversion rounded the 124.79 floating-point value to 125, while the truncated conversion rounded it toward zero, making it 124. You can display the value of the data memory location by using the x/4d command, as the data has been converted to packed doubleword integers:

```
(gdb) x/4d &data
0x80490c0 <data>: 1      125      200      -312
(gdb)
```

As expected, the rounded integer values are displayed.

Summary

This chapter covered a lot of ground regarding how the IA-32 platform deals with numbers. The most basic numeric data type is the integer, which is used to represent whole numbers. Two types of integers are supported: unsigned integers, which only allow positive values, and signed integers, which can contain both positive and negative values. The IA-32 platform supports four sizes of integers, byte, word, doubleword, and quadword. An integer data type represented in one size can be expanded to a larger size without losing its value, as long as it is done using the proper format.

The Intel SIMD technology introduced additional integer data types. The packed byte and doubleword integer types enable multiple signed integer values to be contained in a single 128-bit register. Special instructions are available to perform mathematical operations (such as addition and subtraction) on multiple integer values in parallel, helping to speed up the performance of the application.

The Binary Coded Decimal (BCD) data type enables you to store and use integers using a human-readable decimal format. Each byte represents a single decimal place in a value. Because a decimal number value only requires 4 bits, packed BCD can be used to reduce the space requirements by allowing two decimal places within a single byte.

The floating-point data type is the most useful, but possibly the most complicated, data type available. The floating-point data type is used to represent real numbers in programs. The IA-32 platform uses the IEEE Standard 754 format to define single-precision (32 bit) and double-precision (64 bit) floating-point values. A third format, double-extended-precision floating-point, uses the 80-bit FPU registers to perform more accurate floating-point calculations.

The SSE platform (found in Pentium III processors) and the SSE2 platform (found in Pentium 4 processors) also contribute to the data type list. The SSE platform introduced 80-bit packed byte and doubleword integer values, while the SSE2 platform introduced 128-bit packed byte, doubleword, and quadword integers, and 128-bit packed single- and double-precision floating-point values.

Finally, the chapter discussed the IA-32 instructions that can be used to convert numeric data types between the different formats. These instructions can come in handy when you need to round floating-point values to integer values, or perform floating-point math operations on integer values (such as division).

Now that you know all about the numeric data types, it's time to start doing some math. The next chapter dives into the IA-32 platform's mathematical capabilities and demonstrates how the different data types are used for different mathematical calculations.

Basic Math Functions

Now that you have the different numeric data types under your belt, you can start using them in mathematical operations. This chapter dives into the basic integer math functions that are available in assembly language.

First the chapter describes how integer arithmetic is performed on the processor, and how you can utilize it in your assembly language programs. The instructions used for unsigned and signed addition, subtraction, multiplication, and division are shown, along with examples of how they are used in programs. Next described are the shift instructions, which help you increase the performance of your multiplication and division operations. After that, decimal arithmetic is explained, along with the instructions to implement it. The chapter finishes by describing the basic Boolean logic and bit testing instructions that are available on the IA-32 platform.

Integer Arithmetic

The basic building block for performing mathematical operations in assembly language programs is integer arithmetic. You should have a full understanding of how the processor performs mathematical operations on integers before you try diving into the more complex floating-point math functions.

This section describes how integer math is performed on the processor, and how you can use integer math in your assembly language programs. This includes integer addition, subtraction, multiplication, and division.

Addition

While it would seem that adding two integers together should be a straightforward process, that is not always the case. There are a few bumps in the road that you need to anticipate, and they all revolve around how binary numbers are added. The following sections describe the instructions used for adding integers.

The ADD instruction

The ADD instruction is used to add two integer values. The ADD instruction format is

```
add source, destination
```

where source can be an immediate value, a memory location, or a register. The destination parameter can be either a register or a value stored in a memory location (although you cannot use a memory location for both the source and destination at the same time). The result of the addition is placed in the destination location.

The ADD instruction can add 8-, 16-, or 32-bit values. As with other GNU assembler instructions, you must specify the size of the operands by adding a b (for byte), w (for word), or l (for doubleword) to the end of the ADD mnemonic. Some examples of using the ADD instruction are as follows:

```
addb $10, %al   # adds the immediate value 10 to the 8-bit AL register
addw %bx, %cx   # adds the 16-bit value of the BX register to the CX register
addl data, %eax  # adds the 32-bit integer value at the data label to EAX
addl %eax, %eax  # adds the value of the EAX register to itself
```

These instructions are demonstrated in the addtest1.s program:

```
# addtest1.s - An example of the ADD instruction
.section .data
data:
    .int 40
.section .text
.globl _start
_start:
    nop

    movl $0, %eax
    movl $0, %ebx
    movl $0, %ecx
    movb $20, %al
    addb $10, %al
    movsx %al, %eax
    movw $100, %cx
    addw %cx, %bx
    movsx %bx, %ebx
    movl $100, %edx
    addl %edx, %edx
    addl data, %eax
    addl %eax, data
    movl $1, %eax
    movl $0, %ebx
    int $0x80
```

If you are not using the entire 32-bit register, it is always a good idea to make sure that the destination registers are zeroed out, so there is nothing in the high bits. This can easily be done using the XOR instruction (see the "Logical Operations" section later in this chapter). After ensuring that the destination registers are zeroed, the different ADD instructions are performed. Note that the MOVSX instruction is used to extend the signed integer value of AL to the EAX register, and the BX value to EBX (see Chapter 7, "Using Numbers," for more information about extending signed integers) before the EAX register value can be properly used.

After assembling the program, you can step through the instructions and watch the register values after each instruction. After running all the instructions, you should get the following results:

```
(gdb) print $eax
$1 = 70
(gdb) print $ebx
$2 = 100
(gdb) print $ecx
$3 = 100
(gdb) print $edx
$4 = 200
(gdb) x/d &data
0x804909c <data>:         110
(gdb)
```

All of the additions were performed as expected. As mentioned in Chapter 7, the benefit of using two's complement to represent negative numbers is that the same hardware can be used to add signed and unsigned integers. The addtest2.s program demonstrates adding some signed integers using the ADD instruction:

```
# addtest2.s - An example of the ADD instruction and negative numbers
.section .data
data:
    .int -40
.section .text
.globl _start
_start:
    nop
    movl $-10, %eax
    movl $-200, %ebx
    movl $80, %ecx
    addl data, %eax
    addl %ecx, %eax
    addl %ebx, %eax
    addl %eax, data
    addl $210, data
    movl $1, %eax
    movl $0, %ebx
    int $0x80
```

The ADD instructions perform the addition correctly regardless of the sign of the signed integer value. You should get the following results:

```
(gdb) print $eax
$1 = -170
(gdb) print $ebx
$2 = -200
(gdb) print $ecx
$3 = 80
(gdb) x/d &data
0x80490ac <data>:        0
(gdb)
```

The ADD instruction properly added all of the signed integers used in the program. It is convenient to be able to use the same instruction to add both signed and unsigned integer values.

Detecting a carry or overflow condition

When adding integers, you should always pay attention to the EFLAGS register to ensure that nothing odd happened during the process. For unsigned integers, the *carry flag* is set when an addition results in a carry condition in the binary addition (the result is larger than the maximum value allowed). For signed integers, the *overflow flag* is used when an overflow condition is present (the resulting value is less than the minimum negative value, or greater than the maximum positive value allowed). When these flags are set, you know that the size of the destination operand was too small to hold the value of the result of the addition, and contains an invalid value. The value will be the "overflow" portion of the answer.

*The carry and overflow flags are set relative to the data size used in the addition. For example, in the **ADDB** instruction, the carry flag is set if the result is over 255, but in the **ADDW** instruction, it is not set unless the result is over 65,535.*

The addtest3.s program demonstrates how to detect a carry condition in unsigned integer addition:

```
# addtest3.s - An example of detecting a carry condition
.section .text
.globl _start
_start:
    nop
    movl $0, %ebx
    movb $190, %bl
    movb $100, %al
    addb %al, %bl
    jc over
    movl $1, %eax

    int $0x80
over:
    movl $1, %eax
    movl $0, %ebx
    int $0x80
```

The addtest3.s program performs a simple addition of 2-byte unsigned integer values stored in the AL and BL registers. If the addition results in a carry, the carry flag is set, and the JC instruction will jump to the over label. The result code from the program is either the result of the addition or the value 0 if the result is over 255. Because we set the values in AL and BL, we can control what happens in the program.

Testing the program is easy. First, set the register values to produce a carry, run the program, and view the result code using the echo command:

```
$ ./addtest3
$ echo $?
0
$
```

The result code is 0, indicating that the carry condition was properly detected. Now, change the register values so that the addition does not produce a carry:

```
movb $190, %bl
movb $10, %al
```

After running the program, you should get the following results:

```
$ ./addtest3
$ echo $?
200
$
```

The addition did not produce the carry, the jump was not taken, and the result of the addition was set as the result code.

For unsigned integers, the carry flag is crucial in knowing when the addition result exceeds the data size value limit. If you are not sure of the size of the input values, you should always check the carry flag when performing unsigned integer additions. If you know the limits of the input values, you can avoid checking the carry flag.

When working with signed integers, the carry flag is not as useful. Not only will it be set when the resulting value is too large, it will also be set whenever the value goes below zero. While that is useful for unsigned integers, it is meaningless (and even an annoyance) for signed integers.

Instead, when using signed integers, you must focus on the overflow flag, which will be set whenever the result overflows the negative or positive value limits.

The addtest4.s program demonstrates using the overflow flag to detect an error in a signed integer addition:

```
# addtest4.s - An example of detecting an overflow condition
.section .data
output:
    .asciz "The result is %d\n"
.section .text
.globl _start
_start:
    movl $-1590876934, %ebx
    movl $-1259230143, %eax
    addl %eax, %ebx
    jo over
    pushl %ebx
```

```
    pushl $output
    call printf
    add  $8, %esp
    pushl $0
    call exit
over:
    pushl $0
    pushl $output
    call printf
    add  $8, %esp
    pushl $0
    call exit
```

The `addtest4.s` program attempts to add two large negative numbers, resulting in an overflow condition. The `JO` instruction is used to detect the overflow and transfer control to the `over` label. Because this program uses the `printf` C function, remember to link it with the dynamic linker and the C library for your system (see Chapter 4, "A Sample Assembly Language Program," for details on how to do this).

If you run the program, it should produce the following output:

```
$ ./addtest4
The result is 0
$
```

which indicates that the overflow condition was detected. If you modify the `MOVL` instructions so that the two values do not produce an overflow condition, you will see the result of the addition. For example, the values

```
movl $-190876934, %ebx
movl $-159230143, %eax
```

produce the following result:

```
$ ./addtest4
The result is -350107077
$
```

When adding signed integers, it is important to check the overflow flag for error conditions if you are not sure of the input data sizes.

The ADC instruction

If you must work with extremely large signed or unsigned integers that will not fit in the doubleword data size (the maximum size that can be used with the `ADD` instruction), you can divide the value into multiple doubleword data elements, and perform separate addition operations on each element.

To do this properly, you must detect the carry flag for each addition. If the carry flag is present, it must be carried to the next data element pair that is added, as demonstrated in Figure 8-1.

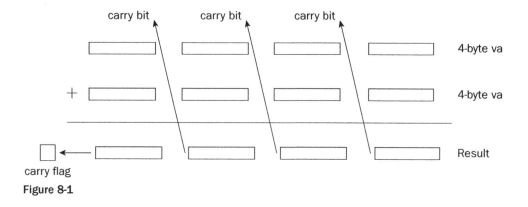

carry flag

Figure 8-1

As shown in Figure 8-1, when the lowest value data element pair is added, the carry flag bit must be carried to the next value data element pair, and so on up to the last data element pair.

To do this manually, you would have to use a combination of ADD and JC (or JO) instructions, producing a complicated web of instructions for determining when a carry (or overflow) condition was present, and when it needed to be added to the next addition operation. Fortunately, you do not have to deal with this, as Intel provides a simple solution.

The ADC instruction can be used to add two unsigned or signed integer values, along with the value contained in the carry flag from a previous ADD instruction. To add multiple groups of bytes, you can chain together multiple ADC instructions, as the ADC instruction also sets the carry and overflow flags as appropriate for the operation. This is shown in Figure 8-2.

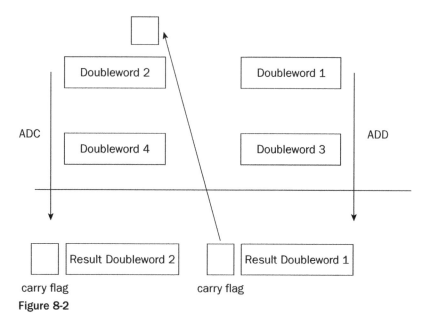

carry flag   carry flag

Figure 8-2

The format of the ADC instruction is

```
adc source, destination
```

where source can be an immediate value or an 8-, 16-, or 32-bit register or memory location value, and destination can be an 8-, 16-, or 32-bit register or memory location value. (Similar to the ADD instruction, source and destination cannot both be memory locations at one time). Also, as with the ADD instruction, the GNU assembler requires an additional character in the mnemonic to indicate the size of the operands (b, w, or l).

An ADC example

To demonstrate using the ADC instruction, let's write a program to add two large numbers, 7,252,051,615 and 5,732,348,928. Since they are both larger than the limit of the 32-bit unsigned integer, we must use a 64-bit unsigned integer value, using two 32-bit registers to hold the value. Because two registers are used to hold the 64-bit value, they must be added separately as two 32-bit additions. After the low-order 32-bits are added, if a carry bit is present, it must be added to the upper 32-bit addition. This can be done using the ADC instruction.

To start off, we need to determine which registers will be used to contain the 64-bit values, and how they will be added. This is shown in Figure 8-3.

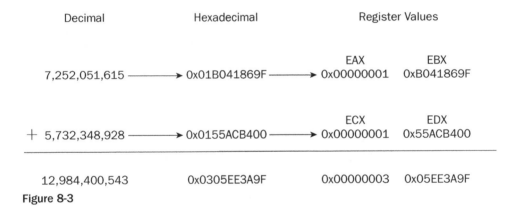

Figure 8-3

As shown in Figure 8-3, the EAX:EBX register combination holds the first value, while the ECX:EDX register combination holds the second value. To add the 64-bit values, first the EBX and EDX registers must be added using the ADD instruction. As you can see from the values in the EBX and EDX registers, the addition will produce a carry bit. Following that, the EAX and ECX registers are added, along with the carry bit from the first addition.

The adctest.s program demonstrates how to implement this operation. It adds two 64-bit values, one held in the EAX:EBX register combination and the other in the ECX:EDX register combination:

```
# adctest.s - An example of using the ADC instruction
.section .data
data1:
    .quad 7252051615
```

```
data2:
    .quad 5732348928
output:
    .asciz "The result is %qd\n"
.section .text
.globl _start
_start:
    movl data1, %ebx
    movl data1+4, %eax
    movl data2, %edx
    movl data2+4, %ecx
    addl %ebx, %edx
    adcl %eax, %ecx
    pushl %ecx
    pushl %edx
    push $output
    call printf
    addl $12, %esp
    pushl $0
    call exit
```

The adctest.s program first defines two 64-bit integer values that will be added together, along with the text for the printf function:

```
data1:
    .quad 7252051615
data2:
    .quad 5732348928
output:
    .asciz "The result is %qd\n"
```

The %qd parameter is used in the printf function to display 64-bit signed integer values (if you just use the standard %d parameter it will only use a 32-bit value). The 64-bit values are loaded into the EAX:EBX and ECX:EDX register pairs using indexed addressing:

```
movl data1, %ebx
movl data1+4, %eax
movl data2, %edx
movl data2+4, %ecx
```

The low 32-bits of the data1 value are loaded into the EBX register, and the high 32-bit value is loaded into the EAX register. The same procedure is used to load the data2 value into the ECX:EDX register pair.

After all that, the addition is performed in two instructions:

```
addl %ebx, %edx
adcl %eax, %ecx
```

The ADDL instruction is used to add the two low-order registers, and then the ADCL instruction is used to add the two high-order registers, along with the carry flag. This ensures that if the low-order registers overflow, it will be caught and added to the high-order registers.

After the addition, the 64-bit result will be in the ECX:EDX register pair. To use them in the printf function, you must push them onto the stack, with the register containing the high-order bytes (ECX) first. The combination of the ECX and EDX pair will be read by the C printf function as a single 64-bit value.

After assembling and linking the file, you can directly display the output, or run the debugger to watch the various steps along the process. For example, after the registers are loaded with the operands, but before the addition takes place, the registers should look like this:

```
(gdb) info reg
eax            0x1        1
ecx            0x1        1
edx            0x55acb400       1437381632
ebx            0xb041869f       -1337882977
```

The hex values of the 64-bit integers have been loaded into the registers as planned. The debugger assumes the register values are signed integers, so the third column values will be meaningless. After the addition instructions, you can look at the registers again:

```
(gdb) info reg
eax            0x1        1
ecx            0x3        3
edx            0x5ee3a9f        99498655
ebx            0xb041869f       -1337882977
```

The ECX:EDX register pair contains the result information, as shown in Figure 8-3. The result is also displayed using the printf function in decimal form:

```
$ ./adctest1
The result is 12984400543
$
```

You can play around with the values in the data1 and data2 variables, changing them and watching how the registers are loaded during the program execution. You can change them to negative values as well, and still come up with the correct results (because the ADD and ADC instruction work with signed integers as well as unsigned integers).

Subtraction

Now that you have integer addition under your belt, integer subtraction should be a breeze. The following sections describe the ins and outs of integer subtraction in assembly language.

The SUB instruction

The basic form for subtraction is the SUB instruction. Just like the ADD instruction, it can be used to subtract both unsigned and signed integers. The format of the SUB instruction is

```
sub source, destination
```

where the source value is subtracted from the destination value, with the result stored in the destination operand location. The source and destination operands can be 8-, 16-, or 32-bit registers or values stored in memory (but again, they cannot both be memory locations at the same time). The source value can also be an immediate data value.

As with the ADD instruction, the GNU assembler requires a size character to be added to the mnemonic. The usual characters apply (b for byte, w for word, and l for doubleword).

The subtest.s program demonstrates using the SUB instruction in an assembly language program:

```
# subtest1.s - An example of the SUB instruction
.section .data
data:
    .int 40
.section .text
.globl _start
_start:
  nop

  movl $0, %eax
  movl $0, %ebx
  movl $0, %ecx
  movb $20, %al
  subb $10, %al
  movsx %al, %eax
  movw $100, %cx
  subw %cx, %bx
  movsx %bx, %ebx
  movl $100, %edx
  subl %eax, %edx
  subl data, %eax
  subl %eax, data
  movl $1, %eax
  movl $0, %ebx
  int $0x80
```

The subtest1.s program performs various basic subtractions using immediate values, registers, and memory locations. After assembling the program, you can watch the registers and memory location in the debugger as it is running. Note the values as the SUB instructions are executed. Note particularly the last SUB instruction, which subtracts the value in the EAX register (-30) from the value at the data1 memory location (40):

```
(gdb) print $eax
$1 = -30
(gdb) x/d &data
0x80490ac <data>:        40
(gdb) s
_start () at subtest1.s:23
23          movl $1, %eax
(gdb) x/d &data
0x80490ac <data>:        70
(gdb)
```

The processor subtracted -30 from 40, and got the correct answer, 70.

*It is extremely important to remember the order of the **SUB** instruction for the GNU assembler. Using the Intel syntax will produce the wrong results!*

A close relative of the SUB instruction is the NEG instruction. It produces the two's complement of a value. This is the same as using the SUB instruction to subtract the value from zero, but quicker.

Carry and overflow with subtraction

Similar to the ADD instruction, the SUB instruction modifies several of the EFLAGS register bits after it performs the subtraction operation. However, the concept of carry and overflow are different in subtraction.

In addition, the carry flag is set when the addition result is too large of a positive value for the data size used to hold the operands. Obviously, with subtraction, the problem arises when the subtraction result becomes too large of a negative value for the data size.

For example, with unsigned integers, what happens when you subtract 5 from 2? The subtest2.s program demonstrates this problem:

```
# subtest2.s - An example of a subtraction carry
.section .text
.globl _start
_start:
    nop
    movl $5, %eax
    movl $2, %ebx
    subl %eax, %ebx
    jc under
    movl $1, %eax
    int $0x80
under:
    movl $1, %eax
    movl $0, %ebx
    int $0x80
```

The subtest2.s program simply places the 5 value in the EAX register, and the 2 value in the EBX register, and then subtracts the EAX register from the EBX register. The JC instruction is used to jump if the carry flag is set. The result code from the program will be either the subtraction value or a 0 if the carry flag is set.

After assembling the program, run it and see what happens:

```
$ ./subtest2
$ echo $?
0
$
```

The carry flag was set when the result was less than zero (which is invalid in unsigned integers). However, by examining the value of the EBX register in the debugger, you should see something interesting:

```
(gdb) print $ebx
$1 = -3
(gdb)
```

The EBX register contained the correct value, even though it was "supposed" to be unsigned. The processor does not know if you are using unsigned or signed integers. It is up to your program to determine when a value is outside of the range of the unsigned (or signed) values.

The carry flag is used to determine when subtracting unsigned integers produces a negative result.

As with adding signed integers, if you are subtracting signed integers, the carry flag is not useful, as the result can often be negative. Instead, you must rely on the overflow flag to tell you when you have reached the data size limits. This is demonstrated in the subtest3.s program:

```
# subtest3.s - An example of an overflow condition in a SUB instruction
.section .data
output:
    .asciz "The result is %d\n"
.section .text
.globl _start
_start:
    movl $-1590876934, %ebx
    movl $1259230143, %eax
    subl %eax, %ebx
    jo over
    pushl %ebx
    pushl $output
    call printf
    add  $8, %esp
    pushl $0
    call exit
over:
    pushl $0
    pushl $output
    call printf
    add  $8, %esp
    pushl $0
    call exit
```

The subtest3.s program demonstrates subtracting a positive value stored in the EAX register from a negative value stored in the EBX register, producing a value too large for the 32-bit EBX register. The JO instruction is used to detect the overflow flag, and send the program to the over: label, setting the output value to 0. After assembling the program and linking it with the C libraries, you can run it to see the output:

```
$ ./subtest3
The result is 0
$
```

The overflow condition was detected and the JO instruction was executed and followed. You can test to determine whether the opposite condition works by changing the value assigned to the EAX to a negative value:

```
movl $-1259230143, %eax
```

and running the program again:

```
$ ./subtest3
The result is -331646791
$
```

This time, subtracting a negative number produced a smaller negative number, well within the data size limits, and not setting the overflow flag.

The SBB instruction

Just like in addition, you can use the carry condition to your advantage to subtract large signed integer values. The SBB instruction utilizes the carry and overflow flags in multibyte subtractions to implement the borrow feature across data boundaries.

The format of the SBB instruction is

```
sbb source, destination
```

where the carry bit is added to the source value, and the result is subtracted from the destination value. The result is stored in the destination location. As usual, the source and destination values can be 8-, 16-, or 32-bit registers or values in memory, and of course you can't use memory locations for both the source and destination values at the same time.

The SBB instruction is most often used to "scoop up" the carry flag from a previous SUB instruction. When the previous SUB instruction is executed and a carry results, the carry bit is "borrowed" by the SBB instruction to continue the subtraction on the next data pair. This is demonstrated in Figure 8-4.

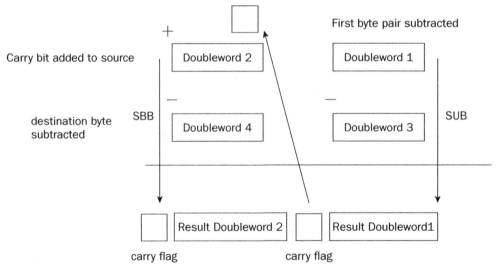

Figure 8-4

The following `sbbtest.s` program demonstrates using the SBB instruction in a multibyte subtraction problem:

```
# sbbtest.s - An example of using the SBB instruction
.section .data
data1:
    .quad 7252051615
data2:
    .quad 5732348928
output:
    .asciz "The result is %qd\n"
.section .text
.globl _start
_start:
    nop
    movl data1, %ebx
    movl data1+4, %eax
    movl data2, %edx
    movl data2+4, %ecx
    subl %ebx, %edx
    sbbl %eax, %ecx
    pushl %ecx
    pushl %edx
    push $output
    call printf
    add  $12, %esp
    pushl $0
    call exit
```

You may notice that the `sbbtest.s` program looks exactly like the `adctest.s` program except for the use of the SUB and SBB instructions instead of the ADD and ADC instructions. Two quadword values are defined, loaded into registers, and then subtracted using the SUB/SBB combination.

After assembling the program and linking it with the C libraries, you should get the following result:

```
$ ./sbbtest
The result is -1519702687
$
```

You can play around with the values of the `data1` and `data2` quadwords to make sure that this works for any combination of valid 64-bit values.

Incrementing and decrementing

Often, when you are creating assembly language programs, you must step through a data array to process each element. This is so common of an occurrence in the programming field that Intel provided special instructions for automatically providing a counting function.

The INC and DEC instructions are used to increment (INC) and decrement (DEC) an unsigned integer value. The INC and DEC instructions don't affect the carry flag, so you can increment or decrement a counter value without affecting any other additions or subtractions in a programming loop involving carry operations.

The format of the instructions is

```
dec destination
inc destination
```

where destination can be an 8-, 16-, or 32-bit register or value in memory.

Remember that the INC and DEC instructions are mainly used for unsigned integers. If you decrement a 32-bit register that is set to 0, the new value will be 0xFFFFFFFF, which may look like -1 as a signed integer, but it is treated like 4294967295 as an unsigned integer (the proper flags will not be set). If you use them for signed integers, be careful of the sign changes.

Multiplication

One of the more complicated functions in integer arithmetic is multiplication. Unlike addition and subtraction, multiplication requires separate instructions for operating on unsigned and signed integers. This section shows the instructions for multiplying integers, and how to use them in your programs.

Unsigned integer multiplication using MUL

The MUL instruction is used to multiply two unsigned integers. Its format is somewhat different from what you would expect. The format for the MUL instruction is

```
mul source
```

where source can be an 8-, 16-, or 32-bit register or memory value. You might be wondering how you can multiply two values by only supplying one operand in the instruction line. The answer is that the destination operand is implied.

Working with the implied destination operand is somewhat complicated. For one thing, the destination location always uses some form of the EAX register, depending on the size of the source operand. Thus, one of the operands used in the multiplication must be placed in the AL, AX, or EAX registers, depending on the size of the value.

Due to the large values that can result from the multiplication, the destination location of the MUL instruction must be twice the size of the source operand. If the source value is 8 bits, the destination operand is the AX register, as the result is 16 bits. It gets even more complicated when the source operand is larger.

Unfortunately, when multiplying a 16-bit source operand, the EAX register is not used to hold the 32-bit result. In order to be backwardly compatible with older processors, Intel uses the DX:AX register pair to hold the 32-bit multiplication result value (this format started back in the 16-bit processor days). The high-order word of the result is stored in the DX register, while the low-order word is stored in the AX register.

For 32-bit source values, the 64-bit EDX:EAX register pair is used, again with the high-order doubleword in the EDX register, and the low-order doubleword in the EAX. Make sure that if you have data stored in the EDX (or DX) register that you save it elsewhere when using the 16- or 32-bit versions of MUL.

To help sum this up, the following table outlines the unsigned integer multiplication requirements.

Source Operand Size	Destination Operand	Destination Location
8 bits	AL	AX
16 bits	AX	DX:AX
32 bits	EAX	EDX:EAX

Also, it is important to remember that with the GNU assembler, you must append the correct size character to the end of the mnemonic.

A MUL instruction example

As an example of using the MUL instruction, let's compute 315,814 times 165,432. Figure 8-5 demonstrates how these values will be handled by the MUL instruction.

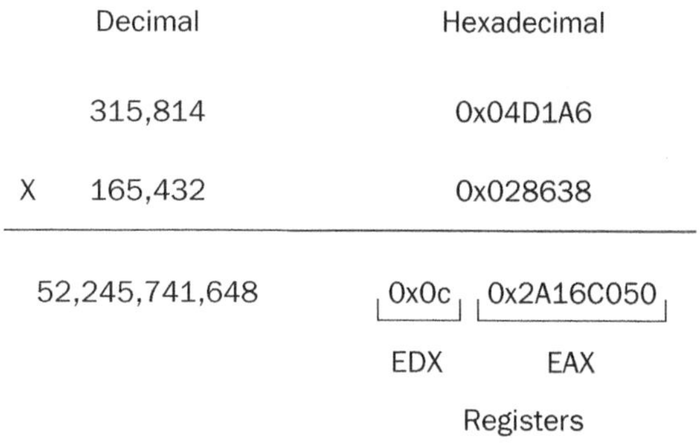

Figure 8-5

The two operands used in the MUL instruction are both 32-bit values. The result of the multiplication is stored as a 64-bit value, split in the EDX and the EAX registers.

The multest.s program demonstrates multiplying the two 32-bit unsigned integers, and retrieving the result from the EDX:EAX registers:

```
# multest.s - An example of using the MUL instruction
.section .data
data1:
    .int 315814
data2:
    .int 165432
result:
    .quad 0
output:
    .asciz "The result is %qd\n"
.section .text
.globl _start
```

```
_start:
    nop
    movl data1, %eax
    mull data2
    movl %eax, result
    movl %edx, result+4
    pushl %edx
    pushl %eax
    pushl $output
    call printf
    add $12, %esp
    pushl $0
    call exit
```

The multtest.s program defines the two integer values in memory (remember that when using the MUL instruction, they must be unsigned values), loads one of them into the EAX register, and then uses the MUL instruction to multiple the other one with the EAX register. The result from the EDX:EAX register pair is both loaded into a 64-bit memory location (using indexed memory access) and displayed using the printf C function.

After assembling the program and linking it with the C library, you can run it directly to see the output, and run it in the debugger to watch the registers in action. The debugger output after the MUL instruction should look something like the following:

```
(gdb) print/x $eax
$3 = 0x2a16c050
(gdb) print/x $edx
$4 = 0xc
(gdb) x/gd &result
0x80491c4 <result>:       52245741648
(gdb) x/8b &result
0x80491c4 <result>: 0x50  0xc0  0x16  0x2a  0x0c  0x00 0x00 0x00
(gdb)
```

The EDX:EAX register pair combine to produce the resulting value, which is stored in the result memory location, and displayed by the printf function.

Signed integer multiplication using IMUL

While the MUL instruction can only be used for unsigned integers, the IMUL instruction can be used by both signed and unsigned integers, although you must be careful that the result does not use the most significant bit of the destination. For larger values, the IMUL instruction is only valid for signed integers. To complicate things even more, there are three different instruction formats of the IMUL instruction.

The first format of the IMUL instruction takes one operand, and behaves exactly the same as the MUL instruction:

```
imul source
```

The source operand can be an 8-, 16-, or 32-bit register or value in memory, and it is multiplied with the implied operand located in the AL, AX, or EAX registers (depending on the source operand size). The result is then placed in the AX register, the DX:AX register pair, or the EDX:EAX register pair.

The second format of the IMUL instruction enables you to specify a destination operand other than the EAX register:

```
imul source, destination
```

where source can be a 16- or 32-bit register or value in memory, and destination must be a 16- or 32-bit general-purpose register. This format enables you to specify where the result of the multiplication will go (instead of being forced to use the AX and DX registers).

The downside to this format is that the multiplication result is forced into the size of the single destination register (no 64-bit results). Extreme care must be taken when using this format that you do not overflow the destination register (check the carry or overflow flags using the standard methods shown in Chapter 6, "Controlling Execution Flow," after the multiplication to ensure that the result fits in the destination register).

The third format of the IMUL instruction enables you to specify three operands:

```
imul multiplier, source, destination
```

where multiplier is an immediate value, source is a 16- or 32-bit register or value in memory, and destination must be a general-purpose register. This format enables you to perform a quick multiplication of a value (the source) with a signed integer (the multiplier), storing the result in a general-purpose register (the destination).

Just like the MUL instruction, remember to add the size character to the end of the IMUL mnemonic when using it in the GNU assembler to specify the size of the source and destination operands.

An IMUL instruction example

The first format of the IMUL instruction is somewhat trivial once you are comfortable with the MUL instruction. The other two formats may need some examples, so here's the imultest.s program, which demonstrates the last two IMUL instruction formats:

```
# imultest.s - An example of the IMUL instruction formats
.section .data
value1:
    .int 10
value2:
    .int -35
value3:
    .int 400
.section .text
.globl _start
_start:
    nop
    movl value1, %ebx
    movl value2, %ecx
    imull %ebx, %ecx
    movl value3, %edx
    imull $2, %edx, %eax
    movl $1, %eax
    movl $0, %ebx
    int $0x80
```

The imultest.s program creates some signed integer values to work with (value1, value2, and value3), moves them into registers, and performs some multiplication using the various IMUL instruction formats.

After assembling and linking the program, you can use the debugger to watch the register values during the program. After stepping through the IMUL instructions, the registers should look like this:

```
(gdb) info reg
eax            0x320    800
ecx            0xffffffea2      -350
edx            0x190    400
ebx            0xa      10
```

The EAX register contains the value of EDX (400) multiplied by the immediate value 2. The ECX register contains the value of the EBX register (10) multiplied by the value originally loaded into the ECX register (-35). Notice that the result was placed in the ECX register as a signed integer value.

Detecting overflows

Remember that when using signed integers and the IMUL instruction, it is important to always detect overflows in the result. One way to do this is to check the overflow flag using the JO instruction (the other way is to check the carry flag).

The imultest2.s program demonstrates this:

```
# imultest2.s - An example of detecting an IMUL overflow
.section .text
.globl _start
_start:
    nop
    movw $680, %ax
    movw $100, %cx
    imulw %cx
    jo over
    movl $1, %eax
    movl $0, %ebx
    int $0x80
over:
    movl $1, %eax
    movl $1, %ebx
    int $0x80
```

The imultest2.s program moves two values into 16-bit registers (AX and CX), and then uses the 16-bit IMUL instruction to multiply them. The result is set so that it will overflow the 16-bit register, and the JO instruction jumps to the over label, which exits the program with a result code of 1. If you modify the immediate data values loaded into the registers so the result is less than 65,535, the overflow flag is not set by the IMUL instruction, the JO instruction is not executed, and the program exits with a result code of 0.

Division

Similar to multiplication, division requires using a specific instruction depending on whether you are using unsigned or signed integers. The tricky part about integer division is that the answer is not always an exact integer, such as if you divide 9 by 2. This produces two parts to the answer. The quotient is the number of times the divisor goes into the dividend. The remainder is how much is left over (the fractional part of the answer). The division instructions produce both the quotient and remainder parts as results of the division.

This section describes and demonstrates the DIV and IDIV instructions used for integer division.

Unsigned division

The DIV instruction is used for dividing unsigned integers. The format of the DIV instruction is

```
div divisor
```

where divisor is the value that is divided into the implied dividend, and can be an 8-, 16-, or 32-bit register or value in memory. The dividend must already be stored in the AX register (for a 16-bit value), the DX:AX register pair (for a 32-bit value), or the EDX:EAX register pair (for a 64-bit value) before the DIV instruction is performed.

The maximum value allowed for the divisor depends on the size of the dividend. For a 16-bit dividend, the divisor can only be 8 bits, for a 32-bit dividend 16 bits, and for a 64-bit dividend the divisor can only be 32 bits.

The result of the division is two separate numbers: the quotient and the remainder. Both values are stored in the same registers used for the dividend value. The following table shows how this is set up.

Dividend	Dividend Size	Quotient	Remainder
AX	16 bits	AL	AH
DX:AX	32 bits	AX	DX
EDX:EAX	64 bits	EAX	EDX

This means that you will lose the value of the dividend when the division completes, so make sure that this is not your only copy of the value (or that you don't care about the value of the dividend after the division). Also remember that the result will alter the value of the DX or EDX registers, so be careful what is stored there as well.

The divtest.s program demonstrates a simple division example:

```
# divtest.s - An example of the DIV instruction
.section .data
dividend:
    .quad 8335
divisor:
    .int 25
```

```
quotient:
    .int 0
remainder:
    .int 0
output:
    .asciz "The quotient is %d, and the remainder is %d\n"
.section .text
.globl _start
_start:
    nop
    movl dividend, %eax
    movl dividend+4, %edx
    divl divisor
    movl %eax, quotient
    movl %edx, remainder
    pushl remainder
    pushl quotient
    pushl $output
    call printf
    add  $12, %esp
    pushl $0
    call exit
```

The divtest.s program loads a 64-bit quadword integer into the EDX:EAX register pair (remember the little-endian order in memory versus the big-endian order in registers, discussed in Chapter 5, "Moving Data"), and divides that value by a 32-bit doubleword integer value stored in memory. The 32-bit quotient value is stored in one memory location, and the 32-bit remainder value is stored in another memory location.

After assembling the program and linking it with the C library, you can run it using different values of the dividend and divisor (remember these must be positive values, and less than the maximum allowed values for their data sizes). You can watch how the values are manipulated in the registers using the debugger.

Signed division

The IDIV instruction is used exactly like the DIV instruction, but for dividing signed integers. It too uses an implied dividend, located in the AX register, the DX:AX register pair, or the EDX:EAX register pair.

Unlike the IMUL instruction, there is only one format for the IDIV instruction, which specifies the divisor used in the division:

```
idiv divisor
```

where divisor can again be an 8-, 16-, or 32-bit register or value in memory.

The IDIV instruction returns the results using the same registers as the DIV instruction, and in the same format of quotient and remainder (except that the results are signed integers).

For signed integer division, the sign of the remainder is always the sign of the dividend.

Another thing to remember about signed division is the size of the dividend. Because it must be twice the size of the divisor, sometimes you must extend the integer value to the proper data size (see Chapter 7). It is important to use the sign extension instructions (such as MOVSX) to extend the dividend to the proper data size for the division. Failure to do so will corrupt the dividend value and produce errors in your results.

Detecting division errors

The biggest problem with integer division is detecting when an error condition has occurred, such as when a division by zero happens, or the quotient (or remainder) overflows the destination register.

When an error occurs, the system produces an interrupt, which will produce an error on the Linux system, such as the following:

```
$ ./divtest
Floating point exception
$
```

This error was produced by setting the divisor value in the divtest.s program to 0.

It is your responsibility to check the divisor and dividend values before performing the DIV or IDIV instructions in your programs. Not doing so can result in erratic behavior in your applications.

Shift Instructions

Multiplying and dividing are two of the most time-consuming operations on the processor. However, there are some tricks that you can use to help speed things up. The shift instructions provide a quick and easy way to perform multiplication and division based on powers of 2. This section describes the methods used to perform multiplication and division using the shift instructions.

Shifting utilizes a feature of binary arithmetic that makes multiplying and dividing by powers of 2 simple. You are probably familiar with the decimal world, and how shifting a decimal value into another decimal place automatically multiplies or divides it by a power of 10 (for example, moving the value 2 over one decimal place to 20 is the same as multiplying it by 10).

The same principle applies to binary numbers, except using powers of 2. Shifting a binary number to the left one space multiplies it by 2, two spaces multiplies it by 4, three spaces multiplies it by 8, and so on. Shifting bits in a data element is much quicker than performing binary multiplication and can be used to increase the performance of mathematically intensive programs.

The following sections describe how to implement the shift instructions in your programs.

Multiply by shifting

To multiply integers by a power of 2, you must shift the value to the left. Two instructions can be used to left shift integer values, SAL (shift arithmetic left) and SHL (shift logical left). Both of these instructions perform the same operation, and are interchangeable. They have three different formats:

```
sal destination
sal %cl, destination
sal shifter, destination
```

The first format shifts the destination value left one position, which is the equivalent of multiplying the value by 2.

The second format shifts the destination value left by the number of times specified in the CL register.

The final version shifts the destination value left the number of times indicated by the shifter value. In all formats, the destination operand can be an 8-, 16-, or 32-bit register or value in memory.

As always, the GNU assembler requires the usual one-character letter appended to the mnemonic to indicate the size of the destination value.

The shift left instructions can be performed on both signed and unsigned integers. The bits emptied by the shift are filled with zeroes. Any bits that are shifted out of the data size are first placed in the carry flag, and then dropped in the next shift. Thus, if a value contains a 1 value in the most significant bit, and is shifted left twice, the most significant bit will be dropped from the carry flag. This is demonstrated in Figure 8-6.

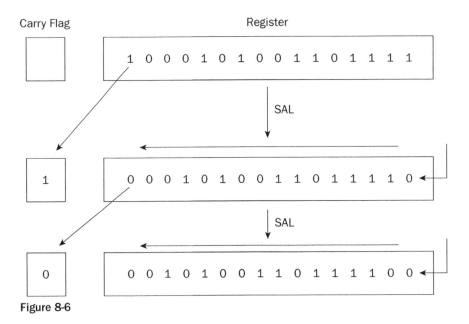

Figure 8-6

The `saltest.s` program demonstrates the basics of using the SAL instruction:

```
# saltest.s - An example of the SAL instruction
.section .data
value1:
    .int 25
.section .text
.globl _start
_start:
    nop
    movl $10, %ebx
    sall %ebx
    movb $2, %cl
    sall %cl, %ebx
    sall $2, %ebx
    sall value1
    sall $2, value1
    movl $1, %eax
    movl $0, %ebx
    int $0x80
```

The `saltest.s` program demonstrates all three formats of the SAL instruction, using the EBX register to hold the value to shift. After assembling the program, you can use the debugger to watch the register values:

```
(gdb) info reg
eax              0x0        0
ecx              0x2        2
edx              0x0        0
ebx              0x140      320
(gdb) x/d &value1
0x804909c <value1>:        200
(gdb)
```

To follow along, the decimal value 10 is loaded into the EBX register. The first SAL instruction shifts it one place (multiplying by 2, making 20). The second SAL instruction shifts it two places (multiplying by four, making 80), and the third SAL instruction shifts it two more places (multiplying by four, making 320). The value in the `value1` location (25) is shifted one place (making it 50), and then shifted two more places (making 200).

Dividing by shifting

Dividing by shifting involves shifting the binary value to the right. However, as you shift an integer value to the right, you must pay attention to the sign of the integer.

For unsigned integers, the bits to the left that are emptied can be filled with zeroes without any problems. Unfortunately, with signed integers, a negative number will be adversely affected by zero-filling the leading bits.

To solve this problem there are two right-shift instructions. The SHR instruction clears the bits emptied by the shift, which makes it useful only for shifting unsigned integers. The SAR instruction either clears or sets the bits emptied by the shift, depending on the sign bit of the integer. For negative numbers, the bits are set to 1, but for positive numbers, they are cleared to zero.

As with the left-shift instructions, the right-shift instructions shift bits out of the data element. Any bits shifted out of the data element (the least significant bits) are first moved to the carry flag, and then shifted out (lost). This is demonstrated in Figure 8-7.

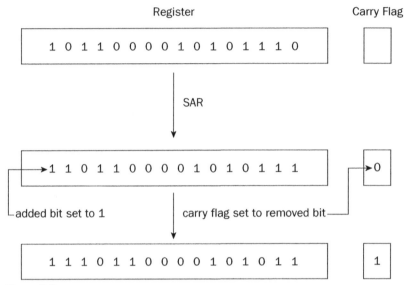

Figure 8-7

Rotating bits

Close relatives to the shift instructions are the rotate instructions. The rotate instructions perform just like the shift instructions, except the overflow bits are pushed back into the other end of the value instead of being dropped. For example, a left rotate of a byte value takes the value in bit position 7 and places it in bit position 0, with each of the other bit positions shifted one place left.

The following table shows the various rotate instructions that can be used.

Instruction	Description
ROL	Rotate value left
ROR	Rotate value right
RCL	Rotate left and include carry flag
RCR	Rotate right and include carry flag

The last two instructions use the carry flag as an additional bit position, to allow 9-bit shifting. The formats of the rotate instructions are the same as the shift instructions, providing three options for their use:

❑ A single operand that is shifted once in the indicated direction

❑ Two operands: The %cl register to indicate the number of times to rotate and the destination operand

❑ Two operands: An immediate value to indicate the number of times to rotate and the destination operand

Decimal Arithmetic

As described in Chapter 7, Binary Coded Decimal (BCD) format is a popular method to handle human-readable numbers, and quickly process them in the processor. Although much of the advanced BCD-handling operations are located in the FPU, the core processor contains some simplistic instructions for performing arithmetic using BCD values.

This section describes the basic BCD arithmetic instructions available, and demonstrates how they are used within the assembly language program.

Unpacked BCD arithmetic

As described in Chapter 7, unpacked BCD values contain a single decimal digit (0 through 9) in a byte. Multiple decimal digits are stored in multiple bytes, 1 byte per digit. When an application is required to perform a mathematical operation on the unpacked BCD values, it is assumed that the result should also be in unpacked BCD format. Fortunately, the IA-32 platform provides special instructions for producing unpacked BCD results from common mathematical operations.

Four instructions are used to convert binary arithmetic results to unpacked BCD format:

❑ **AAA:** Adjusts the result of an addition process

❑ **AAS:** Adjusts the result of a subtraction process

❑ **AAM:** Adjusts the result of a multiplication process

❑ **AAD:** Prepares the dividend of a division process

These instructions must be used in combination with the normal unsigned integer ADD, ADC, SUB, SBB, MUL, and DIV instructions. The AAA, AAS, and AAM instructions are used after their respective operation to convert a binary result into unpacked BCD format. The AAD instruction is somewhat different in that it is used before the DIV instruction to prepare the dividend value to produce an unpacked BCD result.

Each of these instructions uses an implied operand, the AL register. The AAA, AAS, and AAM instructions assume that the previous operation result is placed in the AL register, and converts that value to unpacked BCD format. The AAD instruction assumes that the dividend value is placed in the AX register in unpacked BCD format, and converts it to binary format for the DIV instruction to handle. The result is a proper unpacked BCD value, the quotient in the AL register, and the remainder in the AH register (in unpacked BCD format).

When working with multibyte unpacked BCD values, the carry and overflow flags must be used to ensure that the proper values are calculated. Figure 8-8 demonstrates this problem.

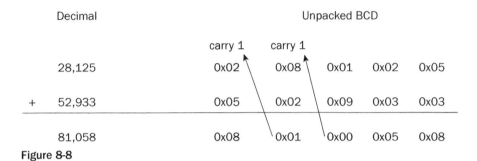

Figure 8-8

The addition performed on the first unpacked BCD values produces a carry, which must be carried to the next BCD value to create the proper result. The AAA, AAS, and AAM instructions all use the AH register along with the carry flag to indicate when a carry operation is required.

This is best shown in a sample program. The aaatest.s program demonstrates adding two multibyte unpacked BCD values:

```
# aaatest.s - An example of using the AAA instruction
.section .data
value1:
    .byte 0x05, 0x02, 0x01, 0x08, 0x02
value2:
    .byte 0x03, 0x03, 0x09, 0x02, 0x05
.section .bss
    .lcomm sum, 6
.section .text
.globl _start
_start:
    nop
    xor %edi, %edi
    movl $5, %ecx
    clc
loop1:
    movb value1(, %edi, 1), %al
    adcb value2(, %edi, 1), %al
    aaa
    movb %al, sum(, %edi, 1)
    inc %edi
    loop loop1
    adcb $0, sum(, %edi, 4)
    movl $1, %eax
    movl $0, %ebx
    int $0x80
```

The unpacked BCD values are stored in memory locations in little-endian format. The first value is read into the AL register 1 byte at a time, and added with the same place value of the second value using the ADC instruction. The ADC instruction is used to ensure that any carry bits are added from the previous additions (don't forget the CLC instruction before the loop to ensure that the carry flag is cleared). The AAA instruction is used after the ADC instruction to convert the binary result in the AL register to unpacked BCD format before it is stored in the same place value location in the sum location. The ECX register is used to count the value places so the LOOP instruction knows when to quit.

After assembling the program, you can test it by running it through the debugger and watching what happens during each step in the process. For example, after the third time the ADC instruction is executed (the third value place), the AL register contains the value

```
(gdb) info reg
eax              0xa      10
(gdb)
```

which shows that the binary addition of the 9 and 1 is 10. However, after the AAA instruction is executed, the AX register has the value

```
(gdb) info reg
eax              0x100    256
(gdb)
```

which shows the unpacked value 1 in the AH register, and 0 in the AL register. The 1 is carried to the next place value addition. In the end, the result is placed in the sum memory location in unpacked BCD format:

```
(gdb) x/6b &sum
0x80490b8 <sum>:        0x08     0x05     0x00     0x01     0x08     0x00
(gdb)
```

Thus, the addition of 28,125 and 52,933 is 81,058.

Packed BCD arithmetic

When working with packed BCD values, only two instructions are available for use:

❑ **DAA:** Adjusts the result of the ADD or ADC instructions

❑ **DAS:** Adjusts the result of the SUB or SBB instructions

These instructions perform the same functions as the AAA and AAS instructions, but with packed BCD values. They also use the implied operand located in the AL register, and place the result of the conversion in the AL register, with the carry bit placed in the AH register and the auxiliary carry flag bit.

An example of packed BCD arithmetic is shown in Figure 8-9.

Decimal	packed BCD	little-endian packed BCD
52,933	0x05 0x29 0x33	0x33 0x29 0x05
— 28,125	0x02 0x81 0x25	0x25 0x81 0x02
24,808	0x02 0x48 0x08	0x08 0x48 0x02

Figure 8-9

The packed BCD value 52,933 is loaded into memory using little-endian format (0x332905), and has the BCD value 28,125 (0x258102) subtracted from it. The result in packed BCD format is 0x084802.

The dastest.s program demonstrates performing the subtraction using the SBB and DAS instructions:

```
# dastest.s - An example of using the DAS instruction
.section .data
value1:
    .byte 0x25, 0x81, 0x02
value2:
    .byte 0x33, 0x29, 0x05
.section .bss
    .lcomm result, 4
.section .text
.globl _start
_start:
    nop
    xor %edi, %edi
    movl $3, %ecx
loop1:
    movb value2(, %edi, 1), %al
    sbbb value1(, %edi, 1), %al
    das
    movb %al, result(, %edi, 1)
    inc %edi
    loop loop1
    sbbb $0, result(, %edi, 4)
    movl $1, %eax
    movl $0, %ebx
    int $0x80
```

The dastest.s program loads the first packed BCD value into the AL register (one decimal place at a time), and subtracts the second packed BCD value from it using the SBB instruction. This way, any carry bits left over from the previous subtraction are accounted for. The DAS instruction is then used to convert the result into packed BCD format to store in the result memory location. The ECX register is used to control the number of times the process must be looped through (once for each packed BCD byte). After the conversion, if there is a left-over carry bit, it is placed in the result value.

After assembling and linking the program, you can run it in the debugger and watch the EAX register value as the subtraction values are computed by the SBB instruction, and then changed to packed BCD format by the DAS instruction. For example, after the first subtraction, the EAX register has the following value:

```
(gdb) info reg
eax            0x0e        14
(gdb)
```

But after the DAS instruction is executed, the value is changed to

```
(gdb) info reg
eax            0x08         8
(gdb)
```

which represents the first decimal place of the result.

Logical Operations

Besides the standard arithmetic functions of addition, subtraction, multiplication, and division, assembly language also provides instructions to perform various operations on the raw bits contained in the byte values. This section looks at two common types of bit functions that assembly programmers often use: Boolean logic and bit testing.

Boolean logic

When working with binary numbers, it is handy to have the standard Boolean logic functions available. The following Boolean logic operations are provided:

- ❏ AND
- ❏ NOT
- ❏ OR
- ❏ XOR

The AND, OR, and XOR instructions use the same format:

```
    and source, destination
```

where source can be an 8-, 16-, or 32-bit immediate value, register, or value in memory, and destination can be an 8-, 16-, or 32-bit register or value in memory (but as usual, you cannot use memory values for both the source and destination). The NOT instruction uses a single operand, which is both the source value and location of the destination result.

The Boolean logic functions perform bit-wise operations on the source and destination. That is, each bit of the data elements is compared individually in order, using the logic function specified. You have already seen some examples of using Boolean logic instructions in assembly language programs. Several example programs used the XOR instruction to zero the value of a register. The most efficient way to clear out a register is to exclusive OR the register with itself using the XOR instruction. Each bit that was set to 1 when XOR'd with itself becomes 0, and each bit that was set to 0 when XOR'd with itself also becomes 0. This ensures that all of the bits in the register will be set to 0, faster than what it would take to load the immediate value of 0 using the MOV instruction.

Bit testing

Sometimes it is necessary to determine whether a single bit within a value is set or not. The most common use for this feature is when checking the values of the EFLAGS register flags. Instead of trying to compare the value of the entire register, it would be nice to detect the value of a single flag.

One way to do this is to use the AND instruction, comparing the EFLAGS register to a known bit value to single out the bit(s) you want to check. However, you may not want to alter the value of the register containing the EFLAGS bits.

To solve this problem, the IA-32 platform provides the TEST instruction. The TEST instruction performs a bit-wise logical AND between two 8-, 16-, or 32-bit values, and sets the sign, zero, and parity flags accordingly, without modifying the destination value.

The format of the TEST instruction is the same as for the AND instruction. Even though no data is written to the destination location, you still must specify any immediate values as the source value. This is similar to how the CMP instruction works like the SUB instruction, but it does not store the result anywhere.

As mentioned, the most common use of the TEST instruction is to check for flags in the EFLAGS register. For example, if you want to use the CPUID instruction to check processor properties, you should first ensure that the processor supports the CPUID instruction.

The ID flag in the EFLAGS register (bit 21) is used to determine whether the CPUID instruction is supported by the processor. If the ID flag can be modified, the CPUID instruction is available. To test this, you must retrieve the EFLAGS register, invert the ID flag bit, and then test to see if it was really changed. The cpuidtest.s program performs these functions:

```
# cpuidtest.s - An example of using the TEST instruction
.section .data
output_cpuid:
    .asciz "This processor supports the CPUID instruction\n"
output_nocpuid:
    .asciz "This processor does not support the CPUID instruction\n"
.section .text
.globl _start
_start:
    nop
    pushfl
    popl %eax
    movl %eax, %edx
    xor $0x00200000, %eax
    pushl %eax
    popfl
```

```
        pushfl
        popl %eax
        xor %edx, %eax
        test $0x00200000, %eax
        jnz cpuid
        pushl $output_nocpuid
        call printf
        add  $4, %esp
        pushl $0
        call exit
cpuid:
        pushl $output_cpuid
        call printf
        add  $4, %esp
        pushl $0
        call exit
```

The cpuidtest.s program first saves the value of the EFLAGS register to the top of the stack using the PUSHFL instruction. Next, the POPL instruction is used to retrieve the EFLAGS value into the EAX register.

The next step demonstrates how the XOR instruction is used to set a bit in a register. A copy of the EFLAGS value is saved into the EDX register using the MOVL instruction, and then the XOR instruction is used to set the ID bit (still in the EAX register) to a one value. The XOR instruction uses an immediate data value set to the bit setting of the ID bit. When exclusive-OR'd with the EAX register value, it ensures that the ID bit is set to one. The next step is to push the new EAX register value onto the stack, and use the POPFL instruction to store it in the EFLAGS register.

Now you must determine whether setting the ID flag worked. Again, the PUSHFL instruction is used to push the EFLAGS register onto the stack, and the POPL instruction is used to pop it into the EAX register. The value is XOR'd with the original EFLAGS value (stored in EDX earlier) to see what values have changed.

Finally, the TEST instruction is used to see if the ID flag bit changed. If so, the value in EAX will not be zero, and the JNZ instruction jumps to print out the appropriate message.

Summary

A lot ground was covered in this chapter. The basics of integer arithmetic were discussed, showing how to perform basic addition, subtraction, multiplication, and division with both unsigned and signed integers.

The ADD and ADC instructions are used to add both unsigned and signed integers, with the ADC instruction used to include the carry flag for multibyte values. The SUB and SBB instructions are used to subtract unsigned and signed integers, with the SBB instruction used to include the carry flag for multibyte values.

Next, the multiplication and division functions were discussed. Unfortunately, separate unsigned and signed instructions are required for both multiplication and division. The MUL and DIV instructions are used for multiplying and dividing unsigned integers, and the IMUL and IDIV instructions are used for multiplying and dividing signed integers. A quicker way of performing multiplication and division by powers of two was also shown, using the shift instructions. The SAL and SHL instructions perform arithmetic or logical left-shifts of values, producing an easy way to multiply values. The SAR and SHR instructions perform arithmetic or logical right-shifts of values, producing a quick way to divide values.

Decimal arithmetic enables you to use both packed and unpacked BCD values in mathematical functions. The BCD values are used to provide an easier method to display integer values, rather than in binary mode. The AAA, AAS, AAM, and AAD instructions provide methods to produce unpacked BCD values from addition, subtraction, multiplication, and division operations. They must be used in conjunction with the binary arithmetic instructions. The packed BCD functions include DAA and DAS, for addition and subtraction of packed BCD values.

Finally, the chapter discussed how to implement common Boolean logic functions using the AND, OR, NOT, and XOR instructions. These instructions enable you to perform bit-wise Boolean operations with binary values in registers and in memory. The TEST instructions provide a simple way to perform an AND instruction without modifying the destination value. This is ideal for testing binary values, such as the flag values within the EFLAGS register.

The next chapter dives into the world of the FPU. The FPU provides advanced mathematical functions for handling floating-point arithmetic and additional BCD arithmetic. These functions are crucial if you must program in an engineering or scientific environment.

Advanced Math Functions

In the old days, floating-point math required using either software emulation or a separate math co-processor. Since the 80486, Intel has incorporated the floating-point operations in an onboard FPU (see Chapter 2, "The IA-32 Platform"). This chapter describes the floating-point operations contained within the FPU and demonstrates how to perform floating-point math on the IA-32 platform.

The first part of this chapter describes the layout of the FPU, and recaps the instructions demonstrated in Chapter 7, "Using Numbers," for loading numbers into the FPU and retrieving results from the FPU. Next, the basic floating-point math functions are shown: addition, subtraction, multiplication, and division. Following that, you will learn how to work with the more advanced floating-point math functions, such as square roots and trigonometric functions. After that, the methods used for comparing floating-point numbers are described, followed by the methods used for storing the FPU environment in memory, and restoring the FPU environment from the backup.

The FPU Environment

Chapter 2 described the basics of the FPU environment on the IA-32 platform. Now that you are more familiar with the layout and operation of the IA-32 platform, it's time to dig a little deeper and examine both the FPU infrastructure and the instructions that are used to control it. This section describes the FPU register stack: the control word, which controls how the FPU operates; the status word, which indicates what is happening in the FPU; and the tag word, which defines the values contained in the FPU register stack.

The FPU register stack

As mentioned in Chapter 2, the FPU is a self-contained unit that handles floating-point operations using a set of registers that are set apart from the standard processor registers. The additional FPU registers include eight 80-bit data registers, and three 16-bit registers called the *control, status,* and *tag* registers.

The FPU data registers are called R0 through R7 (although as you will see, they are not accessed by these names). They operate somewhat differently than the standard registers in that they are linked together to form a stack. Unlike the stack in memory, the FPU register stack is circular — that is, the last register in the stack links back to the first register in the stack.

The register that is considered the top of the stack is defined in the FPU control word register. It is referenced by the name ST(0). Each of the other registers is referenced relative to the top register, by the name ST(x), where x can be 1 through 7. This is shown in Figure 9-1.

FPU Register Stack

Figure 9-1

As data is loaded into the FPU stack, the stack top moves downward in the registers. When eight values have been loaded into the stack, all eight FPU data registers have been utilized. If a ninth value is loaded into the stack, the stack pointer wraps around to the first register and replaces the value in that register with the new value, producing an FPU exception error.

Chapter 7 showed how floating-point values can be placed onto the FPU stack using the FLD instruction, integers using the FILD instruction, and BCD data using the FBLD instruction. Various floating-point constant values are also available to load constant values into the stack. There are also commands for storing the values in the FPU register into memory locations in each of the different data types.

The FPU status, control, and tag registers

Because the FPU is independent of the main processor, it does not normally use the EFLAGS register to indicate results and determine behavior. The FPU contains its own set of registers to perform these functions. The status, control, and tag registers are used to access features and determine the status of the FPU.

This section describes these three FPU registers and shows how to access them in your programs.

The status register

The status register indicates the operating condition of the FPU. It is contained in a 16-bit register, with different bits assigned as different flags. The following table describes the status register bits.

Status Bit	Description
0	Invalid operation exception flag
1	Denormalized operand exception flag
2	Zero divide exception flag
3	Overflow exception flag
4	Underflow exception flag
5	Precision exception flag
6	Stack fault
7	Error summary status
8	Condition code bit 0 (C0)
9	Condition code bit 1 (C1)
10	Condition code bit 2 (C2)
11-13	Top of stack pointer
14	Condition code bit 3 (C3)
15	FPU busy flag

The four condition code bits (8, 9, 10, and 14) are used together to indicate specific error codes from the result of floating-point operations. They are often used with the exception flags to indicate a specific exception condition. You will see more of these bits in action later in this chapter.

The first six bits are the FPU exception flags. They are set by the FPU when a floating-point exception has occurred during processing. The flags remain set until a program manually clears them. The stack fault flag is set when a stack overflow or underflow condition is detected (values too large or too small for the 80-bit stack registers).

The top of stack bits are used to indicate which FPU data register is set as the ST0 register. Any of the eight registers can be designated as the top of the stack. Each of the subsequent registers is assigned the ST(x) values accordingly.

*When values are loaded into the stack, the **TOP** value is decremented by one before the value is loaded. Thus, because the default **TOS** value is zero, the **R7** register is the default location of the top of stack value (**ST0**). This can be confusing, but don't worry — the FPU stack takes care of all this for you.*

The status register can be read into a doubleword memory location or the AX register, using the FSTSW instruction. This is demonstrated in the getstatus.s program.

```
# getstatus.s - Get the FPU Status register contents
.section .bss
    .lcomm status, 2
.section .text
.globl _start
_start:
    nop
    fstsw %ax
    fstsw status

    movl $1, %eax
    movl $0, %ebx
    int $0x80
```

After assembling and linking the program, you can run it in the debugger to see the value that is placed in the AX register and the status memory location:

```
(gdb) x/x &status
0x804908c <status>:      0x00000000
(gdb) print/x $eax
$1 = 0x0
(gdb)
```

Both produce the same value, showing that all of the bits in the FPU status register are set to zero by default. You can also view the status, control, and tag FPU registers from the debugger using the info all command:

```
(gdb) info all
.
.
.
fctrl           0x37f      895
fstat           0x0        0
ftag            0x55555    349525
(gdb)
```

This shows the current values of the three registers.

The control register

The control register controls the floating-point functions within the FPU. Defined here are settings such as the precision the FPU uses to calculate floating-point values, and the method used to round the floating-point results.

The control register uses a 16-bit register, with the bits shown in the following table.

Control Bits	Description
0	Invalid operation exception mask
1	Denormal operand exception mask
2	Zero divide exception mask
3	Overflow exception mask
4	Underflow exception mask
5	Precision exception mask
6–7	Reserved
8–9	Precision control
10–11	Rounding control
12	Infinity control
13–15	Reserved

The first six bits of the control register are used to control which exception flags in the status register are used. When one of these bits is set, the corresponding exception flag in the status register is prevented from being set. By default, the mask bits are all set, masking all exceptions.

The precision control bits enable you to set the floating-point precision used for mathematical calculations within the FPU. This is a great control feature, enabling you to change the time the FPU takes to calculate floating-point values. The possible settings of the precision control bits are as follows:

- ❑ 00 — single-precision (24-bit significand)
- ❑ 01 — not used
- ❑ 10 — double-precision (53-bit significand)
- ❑ 11 — double-extended-precision (64-bit significand)

By default, the FPU precision is set to double-extended-precision. This is the most accurate, but also most time-consuming, value. If you are not interested in such high precision, you can set this value to single-precision to speed up your floating-point calculations.

Similarly, the rounding control bits enable you to set how the FPU rounds the results of floating-point calculations. The possible settings of the rounding control bits are as follows:

❏   00 — round to nearest

❏   01 — round down (toward negative infinity)

❏   10 — round up (toward positive infinity)

❏   11 — round toward zero

By default, the rounding control bits are set to round to the nearest value.

The default values of the control register are set to 0x037F. You can use the FSTCW instruction to load the control register settings into a doubleword memory location to see what the settings are. You can also change the settings by using the FLDCW instruction. This instruction loads a doubleword memory value into the control register. The setprec.s program uses the FLDCW instruction to change the FPU precision setting from double-extended to single-precision:

```
# setprec.s - An example of setting the precision bits in the Control Register
.section .data
newvalue:
    .byte 0x7f, 0x00
.section .bss
    .lcomm control, 2
.section .text
.globl _start
_start:
    nop
    fstcw control
    fldcw newvalue
    fstcw control

    movl $1, %eax
    movl $0, %ebx
    int $0x80
```

The setprec.s program defines a doubleword value newvalue as 0x07f (remember to use little-endian format when storing the bytes in memory). This value sets the precision bits to 00, which sets the FPU precision to single-precision floating-point. It then uses the FSTCW instruction to retrieve the current control register settings into the control doubleword memory location, and uses the FLDCW instruction to load the newvalue value into the control register. To ensure that the value was stored properly, the FSTCW instruction is used again to check the current control register value.

After assembling and linking the program, you can step through the instructions and watch the value of the control register in the debugger:

```
(gdb) run
Starting program: /home/rich/palp/chap09/setprec

Breakpoint 1, _start () at setprec.s:11
11          fstcw control
(gdb) x/x &control
0x804909c <control>:    0x00000000
(gdb) s
12          fldcw newvalue
```

```
(gdb) x/x &control
0x804909c <control>:      0x0000037f
(gdb) s
13          fstcw control
(gdb) s
15          movl $1, %eax
(gdb) x/x &control
0x804909c <control>:      0x0000007f
(gdb) info all
  .

  .
fctrl           0x7f      127
(gdb)
```

The control register was successfully set to 0x07f, so the FPU is now using single-precision floating-point calculations.

This does not necessarily speed up all floating-point calculations. The most common functions that will show improvement are division and square root calculations.

The tag register

The tag register is used to identify the values within the eight 80-bit FPU data registers. The tag register uses 16 bits (2 bits per register) to identify the contents of each FPU data register. This is shown in Figure 9-2.

16-bit Tag Register

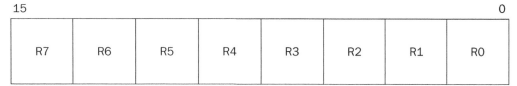

15							0
R7	R6	R5	R4	R3	R2	R1	R0

Figure 9-2

Each tag value corresponds to a physical FPU register. The 2-bit value for each register can contain one of four special codes indicating the content of the register. At any given time, an FPU data register can contain the following:

❑   A valid double-extended-precision value (code 00)

❑   A zero value (code 01)

❑   A special floating-point value (code 10)

❑   Nothing (empty) (code 11)

This enables programmers to perform a quick check of the tag register to determine whether valid data may be in an FPU register, instead of having to read and analyze the contents of the register, although in practice, because you are the one putting the values into the register stack, you should know what is there.

Using the FPU stack

Chapter 7 touched on loading floating-point values into the FPU register stack. In order to perform floating-point math, it is crucial that you understand how data is manipulated on the FPU stack. This is where all of the FPU mathematical operations are performed. You must know how to maneuver data onto and within the stack to process your calculations. The following stacktest.s program demonstrates how to load various data types onto the FPU stack, as well as some common stack functions used when working with the FPU stack:

```
# stacktest.s - An example of working with the FPU stack
.section .data
value1:
    .int 40
value2:
    .float 92.4405
value3:
    .double 221.440321
.section .bss
    .lcomm int1, 4
    .lcomm control, 2
    .lcomm status, 2
    .lcomm result, 4
.section .text
.globl _start
_start:
    nop
    finit
    fstcw control
    fstsw status
    filds value1
    fists int1
    flds value2
    fldl value3
    fst %st(4)
    fxch %st(1)
    fstps result
    movl $1, %eax
    movl $0, %ebx
    int $0x80
```

There's a lot going on in this simple program, so let's take this slowly. First, the FINIT instruction is used to initialize the FPU. It sets the control and status registers to their default values, but it does not alter the data contained in the FPU data registers. It is always a good idea to include this instruction in any program that utilizes the FPU.

Following that, the FPU control and status registers are copied to memory locations using the FSTCW and FSTSW instructions. You can view the default values of these resisters by observing these memory locations after the instructions execute:

```
(gdb) x/2b &control
0x80490cc <control>:      0x7f      0x03
(gdb) x/2b &status
0x80490ce <status>:       0x00      0x00
(gdb)
```

The output shows that the control register defaulted to the value 0x037f (remember that the value is placed in memory in little-endian format), and the status register defaulted to 0x0000.

The next instruction (FILDS) loads a doubleword integer value into the FPU register stack. The FISTS instruction retrieves the value at the top of the register stack (the value you just placed there) and places it into the destination (which was set to the int1 memory location):

```
(gdb) info all
.
.
.
st0             40        (raw 0x4004a000000000000000)
(gdb) x/d &int1
0x80490c8 <int1>:       40
(gdb)
```

The integer value of 40 was stored in the register tagged as the top of the stack (denoted as ST0). However, notice the hexadecimal value of the stored value. It is pretty easy to see that it is not stored as a normal signed integer value. Instead, the value was converted to the double-extended floating-point data type when it was stored in the FPU register. When the value was retrieved from the FPU register stack and placed in memory, it was automatically converted back to a doubleword integer (because the S character was specified on the FIST mnemonic). You can check that by looking at the hexadecimal value of the memory location:

```
(gdb) x/4b &int1
0x80490c8 <int1>:       0x28    0x00    0x00    0x00
(gdb)
```

As expected, the value was stored as a doubleword signed integer value in memory.

The next two instructions load floating-point values into the FPU register stack. The first one uses the FLDS instruction to load a single-precision floating-point value located in the value2 memory location. The second uses the FLDL instruction to load a double-precision floating-point value located in the value3 memory location. Now there are three values loaded into the FPU register stack. As each value is loaded, the preceding values shift down the stack, relative to the top of the stack.

After the FLD instructions, your FPU register stack should look like this:

```
(gdb) info all
.
.
.
st0    221.44032100000001150874595623463392   (raw 0x4006dd70b8e086bdf800)
st1    92.44049835205078125   (raw 0x4005b8e1890000000000)
st2    40     (raw 0x4004a000000000000000)
(gdb)
```

When you display the FPU registers using the info all command, you may notice that the other FPU data registers may or may not contain extraneous data. When the FINIT instruction is executed, it does not initialize the FPU data registers but changes the tag values to show that they are empty. It is possible that extraneous data remains from other operations. It is your job to keep track of what FPU data registers your program uses, and what registers have valid data in them.

Finally, the last three FPU instructions do some data-moving between registers. The FST instruction is used to move data from the ST0 register to another FPU register. Notice the format that is used to specify the fifth FPU register from the top of the stack. The GNU assembler uses the percent sign to indicate a register value, and the FPU register reference number must be enclosed in parentheses.

After the FST instruction, the FXCH instruction is used to exchange the value of the ST0 register with another FPU register — in this case, ST1. After these two instructions, the FPU registers should look like the following:

```
(gdb) info all
 .
 .
 .
st0     92.44049835205078125   (raw 0x4005b8e1890000000000)
st1     221.44032100000000115087459562346339  (raw 0x4006dd70b8e086bdf800)
st2     40     (raw 0x4004a000000000000000)
st3     0      (raw 0x00000000000000000000)
st4     221.44032100000000115087459562346339  (raw 0x4006dd70b8e086bdf800)
(gdb)
```

After you have maneuvered the data around the FPU register stack and performed your required mathematical operations, you will most likely need to retrieve the results from the FPU register stack. The FST and FSTP instructions can also be used to move data from an FPU register to a memory location. The FST instruction copies data from the ST0 FTP register to a memory location (or another FPU register) while keeping the original value in the ST0 register.

The FSTP instruction also copies the ST0 FPU register value, but then pops it from the FPU register stack. This shifts all of the FPU stack values up one place in the stack.

Don't forget to add the data size character to the end of the FST and FSTP mnemonics to specify the proper size of the resulting data value. In this example, the FSTPS instruction is used to create a single-precision floating-point value stored in 4 bytes (32 bits) of memory from the value in the ST0 FPU stack position:

```
(gdb) x/f &result
0x80490cc <result>:     92.4404984
(gdb) x/4b &result
0x80490cc <result>:     0x89    0xe1    0xb8    0x42
(gdb)
```

After the FSTPS instruction, you can see that the value was removed from the stack, and the other values were "shifted" up one position:

```
(gdb) info all
 .
 .
 .
st0     221.44032100000000115087459562346339       (raw 0x4006dd70b8e086800)
st1     40         (raw 0x4004a000000000000000)
st2     0          (raw 0x00000000000000000000)
st3     221.44032100000000115087459562346339       (raw 0x4006dd70b8e086800)
(gdb)
```

Now that you are comfortable with manipulating floating-point values within the FPU, it's time to start working on performing mathematical operations on the data.

Basic Floating-Point Math

As would be expected, the FPU provides instructions for performing the basic math functions on floating-point values. These basic functions are described in the following table.

Instruction	Description
FADD	Floating-point addition
FDIV	Floating-point division
FDIVR	Reverse floating-point division
FMUL	Floating-point multiplication
FSUB	Floating-point subtraction
FSUBR	Reverse floating-point subtraction

Actually, each of these functions has separate instructions and formats that can be used to produce six possible functions, depending on exactly what operation you want to perform. For example, the FADD instruction can be used as follows:

- ❑   FADD source: Add a 32- or 64-bit value from memory to the ST0 register

- ❑   FADD %st(x), %st(0): Add st(x) to st(0) and store the result in st(0)

- ❑   FADD %st(0), %st(x): Add st(0) to st(x) and store the result in st(x)

- ❑   FADDP %st(0), %st(x): Add st(0) to st(x), store the result in st(x), and pop st(0)

- ❑   FADDP: Add st(0) to st(1), store the result in st(1), and pop st(0)

- ❑   FIADD source: Add a 16- or 32-bit integer value to st(0) and store the result in st(0)

Each of the different formats specifies which FPU register is used in the operation, along with how the register is handled after the operation (whether it is kept or popped off of the stack). It is important that you keep track of the status of the FPU register values. Sometimes this can be difficult with complex mathematical operations that perform multiple operations, which store various values in different registers.

With the GNU assembler, things become even more complicated. The instructions that specify a value from memory must also include a one-character size indicator with the mnemonic (s for 32-bit single-precision floating-point values, and l for double-precision floating-point values). And, as usual, the source and destination operands are reversed from what is shown in the Intel literature.

Following are some examples of using the floating-point math instructions:

```
fadds data1          # add the 32-bit value at data1 to the ST0 register
fmull data1          # multiply the 64-bit value at data1 with the ST0 register
fidiv data1          # divide ST0 by the 32-bit integer value at data1
fsub %st, %st(1)     # subtract the value in ST0 from ST1, and store in ST1
fsub %st(0), %st(1)  # subtract the value in ST0 from ST1, and store in ST1
fsub %st(1), %st(0)  #subtract the value in ST1 from ST0, and store in ST0
```

The FSUBR and FDIVR instructions are used to perform reverse subtractions and divisions — that is, the result is the source value subtracted from (or divided by) the destination value, with the result placed in the destination operand location. This is opposite (reverse) of how the FSUB and FDIV instructions perform the calculations. These instructions are handy when you want to swap the order in the mathematical expression without having to use additional instructions to move data between FPU registers.

To demonstrate how these instructions work, let's work out a complex mathematical operation using the IA-32 FPU instructions. The mathematical operation to compute is the following:

```
((43.65 / 22) + (76.34 * 3.1)) / ((12.43 * 6) - (140.2 / 94.21))
```

To tackle such a problem, it is best to determine how the values will be stored and shifted within the FPU registers. It is always quickest to load as many of the values into the FPU as possible to perform the mathematical operations, without having to swap values back and forth between FPU registers and memory. As new values are loaded, the original values "move down" in the FPU register stack. It is important to keep track of how values are arranged within the stack.

First, you must think about how the values will be loaded into the FPU stack, and how the operations will affect how (and where) the answers are located. Here's a step-by-step analysis of what should happen to perform the calculation:

1. Load 43.65 into ST0.
2. Divide ST0 by 22, saving the results in ST0 .
3. Load 76.34 in ST0 (the answer from step 2 moves to ST1).
4. Load 3.1 in ST0 (the value in step 3 moves to ST1, and the answer from Step 2 moves to ST2).
5. Multiply ST0 and ST1, leaving the answer in ST0.
6. Add ST0 and ST2, leaving the answer in ST0 (this is the left side of the equation).
7. Load 12.43 into ST0 (the answer from Step 6 moves to ST1).
8. Multiply ST0 by 6, leaving the answer in ST0.
9. Load 140.2 into ST0 (the answer from Step 8 moves to ST1, and from Step 6 to ST2).
10. Load 94.21 into ST0 (the answer from Step 8 moves to ST2, and from Step 6 to ST3).
11. Divide ST1 by ST0, popping the stack and saving the results in ST0 (the answer from Step 8 moves to ST1, and from Step 6 to ST2).
12. Subtract ST0 from ST1, storing the result in ST0 (this is the right side of the equation).
13. Divide ST2 by ST0, storing the result in ST0 (this is the final answer).

Often, it is easy to get sidetracked trying to figure out where the individual values are located within the FPU register stack. Sometimes it helps to visualize what is happening. The preceding calculation sequence is illustrated in Figure 9-3.

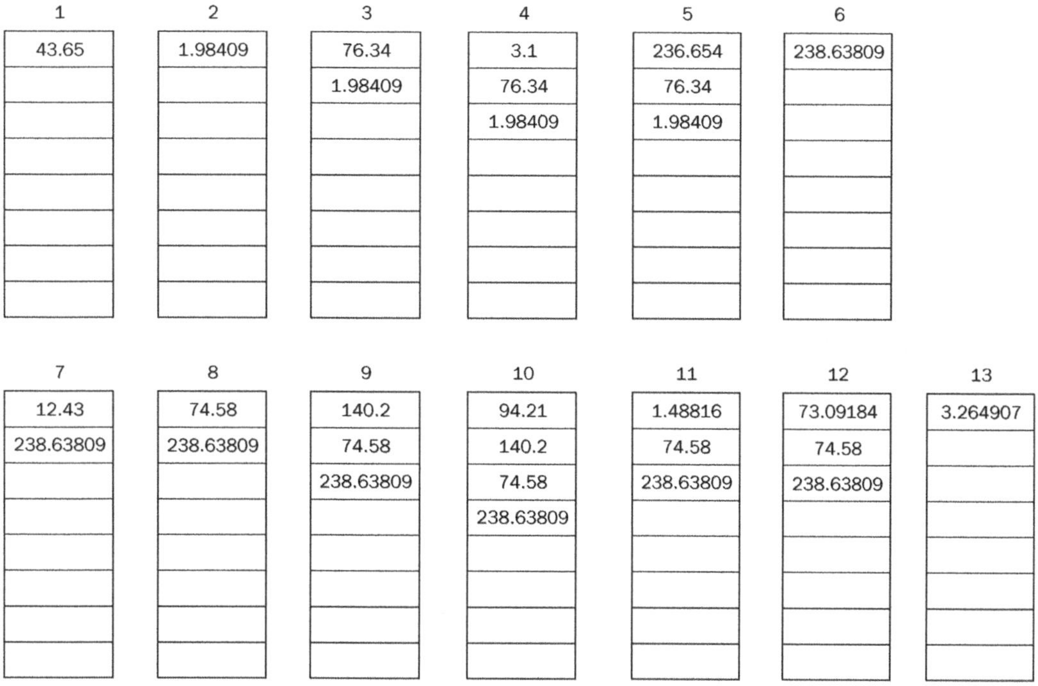

1	2	3	4	5	6
43.65	1.98409	76.34	3.1	236.654	238.63809
		1.98409	76.34	76.34	
			1.98409	1.98409	

7	8	9	10	11	12	13
12.43	74.58	140.2	94.21	1.48816	73.09184	3.264907
238.63809	238.63809	74.58	140.2	74.58	74.58	
		238.63809	74.58	238.63809	238.63809	
			238.63809			

Figure 9-3

With the individual steps mapped out on the stack chart, it's pretty easy to see where the values are stored. Now that you have a plan of attack, you can start writing the code to implement it. The fpmath1.s program uses the FPU instructions to carry out this plan:

```
# fpmath1.s - An example of basic FPU math
.section .data
value1:
    .float 43.65
value2:
    .int 22
value3:
    .float 76.34
value4:
    .float 3.1
value5:
    .float 12.43
value6:
    .int 6
value7:
    .float 140.2
```

```
value8:
   .float 94.21
output:
   .asciz "The result is %f\n"
.section .text
.globl _start
_start:
nop
   finit
   flds value1
   fidiv value2
   flds value3
   flds value4
   fmul %st(1), %st(0)
   fadd %st(2), %st(0)
   flds value5
   fimul value6
   flds value7
   flds value8
   fdivrp
   fsubr %st(1), %st(0)
   fdivr %st(2), %st(0)
   subl  $8, %esp
   fstpl (%esp)
   pushl $output
   call printf
   add   $12, %esp
   pushl $0
   call exit
```

The fpmath1.s program defines all of the variables that will be used in the calculation in the data section. It then proceeds through the calculations, loading some values into the FPU registers, and using some values as instruction operands when possible. One specific thing to notice is that the FDIVR and FSUBR instructions came in handy when the destination address (ST0) was the value that was the divisor (or the number to subtract).

After the calculations are complete, the answer is in the ST0 FPU register. The FSTPL instruction is used to pop the value off of the FPU register stack, and in this case it is placed on the top of the program stack using the ESP register value (after reserving 8 bytes on the stack by subtracting eight from ESP). This ensures that the value is available for the printf C function. The printf function requires the floating-point value to be in double-precision format, so the FSTPL instruction must be used.

After assembling the program and linking it with the C libraries, you can run it from the command line to see if you get the correct answer:

```
$ ./fpmath1
The result is 3.264907
$
```

The answer produced matches the answer I arrived at (using a calculator, of course). If you are curious to see what is happening under the hood, run the program in the debugger and watch as the FPU registers are manipulated by the instructions.

Advanced Floating-Point Math

There is a lot more to floating-point math than simple addition, subtraction, multiplication, and division. Many advanced functions can be performed with floating-point numbers that are provided by the FPU. If you are writing assembly language programs for scientific or engineering applications, you most likely will have to incorporate advanced math functions in your programs.

The following table describes the advanced functions available.

Instruction	Description
F2XM1	Computes 2 to the power of the value in ST0, minus 1
FABS	Computes the absolute value of the value in ST0
FCHS	Changes the sign of the value in ST0
FCOS	Computes the cosine of the value in ST0
FPATAN	Computes the partial arctangent of the value in ST0
FPREM	Computes the partial remainders from dividing the value in ST0 by the value in ST1
FPREM1	Computes the IEEE partial remainders from dividing the value in ST0 by the value in ST1
FPTAN	Computes the partial tangent of the value in ST0
FRNDINT	Rounds the value in ST0 to the nearest integer
FSCALE	Computes ST0 to the ST1st power
FSIN	Computes the sine of the value in ST0
FSINCOS	Computes both the sine and cosine of the value in ST0
FSQRT	Computes the square root of the value in ST0
FYL2X	Computes the value ST1 * log ST0 (base 2 log)
FYL2XP1	Computes the value ST1 * log (ST0 + 1) (base 2 log)

Most of the preceding functions are self-explanatory. The following sections describe some of these functions in more detail.

Floating-point functions

The FABS, FCHS, FRNDINT, and FSQRT instructions perform simple mathematical functions on the floating-point values. The FABS instruction computes the absolute value of ST(0). The FCHS instruction changes the sign bit of the value. The FSQRT computes the square root of ST(0).

The fpmath2.s demonstrates using these functions:

```
# fpmath2.s - An example of the FABS, FCHS, and FSQRT instructions
.section .data
value1:
    .float 395.21
value2:
    .float -9145.290
value3:
    .float 64.0
.section .text
.globl _start
_start:
    nop
    finit
    flds value1
    fchs
    flds value2
    fabs
    flds value3
    fsqrt

    movl $1, %eax
    movl $0, %ebx
    int $0x80
```

After assembling and linking the program, you can watch the FPU registers in the debugger. At the end of the instructions, the FPU registers should look like this:

```
(gdb) info all
.
.
.
st0      8            (raw 0x40028000000000000000)
st1      9145.2900390625   (raw 0x400c8ee5290000000000)
st2      -395.209991455078125     (raw 0xc007c59ae10000000000)
(gdb)
```

Remember that the values are in reverse order as they are pushed onto the FPU stack. The ST0 register holds the result from the FSQRT instruction, and the ST2 register holds the result from the FCHS instruction.

The FRNDINT instruction is different in that its behavior is dependent on the value of the rounding bits in the FPU control register. The FRNDINT instruction rounds the floating-point value in ST0 to the nearest integer value, according to one of the four rounding methods described earlier in the "The control register" section. This is demonstrated in the roundtest.s program:

```
# roundtest.s - An example of the FRNDINT instruction
.section .data
value1:
    .float 3.65
rdown:
    .byte 0x7f, 0x07
```

```
rup:
    .byte 0x7f, 0x0b
.section .bss
    .lcomm result1, 4
    .lcomm result2, 4
    .lcomm result3, 4
.section .text
.globl _start
_start:
    nop
    finit
    flds value1
    frndint
    fists result1

    fldcw rdown
    flds value1
    frndint
    fists result2

    fldcw rup
    flds value1
    frndint
    fists result3

    movl $1, %eax
    movl $0, %ebx
    int $0x80
```

The roundtest.s program defines two doubleword values (rdown and rup) that are used to change the rounding bits in the FPU control register. Because no other values need to be changed, we can do this with a static value. To set rounding to round down, the rounding bits are set to the binary value 01, which makes the control register have the value 0x77F. To set the rounding to round up, the rounding bits are set to the binary value 10, which makes the control register have the value 0xB7F.

The first group of instructions initializes the FPU, loads the test value into ST0, performs the FRNDINT instruction (using the default rounding setting), and moves the result to the result1 memory location (as an integer value):

```
finit
flds value1
frndint
fists result1
```

The next group of instructions loads the control register with the value to set rounding to round down, load the ST0 register with the test value, perform the rounding, and then store the result in the result2 memory location:

```
fldcw rdown
flds value1
frndint
fists result2
```

The last group of instructions loads the control register with the value to set rounding to round up, load the ST0 register with the test value, perform the rounding, and then store the result in the result3 memory location.

After assembling and linking the program, you can watch how it works by running it in the debugger. After the first group of instructions, the rounded value should be in the result1 memory location:

```
(gdb) x/d &result1
0x80490c4 <result1>:     4
(gdb)
```

By default, the floating-point value was rounded up to the integer value 4. After the next group of instructions, the rounded value should be in the result2 memory location:

```
(gdb) x/d &result2
0x80490c8 <result2>:     3
(gdb)
```

As expected, by setting the rounding bits to round down, the new rounded value was set to the integer value 3. Finally, after the last group of instructions, the rounded value should be in the result3 memory location:

```
(gdb) x/d &result3
0x80490cc <result3>:     4
(gdb)
```

The result shows that the rounding bits are now rounding the values up to the nearest integer.

Partial remainders

Partial remainders are a tricky part of floating-point division. The concept of a partial remainder relates to how floating-point division is performed. The remainder of the division operation is determined through a series of subtractions of the divisor from the dividend. Through each subtraction iteration, the intermediate remainder is called the *partial remainder*. The iterations stop when the partial remainder is less than the divisor (no more subtractions can be performed without creating a negative number). At the end of the division, the final answer is an integer value representing the number of subtraction iterations (called the *quotient*), and a floating-point value representing the final partial remainder (now called the *remainder*).

Depending on how many iterations are required to perform the division, there can be many partial remainders. The number of iterations required depends on the difference between the exponent values of the dividend and the divisor. Each subtraction cannot reduce the exponent value of the dividend by more than 63.

The FPREM and FPREM1 instructions both compute the remainder value of a floating-point division, but do it using slightly different methods.

The basic method for determining a division remainder is to determine the floating-point quotient of the division of the dividend and divisor, and then round that value to the nearest integer. The remainder is then the difference of the quotient multiplied by the divisor, and the dividend. For example, to find the remainder for 20.65 divided by 3.97, you would perform the following steps:

1. 20.65 / 3.97 = 5.201511335, rounded = 5 (this is the quotient)

2. 5 * 3.97 = 19.85

3. 20.65 – 19.85 = 0.8 (this is the remainder)

The tricky part is the rounding procedure. Intel developed the FPREM instruction before any standards in partial remainders were created. The Intel developers chose to use the default FPU round toward zero method to find the integer quotient value, and then determine the remainder.

Unfortunately, when the IEEE produced a standard, it chose to round the quotient value up to the nearest integer value before finding the remainder. While this seems to be a subtle difference, it has huge implications when calculating partial remainders along the process. Because of this, Intel chose to keep the original FPREM instruction in its original form, and create the FPREM1 instruction, which uses the IEEE method of calculating the partial remainders.

The problem with calculating partial remainders is that you must know when the iteration process is complete. Both the FPREM and FPREM1 instructions use the FPU status register condition code bit 2 (bit 10 of the status register) to indicate when the iterations are complete. When more iterations are required, the C2 bit is set. When the iterations are complete, the C2 bit is cleared.

To check the C2 bit, you must first use the FSTSW instruction to copy the contents of the status register into either a memory location or the AX register, and then use the TEST instruction to determine whether the bit has been set.

The premtest.s program performs a simple floating-point division using the FPREM1 instruction:

```
# premtest.s - An example of using the FPREM1 instruction
.section .data
value1:
    .float 20.65
value2:
    .float 3.97
.section .bss
    .lcomm result, 4
.section .text
.globl _start
_start:
    nop
    finit
    flds value2
    flds value1
loop:
    fprem1
    fstsw %ax
    testb $4, %ah
    jnz loop

    fsts result
```

```
movl $1, %eax
movl $0, %ebx
int $0x80
```

Because the FPREM1 instruction is an iterative process, there is no guarantee that it will have the final answer on the first pass. The TEST instruction is used to check the value of the C2 condition bit (moved to the AX register with the FSTSW instruction). If the bit is set, the TEST instruction will produce a nonzero value, and the JNZ instruction will jump back to the loop point. When the bit is clear, the TEST instruction produces a zero value, and the JNZ instruction falls through. The remainder value is stored in the ST0 register, which is copied using the FSTS instruction to the result memory location.

After assembling and linking the program, you can run it in the debugger and watch how the FPREM1 instruction determines the remainder value. For the example values shown, the remainder value should look like this:

```
(gdb) x/f &result
0x80490a8 <result>: 0.799999475
(gdb)
```

While the remainder value is stored in the ST0 register, the actual quotient value is not stored in a register. The three least significant bits of the quotient value are stored in the control register using the left-over condition code bits as follows:

❑   Quotient bit 0 in condition bit 1

❑   Quotient bit 1 in condition bit 3

❑   Quotient bit 2 in condition bit 0

You must manually extract these bits to form the lower three bits of the quotient value.

> *While the **FPREM** instruction output may seem odd, there was a reason for it. In the old 80287 FPU co-processor days, the **FPTAN** instruction could not handle angle radians larger than pi/4. The **FPREM** instruction was crucial in determining the quadrant in which a source angle value was located. Because this involved quadrants, only the lower three bits of the quotient were required. Since the 80387 FPU co-processor, the **FPTAN** instruction does not have this limitation, and the quotient value from the **FPREM** instruction is hardly ever used.*

Trigonometric functions

Another huge advantage to the FPU is its ability to calculate trigonometric functions. Normal trig functions such as sine, cosine, and tangent are simple to obtain from the FPU. The following sections demonstrate using the FPU trig functions in assembly language programs.

The FSIN and FCOS instructions

The basic trig functions are all implemented the same way in the FPU. The instructions use an implied source operand, which is located in the ST0 register. When the function completes, the result is placed in the ST0 register.

The only trick to these functions is that they all use radians for the source operand units. If you are working with an application that uses degrees, the values must be converted to radians before you can use the FPU trig functions. The formula for doing this is as follows:

```
radians = (degrees * pi) / 180
```

This calculation can easily be done in the FPU using the following code snippet:

```
fsts degree1           # load the degrees value stored in memory into ST0
fidivs val180          # divide by the 180 value stored in memory
fldpi                  # load pi into ST0, degree/180 now in ST1
fmul %st(1), %st(0)    # multiply degree/180 and pi, saving in ST0
fsin                   # perform trig function on value in ST0
```

The trigtest1.s program demonstrates these functions:

```
# trigtest1.s - An example of using the FSIN and FCOS instructions
.section .data
degree1:
    .float 90.0
val180:
    .int 180
.section .bss
    .lcomm radian1, 4
    .lcomm result1, 4
    .lcomm result2, 4
.section .text
.globl _start
_start:
    nop
    finit
    flds degree1
    fidivs val180
    fldpi
    fmul %st(1), %st(0)
    fsts radian1
    fsin
    fsts result1
    flds radian1
    flds radian1
    fcos
    fsts result2

    movl $1, %eax
    movl $0, %ebx
    int $0x80
```

After the angle is converted from degrees to radians, it is stored in the radian1 memory location. The FSIN instruction is then used to calculate the sine value of the angle, and the FCOS instruction is used to calculate the cosine value. After the program runs, you can view the results in the result1 and result2 memory locations:

```
(gdb) x/f &result1
0x80490bc <result1>:    1
(gdb) x/f &result2
0x80490c0 <result2>:    -4.37113883e-08
(gdb)
```

Of course, the sine for a 90-degree angle is one, and the cosine is zero. You can test this with other degree values as well.

In a production program, it would obviously be much faster to precompute the value of pi/180, and store that value in the FPU, rather than have the processor do that all the time.

The FSINCOS instruction

If you need to obtain both the sine and cosine values of an angle, the FSINCOS instruction enables you to do that in one easy step. The instruction places the sine result in the ST0 register, and then pushes the cosine result onto the FPU register. This normally results in the cosine value being in ST0, and the sine value being in ST1. The trigtest2.s program demonstrates using this instruction:

```
# trigtest2.s - An example of using the FSINCOS instruction
.section .data
degree1:
    .float 90.0
val180:
    .int 180
.section .bss
    .lcomm sinresult, 4
    .lcomm cosresult, 4
.section .text
.globl _start
_start:
    nop
    finit
    flds degree1
    fidivs val180
    fldpi
    fmul %st(1), %st(0)
    fsincos
    fstps cosresult
    fsts sinresult

    movl $1, %eax
    movl $0, %ebx
    int $0x80
```

The results of the trigtest2.s program can be seen in the cosresult and sinresult memory locations:

```
(gdb) x/f &cosresult
0x80490b0 <cosresult>:  -2.71050543e-20
(gdb) x/f &sinresult
0x80490ac <sinresult>:  1
(gdb)
```

The value of cosresult is not exactly 0 as it should be, but pretty close. The value of sinresult is the correct value of 1.

The FPTAN and FPATAN instructions

The FPTAN and FPATAN instructions are somewhat different from their sine and cosine counterparts. While they compute the tangent and arctangent trig functions, the input and output requirements are slightly different.

The FPTAN instruction uses the standard implied operand located in the ST0 register (again, the angle must be in radians, not degrees). The tangent value is calculated and placed in the ST0 register as expected. After that, a value of 1.0 is pushed onto the FPU stack, shifting the tangent result value down to the ST1 register.

The reason for this is to achieve backward compatibility with applications written for the 80287 FPU co-processor. The FSIN and FCOS instructions were not available then, and calculating these required using the reciprocal of the tangent value. By issuing a simple FDIVR instruction after the FPTAN instruction, the cotangent value can be calculated.

The FPATAN instruction uses two implied source operands. It calculates the arctangent of the angle value ST1/ST0 and places the result in ST1, and then pops the FPU stack, moving the value to ST0. This form is available to support finding the arctangent of an infinite ratio — that is, when ST0 is zero. The standard ANSI C function atan2(double x, double y) uses the same idea.

Logarithmic functions

The FPU logarithmic functions provide instructions for performing log base 2 calculations. The FYL2X instruction performs the following calculation:

```
ST(1) * log2 (ST(0))
```

The FYL2X1 instruction performs this calculation:

```
ST(1) * log2 (ST(0) + 1.0)
```

The FSCALE instruction scales a value in ST(0) by 2 to the power of the value in ST(1). This can be used for both scaling up (by using a positive value in ST(1)) and for scaling down (by using a negative value in ST(1)). The fscaletest.s program demonstrates this principle:

```
# fscaletest.s - An example of the FSCALE instruction
.section .data
value:
    .float 10.0
scale1:
    .float 2.0
scale2:
    .float -2.0
.section .bss
    .lcomm result1, 4
    .lcomm result2, 4
.section .text
```

```
.globl _start
_start:
    nop
    finit
    flds scale1
    flds value
    fscale
    fsts result1

    flds scale2
    flds value
    fscale
    fsts result2

    movl $1, %eax
    movl $0, %ebx
    int $0x80
```

The first scale value (set to 2.0) is loaded into the ST(0) register, and then the test value (10.0) is loaded (moving the scale value to ST(1) where it belongs). After the FSCALE instruction, the test value is multiplied by 2 to the power of the scale value, which results in multiplying the test value by 4.

Next, the second scale value (set to –2.0) is loaded, along with the test value, and the FSCALE instruction is executed again. This time the negative scale factor divides the test value by 4.

After assembling and linking the program, you can step through the instructions and display the results in the result1 and result2 memory locations:

```
(gdb) x/f &result1
0x80490b8 <result1>:    40
(gdb) x/f &result2
0x80490bc <result2>:    2.5
(gdb)
```

The values produced were as expected.

> *Note that the **FSCALE** instruction provided a handy way to multiply and divide the floating-point values by powers of 2, similar to the effect of the shift instructions used for integers in Chapter 8, "Basic Math Functions."*

Although the FPU log functions only provide base 2 logarithms, it is possible to perform calculations using other logarithmic bases. To find a logarithm of another base using base 2 logarithms, you can use the following equation:

```
log (base b) X = (1/log(base 2) b) * log(base 2) X
```

This can be easily implemented using the FYL2X instruction. The logtest.s program calculates the base 10 log of a value in memory:

```
# logtest.s - An example of using the FYL2X instruction
.section .data
```

```
value:
    .float 12.0
base:
    .float 10.0
.section .bss
    .lcomm result, 4
.section .text
.globl _start
_start:
    nop
    finit
    fld1
    flds base
    fyl2x
    fld1
    fdivp
    flds value
    fyl2x
    fsts result

    movl $1, %eax
    movl $0, %ebx
    int $0x80
```

The logtest.s program implements the equation to perform a log base 10 calculation of the value 12.0. It starts off by loading the value 1.0 in the FPU register (the Y value for the first log function), then the value of the base (10.0), performing the base 2 log of the value. This produces the value for the first half of the equation (note that in this example, because the base was chosen as 10, the FLDL2T instruction could be used to load the value into ST(0) with one instruction). This value becomes the new Y value for the next FYL2X instruction, with the X value being the original value (12.0). The final result should be equal to the base 10 log of 12, or 1.07918119.

After assembling and linking the program, the result can be seen by running the program in the debugger and looking at the result memory location:

```
(gdb) x/f &result
0x80490a8 <result>: 1.07918119
(gdb)
```

Yes, the logtest.s program produced the correct result for the base 10 log of 12.

Floating-Point Conditional Branches

Unfortunately, comparing floating-point numbers is not as easy as with integers. When working with integers, it's easy to use the CMP instruction and evaluate the values in the EFLAGS register to determine whether the values were less than, equal to, or greater than.

With floating-point numbers, you do not have the luxury of using the CMP instruction. Instead, the FPU provides some instructions of its own to use when comparing floating-point values

The FCOM instruction family

The FCOM family of instructions is used to compare two floating-point values in the FPU. The instructions compare the value loaded in the ST0 FPU register with either another FPU register or a floating-point value in memory. There are also options for popping one or both values off of the FPU stack after the compare. The following table describes the different versions that can be used.

Instruction	Description
FCOM	Compare the ST0 register with the ST1 register.
FCOM ST(x)	Compare the ST0 register with another FPU register.
FCOM source	Compare the ST0 register with a 32- or 64-bit memory value.
FCOMP	Compare the ST0 register with the ST1 register value and pop the stack.
FCOMP ST(x)	Compare the ST0 register with another FPU register value and pop the stack.
FCOMP source	Compare the ST0 register with a 32 or 64-bit memory value and pop the stack.
FCOMPP	Compare the ST0 register with the ST1 register and pop the stack twice.
FTST	Compare the ST0 register with the value 0.0.

The result of the comparison is set in the C0, C2, and C3 condition code bits of the status register. The possible results from the comparison are shown in the following table.

Condition	C3	C2	C0
ST0 > source	0	0	0
ST0 < source	0	0	1
ST0 = source	1	0	0

You must use the FSTSW instruction to copy the status register value to the AX register or a memory location, and then use the TEST instruction to determine the result of the comparison.

The fcomtest.s program demonstrates this principle:

```
# fcomtest.s - An example of the FCOM instruction
.section .data
value1:
    .float 10.923
value2:
    .float 4.5532
.section .text
```

```
        .globl _start
_start:
        nop
        flds value1
        fcoms value2
        fstsw
        sahf
        ja greater
        jb lessthan
        movl $1, %eax
        movl $0, %ebx
        int $0x80
greater:
        movl $1, %eax
        movl $2, %ebx
        int $0x80
lessthan:
        movl $1, %eax
        movl $1, %ebx
        int $0x80
```

The fcomtest.s program uses some trickery to determine the result of the FCOM instruction After retrieving the status register from the FPU and saving it in the AX register using the FSTSW instruction, the SAHF instruction is used to load the EFLAGS register from the AH register values.

The SAHF instruction moves bits 0, 2, 4, 6, and 7 of the AH register to the carry, parity, aligned, zero, and sign flags, respectively. The other bits in the EFLAGS register are unaffected. It just so happens (thanks to the Intel software engineers) that these bits in the AH register contain the FPU status register condition code values. Combining the FSTSW and SAHF instructions moves the following:

❏   The C0 bit to the EFLAGS carry flag

❏   The C2 bit to the EFLAGS parity flag

❏   The C3 bit to the EFLAGS zero flag

Once this is done, the EFLAGS carry, parity, and zero flags line up with the C0, C2, and C3 condition code bits, which produces a nice translation for using the JA, JB, and JZ instructions to determine the comparison of the two floating-point values.

The fcomtest.s program produces different result code depending on the values set in memory. The result code can be seen using the echo command:

```
$ ./fcomtest
$ echo $?
2
$
```

The result code of 2 indicates that the first value (stored in the value1 memory location) was greater than the second value (stored in the value2 memory location). You can change the values within the program to ensure that the comparisons work properly.

One word about the equal comparison: Remember that when a floating-point value is loaded into a FPU register, it is converted to a double-extended-precision floating-point value. This process may lead to some rounding errors. It is possible that a single- or double-precision value, after being loaded into the FPU register, will not be equal to the original value. It is not a good idea to test floating-point values for equality, but rather to test them to within a small tolerance of the expected value.

The FCOMI instruction family

You may be wondering why, if using the FSTSW and SAHF instruction combination after the comparison instruction works so well, it is not incorporated into a single instruction. The answer is that it was. Starting in the Pentium Pro processor line, the FCOMI instruction is available to do just that. The FCOMI family of instructions performs the floating-point comparisons and places the results in the EFLAGS registers using the carry, parity, and zero flags.

The following table describes the instructions in the FCOMI family.

Instruction	Description
FCOMI	Compare the ST0 register with the ST(x) register.
FCOMIP	Compare the ST0 register with the ST(x) register and pop the stack.
FUCOMI	Check for unordered values before the comparison.
FUCOMIP	Check for unordered values before the comparison and pop the stack afterward.

As you can tell from the table descriptions, one limitation to the FCOMI instruction family is that they can only compare two values in the FPU registers, not a FPU register with a value in memory.

The last two instructions in the table perform a service that is not available with the FCOM instruction family. The FUCOMI and FUCOMIP instructions ensure that the values being compared are valid floating-point numbers (using the FPU tag register). If an unordered value is present, an exception is thrown.

The output of the FCOMI instructions uses the EFLAGS registers, as shown in the following table.

Condition	ZF	PF	CF
ST0 > ST(x)	0	0	0
ST0 < ST(x)	0	0	1
ST0 = ST(x)	1	0	0

To prove that the FCOMI instruction works as advertised, the following fcomitest.s program duplicates the scenario of the fcomtest.s program, but using the FCOMI instruction:

```
# fcomitest.s - An example of the FCOMI instruction
.section .data
value1:
    .float 10.923
value2:
    .float 4.5532
.section .text
.globl _start
_start:
    nop
    flds value2
    flds value1
    fcomi %st(1), %st(0)
    ja greater
    jb lessthan
    movl $1, %eax
    movl $0, %ebx
    int $0x80
greater:
    movl $1, %eax
    movl $2, %ebx
    int $0x80
lessthan:
    movl $1, %eax
    movl $1, %ebx
    int $0x80
```

Because the FCOMI instruction requires both values to be in the FPU register, they are loaded in opposite order so the value1 value will be in the ST0 register when the comparison is made. After assembling and linking the program, you can run it and view the result code:

```
$ ./fcomitest
$ echo $?
2
$
```

The FCOMI instruction produced the same result as the FCOM instruction test program. Again, you can play around with the values to make sure the code does indeed produce the proper result code for different comparisons.

The FCMOV instruction family

Similar to the CMOV instructions for integers, the FCMOV instructions enable you to program conditional moves of floating-point values. Each of the instructions in the FCMOV family moves the source operand in the ST(x) FPU register with the destination operand in the ST(0) FPU register based on the value of the EFLAGS register. If the condition is true, the value in the ST(x) register is moved to the ST(0) register.

Because the move is based on the EFLAGS register, it is more common for the FCMOV instruction to be preceded by an FCOMI instruction.

The following table outlines the available instructions in the FCMOV family.

Instruction	Description
FCMOVB	Move if ST(0) is below ST(x).
FCMOVE	Move if ST(0) is equal to ST(x).
FCMOVBE	Move if ST(0) is below or equal to ST(x).
FCMOVU	Move if ST(0) is unordered.
FCMOVNB	Move if ST(0) is not below ST(x).
FCMOVNE	Move it ST(0) is not equal to ST(x).
FCMOVNBE	Move if ST(0) is not below or equal to ST(x).
FCMOVNU	Move if ST(0) is not unordered.

The GNU format of the instructions is

```
fcmovxx source, destination
```

where source is the ST(x) register, and destination is the ST(0) register.

The fcmovtest.s program demonstrates some simple moves:

```
# fcmovtest.s - An example of the FCMOVxx instructions
.section .data
value1:
    .float 20.5
value2:
    .float 10.90
.section .text
.globl _start
_start:
    nop
    finit
    flds value1
    flds value2
    fcomi %st(1), %st(0)
    fcmovb %st(1), %st(0)

    movl $1, %eax
    movl $0, %ebx
    int $0x80
```

The values are loaded into the FPU registers (ST0 = 10.90, and ST1 = 20.5). The FCOMI instruction sets the EFLAGS registers depending on the values in ST0 and ST1. The FCMOVB instruction moves the value in ST1 to ST0 if the value of ST0 is below that of ST1 (which in this case it is).

When the program is assembled and linked, you can check the FPU registers while the program is running to see what happens. After the FCMOVB instruction, both the ST0 and ST1 registers should contain the 20.5 value.

*The **FCMOV** instructions are available in the Pentium Pro and later processors. These instructions will not work on earlier IA-32 processors.*

Saving and Restoring the FPU State

Unfortunately, with modern IA-32 processors, the FPU data registers must do double duty. The MMX technology utilizes the FPU data registers as MMX data registers, storing 80-bit packed integer values for calculations. If you use both FPU and MMX functions in the same program, it is possible that you will "step on" your data registers.

To help prevent this, the IA-32 platform has included several instructions that enable you to save the FPU processor state and return to that state after other processing has completed. This section describes the different instructions that can be used to store and retrieve the FPU processor state.

Saving and restoring the FPU environment

The FSTENV instruction is used for storing the FPU environment in a block of memory. The following FPU registers are stored:

- ❏ Control register
- ❏ Status register
- ❏ Tag register
- ❏ FPU instruction pointer offset
- ❏ FPU data pointer
- ❏ FPU last opcode executed

The values are stored in a 28-byte block of memory. The FLDENV instruction is used to load the memory block values back into the FPU environment. The fpuenv.s program demonstrates these instructions:

```
# fpuenv.s - An example of the FSTENV and FLDENV instructions
.section .data
value1:
    .float 12.34
value2:
    .float 56.789
rup:
    .byte 0x7f, 0x0b
.section .bss
    .lcomm buffer, 28
```

```
.section .text
.globl _start
_start:
    nop
    finit
    flds value1
    flds value2
    fldcw rup
    fstenv buffer

    finit
    flds value2
    flds value1

    fldenv buffer

    movl $1, %eax
    movl $0, %ebx
    int $0x80
```

The fpuenv.s program initializes the FPU, loads a couple of values into the FPU data registers, modifies the control register to alter the rounding bits, and then stores the result in the buffer memory location. If you look at the buffer location after the FSTENV instruction, it should look like this:

```
(gdb) x/28b &buffer
0x80490c0 <buffer>:      0x7f    0x0b    0xff    0xff    0x00    0x30    0xff    0xff
0x80490c8 <buffer+8>:    0xff    0x0f    0xff    0xff    0x7e    0x80    0x04    0x08
0x80490d0 <buffer+16>:   0x23    0x00    0x00    0x00    0xb8    0x90    0x04    0x08
0x80490d8 <buffer+24>:   0x2b    0x00    0xff    0xff
(gdb)
```

You may notice the control register (0x7f 0x0b) and the status register (0x00 0x30) in the memory locations. After the FPU environment is stored, the FPU is initialized, and a few more data values are placed in the FPU data registers. Look at the FPU registers using the info all command.

The FPU environment is then restored from the buffer using the FLDENV instruction. After the restore, look at the registers within the FPU. Notice that the FPU data registers were not restored to their previous values, but the control register is again set to round up the rounding bits.

Saving and restoring the FPU state

The FSTENV instruction stored the FPU environment, but as you saw in the programming example, the data within the FPU was not saved. To save the complete FPU environment plus data, you must use the FSAVE instruction.

The FSAVE instruction copies all of the FPU registers to a 108-byte memory location, and then initializes the FPU state. When the FPU is restored using the FRSTOR instruction, all of the FPU registers (including the data registers) are restored to how they were when the FSAVE instruction was executed:

```
# fpusave.s - An example of the FSAVE and FRSTOR instructions
.section .data
value1:
    .float 12.34
value2:
    .float 56.789
rup:
    .byte 0x7f, 0x0b
.section .bss
    .lcomm buffer, 108
.section .text
.globl _start
_start:
    nop
    finit
    flds value1
    flds value2
    fldcw rup
    fsave buffer

    flds value2
    flds value1

    frstor buffer

    movl $1, %eax
    movl $0, %ebx
    int $0x80
```

After loading a couple of values in the FPU data registers and setting the rounding bits, the FPU state is stored in the buffer location using the FSAVE instruction. Before the FSAVE, you can look at the FPU state using the debugger info all command:

```
(gdb) info all
.
.
.
st0            56.78900146484375      (raw 0x4004e327f00000000000)
st1            12.340000152587890625  (raw 0x4002c570a40000000000)
st2            0           (raw 0x00000000000000000000)
st3            0           (raw 0x00000000000000000000)
st4            0           (raw 0x00000000000000000000)
st5            0           (raw 0x00000000000000000000)
st6            0           (raw 0x00000000000000000000)
st7            0           (raw 0x00000000000000000000)
fctrl          0xb7f       2943
fstat          0x3000      12288
ftag           0xfff       4095
fiseg          0x23        35
fioff          0x804807e        134512766
foseg          0x2b        43
fooff          0x80490b4        134516916
fop            0x0         0
(gdb)
```

The two data values, and the new control register setting, can be seen in the preceding listing. After the FSAVE instruction, you can view the new FPU state:

```
(gdb) info all
.
.
.
st0          0              (raw 0x00000000000000000000)
st1          0              (raw 0x00000000000000000000)
st2          0              (raw 0x00000000000000000000)
st3          0              (raw 0x00000000000000000000)
st4          0              (raw 0x00000000000000000000)
st5          0              (raw 0x00000000000000000000)
st6          56.78900146484375      (raw 0x4004e327f00000000000)
st7          12.340000152587890625  (raw 0x4002c570a40000000000)
fctrl        0x37f          895
fstat        0x0            0
ftag         0xffff         65535
fiseg        0x0            0
fioff        0x0            0
foseg        0x0            0
fooff        0x0            0
fop          0x0            0
(gdb)
```

Notice that the top of stack value has been moved so that the original top of stack is now at the bottom of the register stack. Also, the control register value has been reset to the default value. You can see what values are in the buffer memory location using the debugger:

```
(gdb) x/108b &buffer
0x80490c0 <buffer>:     0x7f   0x0b   0xff   0xff   0x00   0x30   0xff   0xff
0x80490c8 <buffer+8>:   0xff   0x0f   0xff   0xff   0x7e   0x80   0x04   0x08
0x80490d0 <buffer+16>:  0x23   0x00   0x00   0x00   0xb4   0x90   0x04   0x08
0x80490d8 <buffer+24>:  0x2b   0x00   0xff   0xff   0x00   0x00   0x00   0x00
0x80490e0 <buffer+32>:  0x00   0xf0   0x27   0xe3   0x04   0x40   0x00   0x00
0x80490e8 <buffer+40>:  0x00   0x00   0x00   0xa4   0x70   0xc5   0x02   0x40
0x80490f0 <buffer+48>:  0x00   0x00   0x00   0x00   0x00   0x00   0x00   0x00
0x80490f8 <buffer+56>:  0x00   0x00   0x00   0x00   0x00   0x00   0x00   0x00
0x8049100 <buffer+64>:  0x00   0x00   0x00   0x00   0x00   0x00   0x00   0x00
0x8049108 <buffer+72>:  0x00   0x00   0x00   0x00   0x00   0x00   0x00   0x00
0x8049110 <buffer+80>:  0x00   0x00   0x00   0x00   0x00   0x00   0x00   0x00
0x8049118 <buffer+88>:  0x00   0x00   0x00   0x00   0x00   0x00   0x00   0x00
0x8049120 <buffer+96>:  0x00   0x00   0x00   0x00   0x00   0x00   0x00   0x00
0x8049128 <buffer+104>  0x00   0x00   0x00   0x00
(gdb)
```

The buffer contains not only the control, status, and tag registers, but also the FPU data register values. After executing the FRSTOR instruction, you can look at all the registers and see that they are restored to how they were when the FSAVE was performed:

```
(gdb) info all
 .
 .
 .
st0        56.78900146484375        (raw 0x4004e327f00000000000)
st1        12.340000152587890625    (raw 0x4002c570a40000000000)
st2        0      (raw 0x00000000000000000000)
st3        0      (raw 0x00000000000000000000)
st4        0      (raw 0x00000000000000000000)
st5        0      (raw 0x00000000000000000000)
st6        0      (raw 0x00000000000000000000)
st7        0      (raw 0x00000000000000000000)
fctrl      0xb7f       2943
fstat      0x3000      12288
ftag       0xfff       4095
fiseg      0x23        35
fioff      0x804807e        134512766
foseg      0x2b        43
fooff      0x80490b4        134516916
fop        0x0         0
(gdb)
```

Waiting versus Nonwaiting Instructions

If you are following along in the Intel manual, you probably have noticed that some of the floating-point instructions have nonwaiting counterparts. The terms waiting and nonwaiting refer to how the instructions handle floating-point exceptions.

The floating-point exceptions were discussed earlier in the section "The Status Register." Six types of floating-point exceptions can be generated by the floating-point instructions. They usually indicate that something went wrong with the calculation (such as attempting to divide by zero).

Most floating-point instructions must wait before executing to ensure that no exceptions were thrown by the previous instructions. If an exception is present, it must be handled before the next instruction can be executed.

Alternatively, some instructions include a nonwaiting version of the instruction, which does not wait to check for floating-point exceptions. These instructions allow the program to save or reset the current FPU state without dealing with any pending exceptions. The following table describes the nonwaiting instructions that can be used.

Instruction	Description
FNCLEX	Clear the floating-point exception flags.
FNSAVE	Save the FPU state in memory.
FNSTCW	Save the FPU control register.
FNSTENV	Save the FPU operating environment in memory.
FNSTSW	Save the FPU status register in memory or the AX register.

Optimizing Floating-Point Calculations

Floating-point calculations can represent some of the most time-consuming parts of an assembly language application. Always attempt to optimize your floating-point code as much as possible to help increase the performance of your calculations.

Intel has provided some simple tips to follow when coding floating-point programs:

❑   Make sure the floating-point values do not overflow or underflow the data elements.

❑   Set the precision control bit for single precision.

❑   Use lookup tables for simple trig functions.

❑   Break dependence chains when possible. For example, instead of calculating $z = a + b + c + d$, calculate $x = a + b$; $y = c + d$; $z = x + y$.

❑   Keep equation values in the FPU registers as much as possible.

❑   When working with integers and floating-point values, loading the integers into the FPU registers and performing a calculation is quicker than using a floating-point instruction with the integer. For example, instead of using FIDIV, use FILD to load the integer, and then the FDIVP instruction on the values in the FPU registers.

❑   Use FCOMI instructions instead of FCOM instructions as much as possible.

Summary

This chapter discusses the floating-point math functions available on the FPU in the IA-32 platform. First a review of the FPU environment was presented, which described the FPU data registers (which are combined to make a stack), the status register (which maintains the operating status of the FPU), the control register (which provides a method to control operations with the FPU), and the tag register (which is an easy way to determine the state of the FPU data registers).

After the brief FPU environment review, the basics of FPU math were covered, including the instructions available for performing simple floating-point addition, subtraction, multiplication, and division. There are six versions of each instruction, providing methods for using operands both from the FPU data registers and from memory, as well as instructions for performing calculations using integer and floating-point values. You also looked at a demonstration of how to perform complex mathematical equations by keeping all of the values in the FPU register to increase performance.

The next section tackled advanced floating-point math functions. First discussed were functions that convert floating-point values from one form to another (such as absolute values and change sign instructions). Next, the instructions used to calculate partial remainders were discussed, including how floating-point partial remainders are calculated and how the FPU displays the results of the calculation using the condition code bits of the status register. After that, you learned about the trigonometric functions. The FPU provides all the basic trig functions: FSIN, FCOS, and FPTAN. The important thing to remember when working with FPU trig functions is that all of the angle values must be in radians. A simple method of converting degrees to radians was shown, as well as how to utilize that method within a program. Finally, the advanced math section showed the FPU logarithmic functions and demonstrated how you can use them to calculate any base logarithm needed.

Next up were the FPU conditional branch instructions. Similar to integer conditional branching, the FPU provides instructions that enable you to create branches within your floating-point applications depending on the values of floating-point variables. The FCOM instruction uses the status register condition code bits to indicate whether two variables are equal, less than, or greater than. You can use the FSTSW and SAHF instructions to load the condition code bits into the standard EFLAGS register to perform the comparison branches. Newer IA-32 processors also include the FCOMI instruction, which performs the comparisons and automatically loads the condition code bits into the EFLAGS register, using the carry, parity, and zero flags as indicators. Finally, the FCMOV family of instructions is a great tool to have to move values around within the FPU based on comparisons without having to perform branching instructions. This can greatly increase performance by not corrupting the processor instruction prefetch cache.

You also learned how to store and retrieve the FPU environment and state. Because the FPU shares its resources with the newer MMX technology, programs that utilize both must be able to store and recover the FPU values. The FPU environment consists of the control and status registers, along with the FPU instruction and data pointers. They can be stored in a 28-bit memory location using the FSTENV instruction, and retrieved at any time using the FLDENV instruction. If you need to also store the values of the FPU data registers, the FSAVE instruction saves both the FPU environment as well as all of the data registers. This requires a 108-bit memory location to hold all of the values. Be careful when using the FSAVE instruction, however, as the FPU state is reinitialized after the instruction completes. You will lose any settings that were set in the control register. The FRSTOR instruction can then be used at any time to return the FPU state back to the way it was (including data values) when the FSAVE was performed.

Also presented in this chapter were two short sections on waiting versus nonwaiting instruction calls, and on optimizing floating-point programs. For each FPU instruction, it is possible that an error will occur. The FPU normally attempts to wait for errors to appear before continuing with the next instruction. However, there may be certain circumstances in which you do not want to wait, such as when you are trying to save the FPU state before the exception happens. Several FPU instructions (all beginning with FN) can be performed without waiting for any FPU exceptions. The Intel documentation also provides some basic tips to keep in mind while programming in the FPU environment. If your application requires as much processing speed as possible, it is a good idea to attempt to follow the floating-point optimization tips.

The next chapter departs from the math world (finally) and enters the world of strings. While the processor is not too excited about strings, we humans can't live without them. To make our lives easier, Intel has provided some instructions to help manipulate string values within the processor. These are all covered in the next chapter.

10

Working with Strings

For humans, written communication is crucial. Unfortunately, computers were not specifically designed for ease of communication with humans. Most high-level languages provide specific functions for helping programmers write programs to interact with humans. As an assembly language programmer, you do not have the luxury of these functions. It is up to you to code your programs to interact with humans in their own language.

The use of strings helps programs communicate with humans in their own language. While using strings is not a simple matter in assembly language programming, it is not impossible. This chapter guides you through working with strings. The first section discusses the instructions used to move strings around in memory by copying them from one memory location to another. The next section shows how, similar to integers, strings can be compared for equality. The last section describes the instructions that are used to scan strings for a search character or character string. This feature comes in handy when searching for specific characters within text.

> *Note that the string instructions presented in this chapter also can be applied to nonstring data. Moving, modifying, and comparing blocks of numerical data can also be accomplished using the IA-32 string instructions.*

Moving Strings

One of the most useful functions when dealing with strings is the capability to copy a string from one memory location to another. If you remember from Chapter 5, "Moving Data," you cannot use the MOV instruction to move data from one memory location to another.

Fortunately, Intel has created a complete family of instructions to use when working with string data. This section describes the IA-32 string moving instructions, and shows how to use them in your programs.

The MOVS instruction

The MOVS instruction was created to provide a simple way for programmers to move string data from one memory location to another. There are three formats of the MOVS instruction:

❑ **MOVSB:** Moves a single byte

❑ **MOVSW:** Moves a word (2 bytes)

❑ **MOVSL:** Moves a doubleword (4 bytes)

> *The Intel documentation uses* **MOVSD** *for moving a doubleword. The GNU assembler decided to use* **MOVSL.**

The MOVS instructions use implied source and destination operands. The implied source operand is the ESI register. It points to the memory location for the source string. The implied destination operand is the EDI register. It points to the destination memory location to which the string is copied. The obvious way to remember this is that the S in ESI stands for source, and the D in EDI stands for destination.

With the GNU assembler, there are two ways to load the ESI and EDI values. The first way is to use indirect addressing (see Chapter 5). By placing a dollar sign in front of the memory location label, the address of the memory location is loaded into the ESI or EDI registers:

```
movl $output, %edi
```

This instruction moves the 32-bit memory location of the output label to the EDI register.

Another method of specifying the memory locations is the LEA instruction. The LEA instruction loads the effective address of an object. Because Linux uses 32-bit values to reference memory locations, the memory address of the object must be stored in a 32-bit destination value. The source operand must point to a memory location, such as a label used in the .data section. The instruction

```
leal output, %edi
```

loads the 32-bit memory location of the output label to the EDI register.

The following movstest1.s program uses the MOVS instruction to move some strings:

```
# movstest1.s - An example of the MOVS instructions
.section .data
value1:
    .ascii "This is a test string.\n"
.section .bss
    .lcomm output, 23
.section .text
.globl _start
_start:
```

```
nop
leal value1, %esi
leal output, %edi
movsb
movsw
movsl

movl $1, %eax
movl $0, %ebx
int $0x80
```

The movstest1.s program loads the location of the value1 memory location into the ESI register, and the location of the output memory location into the EDI register. When the MOVSB instruction is executed, it moves 1 byte of data from the value1 location to the output location. Because the output variable was declared in the .bss section, any string data placed there will automatically be null terminated.

The interesting thing is what happens when the MOVSW instruction is executed. If you run the program in the debugger, you can see the output after each of the MOVS instructions:

```
(gdb) s
13            movsb
(gdb) s
14            movsw
(gdb) x/s &output
0x80490b0 <output>:       "T"
(gdb) s
15            movsl
(gdb) x/s &output
0x80490b0 <output>:       "Thi"
(gdb) s
17            movl $1, %eax
(gdb) x/s &output
0x80490b0 <output>:       "This is"
(gdb)
```

The MOVSB instruction moved the "T" from the value1 location to the output location as expected. However, without changing the ESI and EDI registers, when the MOVSW instruction ran, instead of moving the "Th" (the first 2 bytes of the string), it moved the "hi" from the value1 location to the output location. Then the MOVSL instruction continues by adding the next 4 byte values. There is a reason for this.

Each time a MOVS instruction is executed, when the data is moved, the ESI and EDI registers are automatically changed in preparation for another move. While this is usually a good thing, sometimes it can be somewhat tricky.

One of the tricky parts of this operation is the direction in which the registers are changed. The ESI and EDI registers can be either automatically incremented or automatically decremented, depending on the value of the DF flag in the EFLAGS register.

If the DF flag is cleared, the ESI and EDI registers are incremented after each MOVS instruction. If the DF flag is set, the ESI and EDI registers are decremented after each MOVS instruction. Because the movstest.s program did not specifically set the DF flag, we are at the mercy of the current setting. To ensure that the DF flag is set in the proper direction, you can use the following commands:

❑   CLD to clear the DF flag

❑   STD to set the DF flag

When the STD instruction is used, the ESI and EDI registers are decremented after each MOVS instruction, so they should point to the end of the string locations instead of the beginning. The movstest2.s program demonstrates this:

```
# movstest2.s - A second example of the MOVS instructions
.section .data
value1:
    .ascii "This is a test string.\n"
.section .bss
    .lcomm output, 23
.section .text
.globl _start
_start:
    nop
    leal value1+22, %esi

    leal output+22, %edi

    std
    movsb
    movsw
    movsl

    movl $1, %eax
    movl $0, %ebx
    int $0x80
```

This time, the address location of the value1 memory location is placed in the EAX register, the length of the test string (minus one because it starts at address 0) is added to it, and the value is placed in the ESI register. This causes the ESI register to point to the end of the test string. The same is done for the EDI register, so it points to the end of the output memory location. The STD instruction is used to set the DF flag so the ESI and EDI registers are decremented after each MOVS instruction.

The three MOVS instructions move 1, 2, and 4 bytes of data between the two string locations. However, this time, there is a difference. After the three MOVS instructions have been executed, you can look at the end of the output memory location using the debugger:

```
(gdb) x/23b &output
0x80490b8 <output>:      0x00   0x00   0x00   0x00   0x00   0x00   0x00  0x00
0x80490c0 <output+8>:    0x00   0x00   0x00   0x00   0x00   0x00   0x00  0x00
0x80490c8 <output+16>:  0x00   0x00   0x00   0x6e   0x67   0x2e   0x0a
(gdb)
```

Notice that the output string was beginning to fill in from the end of the string, but after the three MOVS instructions, only four memory locations have been filled in. In the movstest.s program, which ran forward, seven memory locations were filled in using the same three instructions. Why is that?

The answer relates to how the values are copied. Even though the ESI and EDI registers are counting backward, the MOVW and MOVL instructions are getting the memory locations in forward order. When the MOVSB instruction finished, it decremented the ESI and EDI registers one, but the MOVSW instruction gets two memory locations. Likewise, when the MOVSW instruction finished, it decremented the ESI and EDI registers two, but the MOVSL instruction gets four memory locations. This is demonstrated in Figure 10-1.

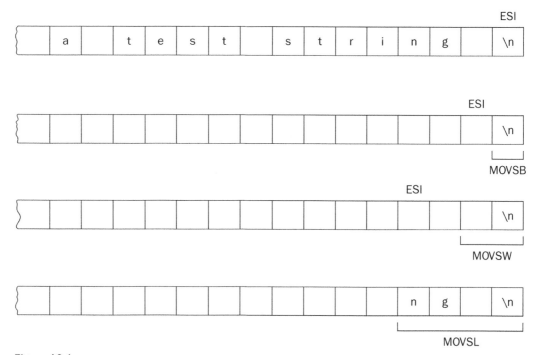

Figure 10-1

Of course, the way to solve this problem is to consistently use the same size blocks to move for every instruction. If all three instructions were MOVSW instructions, the ESI value would be decremented by two each time, and 2 bytes would be moved.

> It is important to remember that if you use the **STD** instruction to work backward from a string, the **MOVSW** and **MOVSL** instructions are still working forward in retrieving memory locations.

If you are copying a large string, it is easy to see that it could take a lot of MOVL instructions to get all of the data. To make things easier, you might be tempted to put the MOVL instruction in a loop, controlled by the ECX register set to the length of the string. The movstest3.s program demonstrates this:

```
# movstest3.s - An example of moving an entire string
.section .data
value1:
    .ascii "This is a test string.\n"
.section .bss
    .lcomm output, 23
```

277

```
.section .text
.globl _start
_start:
    nop
    leal value1, %esi
    leal output, %edi
    movl $23, %ecx
    cld
loop1:
    movsb
    loop loop1

    movl $1, %eax
    movl $0, %ebx
    int $0x80
```

The ESI and EDI registers are loaded as before with the source and destination memory locations. The ECX register is loaded with the length of the string to move. The loop section continually performs the MOVSB instruction until the entire string has been moved. Viewing the string value at the output memory location can check this:

```
(gdb) x/s &output
0x80490b0 <output>:      "This is a test string.\n"
(gdb)
```

While this method works, Intel has provided a simpler way to do this: using the REP instruction.

The REP prefix

The REP instruction is special in that it does nothing by itself. It is used to repeat a string instruction a specific number of times, controlled by the value in the ECX register, similar to using a loop, but without the extra LOOP instruction. The REP instruction repeats the string instruction immediately following it until the value in the ECX register is zero. That is why it is called a prefix.

Moving a string byte by byte

The MOVSB instruction can be used with the REP instruction to move a string 1 byte at a time to another location. The reptest1.s program demonstrates how this works:

```
# reptest1.s - An example of the REP instruction
.section .data
value1:
    .ascii "This is a test string.\n"
.section .bss
    .lcomm output, 23
.section .text
.globl _start
_start:
    nop
    leal value1, %esi
    leal output, %edi
```

```
movl $23, %ecx
cld
rep movsb

movl $1, %eax
movl $0, %ebx
int $0x80
```

The size of the string to move is loaded into the ECX register, and the REP instruction is used with the MOVSB instruction to move a single byte of data 23 times (the length of the string). When you step through the program in the debugger, the REP instruction still only counts as one instruction step, not 23. You should see the following output from the debugger:

```
$ gdb -q reptest1
(gdb) break *_start+1
Breakpoint 1 at 0x8048075: file reptest1.s, line 11.
(gdb) run
Starting program: /home/rich/palp/chap10/reptest1

Breakpoint 1, _start () at reptest1.s:11
11          leal value1, %esi
Current language:  auto; currently asm
(gdb) s
12          leal output, %edi
(gdb) s
13          movl $23, %ecx
(gdb) s
14          cld
(gdb) s
15          rep movsb
(gdb) s
17          movl $1, %eax
(gdb) x/s &output
0x80490b0 <output>:      "This is a test string.\n"
(gdb)
```

While stepping through the instructions, the REP instruction took only one step, but after that step, all 23 bytes of the source string were moved to the destination string location.

Moving strings block by block

You are not limited to moving the strings byte by byte. You can also use the MOVSW and MOVSL instructions to move more than 1 byte per iteration.

If you are using the MOVSW or MOVSL instructions, the ECX register should contain the number of iterations required to walk through the string. For example, if you are moving an 8-byte string, you would need to set ECX to 8 if you are using the MOVSB instruction, to 4 if you are using the MOVSW instruction, or to 2 if you are using the MOVSL instruction.

When walking through the string using MOVSW or MOVSL, be careful that you do not overstep the string boundaries. If you do, look at what happens in the reptest2.s program:

```
# reptest2.s - An incorrect example of using the REP instruction
.section .data
value1:
    .ascii "This is a test string.\n"
value2:
    .ascii "Oops"
.section .bss
    .lcomm output, 23
.section .text
.globl _start
_start:
    nop
    leal value1, %esi
    leal output, %edi
    movl $6, %ecx
    cld
    rep movsl

    movl $1, %eax
    movl $0, %ebx
    int $0x80
```

The preceding example attempts to be resourceful by looping only six times to move blocks of 4 bytes of data. The only problem is that the total data size of the source string is not an even multiple of four. The last time the MOVSL instruction executes, it will not only get the end of the value1 string, it will also erroneously pick up a byte from the next string defined. You can see this from the debugger output:

```
$ gdb -q reptest2
(gdb) break *_start+1
Breakpoint 1 at 0x8048075: file reptest2.s, line 13.
(gdb) run
Starting program: /home/rich/palp/chap10/reptest2

Breakpoint 1, _start () at reptest2.s:13
13          leal value1, %esi
Current language:  auto; currently asm
(gdb) s
14          leal output, %edi
(gdb) s
15          movl $6, %ecx
(gdb) s
16          cld
(gdb) s
17          rep movsl
(gdb) s
19          movl $1, %eax
(gdb) x/s &output
0x80490b0 <output>:     "This is a test string.\nO"
(gdb)
```

The output string now contains the first character from the value2 string tacked onto the data from the value1 string. That is not at all what we would want to have happen.

Moving large strings

Obviously, it is more efficient to move string characters using the MOVSL instruction as much as possible. The problem, as demonstrated in the reptest2.s program, is that you must know when to stop using the MOVSL instruction and convert back to the MOVSB. The trick is in matching the length of the string.

When you know the length of the string, it is easy to perform an integer division (see Chapter 8, "Basic Math Functions") to determine how many doublewords would be in the string. The remainder can then use the MOVSB instruction (which should be no more than three iterations). This is demonstrated in the following reptest3.s program:

```
# reptest3.s - Moving a large string using MOVSL and MOVSB
.section .data
string1:
    .asciz "This is a test of the conversion program!\n"
length:
    .int 43
divisor:
    .int 4
.section .bss
    .lcomm buffer, 43
.section .text
.globl _start
_start:
    nop

    leal string1, %esi
    leal buffer, %edi
    movl length, %ecx
    shrl $2, %ecx

    cld
    rep movsl
    movl length, %ecx
    andl $3, %ecx
    rep movsb

    movl $1, %eax
    movl $0, %ebx
    int $0x80
```

The reptest3.s program loads the source and destination memory locations into the ESI and EDI registers as normal, but then loads the string length value into the AX register. To divide the string length by four, the SHR instruction is used to shift the length value right 2 bits (which is the same as dividing by four), which leaves the quotient value loaded into the ECX register. The REP MOVSL instruction pair is then performed that number of times. After that completes, the remainder value is determined using a common math trick.

If the divisor is a power of two (which four is) you can quickly find the remainder by subtracting one from the divisor and ANDing it with the dividend. This value is then loaded into the ECX register, and the REP MOVSB instruction pair is performed to move the remaining characters.

You can watch this as it happens in the debugger. First, stop the program after the REP MOVSL instruction pair are performed, and display the buffer memory location contents:

```
(gdb) s
22          movl %edx, %ecx
(gdb) x/s &buffer
0x80490d8 <buffer>:        "This is a test of the conversion program"
(gdb)
```

Notice that the first 40 characters were moved from the source string to the destination string. Next, execute the REP MOVSB instruction pair, and look at the buffer memory location contents again:

```
(gdb) s
23          rep movsb
(gdb) s
25          movl $1, %eax
(gdb) x/s &buffer
0x80490d8 <buffer>:        "This is a test of the conversion program!\n"
(gdb)
```

The final two characters in the string were successfully moved. Again, try different combinations of strings and string lengths to verify that this method works properly.

Moving a string in reverse order

The REP instruction works equally well backward and forward. The DF flag can be set to work backward on a string, moving it in reverse order between memory locations. This is demonstrated in the reptest4.s program:

```
# reptest4.s - An example of using REP backwards
.section .data
value1:
    .asciz "This is a test string.\n"
.section .bss
    .lcomm output, 24
.section .text
.globl _start
_start:
    nop
    leal value1+22, %esi
    leal output+22, %edi
    movl $23, %ecx
    std
    rep movsb

    movl $1, %eax
    movl $0, %ebx
    int $0x80
```

Similar to the movstest2.s program, the reptest4.s program loads the location of the end of the source and destination strings into the ESI and EDI registers, and then sets the DF flag using the STD instruction. This causes the destination string to be stored in reverse order (although you won't be able to see that from the debugger, as the REP instruction still moves all of the bytes in one step):

```
(gdb) s
20        std
(gdb) s
21        rep movsb
(gdb) s
23        movl $1, %eax
(gdb) x/s &output
0x80490c0 <output>:        "This is a test string.\n"
(gdb)
```

Other REP instructions

While the REP instruction is handy, you can use a few other versions of it when working with strings. Besides monitoring the value of the ECX register, there are REP instructions that also monitor the status of the zero flag (ZF). The following table describes the other REP instructions that can be used.

Instruction	Description
REPE	Repeat while equal
REPNE	Repeat while not equal
REPNZ	Repeat while not zero
REPZ	Repeat while zero

The REPE and REPZ instructions are synonyms for the same instruction, and the REPNE and REPNZ instructions are synonymous.

*While the **MOVS** instructions do not lend themselves to using these **REP** variations, the comparing and scanning string functions discussed later in this chapter make extensive use of them.*

Storing and Loading Strings

Besides moving strings from one memory location to another, there are also instructions for loading string values in memory into registers, and then back into memory locations. This section describes the STOS and LODS instructions that are used for this purpose.

The LODS instruction

The LODS instruction is used to move a string value in memory into the EAX register. As with the MOVS instruction, there are three different formats of the LODS instruction:

❑ **LODSB:** Loads a byte into the AL register

❑ **LODSW:** Loads a word (2 bytes) into the AX register

❑ **LODSL:** Loads a doubleword (4 bytes) into the EAX register

*The Intel documents use **LODSD** for loading doublewords. The GNU assembler uses **LODSL**.*

The LODS instructions use an implied source operand of the ESI register. The ESI register must contain the memory address of the location of the string to load. The LODS instruction increments or decrements (depending on the DF flag status) the ESI register by the amount of data loaded after the data is moved.

The STOS and SCAS instructions described later in this chapter both utilize data stored in the EAX register. The LODS instruction is useful in placing string values into the EAX register for these instructions. While you can use the REP instruction to repeat LODS instructions, it is unlikely you would ever do that, as the most you can load into the EAX register is 4 bytes, which can be done with a single LODSL instruction.

The STOS instruction

After the LODS instruction is used to place a string value in the EAX register, the STOS instruction can be used to place it in another memory location. Similar to the LODS instruction, the STOS instruction has three formats, depending on the amount of data to move:

❑ **STOSB:** Stores a byte of data from the AL register

❑ **STOSW:** Stores a word (2 bytes) of data from the AX register

❑ **STOSL:** Stores a doubleword (4 bytes) of data from the EAX register

The STOS instruction uses an implied destination operand of the EDI register. When the STOS instruction is executed, it will either increment or decrement the EDI register value by the data size used.

The STOS instruction by itself is not too exciting. Just placing a single byte, word, or doubleword string value into a memory location is not too difficult of a task. Where the STOS instruction really comes handy is when it is used with the REP instruction to replicate a string value multiple times within a large string value — for example, copying a space character (ASCII value 0x20) to a 256-byte buffer area.

The stostest1.s program demonstrates this concept:

```
# stostest1.s - An example of using the STOS instruction
.section .data
space:
    .ascii " "
.section .bss
    .lcomm buffer, 256
.section .text
.globl _start
_start:
    nop
    leal space, %esi
    leal buffer, %edi
    movl $256, %ecx
    cld
    lodsb
    rep stosb

    movl $1, %eax
    movl $0, %ebx
    int $0x80
```

The stostest1.s program loads an ASCII space character into the AL register, then copies it 256 times into the memory locations pointed to by the buffer label. You can see the before and after values of the buffer memory locations using the debugger:

```
(gdb) s
15          lodsb
(gdb) s
16          rep stosb
(gdb) print/x $eax
$1 = 0x20
(gdb) x/10b &buffer
0x80490a0 <buffer>:      0x00    0x00    0x00    0x00    0x00    0x00    0x00    0x00
0x80490a8 <buffer+8>:    0x00    0x00
(gdb) s
18          movl $1, %eax
(gdb) x/10b &buffer
0x80490a0 <buffer>:      0x20    0x20    0x20    0x20    0x20    0x20    0x20    0x20
0x80490a8 <buffer+8>:    0x20    0x20
(gdb)
```

This output shows that the space character was loaded into the AL register by the LODSB instruction. Before the STOSB instruction, the buffer memory location contained zeros (which is what we would expect because it was constructed in the .bss section). After the STOSB instruction, the buffer contained all spaces.

Building your own string functions

The STOS and LODS instructions come in handy for a variety of string operations. By pointing the ESI and EDI registers to the same string, you can perform simple functions on the string. You can use the LODS instruction to walk your way through a string, load each character one at a time into the AL register, perform some operation on that character, and then load the new character back into the string using the STOS instruction.

The convert.s program demonstrates this principle by converting an ASCII string into all capital letters:

```
# convert.s - Converting lower to upper case
.section .data
string1:
    .asciz "This is a TEST, of the conversion program!\n"
length:
    .int 43
.section .text
.globl _start
_start:
    nop
    leal string1, %esi
    movl %esi, %edi
    movl length, %ecx
    cld
```

```
loop1:
    lodsb
    cmpb $'a', %al
    jl skip
    cmpb $'z', %al
    jg skip
    subb $0x20, %al
skip:
    stosb
    loop loop1
end:
    pushl $string1
    call printf
    addl $4, %esp
    pushl $0
    call exit
```

The convert.s program loads the string1 memory location into both the ESI and EDI registers, and the string length into the ECX register. It then uses the LOOP instruction to perform a character check for each character in the string. It checks the characters by loading each individual character into the AL register, and determining whether it is less than the ASCII value for the letter a (0x61) or greater than the ASCII value for the letter z (0x7a). If the character is within these ranges, it must be a lowercase letter that can be converted to uppercase by subtracting 0x20 from it.

Whether the character was converted or not, it must be placed back into the string to keep the ESI and EDI registers in sync. The STOSB instruction is run on each character, and then the code loops back for the next character until it runs out of characters in the string.

After assembling the program and linking it with the C library, you can run it to see if it works right:

```
$ ./convert
THIS IS A TEST, OF THE CONVERSION PROGRAM!
$
```

Indeed, it performed as expected. You can test the program by using different types of ASCII characters within the string (remember to change the length value to match your new string).

Comparing Strings

Moving strings from one place to another is useful, but there are other string functions that can really help out when working with strings. One of the most useful string functions available is the capability to compare strings. Many programs need to compare input values from users, or compare string records with search values. This section describes the methods used to compare string values in assembly language programs.

The CMPS instruction

The CMPS family of instructions is used to compare string values. As with the other string instructions, there are three formats of the CMPS instruction:

❑ **CMPSB:** Compares a byte value

❑ **CMPSW:** Compares a word (2 bytes) value

❑ **CMPSL:** Compares a doubleword (4 bytes) value

As with the other string instructions, the locations of the implied source and destination operands are again stored in the ESI and EDI registers. Each time the CMPS instruction is executed, the ESI and EDI registers are incremented or decremented by the amount of the data size compared, depending on the DF flag setting.

The CMPS instruction subtracts the destination string from the source string, and sets the carry, sign, overflow, zero, parity, and adjust flags in the EFLAGS register appropriately. After the CMPS instruction, you can use the normal conditional jump instructions to branch, depending on the values of the strings.

The cmpstest1.s program demonstrates a simple example of using the CMPS instruction:

```
# cmpstest1.s - A simple example of the CMPS instruction
.section .data
value1:
    .ascii "Test"
value2:
    .ascii "Test"
.section .text
.globl _start
_start:
    nop
    movl $1, %eax
    leal value1, %esi
    leal value2, %edi
    cld
    cmpsl
    je equal
    movl $1, %ebx
    int $0x80
equal:
    movl $0, %ebx
    int $0x80
```

The cmptest1.s program compares two string values, and sets the return code for the program depending on the result of the comparison. First the exit system call value is loaded into the EAX register. After loading the location of the two strings to test into the ESI and EDI registers, the cmpstest1.s program uses the CMPSL instruction to compare the first four bytes of the strings. The JE instruction is used to jump to the equal label if the strings are equal, which sets the program result code to 0 and exits. If the strings are not equal, the branch is not taken, and execution falls through to set the result code to 1 and exit.

After assembling and linking the program, you can test it by running it and checking the result code:

```
$ ./cmpstest1
$ echo $?
0
$
```

The result code was 0, indicating that the strings matched. To test this, you can change one of the strings and assemble the program again to see whether the result code changes to 1.

This technique works well for matching strings up to four characters long, but what about longer strings? The answer lies in the REP instruction, described in the next section.

Using REP with CMPS

The REP instruction can be used to repeat the string comparisons over multiple bytes, but there is a problem. Unfortunately, the REP instruction does not check the status of the flags between repetitions; remember that it is only concerned about the count value in the ECX register.

The solution is to use the other instructions in the REP family: REPE, REPNE, REPZ, and REPNZ. These instructions check the zero flag for each repetition and stop the repetitions if the zero flag is set. This enables you to check strings byte by byte to determine whether they match up. As soon as one of the character pairs does not match, the REP instruction will stop repeating.

The cmpstest2.s program demonstrates how this is accomplished:

```
# cmpstest2.s - An example of using the REPE CMPS instruction
.section .data
value1:
    .ascii "This is a test of the CMPS instructions"
value2:
    .ascii "This is a test of the CMPS Instructions"
.section .text
.globl _start
_start:
    nop
    movl $1, %eax
    lea value1, %esi
    leal value2, %edi
    movl $39, %ecx
    cld
    repe cmpsb
    je equal
    movl %ecx, %ebx
    int $0x80
equal:
    movl $0, %ebx
    int $0x80
```

The cmpstest2.s program loads the source and destination string locations into the ESI and EDI registers, as well as the string length in the ECX register. The REPE CMPSB instructions repeat the string compare byte by byte until either the ECX register runs out or the zero flag is set, indicating a nonmatch.

After the REPE instruction, the JE instruction is used as normal to check the EFLAGS registers to determine whether the strings were equal. If the REPE instruction exited, the zero flag will be set, and the JE instruction will not branch, indicating the strings were not the same. The ESI and EDI registers will then contain the location of the mismatched character in the strings, and the ECX register will contain the position of the mismatched character (counting back from the end of the string).

This example also demonstrates how sensitive the string comparisons are. The two strings differ only in the capitalization of one character, which will be detected by the comparison:

```
$ ./cmpstest2
$ echo $?
11
$
```

The CMPS instructions subtract the hexadecimal values of the source and destination strings. The ASCII codes for each individual character are different, so any difference between the strings will be detected.

String inequality

While on the topic of comparing strings, it is a good idea to discuss the concept of unequal strings. When comparing strings, it is easy to determine when two strings are equal. The string "test" is always equal to the string "test." However, what about the string "test1"? Should that be less than or greater than the string "test"?

Unlike integers, where it is easy to understand why the value 100 would be greater than 10, determining string inequalities is not as simple of a concept. Trying to determine whether the string "less" is less than or greater than the string "greater" is not easy to understand. If your application must determine string inequalities, you must have a specific method for determining them.

The method most often used to compare strings is called *lexicographical ordering*. This is most often referred to as *dictionary ordering,* as it is the standard by which dictionaries order words. As you page through a dictionary, you can see how the words are ordered. The basic rules for lexicographical ordering are as follows:

- ❑ Alphabetically lower letters are less than alphabetically higher letters
- ❑ Uppercase letters are less than lowercase letters

You may notice that these rules follow the standard ASCII character coding values. It is easy to apply these rules to strings that are the same length. The string `"test"` would be less than the string `"west"`, but greater than the string `"Test"`. When working with strings of different lengths, things get tricky.

When comparing two strings of different lengths, the comparison is based on the number of characters in the shorter string. If the shorter string would be greater than the same number of characters in the longer string, then the shorter string is greater than the longer string. If the shorter string would be less than the same number of characters in the longer string, then the shorter string would be less than the longer string. If the shorter string is equal to the same number of characters in the longer string, the longer string is greater than the shorter string.

Using this rule, the following examples would be true:

- ❑ `"test"` is greater than `"boomerang"`
- ❑ `"test"` is less than `"velocity"`
- ❑ `"test"` is less than `"test1"`

The `strcomp.s` program demonstrates comparing strings for both inequality and equality:

```
# strcomp.s - An example of comparing strings
.section .data
string1:
    .ascii "test"
length1:
    .int 4
string2:
    .ascii "test1"
length2:
    .int 5
.section .text
.globl _start
_start:
    nop
    lea string1, %esi
    lea string2, %edi
    movl length1, %ecx
    movl length2, %eax
    cmpl %eax, %ecx
    ja longer
    xchg %ecx, %eax
longer:
    cld
    repe cmpsb
    je equal
    jg greater
less:
    movl $1, %eax
    movl $255, %ebx
    int $0x80
greater:
    movl $1, %eax
    movl $1, %ebx
    int $0x80
equal:
    movl length1, %ecx
    movl length2, %eax
    cmpl %ecx, %eax
    jg greater
    jl less
    movl $1, %eax
    movl $0, %ebx
    int $0x80
```

The `strcomp.s` program defines two strings, `string1` and `string2`, along with their lengths (`length1` and `length2`). The result code produced from the program reflects the comparison of the two strings, shown in the following table.

Result Code	Description
255	string1 is less than string2
0	string1 is equal to string2
1	string1 is greater than string2

To perform the lexicographical ordering, first the shorter string length must be determined. This is done by loading the two string lengths into registers and using the CMP instruction to compare them. The shorter number is loaded into the ECX register for the REPE instruction.

Next, the two strings are compared byte by byte using the REPE and CMPSB instructions for the length of the shorter string. If the first string is greater than the second string, the program branches to the greater label and sets the result code to 1 and exits. If the first string is less than the second string, the program falls through and sets the result code to 255 and exits.

If the two strings are equal, there is more work to be done — the program must still determine which of the two strings is longer. If the first string is longer, then it is greater, and the program branches to the greater label, sets the result code to 1, and exits. If the second string is longer, then the first string is less, and the program branches to the less label, sets the result code to 255, and exits. If the two lengths are not greater or less, then not only did the strings match, but their lengths are equal, so the strings are equal.

You can set various strings in the string1 and string2 locations to test the lexicographical ordering (just remember to change the string length values accordingly). Using the values shown in the strcomp.s program listing, the output should be as follows:

```
$ ./strcomp
$ echo $?
255
$
```

as the first string, "test", is less than the second string, "test1".

Scanning Strings

Sometimes it is useful to scan a string for a specific character or character sequence. One method would be to walk through the string using the LODS instruction, putting each character in the AL register, and comparing the characters with the search character. This would certainly work, but would be a time-consuming process.

Intel provides a better way to do this with another string instruction. The SCAS instruction provides a way for you to scan a string looking for a specific character, or group of characters. This section describes how to use the SCAS instruction in your programs.

The SCAS instruction

The SCAS family of instructions is used to scan strings for one or more search characters. As with the other string instructions, there are three versions of the SCAS instruction:

- ❑ **SCASB:** Compares a byte in memory with the AL register value
- ❑ **SCASW:** Compares a word in memory with the AX register value
- ❑ **SCASL:** Compares a doubleword in memory with the EAX register value

The SCAS instructions use an implied destination operand of the EDI register. The EDI register must contain the memory address of the string to scan. As with the other string instructions, when the SCAS instruction is executed, the EDI register value is incremented or decremented (depending on the DF flag value) by the data size amount of the search character.

When the comparison is made, the EFLAGS adjust, carry, parity, overflow, sign, and zero flags are set accordingly. You can use the standard conditional branch instructions to detect the outcome of the scan.

By itself, the SCAS instruction is not too exciting. It will only check the current character pointed to by the EDI register against the character in the AL register, similar to the CMPS instruction. Where the SCAS instruction comes in handy is when it is used with the REPE and REPNE prefixes.

These two prefixes enable you to scan the entire length of a string looking for a specific search character (or character sequence). The REPE and REPNE instructions are usually used to stop the scan when the search character is found. Be careful, however, when using these two instructions, as their behavior might be opposite from what you would think:

- ❑ REPE: Scans the string characters looking for a character that does not match the search character
- ❑ REPNE: Scans the string characters looking for a character that matches the search character

For most string scans, you would use the REPNE instruction, as it will stop the scan when the search character is found in the string. When the character is found, the EDI register contains the memory address immediately after where the character is located. This is because the REPNE instruction increments the EDI register after the SCAS instruction is performed. The ECX register contains the position from the end of the string that contains the search character. Be careful with this value, as it is counted from the end of the string. To get the position from the start of the string, subtract the string length from this value and reverse the sign.

The scastest1.s program demonstrates searching for a character in a string using the REPNE and SCAS instructions:

```
# scastest1.s - An example of the SCAS instruction
.section .data
string1:
    .ascii "This is a test - a long text string to scan."
length:
    .int 44
string2:
    .ascii "-"
```

```
.section .text
.globl _start
_start:
    nop
    leal string1, %edi
    leal string2, %esi
    movl length, %ecx
    lodsb
    cld
    repne scasb
    jne notfound
    subw length, %cx
    neg %cx
    movl $1, %eax
    movl %ecx, %ebx
    int $0x80
notfound:
    movl $1, %eax
    movl $0, %ebx
    int $0x80
```

The scastest1.s program loads the memory location of the string to scan into the EDI register, uses the LODSB instruction to load the AL register with the character to search for, and places the length of the string in the ECX register. When all of that is done, the REPNE SCASB instruction is used to scan the string for the location of the search character. If the character is not found, the JNE instruction will branch to the notfound label. If the character is found, its location from the end of the string is now in ECX. The length of the string is subtracted from ECX, and the NEG instruction is used to change the sign of the value to produce the location in the string where the search character is found. The location is loaded into the EBX register so it becomes the result code after the program terminates:

```
$ ./scastest1
$ echo $?
16
$
```

The output shows that the "-" character was found in position 16 of the string.

Scanning for multiple characters

While the SCASW and SCASL instructions can be used to scan for a sequence of two or four characters, care must be taken when using them. They might not perform just as you are expecting.

The SCASW and SCASL instructions walk down the string looking for the character sequence in the AX or EAX registers, but they do not perform a character-by-character comparison. Instead, the EDI register is incremented by either 2 (for SCASW) or 4 (for SCASL) after each comparison, not by 1. This means that the character sequence must also be present in the proper sequence within the string. The scastest2.s program demonstrates this problem:

```
# scastest2.s - An example of incorrectly using the SCAS instruction
.section .data
string1:
    .ascii "This is a test - a long text string to scan."
```

```
length:
    .int 11
string2:
    .ascii "test"
.section .text
.globl _start
_start:
    nop
    leal string1, %edi
    leal string2, %esi
    movl length, %ecx
    lodsl
    cld
    repne scasl
    jne notfound
    subw length, %cx
    neg %cx
    movl $1, %eax
    movl %ecx, %ebx
    int $0x80
notfound:
    movl $1, %eax
    movl $0, %ebx
    int $0x80
```

The scastest2.s program attempts to find the character sequence "test" within the string. It loads the complete search string into the EAX register, and uses the SCASL instruction to check 4 bytes of the string at a time. Note that the ECX register is not set to the string length, but instead to the number of iterations the REPNE instruction needs to take to complete the string walking. Because each iteration checks 4 bytes, the ECX register is one-fourth the total string length of 44.

If you run the program and check the result code, you will see something that you might not expect to see:

```
$ ./scastest2
$ echo $?
0
$
```

The SCASL instruction did not find the character sequence "test" within the string. Obviously, something went wrong. That something was the way in which the REPNE instruction performed the iterations. Figure 10-2 demonstrates how this was done.

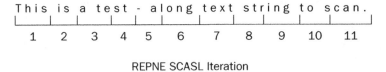

REPNE SCASL Iteration

Figure 10-2

The first iteration of the REPNE instruction checked the 4 bytes "This" against the character sequence in EAX. Because they did not match, it incremented the ECX register by four, and checked the next 4 bytes,

" is ". As you can see from Figure 10-2, no groups of 4 bytes tested matched the character sequence, even though the sequence was in the string.

> *While the SCASW and SCASL instructions don't work well with strings, they are useful when searching for nonstring data sequences in data arrays. The SCASW instruction can be used for 2-byte arrays, while the SCASL instruction can be used with 4-byte arrays.*

Finding a string length

One extremely useful function of the SCAS instruction is to determine the string length of zero-terminated (also called null-terminated) strings. These strings are most commonly used in C programs, but are also used in assembly language programs by using the .asciz declaration. With a zero-terminated string, the obvious thing to search for is the location of the zero, and count how many characters were processed looking for the zero. The strsize.s program demonstrates this:

```
# strsize.s - Finding the size of a string using the SCAS instruction
.section .data
string1:
    .asciz "Testing, one, two, three, testing.\n"
.section .text
.globl _start
_start:
    nop
    leal string1, %edi
    movl $0xffff, %ecx
    movb $0, %al
    cld
    repne scasb
    jne notfound
    subw $0xffff, %cx
    neg %cx
    dec %cx
    movl $1, %eax
    movl %ecx, %ebx
    int $0x80
notfound:
    movl $1, %eax
    movl $0, %ebx
    int $0x80
```

The strsize.s program loads the memory location of the string to test into the EDI register and loads a fictitious string length into the ECX register. The 0xffff string length value indicates that this utility will only work on strings up to 65,535 bytes in length. The ECX register will keep track of how many iterations it takes to find the terminating zero in the string. If the zero is found by the SCASB instruction, the position must be calculated from the value of the ECX register. Subtracting it from the original value and changing the sign of the result does this. Because the length includes the terminating zero, the final value must be decreased by one to show the actual string size. The result of the calculation is placed in the EBX register so it can be retrieved by checking the result code from the program:

```
$ ./strsize
$ echo $?
35
$
```

Summary

Strings are an important part of working with programs that must interact with humans. Creating, moving, comparing, and scanning strings are vital functions that must be performed within assembly language programs. This chapter presented the IA-32 string instructions and demonstrated how they can be used in assembly language programs.

The MOVS instruction family provides methods to move strings from one memory location to another. These instructions move a string referenced by the ESI register to a location referenced by the EDI register. The three formats of the MOVS instruction, MOVSB (for bytes), MOVSW (for words), and MOVSL (for doublewords) provide quick methods for moving large strings in memory. To move even more memory, the REP instruction enables the repetition of the MOVS instructions a preset number of times. The ECX register is used as a counter to determine how many iterations of the MOVS instruction will be performed. It is important to remember that the ECX register counts iterations and not necessarily the string size. The ESI and EDI registers are incremented or decremented automatically by the amount of the data size moved. The EFLAGS DF flag is used to control the direction in which the registers are changed.

The LODS instruction family is used to load a string value into the EAX register. The LODSB instruction moves a byte into the AL register, the LODSW instruction moves a word into the AX register, and the LODSL instruction moves a doubleword into the EAX register. Once a string value is placed in the register, many different functions can be performed on it, such as changing the ASCII value from a lowercase letter to an uppercase letter. After the function is applied, the string character can be moved back into memory using the STOS instruction. The STOS instructions include STOSB (store a byte), STOSW (store a word), and STOSL (store a doubleword).

A very handy function to perform with strings is the capability to compare different string values, which is made possible by the CMPS instruction. The memory locations of the strings to compare are loaded into the ESI and EDI registers. The result of the CMPS instructions is set in the EFLAGS registers, using the usual flags. This enables you to use the standard conditional branching instructions to check the EFLAGS flag settings and branch accordingly. The REPE instruction can be used to compare longer strings, comparing each individual character until two characters are not the same. The length of the strings to compare is set in the ECX register. Again, the EFLAGS registers can be used to determine whether the two strings are the same.

Besides comparing strings, it is often useful to scan a string for a specific character or character sequence. The SCAS instructions are used to scan strings for characters that are stored in the EAX register. The SCAS instruction is often used with the REPNE instruction to repeat the scan function over an entire string length. The scan will continue until the search character is found, or the end of the string is reached. The length of the string to scan is placed in the ECX register, and the results are set in the EFLAGS register.

With all of these specialized string functions, along with the special math functions presented in the previous chapters, you can start building a library of assembly language functions to use in all your programs. Chapter 11, "Using Functions," demonstrates how to separate code functions into self-contained libraries that can be used in any assembly program where they are needed. This can save you a lot of time by not having to repeat the same code functions in all of your programs.

11

Using Functions

After you start coding various types of utilities for different projects, you will realize that you are coding the same utilities multiple times within the same program, or possibly using the same utilities within different programs. Instead of having to retype the code for the utility every time you need to use it, you can create a standalone function that can be called anytime you need the utility.

This chapter describes what functions are and how they are used in programs. You will learn how functions are used in assembly language, including examples of how they are created and used in assembly language programs. After that, you will learn how to create assembly language functions using the C calling convention, as well as how to split assembly language functions into files separate from the main program. Finally, because passing parameters is important to functions as well as programs, you will learn how to read and process command-line parameters from within an assembly language program, and examine a demonstration of how to use command-line parameters in your application.

Defining Functions

Often, applications require that the same procedures or processes be performed multiple times with different data sets. When the same code is required throughout an application, instead of rewriting the code multiple times, it is sometimes best to create a single *function* containing the code, which can then be called from anywhere in the program. A function contains all of the code necessary to complete a specific routine, without requiring any code assistance from the main program. Data is passed to the function from the main program, and the results are returned back to the main program.

When a function is called, the execution path of the program is altered, switching to the first instruction in the function code. The processor executes instructions from that point, until the function indicates that it can return control back to the original location in the main program. This is demonstrated in Figure 11-1.

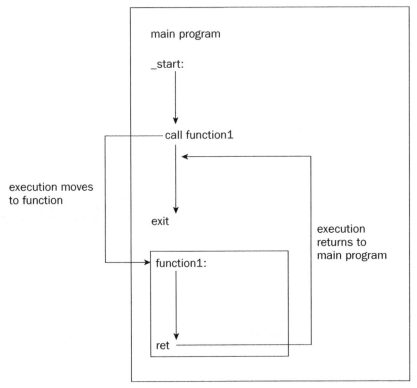

Figure 11-1

Most high-level languages provide a method to write and use functions within programs. Functions can be contained and compiled in the same source code file as the main program, or they can be located in a separate source code file and be linked with the main program.

The `ctest.c` program demonstrates a simple C language function that calculates the area of a circle given the radius:

```
/* ctest.c - An example of using functions in C */
#include <stdio.h>

float function1(int radius)
{
    float result = radius * radius * 3.14159;
    return result;
}

int main()
{
    int i;
    float result;
    i = 10;
    result = function1(i);
    printf("Radius: %d,  Area: %f\n", i, result);
```

```
    i = 2;
    result = function1(i);
    printf("Radius: %d,  Area: %f\n", i, result);

    i = 120;
    result = function1(i);
    printf("Radius: %d,  Area: %f\n", i, result);
    return 0;
}
```

The function defines the required input value, as well as the type of output the function will produce:

```
float function1(int radius)
```

The function definition shows that the input value is an integer, and the function produces a floating-point value for the output. When the function is called within the program, it must use the same format:

```
result = function1(i);
```

The variable placed inside the function call is defined as an integer, and the output of the function is stored in the variable result, which is defined as a floating-point value. To compile the program, you can use the GNU C compiler (gcc):

```
$ gcc -o ctest ctest.c
$./ctest
Radius: 10,  Area: 314.158997
Radius: 2,  Area: 12.566360
Radius: 120,  Area: 45238.894531
$
```

Now that you have seen how functions work in general, it's time to create some functions in assembly language.

Assembly Functions

Writing functions in assembly language is similar to writing them with C. To create a function, you must define its input values, how it processes the input values, and its output values. Once the function is defined, you can code it within your assembly language application.

This section shows how to create functions in assembly language programs, and provides a simple example of using a function within a program.

Writing functions

Three steps are required for creating functions in assembly language programs:

1. Define what input values are required.
2. Define the processes performed on the input values.

3.   Define how the output values are produced and passed to the calling program.

This section walks through these steps using the area of a circle function as an example.

Defining input values

Many (if not most) functions require some sort of input data. You must decide how your program will pass this information along to the function. Basically, three techniques can be employed:

- ❑   Using registers
- ❑   Using global variables
- ❑   Using the stack

The simple example shown in this section uses the registers technique to pass an input value to the function. The second two techniques, global variables and the stack, are covered in detail later in this chapter.

When functions are called from the main program, they pick up execution from where the main program left off when the function was called. Any data located in memory and in the registers is fair game to the function. Using the registers to pass input values to a function is quick and simple.

> *When using registers to pass data between the main program and functions, remember to use the proper data type for the data. The data must be placed in the register in the same data type that the function expects.*

Defining function processes

The function is written as normal assembly language code within the program. The function instructions must be set apart from the rest of the main program instructions in the source code file.

What makes the function different from the rest of the main program is the way it is defined for the assembler. Different assemblers use different methods for defining functions.

To define a function in the GNU assembler, you must declare the name of the function as a label in the program. To declare the function name for the assembler, use the `.type` directive:

```
.type func1, @function
func1:
```

The `.type` directive informs the GNU assembler that the `func1` label defines the start of a function that will be used within the assembly language program. The `func1` label defines the start of the function. The first instruction after the `func1` label is the beginning of the function.

Within the function, code can be used just as with the main program code. Registers and memory locations can be accessed, and special features such as the FPU, MMX, and SSE can be utilized.

The end of the function is defined by a RET instruction. When the RET instruction is reached, program control is returned to the main program, at the instruction immediately following where the function was called with the CALL instruction.

Defining output values

When the function finishes processing the data, most likely you will want to retrieve the result back in the calling program area. The function must have a way to pass the result back to the main program so the main program can utilize the data for further processing or displaying. Similar to the input value techniques, there are multiple ways to accomplish transferring results, although the following two are most popular:

❑　Place the result in one or more registers.

❑　Place the result in a global variable memory location.

The sample function used here uses a single register to pass the result back to the main program. Later in this chapter you will learn how to use the global variable techniques to pass data back to the main program.

Creating the function

Now that you have seen the basics for creating assembly language functions, it's time to create one. This code snippet shows how a function could be created to perform the area function in an assembly language program:

```
.type area, @function
area:
    fldpi
    imull %ebx, %ebx
    movl %ebx, value
    filds value
    fmulp %st(0), %st(1)

    ret
```

The area function uses the FPU to calculate the area of a circle, based on the radius. The input value (the radius) is assumed to be an integer value, located in the EBX register when the function is called.

The pi value needed for the calculation is loaded into the FPU register stack using the FLDPI instruction. Next, the value in the EBX register is squared and stored in a memory location already defined in memory by the main program (remember that the function has full access to the memory locations defined by the main program).

The FILDS instruction is used to load the squared radius value into the top of the FPU stack, moving the pi value to the ST(1) position. Next, the FMULP instruction is used to multiply the first and second FPU stack positions, placing the result in the ST(1) position, and then popping the ST(0) value off of the stack, leaving the final result in the ST(0) register.

The requirements for a program to use the area function are as follows:

❑　The input value must be placed in the EBX register as an integer value.

❑　A 4-byte memory location called value must be created in the main program.

❑　The output value is located in the FPU ST(0) register.

It is crucial to follow these requirements when using the area function within the main program. For example, if you place the radius value in the EBX register as a floating-point data type, the entire area calculation will be incorrect.

The sample area function shown here has a complicated set of requirements that must be followed in order for an application to use it. If you are working with a large application with numerous functions, it would be difficult to keep track of which functions had which sets of requirements. There is a way to remedy this, which is demonstrated in the section "Passing Data Values in C Style."

Accessing functions

Once the function is created, it can be accessed from anywhere in the program. The CALL instruction is used to pass control from the main program to the function. The CALL instruction has a single operand:

```
call function
```

where function is the name of the function to call. Remember to place any input values in the appropriate locations before the CALL instruction.

The functest1.s program demonstrates performing multiple calls to the area function within a program:

```
# functest1.s - An example of using functions
.section .data
precision:
    .byte 0x7f, 0x00
.section .bss
    .lcomm value, 4
.section .text
.globl _start
_start:
    nop
    finit
    fldcw precision

    movl $10, %ebx
    call area

    movl $2, %ebx
    call area

    movl $120, %ebx
    call area

    movl $1, %eax
    movl $0, %ebx
    int $0x80

.type area, @function
area:
    fldpi
    imull %ebx, %ebx
    movl %ebx, value
```

```
filds value
fmulp %st(0), %st(1)
fstps %eax
ret
```

The `area` function is created exactly as the code snippet earlier demonstrated. The main program first initializes the FPU and sets it to use single-precision floating-point results (See Chapter 9, "Advanced Math Functions"). Next, three calls are made to the `area` function, each time using a different value in the EBX register. The output from the function is placed in the EAX register as a single-precision floating-point data type. For this example, the results are not displayed. Instead, they can be viewed from the debugger while running the program.

After assembling and linking the program, run it in the debugger, and watch how the program execution moves. When the CALL instruction is performed, the next instruction executed is the first instruction in the function:

```
$ gdb -q functest1
(gdb) break *_start+1
Breakpoint 1 at 0x8048075: file functest1.s, line 11.
(gdb) run
Starting program: /home/rich/palp/chap11/functest1

Breakpoint 1, _start () at functest1.s:11
11          finit
Current language:  auto; currently asm
(gdb) s
12          fldcw precision
(gdb) s
14          movl $10, %ebx
(gdb) s
15          call area
(gdb) s
29          fldpi
(gdb)
```

Continuing to step through the program, the next instruction in the function is performed, and so on until the RET instruction, which returns to the main program:

```
(gdb) s
37          ret
(gdb) s
17          movl $2, %ebx
(gdb)
```

After returning to the main program, you can view the result value in the ST(0) register as a floating-point value:

```
(gdb) print/f $st0
$1 = 314.159271
(gdb)
```

The function performed as expected, producing the correct area value for the first radius value (10). This process continues for the other values and function calls.

Function placement

You may have noticed that in the `functest1.s` program, the function code was placed after the end of the source code for the main program. You can also place the function code before the source code for the main program. As mentioned in Chapter 4, "A Sample Assembly Language Program," when the source code object file is linked, the linker is looking for the code section labeled `_start` for the first instruction to execute. You can have any number of functions coded before the `_start` label without affecting the start of the main program.

In addition, as demonstrated in the `functest1.s` program, unlike some high-level languages, the functions do not have to be defined before they are called in the main program. All the `CALL` instruction is looking for is the label to define where the function begins for the instruction pointer.

Using registers

While the `area` function used only a single output register in the process, that may not be the case with more complex functions. Often functions use registers for processing data. There is no guarantee that the registers will be in the same state when the function is finished as they were before the function was called.

When calling a function from a program, you should know what registers the function uses for its internal processing. Any registers (and memory locations as well) used within the function may or may not be the same values when execution returns to the main program.

If you are calling a function that modifies registers the main program uses, it is crucial that you save the current state of the registers before calling the function, and then restore them after the function returns. You can either save specific registers individually using the `PUSH` instruction or save all of the registers together using the `PUSHA` instruction before calling the function. Similarly, you can restore the registers back to their original state either individually using the `POP` instruction or together using the `POPA` instruction.

> Be careful when restoring the register values after the function call. If the function returns a value in a register, you must move it to a safe place before restoring the original register values.

Using global data

You have already seen in the sample `area` function that functions can access memory locations defined in the main program. Because these memory locations are accessible by all of the functions in the program, they are called *global variables*. Functions can use global variables for any purpose, including passing data between the main program and the functions.

The `functest2.s` program demonstrates using global variables to pass input and output values between the function and the main program:

```
# functest2.s - An example of using global variables in functions
.section .data
precision:
    .byte 0x7f, 0x00
.section .bss
    .lcomm radius, 4
    .lcomm result, 4
```

```
        .lcomm trash, 4
.section .text
.globl _start
_start:
    nop
    finit
    fldcw precision

    movl $10, radius
    call area

    movl $2, radius
    call area

    movl $120, radius
    call area

    movl $1, %eax
    movl $0, %ebx
    int $0x80

.type area, @function
area:
    fldpi
    filds radius
    fmul %st(0), %st(0)
    fmulp %st(0), %st(1)
    fstps result

    ret
```

The functest2.s program modifies the area function so that it does not need to use any general-purpose registers. Instead, it takes the input value from the radius global variable, loads it into the FPU, performs all of the mathematical operations within the FPU, and then pops the FPU ST(0) register into a global variable that can be accessed by the main program. Because no registers are used to hold input values, the main program must load each input value into the radius global variable instead of a register.

After assembling and linking the program, you can run it in the debugger to watch the global variables as the program progresses. Here are the values after the first call to the area function:

```
(gdb) x/d &radius
0x80490d4 <radius>:      10
(gdb) x/f &result
0x80490d8 <result>:      314.159271
(gdb)
```

The result was properly placed in the result memory location. After the first call to the function, a new value is loaded into the radius memory location, and the function is called again. This continues with the third call as well.

Using global memory locations to pass parameters and return results is not a common programming practice, even in C and C++ programming. The next section describes the more common method of passing values between functions.

Passing Data Values in C Style

As you can tell, numerous options are available for handling input and output values in functions. While this might seem like a good thing, in reality it can become a problem. If you are writing functions for a large project, the documentation required to ensure that each function is used properly can become overwhelming. Trying to keep track of which function uses which registers and global variables, or which registers and global variables are used to pass which parameters, can be a nightmare.

To help solve this problem, a standard must be used to consistently place input parameters for functions to retrieve, and consistently place output values for the main program to retrieve. When creating code for the IA-32 platform, most C compilers use a standard method for handling input and output values in assembly language code compiled from C functions. This method works equally as well for any assembly language program, even if it wasn't derived from a C program.

The C solution for passing input values to functions is to use the stack. The stack is accessible from the main program as well as from any functions used within the program. This creates a clean way to pass data between the main program and the functions in a common location, without having to worry about clobbering registers or defining global variables.

Likewise, the C style defines a common method for returning values to the main program, using the EAX register for 32-bit results (such as short integers), the EDX:EAX register pair for 64-bit integer values, and the FPU ST(0) register for floating-point values.

The following sections review how the stack works and show how it is used to pass input values to functions.

Revisiting the stack

The basic operation of the stack was discussed briefly in Chapter 5, "Moving Data." The stack consists of memory locations reserved at the end of the memory area allocated to the program. The ESP register is used to point to the top of the stack in memory. Data can be placed only on the top of the stack, and it can be removed only from the top of the stack.

Data is usually placed on the stack using the PUSH instruction. This places the data on the bottom of the memory area reserved for the stack and decreases the value in the stack pointer (the ESP register) to the location of the new data.

To retrieve data from the stack, the POP instruction is used. This moves the data to a register or memory location and increases the ESP register value to point to the previous stack data value.

Passing function parameters on the stack

Before a function call is made, the main program places the required input parameters for the function on the top of the stack. Of course, the programmer must know the order in which the function is expecting the data values to be placed on the stack, but that is usually part of the function documentation. The C style requires placing parameters on the stack in reverse order from the prototype for the function.

When the CALL instruction is executed, it places the return address from the calling program onto the top of the stack as well, so the function knows where to return. This leaves the stack in the state shown in Figure 11-2.

Program Stack

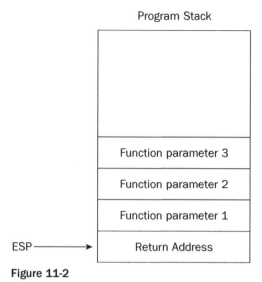

Figure 11-2

The stack pointer (ESP) points to the top of the stack, where the return address is located. All of the input parameters for the function are located "underneath" the return address on the stack. Popping values off of the stack to retrieve the input parameters would cause a problem, as the return address might be lost in the process. Instead, a different method is used to retrieve the input parameters from the stack.

Chapter 5 discussed the topic of indirect addressing using registers. This technique provides a method of accessing locations in memory based on the index value in a register. Because the ESP pointer points to the top of the stack (which contains the return address for the function), the function can use indirect addressing with the ESP register to access the input parameters without having to pop the values off of the stack. Figure 11-3 demonstrates this.

Program Stack

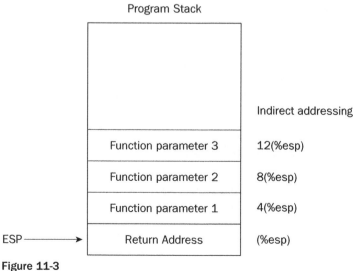

Figure 11-3

Each parameter can be indirectly accessed via the offset from the ESP register, without having to POP values off of the stack.

There is a problem with this technique, however. While in the function, it is possible that part of the function process will include pushing data onto the stack. If this happens, it would change the location of the ESP stack pointer and throw off the indirect addressing values for accessing the parameters in the stack.

To avoid this problem, it is common practice to copy the ESP register value to the EBP register when entering the function. This ensures that there is a register that always contains the correct pointer to the top of the stack when the function is called. Any data pushed onto the stack during the function would not affect the EBP register value. To avoid corrupting the original EBP register if it is used in the main program, before the ESP register value is copied, the EBP register value is also placed on the stack. This produces the scenario shown in Figure 11-4.

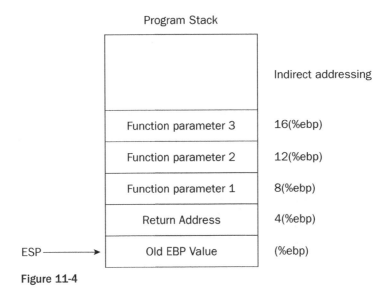

Figure 11-4

Now the EBP register contains the location of the start of the stack (which is now the old EBP register value). The first input parameter from the main program is located at the indirect addressing location 8(%ebp), the second parameter is located at the location 12(%ebp), and so on. These values can be used throughout the function without worrying about what other values are placed onto or taken off of the stack.

Function prologue and epilogue

The technique of using the stack to reference input data for the function has created a standard set of instructions that are found in all functions written using the C function style technique. This code snippet demonstrates what instructions are used for the start and end of the function code:

```
function:
    pushl %ebp
    movl %esp, %ebp
    .
    .
    movl %ebp, %esp
    popl %ebp
    ret
```

The first two instructions at the top of the function code save the original value of EBP to the top of the stack, and then copy the current ESP stack pointer (now pointing to the original value of EBP in the stack) to the EBP register.

After the function processing completes, the last two instructions in the function retrieve the original value in the ESP register that was stored in the EBP register, and restore the original EBP register value. Resetting the ESP register value ensures that any data placed on the stack within the function but not cleaned off will be discarded when execution returns to the main program (otherwise, the RET instruction could return to the wrong memory location).

The ENTER and LEAVE instructions are specifically designed for setting up function prologues (the ENTER instruction) and epilogues (the LEAVE instruction). These can be used instead of creating the prologues by hand.

Defining local function data

While the function code has control of the program, most likely the processes will need to store data elements someplace. As discussed earlier, registers can be used within the function code, but this provides a limited amount of work area. Global variables can also be used for working data, but this presents the problem of creating additional requirements for the main program to provide specific data elements for the function. When looking for an easy location for working storage for data elements within the function, the stack again comes to the rescue.

Once the EBP register is set to point to the top of the stack, any additional data used in the function can be placed on the stack after that point without affecting how the input values are accessed. This is shown in Figure 11-5.

Now that the local variables are defined on the stack, they can easily be referenced using the EBP register. Assuming 4-byte data values, the first local variable would be accessed by referencing -4(%ebp), while the second local variable would be accessed by referencing -8(%ebp).

There is still one lingering problem with this setup. If the function pushes any data onto the stack, the ESP register still points to the location before the local variables were placed and will overwrite those variables.

Program Stack

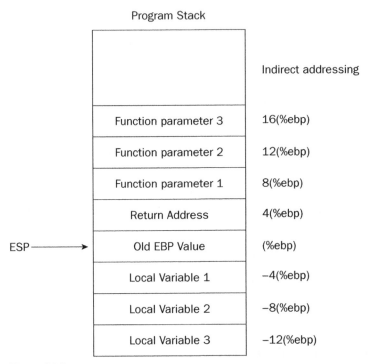

Figure 11-5

To solve this problem, at the start of the function code another line is added to reserve a set amount of stack space for local variables by subtracting the value from the ESP register. Figure 11-6 shows how this looks on the stack.

Now, if any data is pushed onto the stack, it will be placed beneath the local variables, preserving them so they can still be accessed via the EBP register pointer. The normal ESP register can still be used to push data onto the stack and pop it off of the stack without affecting the local variables.

When the end of the function is reached and the ESP register is set back to its original value, the local variables will be lost from the stack and will not be directly accessible using the ESP or EBP registers from the calling program (thus the term local variables).

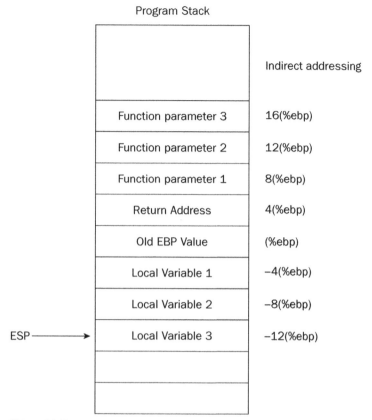

Figure 11-6

The function prologue code now must include one additional line to reserve the space for the local variables by moving the stack pointer down. You must remember to reserve enough space for all of the local variables needed in the function. The new prologue would look like this:

```
function:
    pushl %ebp
    movl %esp, %ebp
    subl $8, %esp
    .
    .
    .
```

This code reserves 8 bytes to be used for local variables. This space can be used as either two-word values or one doubleword value.

Cleaning out the stack

There is just one more detail to consider when using C style function calling. Before the function is called, the calling program places all of the required input values onto the stack. When the function returns, those values are still on the stack (since the function accessed them without popping them off of the stack). If the main program uses the stack for other things, most likely it will want to remove the old input values from the stack to get the stack back to where it was before the function call.

While you can use the POP instruction to do this, you can also just move the ESP stack pointer back to the original location before the function call. Adding back the size of the data elements pushed onto the stack using the ADD instruction does this.

For example, if you place two 4-byte integer values onto the stack and then call a function, you must add 8 to the ESP register to clean the data off of the stack:

```
pushl %eax
pushl %ebx
call compute
addl $8, %esp
```

This ensures that the stack is back to where it should be for the rest of the main program.

An example

Now that you know how to use the stack for passing input values to functions, and for local variables within the functions, it's time for an example. The functest3.s program demonstrates how all of these components can work together to simplify the area function example:

```
# functest3.s - An example of using C style functions
.section .data
precision:
    .byte 0x7f, 0x00
.section .bss
    .lcomm result, 4
.section .text
.globl _start
_start:
    nop
    finit
    fldcw precision

    pushl $10
    call area
    addl $4, %esp
    movl %eax, result

    pushl $2
    call area
    addl $4, %esp
    movl %eax, result

    pushl $120
    call area
```

```
    addl $4, %esp
    movl %eax, result

    movl $1, %eax
    movl $0, %ebx
    int $0x80

.type area, @function
area:
    pushl %ebp
    movl %esp, %ebp
    subl $4, %esp
    fldpi
    filds 8(%ebp)
    fmul %st(0), %st(0)
    fmulp %st(0), %st(1)
    fstps -4(%ebp)
    movl -4(%ebp), %eax

    movl %ebp, %esp
    popl %ebp
    ret
```

The area function code was modified to utilize the stack to retrieve the radius input value, and use a local function variable to move the result from the ST(0) register to the EAX register as a single-precision floating-point value. The result of the function is returned in the EAX register instead of the ST(0) register to help demonstrate using the local variable. In Chapter 14, "Calling Assembly Libraries," you will see that C programs expect the result in the ST(0) register.

After the standard function prologue (including reserving 4 bytes of space on the stack for a local variable), the pi value and the radius value are loaded into the FPU stack:

```
fdpi
filds 8(%ebp)
```

The 8(%ebp) value references the first parameter placed on the stack by the calling program. After the area result is calculated, it is placed in the local variable data:

```
fstps -4(%ebp)
```

The -4(%ebp) value references the first local variable on the stack. That value is placed into the EAX register, where it is retrieved by the main program.

Following that, the standard function epilogue instructions are used to replace the ESP and EBP pointer values and to return control back to the main program.

Notice the new code within the main program used for each radius value:

```
pushl $10
call area
addl $4, %esp
movl %eax, result
```

Each radius value is pushed onto the stack before the call to the `area` function. When the function completes, the stack is reset to its previous location by adding 4 (the data size of the radius value) to the ESP register. The result is then moved from the EAX register to the global variable memory location.

Watching the stack in action

You can watch how all of the data values are placed in the stack area while the program is running by using the debugger. After assembling and linking the program, run the program in the debugger, set a breakpoint at the start of the program, and look at where the stack pointer is set:

```
$ gdb -q functest3
(gdb) break *_start+1
Breakpoint 1 at 0x8048075: file functest3.s, line 11.
(gdb) run
Starting program: /home/rich/palp/chap11/functest3

Breakpoint 1, _start () at functest3.s:11
11              finit
Current language:  auto; currently asm
(gdb) print $esp
$1 = (void *) 0xbffff950
(gdb)
```

The stack point is currently set to the memory address at 0xbffff950. Step through the program until after the first PUSHL instruction before the CALL instruction, and look at the stack pointer value and the value of the data element in the last stack position:

```
(gdb) s
14              pushl $10
(gdb) s
15              call area
(gdb) print $esp
$2 = (void *) 0xbffff94c
(gdb) x/d 0xbffff94c
0xbffff94c:     10
(gdb)
```

After the PUSHL instruction, the new stack pointer value is 4 bytes less than the original (as expected). The data value pushed onto the stack is now shown at that memory location. Now, step through the CALL instruction, and again examine the stack:

```
(gdb) s
35              pushl %ebp
(gdb) print $esp
$3 = (void *) 0xbffff948
(gdb) x/x 0xbffff948
0xbffff948:     0x08048085
(gdb) x/d 0xbffff94c
0xbffff94c:     10
(gdb)
```

Again, the value of the ESP register is decreased, and the value stored there is the memory location of the instruction immediately following the CALL instruction. The input parameter is still located in the next stack position.

Control of the program is now in the area function. After stepping through the PUSHL instruction, the ESP register is again decreased, with the original value of EBP placed in the stack:

```
(gdb) s
36          movl %esp, %ebp
(gdb) print $esp
$5 = (void *) 0xbffff944
  (gdb) x/x 0xbffff944
0xbffff944:      0x00000000
(gdb)
```

Stepping through one more step in the instructions loads the ESP register value into EBP, which can now be used in indirect addressing to access the data on the stack. You can see the three values stored in the stack using the debugger:

```
(gdb) x/3x ($ebp)
0xbffff944:      0x00000000      0x08048085      0x0000000a
(gdb)
```

The stack now contains the original value of EBP, the return address from the CALL instruction, and the input value placed on the stack with the PUSH instruction.

Next, the ESP register is decreased to make room for the local variable:

```
(gdb) s
area () at functest3.s:37
37          subl $4, %esp
(gdb) s
38          fldpi
(gdb) print $esp
$1 = (void *) 0xbffff940
(gdb)
```

The new ESP location is 0xbffff940, while the EBP value is 0xbffff944. This leaves 4 bytes for a 32-bit single-precision floating-point value to be stored.

The pi value, as well as the input parameter, are loaded into the FPU stack, which can be examined using the info all command in the debugger:

```
(gdb) info all
.
.
st0   10       (raw 0x4002a000000000000000)
st1   3.1415926535897932385128089594061862 (raw 0x4000c90fdaa22168c235)
(gdb)
```

The input parameter was successfully loaded into the FPU stack using the FILDS instruction.

Stepping through the rest of the area function instructions, you can stop when the result is placed in the local variable on the stack, and see what happens:

```
(gdb) s
42          fstps -4(%ebp)
(gdb) s
43          movl -4(%ebp), %eax
(gdb) x/4x 0xbffff940
0xbffff940:     0x439d1463      0x00000000      0x08048085      0x0000000a
(gdb) x/f 0xbffff940
0xbffff940:     314.159271
(gdb)
```

The result value was placed into the stack at the −4(%ebp) location. It can be viewed in the debugger by reading the memory location and setting the output to floating-point format using the x/f command.

The last steps in the function reset the ESP and EBP registers back to their original values:

```
(gdb) s
45          movl %ebp, %esp
(gdb) s
46          popl %ebp
(gdb) print $esp
$2 = (void *) 0xbffff944
(gdb) print $ebp
$3 = (void *) 0xbffff944
(gdb) s
area () at functest3.s:47
47          ret
(gdb) print $esp
$4 = (void *) 0xbffff948
(gdb) print $ebp
$5 = (void *) 0x0
(gdb)
```

Now the ESP register points to the return location for the CALL instruction. When the RET instruction is executed, program control returns to the main program:

```
(gdb) s
area () at functest3.s:47
47          ret
(gdb) print $esp
$4 = (void *) 0xbffff948
(gdb) print $ebp
$5 = (void *) 0x0
(gdb) s
16          addl $4, %esp
(gdb) s
17          movl %eax, result
(gdb) print $esp
$6 = (void *) 0xbffff950
(gdb)
```

When control is returned, the ESP value is then increased by four to remove the radius value pushed onto the stack. The new stack pointer value is now 0xbffff950, which is where it was at the start of things. The process is ready to be started all over again with the next radius value.

Using Separate Function Files

Another benefit of using C style function calls is that the function is completely self-contained. No global memory locations need to be defined for accessing data, so .data directives do not need to be included in the functions.

This freedom creates another benefit: You no longer need to include the function source code in the same file as the main program source code. For programmers working on large projects that involve multiple people, this is a great benefit. Individual functions can be self-contained in their own files, and linked together for the final product. With code functions contained in separate files, you can see how it can quickly become a problem to continue using global variables to pass data around. Each function file would need to keep track of the global variables used.

This section demonstrates how to create separate function files, and how to assemble and link them with the main program file.

Creating a separate function file

The self-contained function file is similar to the main program files you are used to creating. The only difference is that instead of the _start section, you must declare the function name as a global label, so other programs can access it. This is done using the .globl directive:

```
.section .text
.type area, @function
.globl area
area:
```

The preceding code snippet defines the global label area, which is the start of the area function used earlier. The .type directive is used to declare that the area label points to the start of a function. The complete function is shown in the file area.s:

```
# area.s - The area function
.section .text
.type area, @function
.globl area
area:
    pushl %ebp
    movl %esp, %ebp
    subl $4, %esp
    fldpi
    filds 8(%ebp)
    fmul %st(0), %st(0)
    fmulp %st(0), %st(1)
    fstps -4(%ebp)
    movl -4(%ebp), %eax
```

```
        movl %ebp, %esp
        popl %ebp
        ret
```

The area.s file contains the complete source code for the area function, as shown in the functtest3.s program. This version uses the C style function calls, so the input value is taken from the stack, which is also used for defining a local variable. The area function uses the EAX register to return the output result.

Finally, the main program must be created, using the normal format for calling the external functions. This is shown in the functtest4.s program:

```
# functtest4.s - An example of using external functions
.section .data
precision:
    .byte 0x7f, 0x00
.section .bss
    .lcomm result, 4
.section .text
.globl _start
_start:
    nop
    finit
    fldcw precision

    pushl $10
    call area
    addl $4, %esp
    movl %eax, result

    pushl $2
    call area
    addl $4, %esp
    movl %eax, result

    pushl $120
    call area
    addl $4, %esp
    movl %eax, result

    movl $1, %eax
    movl $0, %ebx
    int $0x80
```

Because none of the code required for the area function is contained in the main program, the main program listing becomes shorter and less cluttered.

Creating the executable file

Once the function and main program files are created, they must be assembled and linked together. Each program file must be assembled separately, which creates an object file for each file:

```
$ as -gstabs -o area.o area.s
$ as -gstabs -o functtest4.o functtest4.s
$
```

Now there are two object files that are required to be linked together to create the executable file. If you do not link the function object file, the linker will produce an error:

```
$ ld -o functest4 functest4.o
functest4.o:functest4.s:15: undefined reference to 'area'
functest4.o:functest4.s:20: undefined reference to 'area'
functest4.o:functest4.s:25: undefined reference to 'area'
$
```

The linker could not resolve the calls to the area function. To create the executable program, you must include both object files in the linker command line:

```
$ ld -o functest4 functest4.o area.o
$
```

The program can now be run in the debugger as before, with the same results.

Debugging separate function files

You may have noticed that when both the function file and the main program file were assembled, I used the -gstabs command-line option. This ensured that both the function and the main program could be viewed in the debugger. Sometimes, when working on large programs that contain numerous long functions, this is not desired.

Instead of having to step through long functions several times before reaching the function you want to debug, you can choose to not debug individual function files. Instead of using the -gstabs option when assembling all of the functions, use it for only the function you want to debug, along with the main program.

For example, you can assemble the area.s function without the -gstabs option, and then watch what happens when you step through the functest4 program:

```
$ as -o area.o area.s
$ as -gstabs -o functest3.o functest4.s
$ ld -o functest4 functest4.o area.o
$ gdb -q functest4
(gdb) break *_start+1
Breakpoint 1 at 0x8048075: file functest4.s, line 11.
(gdb) run
Starting program: /home/rich/palp/chap11/functest4

Breakpoint 1, _start () at functest4.s:11
11          finit
Current language:  auto; currently asm
(gdb) s
12          fldcw precision
(gdb) s
14          pushl $10
(gdb) s
15          call area
(gdb) s
0x080480b8      31              int $0x80
```

```
(gdb) s
16          addl $4, %esp
(gdb)
```

When stepping through the main program, when the CALL instruction is executed, it is treated as a single instruction, and the next instruction in the debugger is the next instruction in the main program. All of the instructions in the area function were processed without stopping. To see that it worked properly, you can check the return values to verify that the function worked:

```
(gdb) print/f $eax
$1 = 314.159271
(gdb)
```

Indeed, the EAX register contains the result from the first call to the area function.

Using Command-Line Parameters

Related to the topic of passing parameters to functions is the topic of passing parameters to programs. Some applications require input parameters to be specified on the command line when the program is started. This section describes how you can utilize this feature in your assembly language programs.

The anatomy of a program

Different operating systems use different methods for passing command-line parameters to programs. Before trying to explain how command-line parameters are passed to programs in Linux, it's best to first explain how Linux executes programs from the command line in the first place.

When a program is run from a Linux shell prompt, the Linux system creates an area in memory for the program to operate. The memory area assigned to the program can be located anywhere on the system's physical memory. To simplify things, each program is assigned the same virtual memory addresses. The virtual memory addresses are mapped to physical memory addresses by the operating system.

The virtual memory addresses assigned to programs running in Linux start at address 0x8048000 and end at address 0xbfffffff. The Linux OS places the program within the virtual memory address area in a specific format, shown in Figure 11-7.

The first block in the memory area contains all the instructions and data (from both the .bss and .data sections) of the assembly program. The instructions include not only the instruction codes from your assembly program, but also the necessary instruction information from the linking process for Linux to run the program.

The second block in the memory area is the program stack. As mentioned in Chapter 2, "The IA-32 Platform," the stack grows downward from the end of the memory area. Given this information, you would expect the stack pointer to be set to 0xbfffffff each time a program starts, but this is not the case. Before the program loads, Linux places a few things into the stack, which is where the command-line parameters come in.

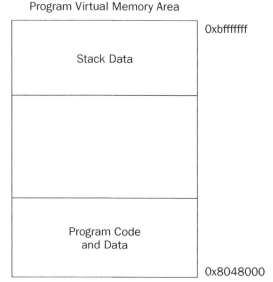

Program Virtual Memory Area

Figure 11-7

Analyzing the stack

Linux places four types of information into the program stack when the program starts:

❏   The number of command-line parameters (including the program name)

❏   The name of the program as executed from the shell prompt

❏   Any command-line parameters included on the command line

❏   All the current Linux environment variables at the start of the program

The program name, command-line parameters, and environment variables are variable-length strings that are null terminated. To make your life a little easier, Linux not only loads the strings into the stack, it also loads pointers to each of these elements into the stack, so you can easily locate them in your program.

The layout of the stack when a program starts generally looks like what is shown in Figure 11-8.

Starting at the stack pointer (ESP), the number of command-line parameters used to start the program is specified as a 4-byte unsigned integer value. Following that, the 4-byte pointer to the program name location is placed in the next location in the stack. After that, pointers to each of the command-line parameters are placed in the stack (again, each 4 bytes in length).

Program Stack

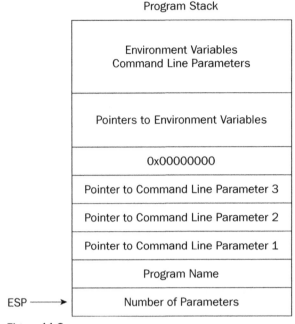

Figure 11-8

You can use the debugger to see how this works. Run the functtest4 program (presented earlier in the section "Creating a separate function file") in the debugger, and watch the stack when the program starts. First, start the program, and give it a command-line parameter (this is done in the run command in the debugger):

```
$ gdb -q functtest4
(gdb) break *_start+1
Breakpoint 1 at 0x8048075: file functtest4.s, line 11.
(gdb) run 10
Starting program: /home/rich/palp/chap11/functtest4 10

Breakpoint 1, _start () at functtest4.s:11
11          finit
Current language:  auto; currently asm
(gdb) print $esp
$1 = (void *) 0xbffff950
(gdb)
```

Notice that the starting program line indicates the command-line parameter specified in the run command. The ESP pointer shows that it is pointing to memory location 0xbffff950. This indicates the top of the stack. You can view the values there using the x command:

```
(gdb) x/20x 0xbffff950
0xbffff950:   0x00000002   0xbffffa36   0xbffffa57   0x00000000
0xbffff960:   0xbffffa5a   0xbffffa75   0xbffffa95   0xbffffaa7
0xbffff970:   0xbffffabf   0xbffffadf   0xbffffaf2   0xbffffb14
```

```
0xbffff980:    0xbffffb26    0xbffffb38    0xbffffb41    0xbffffb4b
0xbffff990:    0xbffffd29    0xbffffd37    0xbffffd58    0xbffffd72
(gdb)
```

The x/20x command displays the first 20 bytes starting at the specified memory location, in hexadecimal format. The first value indicates the number of command-line parameters (including the program name). The next two memory locations contain pointers to the program name and command-line parameter strings as stored later in the stack. You can view the string values using the x command and the pointer address:

```
(gdb) x/s 0xbffffa36
0xbffffa36:       "/home/rich/palp/chap11/functest4"
(gdb) x/s 0xbffffa57
0xbffffa57:       "10"
(gdb)
```

As expected, the first pointer pointed to the program name string stored in the stack area. The second pointer pointed to the string for the command-line parameter.

> *Be careful: It is important to remember that all command-line parameters are specified as strings, even if they look like numbers.*

After the command-line parameters, a 4-byte null value is placed on the stack to separate them from the start of the pointers to the environment variables. Again, you can use the x command to view some of the environment variables stored on the stack:

```
(gdb) x/s 0xbffffa5a
0xbffffa5a:       "PWD=/home/rich/palp/chap11"
(gdb) x/s 0xbffffa75
0xbffffa75:       "http_proxy=http://webproxy:1234"
(gdb) x/s 0xbffffa95
0xbffffa95:       "LC_MESSAGES=en_US"
(gdb) x/s 0xbffffaa7
0xbffffaa7:       "HOSTNAME=test1.blum.lan"
(gdb) x/s 0xbffffabf
0xbffffabf:       "NLSPATH=/usr/share/locale/%l/%N"
(gdb) x/s 0xbffffadf
0xbffffadf:       "LESSKEY=/etc/.less"
(gdb)
```

Depending on what applications you have loaded on your Linux box, numerous environment variables may be loaded here.

Viewing command-line parameters

Now that you know where the command-line parameters are located on the stack, it is easy to write a simple program to access them and list them. The paramtest1.s program does just that.

```
# paramtest1.s - Listing command line parameters
.section .data
output1:
    .asciz "There are %d parameters:\n"
```

```
output2:
    .asciz "%s\n"
.section .text
.globl _start
_start:
    movl (%esp), %ecx
    pushl %ecx
    pushl $output1
    call printf
    addl $4, %esp
    popl %ecx
    movl %esp, %ebp
    addl $4, %ebp
loop1:
    pushl %ecx
    pushl (%ebp)
    pushl $output2
    call printf
    addl $8, %esp
    popl %ecx
    addl $4, %ebp
    loop loop1
    pushl $0
    call exit
```

The paramtest1.s program first reads the number of command-line parameter values from the top of the stack and places the value in the ECX register (so it can be used as a loop value). After that, it pushed the value onto the stack, along with the output text string for the printf C library function to display.

After the call to the printf function, you must clean the pushed values off of the stack. In this case, however, it works to our advantage, as we need to restore the ECX value after the printf function destroyed it. Next, the stack pointer in the ESP register is copied to the EBP pointer, so we can walk through the values without destroying the stack pointer. The EBP pointer is incremented by four to skip over the command-line parameter count value, ready to read the first parameter.

In the loop, first the current value of ECX is pushed onto the stack so it can be restored after the printf function. Next, the pointer to the first command-line parameter string (located in the memory address pointed to by the EBP register) is pushed onto the stack, along with the output string to display it for the printf function. After the printf function returns, the two values pushed onto the stack are removed by adding eight to the ESP pointer, and the ECX value is popped from the stack. The EBP register value is then incremented by four to point to the next command-line parameter pointer value in the stack.

After assembling the program and linking it with the C libraries on the Linux system, you can test it out with any number of command-line parameters:

```
$ ./paramtest1 testing 1 2 3 testing
There are 6 parameters:
./paramtest1
testing
1
2
3
testing
$
```

Remember that the program name is considered the first parameter, with the first command-line parameter being the second parameter, and so on. A common beginner's mistake is to check the number of command-line parameters for a zero value. It will never be zero, as the program name must always be present on the command line.

Viewing environment variables

Just like viewing the command-line parameters, you can walk through the pointers stored in the program stack and view all the system environment variables. The `paramtest2.s` program demonstrates doing this:

```
# paramtest2.s - Listing system environment variables
.section .data
output:
    .asciz "%s\n"
.section .text
.globl _start
_start:
    movl %esp, %ebp
    addl $12, %ebp
loop1:
    cmpl $0, (%ebp)
    je endit
    pushl (%ebp)
    pushl $output
    call printf
    addl $12, %esp
    addl $4, %ebp
    loop loop1
endit:
    pushl $0
    call exit
```

When no command-line parameters are specified, the environment variable section starts at offset 12 of the ESP register. The end of the environment variables section is defined as a NULL string. Comparing the value in the stack with zero checks for this condition. If it is not zero, the pointer location is displayed using the `printf` C function.

After assembling the program and linking it with the C function libraries, you can run the `paramtest2` program on your system to see the active environment variables:

```
$ ./paramtest2
TERM=xterm
SHELL=/bin/bash
SSH_CLIENT=192.168.0.4 1698 22
QTDIR=/usr/share/qt3
OLDPWD=/home/rich
SSH_TTY=/dev/pts/0
USER=rich
KDEDIR=/usr
MAIL=/var/mail/rich
PATH=/bin:/sbin:/usr/bin:/usr/sbin:/usr/X11R6/bin:/usr/local/bin:/usr/local/sbin:/u
sr/games
```

```
PWD=/home/rich/palp/chap11
LANG=en_US
SHLVL=1
HOME=/home/rich
LOGNAME=rich
SSH_CONNECTION=192.168.0.4 1698 192.168.0.100 22
_=./paramtest2
$
```

The environment variables present on your system will vary depending on what applications are running and what local settings are specified. You can test this yourself by creating a new environment variable and running the program again:

```
$ TESTING=/home/rich ; export TESTING
$ ./paramtest2
.
.
.
TESTING=/home/rich
_=./paramtest2
$
```

As expected, the new environment variable shows up in the program stack.

An example using command-line parameters

As mentioned in the "Analyzing the stack" section, command-line parameters are stored in the stack as string values. If you intend for them to be used as numbers, it is up to you to do the conversion.

There are many ways to convert strings to integer or floating-point values. You can do an Internet search for some handy assembly language utilities for performing the conversion. If you are not averse to using the C library functions in your assembly language programs, the standard C conversion utilities are available to use:

❑   **atoi():** Converts an ASCII string to a short integer value

❑   **atol():** Converts an ASCII string to a long integer value

❑   **atof():** Converts an ASCII string to a double-precision floating-point value

Each of these functions requires that a pointer to the parameter string location be placed on the stack before the function call. The result for the atoi() function is returned in the EAX register. The result for the atol() function is placed in the EDX:EAX register pair (since they require 64 bits). The atof() function returns its result in the FPU ST(0) register.

The paramtest3.s program demonstrates how to read a command-line parameter, convert it to an integer value, and then process it by calculating our old friend the area value from it:

```
# paramtest3.s - An example of using command line parameters
.section .data
output:
```

```
        .asciz "The area is: %f\n"
.section .bss
    .lcomm result, 4
.section .text
.globl _start
_start:
    nop
    finit

    pushl 8(%esp)
    call atoi
    addl $4, %esp
    movl %eax, result
    fldpi
    filds result
    fmul %st(0), %st(0)
    fmul %st(1), %st(0)
    fstpl (%esp)
    pushl $output
    call printf
    addl $12, %esp

    pushl $0
    call exit
```

The paramtest3.s program pushes the pointer to the first command-line parameter onto the stack, and calls the atoi() C function to convert the parameter string into an integer value. The integer value is returned in the EAX register, which is copied to a memory location. The stack pointer is moved to remove the parameter from the stack.

Next, the FLDPI instruction is used to load the pi value into the FPU stack, and then the FILDS instruction is used to move the parameter stored as a 4-byte integer value into the FPU stack. After that, the normal calculations to determine the area of the circle are made. When they are finished, the result is located in the ST(0) FPU stack register. The FSTPL instruction is used to push the double-precision floating-point value onto the program stack for the printf function to display.

After assembling the program and linking it with the C libraries, you can easily test different radius values:

```
$ ./paramtest3 10
The area is: 314.159265
$ ./paramtest3 2
The area is: 12.566371
$ ./paramtest3 120
The area is: 45238.934212
$
```

Now this is starting to look like a professional program!

Summary

This chapter discussed the topic of assembly language functions. Functions can save time by eliminating the need to code the same utilities multiple times, and streamline the programming process, by enabling functions to be spread across separate files that different programmers can work on simultaneously.

When creating a function, you must first determine its requirements. These include how data is passed to the function, what registers and memory locations are used for processing the data, and how the results are passed back to the calling program. Three basic techniques are used for passing data between functions and the calling programs: registers, common memory locations defined in the calling program, and the program stack. If the function uses the same registers and memory locations to process data as the calling program, care must be taken. The calling program must save any registers whose values are important before calling the function, and then restore them when the function returns.

Because there are so many options available for passing data between functions and calling programs, a standard method was devised to help simplify things. The C style of functions uses the program stack to pass input values to functions without requiring registers or memory locations. Each input value is pushed onto the stack by the calling program before the function is called. Instead of popping the data from the stack, the function uses indirect addressing with the EBP register as a pointer to access the input values. Additionally, extra space can be reserved on the stack by the function to hold data elements used within the function process. This makes it possible for the function to be completely self-contained, without using any resources supplied by the calling program.

Because C style functions are completely self-contained, they can be created in separate source code files and assembled separately from the main program. This feature enables multiple programmers to work on different functions independently of one another. All that is needed is the knowledge of which functions perform what tasks, and the order in which input values should be passed to the functions.

Passing input parameters is not just a function requirement. Many assembly language programs require input data to process. One method of supplying the input data is on the command line when the program is executed. The Linux operating system provides a standard way of passing command-line parameters to programs within the stack area. You can utilize this information within your assembly language program to access the command-line parameters using indirect addressing.

The first value at the top of the stack when a program starts in Linux is the number of command-line parameters (including the program name itself). The next value in the stack is a pointer to the program name string stored further back in the stack. Following that, a pointer is entered for each command-line parameter entered. Each parameter is stored as a null-terminated string further back in the stack and is accessible via the pointer supplied earlier in the stack. Finally, each system environment variable active at the time the program starts is placed in the stack area. This feature enables programs to utilize environment variables for setting values and options for the program.

The next chapter discusses a different type of function provided by the Linux operating system. The operating system kernel supplies many standard functions, such as displaying data, reading data files, and exiting programs. Assembly language programs can tap into this wealth of information using software interrupts. Similar to a function call, the software interrupt transfers control of the program to the kernel function. Input and output values are passed via registers. This is a handy way to access common Linux functions from your assembly language program.

12

Using Linux System Calls

The previous chapter showed how assembly language routines can be stored as functions that can be accessed by any program. This chapter describes another technique for accessing functions that involves using software interrupts.

Most operating systems provide core functions that application programs can access. Linux is not different. The core of the Linux operating system provides many functions that applications can access to easily access files, determine user and group permissions, access network resources, and retrieve and display data. These functions are called *system calls*.

This chapter first describes how the Linux operating system provides system calls and then examines the resources that can be used. Next, examples are shown for incorporating system calls into your assembly language programs. If you use a lot of system calls in your applications, you will probably need a method to use for debugging. The `strace` application is a great tool to use for watching system calls in action. It is described in this chapter, along with examples of different ways to use it. Finally, you'll see a comparison between using Linux system calls and C library functions.

The Linux Kernel

The core of the Linux operating system is the kernel. Before discussing system calls, it helps to understand what is happening under the hood of the operating system that provides the system calls. This section provides a brief description of the Linux kernel and explains why it provides system calls. If you are already familiar with the Linux kernel, feel free to skip to the next section.

Parts of the kernel

The kernel software is the core of the operating system. It controls the hardware and software on the system, allocating hardware when necessary, and executing software when required. The kernel is primarily responsible for four things:

❑ Memory management

❑ Device management

❑ File system management

❑ Process management

The system calls provided by the kernel provide interfaces so programs can interact with each of these parts of the operating system. Knowing what each of these parts does helps in understanding what the system calls try to accomplish. The following sections describe these features and how the system calls are used to provide interfaces to the features.

Memory management

One of the primary functions of the operating system kernel is memory management. Not only does the kernel manage the physical memory available on the server, it can also create and manage "virtual memory," or memory that does not physically exist on the motherboard.

It does this by using space on the hard disk, called *swap space,* swapping memory locations back and forth from the hard disk to the actual physical memory. This enables the system to assume there is more memory available than what physically exists. The memory locations are grouped into blocks called *pages.* Each page of memory is located either in the physical memory or the swap space. The kernel must maintain a table of the memory pages that indicates which pages are where.

The kernel will automatically copy memory pages that have not been accessed for a period of time to the swap space area on the hard disk. When a program wants to access a memory page that has been "swapped out," the kernel must swap out a different memory page and swap in the required page from the swap space.

On Linux systems, the current status of the virtual memory can be determined by viewing the special /proc/meminfo file. The output of the meminfo file differs between different Linux systems but generally should look something like the following:

```
$ cat /proc/meminfo
        total:    used:     free:  shared: buffers:  cached:
Mem:   129957888 119554048 10403840       0 34099200 37548032
Swap: 254943232  2945024 251998208
MemTotal:       126912 kB
MemFree:         10160 kB
MemShared:           0 kB
Buffers:         33300 kB
Cached:          36668 kB
Active:          23116 kB
Inact_dirty:     46064 kB
Inact_clean:       788 kB
```

```
Inact_target:         12 kB
HighTotal:             0 kB
HighFree:              0 kB
LowTotal:         126912 kB
LowFree:           10160 kB
SwapTotal:        248968 kB
SwapFree:         246092 kB
$
```

The first line shows the Linux command used to view the /proc/meminfo file. The third line shows that this Linux server has 128MB of physical memory. It also shows that about 10MB are not currently being used. The next line shows that about 252MB of swap space memory are available on this system.

Each process running on the Linux system has its own private memory area. One process cannot access memory being used by another process. No processes can access memory used by the kernel processes. To facilitate data sharing, shared memory segments can be created. Multiple processes can read and write to a common shared memory area. The kernel must maintain and administer the shared memory areas. The ipcs command can be used to view the current shared memory segments on the system:

```
# ipcs -m

------ Shared Memory Segments --------
key         shmid      owner     perms   bytes      nattch   status
0x00000000 0          root      600     1056768    5        dest
0x00000000 32769      apache    600     46084      5        dest
0x00000000 65538      root      600     1056768    5        dest
0x00000000 10289155   root      600     520192     5        dest
0x00000000 131076     apache    600     46084      5        dest
0x0052e2ca 163845     postgres  700     144        1
0x0052e2c1 196614     postgres  600     1104896    1
0x0052e2c7 229383     postgres  600     66060      1

#
```

This shows the ipcs command using the -m option to display just the shared memory segments. Each shared memory segment has an owner that created the segment. Each segment also has a standard UNIX permissions setting that sets the availability of the segment to other users. The key value is used to enable other users to gain access to the shared memory segment.

Device management

Another responsibility for the kernel is hardware management. Any device that the Linux system must communicate with needs driver code inserted inside the kernel code. The driver code enables the kernel to pass data back and forth to the device from a common interface. Two methods are used for inserting device driver code in the Linux kernel:

❑   Compiling the driver code into the kernel code

❑   Inserting the driver code into the running kernel

Previously, the only way to insert a device driver code was to recompile the kernel. Each time a new device was added to the system, the kernel code needed to be recompiled. This process became more inefficient as Linux kernels supported more hardware.

A better method was developed to insert driver code into the running kernel. The concept of *kernel modules* was developed to enable driver code to be inserted into a running kernel, and also removed from the kernel when the device was finished being used.

Hardware devices are identified on the UNIX server as special device files. There are three different classifications of device files:

- ❑   Character
- ❑   Block
- ❑   Network

Character files are for devices that can only handle data one character at a time. Most types of terminal interfaces are created as character files. Block files are used for devices that handle data in large blocks at a time, such as disk drives. The network file types are used for devices that use packets to send and receive data. This includes network cards and the special loopback device that enables the Linux system to communicate with itself using common network programming protocols.

Device files are created in the file system as nodes. Each node has a unique number pair that identifies it to the Linux kernel. The number pair includes a major and minor device number. Similar devices are grouped into the same major device number. The minor device number is used to identify the device within the major device numbers. Here's a listing of some sample devices on a Linux system:

```
# ls -al hda*
brw-rw----    1 root     disk        3,    0 Apr 14  2001 hda
brw-rw----    1 root     disk        3,    1 Apr 14  2001 hda1
brw-rw----    1 root     disk        3,   10 Apr 14  2001 hda10
brw-rw----    1 root     disk        3,    2 Apr 14  2001 hda2
brw-rw----    1 root     disk        3,    3 Apr 14  2001 hda3
brw-rw----    1 root     disk        3,    4 Apr 14  2001 hda4
brw-rw----    1 root     disk        3,    5 Apr 14  2001 hda5
# ls -al ttyS*
[root@test2 /dev]# ls -al ttyS* | more
crw-rw----    1 root     uucp        4,   64 Apr 14  2001 ttyS0
crw-rw----    1 root     uucp        4,   65 Apr 14  2001 ttyS1
crw-rw----    1 root     uucp        4,   74 Apr 14  2001 ttyS10
crw-rw----    1 root     uucp        4,  164 Apr 14  2001 ttyS100
crw-rw----    1 root     uucp        4,  165 Apr 14  2001 ttyS101
crw-rw----    1 root     uucp        4,  166 Apr 14  2001 ttyS102
crw-rw----    1 root     uucp        4,  167 Apr 14  2001 ttyS103
#
```

This shows the `ls` command being used to display some of the entries for the hda and ttyS devices. The hda device is the first IDE hard drive partition found on the system, and the ttyS devices are the standard IBM PC COM ports. The listing shows that several hda devices were created on the sample Linux system. Not all of them are actually used, but they are created in case the administrator needs them. Similarly, the listing shows that several ttyS devices were created as well.

The fifth column in the listing is the major device node number. Notice that all of the hda devices have the same major device node, 3, and that all of the ttyS devices use 4. The sixth column is the minor device node number. Each device within a major number has its own unique minor device node number. This is how the kernel accesses each device individually.

The first column indicates the permissions for the device file. The first character of the permissions indicates the type of file. Notice that the IDE hard drive files are all marked as block (b) files, while the COM port device files are marked as character (c) files.

File system management

Unlike some other operating systems, the Linux kernel can support different types of file systems to read and write data to hard drives. Currently, 15 different file system types are available on Linux systems. The kernel must be compiled with support for all the types of file systems that the system will use. The following table describes the standard file systems available on Linux systems.

File System	Description
affs	Amiga file system
ext	Linux Extended file system
ext2	Second extended file system
ext3	Third extended file system
hpfs	OS/2 high-performance file system
iso9660	ISO 9660 file system (CD-ROMs)
minix	MINIX file system
msdos	Microsoft FAT16
ncp	Netware file system
proc	Access to system information
reiserfs	Journaling file system
sysv	Older UNIX file system
ufs	BSD file system
umsdos	UNIX-like file system that resides on top of MS-DOS
vfat	Windows 95 file system (fat32)

Any hard drive that a Linux system accesses must be formatted using one of the file system types listed in the table. Formatting a Linux file system is similar to formatting a Microsoft Windows type disk. The operating system must build the necessary file system information onto the disk before the disk can be used to store information.

The Linux kernel interfaces with each file system using the Virtual File System (VFS). This provides a standard interface for the kernel to communicate with any type of file system. VFS caches information in memory as each file system is mounted and used.

The kernel provides system calls to help manage and access files on each of the different file systems using VFS. A single system call can be used to access files on any file system type.

Process management

The Linux operating system handles programs as processes. The kernel controls how processes are managed in the system. The kernel creates the first process, called the *init* process, to start all other processes on the system. When the kernel starts, the init process is loaded into virtual memory. As each process is started, it is given an area in virtual memory to store data and code that will be executed by the system.

Some Linux implementations contain a table of terminal processes to start automatically on bootup. Each terminal process provides an access point for interactively logging into the Linux system. When the init process starts, it reads the file /etc/inittabs to determine what terminal processes it must start on the system.

The Linux operating system uses an init system that utilizes *run levels*. A run level can be used to direct the init process to run only certain types of processes. There are five init run levels in the Linux operating system.

At run level 1, only the basic system processes are started, along with one console terminal process. This is called *single-user mode*. Single-user mode is most often used for file system maintenance. The standard init run level is 3. At this run level, most application software, such as network support software, is started. Another popular run level in Linux is run level 5. This is the run level on which the X Window software is started. Notice how the Linux system can control overall system functionality by controlling the init run level. By changing the run level from 3 to 5, the system can change from a console-based system to an advanced, graphical X Window system.

To view the currently active process on the Linux system, you can use the ps command. The format of the ps command is

```
ps options
```

where options is a list of options that can modify the output of the ps command. The following table describes the options that are available.

Option	Description
l	Use the long format to display
u	Use user format (shows user name and start time)
j	Use job format (shows process gid and sid)
s	Use signal format
v	Use vm format
m	Displays memory information
f	Use "forest" format (displays processes as a tree)
a	Show processes of other users
x	Show processes without a controlling terminal
S	Show child CPU and time and page faults

Option	Description
c	Command name for task_struct
e	Shows environment after command line and a +
w	Use wide output format
h	Do not display the header
r	Show running processes only
n	Show numeric output for USER and WCHAN
txx	Show the processes that are controlled by terminal ttyxx
O	Order the process listing using sort keys k1, k2, and so on
pids	Show only the specified pids

Numerous options are available to modify the ps command output. Here's a sample output from a ps listing:

```
# ps ax
  PID TTY   STAT    TIME COMMAND
    1 ?     S       1:16 init [5]
    2 ?     SW      0:00 [keventd]
    3 ?     SW  131884:22 [kapm-idled]
    4 ?     SW      5:54 [kswapd]
    5 ?     SW      0:00 [kreclaimd]
    6 ?     SW      2:32 [bdflush]
    7 ?     SW      2:39 [kupdated]
    8 ?     SW<     0:00 [mdrecoveryd]
   63 ?     S       0:00 open -w -s -c 12 /sbin/Monitor-NewStyle-Categorizing-WsLib
   68 tty12 S       0:03 /sbin/Monitor-NewStyle-Categorizing-WsLib
  565 ?     SW      0:00 [khubd]
  663 ?     S       0:00 /sbin/cardmgr
  814 ?     SW      0:00 [eth0]
  876 ?     S       0:11 syslogd -m 0
  885 ?     S       0:00 klogd -2
  981 ?     S       0:00 xinetd -reuse -pidfile /var/run/xinetd.pid
 1292 ?     S       0:23 httpd-perl -f /etc/httpd/conf/httpd-perl.conf -DPERLPROXIED
 1299 ?     S       0:00 httpd-perl -f /etc/httpd/conf/httpd-perl.conf -DPERLPROXIED
 1300 ?     S       0:00 httpd-perl -f /etc/httpd/conf/httpd-perl.conf -DPERLPROXIED
 1301 ?     S       0:00 httpd-perl -f /etc/httpd/conf/httpd-perl.conf -DPERLPROXIED
 1302 ?     S       0:00 httpd-perl -f /etc/httpd/conf/httpd-perl.conf -DPERLPROXIED
 1307 ?     S       0:55 httpd -DPERLPROXIED -DHAVE_SSL -DHAVE_PROXY -DHAVE_ACCESS
 1293 ?     S       0:00 pickup -l -t fifo
 2359 ?     S       0:00 /usr/sbin/sshd
 2360 pts/0 S       0:00 -bash
 2422 pts/0 S       0:00 su
 2423 pts/0 S       0:00 bash
 2966 pts/0 R       0:00 ps ax
#
```

The first line shows the ps command as entered on the command line. Both the a and x options are used for the output to display all processes running on the system. The first column in the output shows the process ID (or PID) of the process. The third line shows the init process started by the kernel. The init process is assigned PID 1. All other processes that start after the init process are assigned PIDs in numerical order. No two processes can have the same PID.

The third column shows the current status of the process. The following table describes the possible process status codes.

Code	Description
D	Uninterruptible sleep
L	Process has pages locked into memory
N	Low-priority task
R	Runable
S	The process has asked for a page replacement (sleeping)
T	Traced or stopped
Z	A defunct (zombie) process
W	Process has no resident pages
<	High-priority process

The process name is shown in the last column. Processes that are in brackets, [], are processes that have been swapped out of memory to the disk swap space due to inactivity. You can see that some of the processes have been swapped out, but most of the running processes have not.

Linux kernel version

Which kernel version the system runs directly affects which system calls are available for your application to use. As each newer version of the kernel is produced, additional system calls are created to assist programmers in different areas.

The development of the Linux kernel has evolved at a very rapid pace. Linux Torvalds maintains strict control over the Linux kernel, although he accepts change requests from anyone, anywhere. Many advances in the Linux kernel design have been made over the years, such as the addition of modules.

The kernel developers use a strict version-control system. The format of a kernel release is

```
linux-a.b.c
```

where a is the major release number, b is the minor release number, and c is the patch number (often there are intermediate patches, so the c value can also be c.d, where x is the intermediate patch number). A convention has been established whereby odd-numbered minor releases are considered developmental releases, and even-numbered minor releases are considered stable production releases.

At the time of this writing, the current stable production release of the Linux kernel is 2.6.8.1, whereas the current development release is 2.4.2-pre1. Although version 2.4.1 is the current kernel release, most Linux distributions have not released versions using this kernel.

To determine the kernel version your Linux system is using, you can use the uname command with the -a option. On my Mandrake Linux 8.0 system, it produces the following output:

```
$ uname -a
Linux test.blum.lan 2.4.3-20mdk #1 Sun Apr 15 23:03:10 CEST 2001 i686 unknown
$
```

The third item in the list is the kernel version. For this system, the core Linux kernel used is version 2.4.3, with some Mandrake extensions added.

System Calls

Now that you know what the Linux kernel is about, it's time to see the kernel system calls that are provided. Many system calls are provided by the kernel, and knowing how to find and use them is beneficial in assembly language programming. This section shows how to utilize Linux system calls in your programs.

Finding system calls

As mentioned, numerous system calls are available for programmers to use. Often, with each release of a new kernel, new system calls are added to the list. It is easy to determine which system calls are available for use on your system — just look at the kernel.

If your Linux system has been configured for a programming development environment (which, if you are assembling programs, it most likely is), the system calls are defined in the following file:

```
/usr/include/asm/unistd.h
```

The unistd.h file contains definitions for each of the system calls available in the kernel. The first few lines of the file look like this:

```
#ifndef _ASM_I386_UNISTD_H_
#define _ASM_I386_UNISTD_H_

/*
 * This file contains the system call numbers.
 */

#define __NR_exit                 1
#define __NR_fork                 2
#define __NR_read                 3
#define __NR_write                4
#define __NR_open                 5
#define __NR_close                6
#define __NR_waitpid              7
```

```
#define __NR_creat          8
#define __NR_link           9
#define __NR_unlink        10
#define __NR_execve        11
#define __NR_chdir         12
#define __NR_time          13
#define __NR_mknod         14
#define __NR_chmod         15
#define __NR_lchown        16
```

Each system call is defined as a name (preceded by __NR_), and its system call number. As you will see in the next section, the system call number is crucial to assembly language programmers, as that is how the assembly program references the system call.

Finding system call definitions

In the unistd.h file on my Linux system, 221 system calls are defined. If you are interested in using any of the system calls, you must know the format of the call for the assembly language program.

Once you find the system call you need to use in the system call list on your system, you can usually find the definition in the system's man pages (if they have been installed). Section 2 of the man pages contains the definitions of all the system calls available.

If the man pages for your system are not installed, consult the Linux distribution documentation for installing them.

To access the system call definitions, use the man command from the command prompt:

```
# man 2 exit
```

The 2 in the command line specifies section 2 of the man pages. Don't forget to include it, as some system calls also contain shell commands that are listed in section 1 of the man pages. These will be shown instead of the system call definition. The exit option specifies the system call name to get information for. The man page contains four main parts:

❑   **Name:** Shows the name of the system call

❑   **Synopsis:** Shows how the system call is used

❑   **Description:** A brief description of the system call

❑   **Return Value:** The value returned when the system call finishes

Here's what it looks like for the exit system call:

```
NAME
        _exit - terminate the current process

SYNOPSIS
        #include <unistd.h>
```

```
        void _exit(int status);

DESCRIPTION
        _exit terminates the calling process immediately. Any open
        file descriptors belonging to the process are closed;  any
        children  of the process are inherited by process 1, init,
        and the process's parent is sent a SIGCHLD signal.

        status is returned to the parent process as the  process's
        exit  status,  and  can be collected using one of the wait
        family of calls.

RETURN VALUE
        _exit never returns.
```

The synopsis section is written for C programmers, but we assembly language programmers can benefit from it as well. The synopsis of the system call shows that it takes a single integer input value (the value in the parentheses), and does not produce a return value.

Common system calls

While there are many system calls from which to choose, most common programming functions require just a few different system calls. This section describes some of the more common system calls used, grouped by kernel features.

The memory-access kernel system calls are described in the following table.

System Call	Description
brk	Change the data segment size.
mlock	Disable paging for parts of memory.
mlockall	Disable paging for the calling process.
mmap	Map files or devices into memory.
mprotect	Control allowable accesses to a region of memory.
mremap	Remap a virtual memory address.
msync	Synchronize the file with a memory map.
munlock	Enable paging for parts of memory.
munlockall	Enable paging for calling process.
munmap	Unmap files or devices from memory.

The common device-access kernel system calls are described in the next table.

339

System Call	Description
access	Check permissions for a device.
chmod	Change permissions for a device.
chown	Change the ownership for a device.
close	Close a device file descriptor.
dup	Duplicate a device file descriptor.
fcntl	Manipulate the file descriptor.
fstat	Get the status of a device.
ioctl	Control a device's parameters.
link	Assign a new name to a file descriptor.
lseek	Reposition the read/write file offset.
mknod	Create a new file descriptor for a device.
open	Open/create a file descriptor for a device or file.
read	Read from a device file descriptor.
write	Write to a device file descriptor.

The file-system system calls are described in the following table.

System Call	Description
chdir	Change the working directory.
chroot	Change the root directory.
flock	Apply or remove an advisory lock on an open file.
statfs	Get file system statistics.
getcwd	Get the current working directory.
mkdir	Create a directory.
rmdir	Remove a directory.
symlink	Make a new name for a file.
umask	Set the file creation mask.
mount	Mount and unmount file systems.
swapon	Start swapping memory to the file system.
swapoff	Stop swapping memory to the file system.

Finally, the process-system calls are described in the next table.

System Call	Description
acct	Turn process accounting on or off.
capget	Get process capabilities.
capset	Set process capabilities.
clone	Create a child process.
execve	Execute a program.
exit	Terminate the current process.
fork	Create a child process.
getgid	Get the group identity.
getpgrp	Get/set the process group.
getppid	Get process identification.
getpriority	Get the program scheduling priority.
getuid	Get the user identity.
kill	Send a signal to kill a process.
nice	Change the process priority.
vfork	Create a child process and block the parent.

Using System Calls

Using system calls in assembly language programs can be complicated. This section describes how to use system calls, and walks through the process of using them in an example program.

The system call format

As you have already seen in the examples in this book, to initiate a system call, the INT instruction is used. The Linux system calls are located at interrupt 0x80. When the INT instruction is performed, all operations transfer to the system call handler in the kernel. When the system call is complete, execution transfers back to the next instruction after the INT instruction (unless, of course, the exit system call is performed).

The following sections show how to create the system call.

System call values

If you have been working along in the book, you already know from the example programs presented that the EAX register is used to hold the system call value. This value defines which system call is used from the list of system calls supported by the kernel.

The integers listed next to the system call names in the unistd.h file are the system call *values*. Each system call is assigned a unique number to identify it. The desired value is moved into the EAX register before the INT instruction is performed. A good example of this is the exit system call that has already been used in this book:

```
movl $1, %eax
int 0x80
```

In the unistd.h file, the exit system call is defined as follows:

```
#define __NR_exit               1
```

This indicates that the system call value to perform the exit system call is 1. This value is loaded into the EAX register using the standard MOVL instruction. After placing the system call value in the EAX register, the INT instruction is performed, using the vector value for the kernel system calls (0x80).

System call input values

Unlike C style functions, where the input values are placed on the stack, system calls require that input values be placed in registers. There is a specific order in which each input value is placed in the registers. Placing the wrong input value in a wrong register can produce catastrophic results.

You have already seen that the EAX register is used to hold the system call value to perform. The EIP, EBP, and ESP registers cannot be used, as that would adversely affect the program operation. This leaves five registers available to hold input values.

As mentioned, the order in which input values are placed in the registers is important. The order in which the system calls expect input values is as follows:

- ❑ EBX (first parameter)
- ❑ ECX (second parameter)
- ❑ EDX (third parameter)
- ❑ ESI (fourth parameter)
- ❑ EDI (fifth parameter)

System calls that require more than six input parameters use a different method of passing the parameters to the system call. The EBX register is used to contain a pointer to the memory location of the input parameters, stored in sequential order. The system call uses the pointer to access the memory location to read the parameters.

The next trick is deciding which parameter in the system call function belongs in which order. To describe this, it's best to walk through an example.

The write() system call is used to write data to a file descriptor. If you look in the man pages, the synopsis of the system call is as follows:

```
SYNOPSIS
       #include <unistd.h>

       ssize_t write(int fd, const void *buf, size_t count);
```

The parameter numbers are set left to right as they appear in the synopsis. The first paramter (fd) is an integer value representing the file descriptor for the output device. The second parameter (buf) is a pointer to the string to write to the device. The third parameter (count) is the size of the string to display.

Using this convention, the input values would be assigned to the following registers:

❑   **EBX:** The integer file descriptor

❑   **ECX:** The pointer (memory address) of the string to display

❑   **EDX:** The size of the string to display

An example of using this system call is shown in the syscalltest1.s program:

```
# syscalltest1.s - An example of passing input values to a system call
.section .data
output:
    .ascii "This is a test message.\n"
output_end:
    .equ len, output_end - output
.section .text
.globl _start
_start:
    movl $4, %eax
    movl $1, %ebx
    movl $output, %ecx
    movl $len, %edx
    int $0x80

    movl $1, %eax
    movl $0, %ebx
    int $0x80
```

By now you are probably comfortable with most of what is happening in the syscalltest1.s program. The system call value for the write() system call (4) is placed in the EAX register. The input values required for the system call are then placed in the appropriate registers.

The file descriptor value for the output location is placed in the EBX. Linux systems contain three special file descriptors:

❑   **0 (STDIN):** The standard input for the terminal device (normally the keyboard)

❑   **1 (STDOUT):** The standard output for the terminal device (normally the terminal screen)

❑   **2 (STDERR):** The standard error output for the terminal device (normally the terminal screen)

The `syscalltest1.s` program uses the STDOUT file descriptor to display the text on the terminal screen. The next input value is the string to display. Notice that direct addressing mode is used when specifying the `output` memory location. This places the actual memory location address to which the `output` label points in the ECX register, instead of the value in the memory location.

The final input parameter is the length of the string to display. Instead of hard-coding a static length value, the `syscalltest1.s` program uses a common assembly language trick to determine the length of the string. As mentioned, the `output` label is used to declare the memory location where the string starts. An additional label is used immediately following the `.ascii` directive. The `output_end` label declares the location immediately after the end of the string. While nothing is stored in that location, the label itself can now be used to point to the end of the string. An `.equ` directive is used to define the length value by subtracting the two labels:

```
.equ len, output_end - output
```

The `len` label can now be used throughout the program to denote the length of the string. Remember that the `len` label is treated as an immediate value, so it must be preceded by a dollar sign when it is used:

```
movl $len, %edx
```

This instruction loads the length of the string into the EDX register. Now all of the registers are loaded, and the system call is ready to be executed by using the INT instruction.

After assembling and linking the program (remember that system calls do not require any C functions, so you do not have to link in the C libraries), you can test it out:

```
$ ./syscalltest1
This is a test message.
$
```

System call return value

As shown in the synopsis for the `write` system call, many system calls return a value after they complete. In the case of the `write` system call, it returns the size of the string written to the file descriptor, or a negative value if the call fails.

The return value from a system call is placed in the EAX register. It is your job to check the value in the EAX register, especially for failure conditions.

You should always be aware of the data type of the returned value. Some system calls use exotic data types to handle data. A good case in point is the `write` system call demonstrated earlier.

According to the synopsis, the `write` system call returns a `ssize_t` data type value. The `ssize_t` data type is not one of the standard assembly language data types available for use. The `ssize_t` data type is a `typedef` (or a synonym) of a signed integer value, which represents the number of characters written to the file descriptor if successful, or -1 if there was an error.

The `syscalltest2.s` program demonstrates handling the return value from a system call:

```
# syscalltest2.s - An example of getting a return value from a system call
.section .bss
    .lcomm pid, 4
```

```
    .lcomm uid, 4
    .lcomm gid, 4
.section .text
.globl _start
_start:
    movl $20, %eax
    int $0x80
    movl %eax, pid

    movl $24, %eax
    int $0x80
    movl %eax, uid

    movl $47, %eax
    int $0x80
    movl %eax, gid
end:
    movl $1, %eax
    movl $0, %ebx
    int $0x80
```

The syscalltest2.s program uses three separate system calls, described in the following table.

System Call Value	System Call	Description
20	getpid	Retrieves the process ID of the running program
24	getuid	Retrieves the user ID of the person running the program
47	getgid	Retrieves the group ID of the person running the program

After moving each system call value to the EAX register and executing the INT instruction, the return value in EAX is placed in the appropriate memory location.

After assembling and linking the program, you can run it in the debugger to watch the values. The end label was created to provide an easy breakpoint location so you can see the values before the program exits. Here's what the output looked like on my system:

```
$ gdb -q syscalltest2
(gdb) break *end
Breakpoint 1 at 0x8048098: file syscalltest2.s, line 21.
(gdb) run
Starting program: /home/rich/palp/chap12/syscalltest2

Breakpoint 1, end () at syscalltest2.s:21
21          movl $1, %eax
Current language:  auto; currently asm
(gdb) x/d &pid
0x80490a4 <pid>:        4758
(gdb) x/d &uid
0x80490a8 <uid>:        501
(gdb) x/d &gid
0x80490ac <gid>:        501
```

```
(gdb) cont
Continuing.

Program exited normally.
(gdb) quit
$
```

The values in the `pid`, `uid`, and `gid` memory locations can be displayed as integer values using the `x/d` debugger command. While the process ID is unique to the running program, you can check the `uid` and `gid` values using the `id` shell command:

```
$ id
uid=501(rich) gid=501(rich) groups=501(rich), 22(cdrom), 43(usb), 80(cdwriter),
81(audio), 503(xgrp)
$
```

As determined from the `syscalltest2` program, the `uid` used was `501`, and the `gid` was also `501`.

Advanced System Call Return Values

Sometimes system calls return complex data involving C style structures. When using them in assembly language programs, it is sometimes difficult to determine how to handle the returned C structure and convert it into a data type that can be handled by the assembly language program.

This section demonstrates using a system call that returns a data structure and shows one method that can be used to handle the returned data.

The sysinfo system call

The `sysinfo` system call can be used to return information about how the system is configured and what resources are available. The man page for the `sysinfo` system call looks like this:

```
NAME
       sysinfo - returns information on overall system statistics

SYNOPSIS
       #include <sys/sysinfo.h>

       int sysinfo(struct sysinfo *info);
```

The `sysinfo` system call uses a single input value, which points to a memory location to hold the structure that contains the returned data. The man page also shows what this structure should look like:

```
struct sysinfo {
        long uptime;                   /* Seconds since boot */
        unsigned long loads[3];        /* 1, 5, and 15 minute load averages */
        unsigned long totalram;        /* Total usable main memory size */
        unsigned long freeram;         /* Available memory size */
        unsigned long sharedram;       /* Amount of shared memory */
        unsigned long bufferram;       /* Memory used by buffers */
```

```
            unsigned long totalswap;  /* Total swap space size */
            unsigned long freeswap;   /* swap space still available */
            unsigned short procs;     /* Number of current processes */
            unsigned long totalhigh;  /* Total high memory size */
            unsigned int mem_unit;    /* Memory unit size in bytes */
            char _f[20-2*sizeof(long)-sizeof(int)]; /* Padding for libc5 */
    }
```

Each of the system values is returned in a specific location within the structure. You must create the structure at a memory location so the values can be returned there:

```
.section .data
result:
uptime:
    .int 0
load1:
    .int 0
load5:
    .int 0
load15:
    .int 0
totalram:
    .int 0
freeram:
    .int 0
sharedram:
    .int 0
bufferram:
    .int 0
totalswap:
    .int 0
freeswap:
    .int 0
totalhigh:
    .int 0
memunit:
    .int 0
```

You may notice the two labels at the start of the data definitions. They will both point to the same memory location when the program is assembled. The result label can be used to reference the structure as a whole, and the uptime label can be used to reference the first value in the structure.

Using the return structure

Once you have defined the return structure, you can use that information within the assembly language program. The sysinfo.s program shown here uses this structure to retrieve the system information from the sysinfo system call:

```
# sysinfo.s - Retrieving system information via kernel system calls
.section .data
result:
uptime:
    .int 0
```

```
load1:
    .int 0
load5:
    .int 0
load15:
    .int 0
totalram:
    .int 0
freeram:
    .int 0
sharedram:
    .int 0
bufferram:
    .int 0
totalswap:
    .int 0
freeswap:
    .int 0
procs:
    .byte 0x00, 0x00
totalhigh:
    .int 0
memunit:
    .int 0
.section .text
.globl _start
_start:
    nop
    movl $result, %ebx
    movl $116, %eax
    int $0x80

    movl $0, %ebx
    movl $1, %eax
    int $0x80
```

The system call value for the `sysinfo` system call is placed in the EAX register, and the memory location of the `result` label is placed in the EBX register as the input value. After the INT instruction is executed, the return structure values are loaded into the memory location, and the memory labels can be used to reference each individual value.

Viewing the results

After the system call completes, the individual data elements can be retrieved by their labels. This is demonstrated by using the debugger and checking the values after the system call:

```
(gdb) x/d &uptime
0x8049090 <uptime>:       27421854
(gdb) x/d &load1
0x8049094 <load1>:        3296
(gdb) x/d &load5
0x8049098 <load5>:        3200
(gdb) x/d &load15
0x804909c <load15>:       448
```

```
(gdb) x/d &totalram
0x80490a0 <totalram>:    129957888
(gdb) x/d &freeram
0x80490a4 <freeram>:     11579392
(gdb) x/d &sharedram
0x80490a8 <sharedram>:   0
(gdb) x/d &bufferram
0x80490ac <bufferram>:   31346688
(gdb) x/d &totalswap
0x80490b0 <totalswap>:   254943232
(gdb) x/d &freeswap
0x80490b4 <freeswap>:    251998208
(gdb) x/d &procs
0x80490b8 <procs>:       53
(gdb) x/d &totalhigh
0x80490ba <totalhigh>:   0
(gdb) x/d &memunit
0x80490be <memunit>:     0
```

Tracing System Calls

When using system calls in assembly language programs, it often helps to be able to see what is happening while the program is running. The Linux system provides the strace program, which traces system calls used within an application while it is running. Many options are available for using the strace program. This section describes the strace program and demonstrates how it can be used to troubleshoot assembly language system call problems.

The strace program

The strace program intercepts system calls made by a program and displays them for you to see. The program can be run from the strace command or it can be an already running process on the system. If you have the proper privileges, you can tap into an existing process and snoop on the system calls being made. This is an invaluable tool to have when debugging programs, assembly language as well as high-level languages.

Often, just using the default values for the strace program produces the required information about a program:

```
$ strace ./syscalltest2
execve("./syscalltest2", ["./syscalltest2"], [/* 38 vars */]) = 0
getpid()                                = 7616
getuid()                                = 501
getgid()                                = 501
_exit(0)                                = ?
$
```

This output shows all of the system calls the syscalltest1 program made, in the order in which they were performed by the application. The left side shows the system call names, and the right side shows the return values produced by the system calls. The execve system call shows how the operating system shell ran the program. This includes the command-line parameters and environment variables that are present in the stack (see Chapter 11, "Using Functions").

The -c command-line parameter creates a report after the program executes, outlining all of the system calls made, and how much time was spent in each call:

```
$ strace -c ./syscalltest2
execve("./syscalltest2", ["./syscalltest2"], [/* 38 vars */]) = 0
% time     seconds  usecs/call     calls    errors syscall
------ ----------- ----------- --------- --------- ----------------
 60.00    0.000006           6         1           getpid
 20.00    0.000002           2         1           getuid
 20.00    0.000002           2         1           getgid
------ ----------- ----------- --------- --------- ----------------
100.00    0.000010                     3           total
$
```

In this trivial example, you don't have too much data to wade through.

Advanced strace parameters

While the basic operation of the strace program produces a lot of data, you can use several command-line parameters to fine-tune strace for your particular application. The following table describes the command-line parameters available.

Parameter	Description
-c	Count the time, calls, and errors for each system call.
-d	Show some debugging output of strace.
-e	Specify a filter expression for the output.
-f	Trace child processes as they are created.
-ff	If writing to an output file, write each child process in a separate file.
-i	Print the instruction pointer at the time of the system call.
-o	Write the output to the file specified.
-p	Attach to the existing process by the PID specified.
-q	Suppress messages about attaching and detaching.
-r	Print a relative timestamp on each system call.
-t	Add the time of day to each line.
-tt	Add the time of day, including microseconds to each line.
-ttt	Add the time of day in epoch (seconds since Jan. 1, 1970), including microseconds.
-T	Show the time spent in each system call.
-v	Print unabbreviated versions of the system call information (verbose).

Parameter	Description
-x	Print all non-ASCII characters in hexadecimal format.
-xx	Print all strings in hexadecimal format.

Most of the command-line parameters are fairly self-explanatory. The -e parameter is handy in that it can be used to display only a subset of system calls instead of seeing all of them. The format for the -e parameter is

```
trace=call_list
```

where `call_list` is a comma-separated list of the system calls you want to trace. For example, if you only want to see the calls to the `getuid` and `getgid` system calls, you would use the following format:

```
$ strace -e trace=getpid,getgid ./syscalltest2
getpid()                            = 7799
getgid()                            = 501
$
```

Watching program system calls

One of the best features of `strace` is that it works on any program on the system (assuming you have privileges to execute the program). You do not have to assemble or compile the program with any special features for the `strace` program to work.

This can provide a wealth of information for you when working with programs that are causing problems. It is also handy to use when you are just curious about how an application performs a particular task.

In the previous section, the `id` command was used to display the current user and group IDs for running the programs. Let's dissect the `strace` output for that command. First, use `strace` in normal mode to watch the `id` command:

```
$ strace -o outfile id
```

This command creates the file `outfile`, which contains all of the system calls produced by the `id` command. You can use the editor to look at the `outfile` file. The file created on my system contains 223 lines of system calls—that's a lot of system calls to have to wade through! To help organize the calls, try using the -c parameter, which will break down the calls by name:

```
$ strace -c id
execve("/usr/bin/id", ["id"], [/* 38 vars */]) = 0
uid=501(rich) gid=501(rich)
groups=501(rich),22(cdrom),43(usb),80(cdwriter),81(audio),503(xgrp)
% time     seconds  usecs/call     calls    errors syscall
------ ----------- ----------- --------- --------- ----------------
 33.98    0.000713          19        37         3 open
 14.68    0.000308          15        21           read
 14.25    0.000299           8        37           old_mmap
  7.29    0.000153          12        13           munmap
  7.24    0.000152           4        36           close
  5.77    0.000121           3        35           fstat64
```

```
  3.86      0.000081           81           1                 write
  3.05      0.000064           32           2       2 connect
  2.72      0.000057           29           2         socket
  2.10      0.000044            9           5         mprotect
  2.05      0.000043            3          16         shmat
  1.33      0.000028            4           7         brk
  0.43      0.000009            9           1         ioctl
  0.38      0.000008            8           1         uname
  0.29      0.000006            3           2         ipc_subcall
  0.14      0.000003            3           1         getpid
  0.14      0.000003            3           1         semop
  0.10      0.000002            2           1         SYS_199
  0.10      0.000002            2           1         ipc_subcall
  0.10      0.000002            2           1         semget
------ ----------- ----------- ---------- ---------- ------------------
100.00     0.002098                      221         5 total
$
```

Now that's much easier to read and dissect. The report shows all of the different system calls made by the id program to perform its task. Notice that in the Errors column, there were three errors in the open system call, and two errors in the connect system call. To investigate this further, you can single out these calls in strace:

```
$ strace -e trace=open,connect id
open("/etc/ld.so.preload", O_RDONLY)     = -1 ENOENT (No such file or directory)
open("/etc/ld.so.cache", O_RDONLY)       = 3
open("/lib/libpam.so.0", O_RDONLY)       = 3
open("/lib/libpam_misc.so.0", O_RDONLY)  = 3
open("/lib/libc.so.6", O_RDONLY)         = 3
open("/lib/libc.so.6", O_RDONLY)         = 3
open("/lib/libdl.so.2", O_RDONLY)        = 3
open("/lib/libc.so.6", O_RDONLY)         = 3
open("/lib/libdl.so.2", O_RDONLY)        = 3
open("/lib/libc.so.6", O_RDONLY)         = 3
open("/usr/share/locale/locale.alias", O_RDONLY) = 3
open("/usr/share/locale/en/LC_IDENTIFICATION", O_RDONLY) = 3
open("/usr/share/locale/en/LC_MEASUREMENT", O_RDONLY) = 3
open("/usr/share/locale/en/LC_TELEPHONE", O_RDONLY) = 3
open("/usr/share/locale/en/LC_ADDRESS", O_RDONLY) = 3
open("/usr/share/locale/en/LC_NAME", O_RDONLY) = 3
open("/usr/share/locale/en/LC_PAPER", O_RDONLY) = 3
open("/usr/share/locale/en_US/LC_MESSAGES", O_RDONLY) = 3
open("/usr/share/locale/en_US/LC_MESSAGES/SYS_LC_MESSAGES", O_RDONLY) = 3
open("/usr/share/locale/en_US/LC_MONETARY", O_RDONLY) = 3
open("/usr/share/locale/en_US/LC_COLLATE", O_RDONLY) = 3
open("/usr/share/locale/en_US/LC_TIME", O_RDONLY) = 3
open("/usr/share/locale/en_US/LC_NUMERIC", O_RDONLY) = 3
open("/usr/share/locale/en_US/LC_CTYPE", O_RDONLY) = 3
connect(3, {sin_family=AF_UNIX, path="
/var/run/.nscd_socket"}, 110) = -1 ENOENT (No such file or directory)
open("/etc/nsswitch.conf", O_RDONLY)     = 3
open("/etc/ld.so.cache", O_RDONLY)       = 3
open("/lib/libnss_files.so.2", O_RDONLY) = 3
open("/etc/passwd", O_RDONLY)            = 3
```

```
connect(3, {sin_family=AF_UNIX, path="
/var/run/.nscd_socket"}, 110) = -1 ENOENT (No such file or directory)
open("/etc/group", O_RDONLY)            = 3
open("/usr/share/locale/en_US/LC_MESSAGES/sh-utils.mo", O_RDONLY) = -1 ENOENT (No
such file or directory)
open("/usr/share/locale/en/LC_MESSAGES/sh-utils.mo", O_RDONLY) = -1 ENOENT (No such
file or directory)
open("/etc/group", O_RDONLY)            = 3
open("/etc/group", O_RDONLY)            = 3
open("/etc/group", O_RDONLY)            = 3
open("/etc/group", O_RDONLY)            = 3
open("/etc/group", O_RDONLY)            = 3
open("/etc/group", O_RDONLY)            = 3
uid=501(rich) gid=501(rich)
groups=501(rich),22(cdrom),43(usb),80(cdwriter),81(audio),503(xgrp)
$
```

From this report you can see the three instances where the open system call failed to open library files and the two times the connect system call failed to connect to a local socket.

Attaching to a running program

Another great feature of the strace program is the capability to watch a program that is already running on the system. The -p parameter enables you to attach to a PID and capture system calls.

To demonstrate this feature, we need a program that we can run in background mode and which will stay running for a while. The nanotest.s program can do just that:

```
# nanotest.s - Another example of using system calls
.section .data
timespec:
    .int 5, 0
output:
    .ascii "This is a test\n"
output_end:
    .equ len, output_end - output
.section .bss
    .lcomm rem, 8
.section .text
.globl _start
_start:
    nop
    movl $10, %ecx
loop1:
    pushl %ecx
    movl $4, %eax
    movl $1, %ebx
    movl $output, %ecx
    movl $len, %edx
    int $0x80

    movl $162, %eax
```

```
        movl $timespec, %ebx
        movl $rem, %ecx
        int $0x80
        popl %ecx
        loop loop1

        movl $1, %eax
        movl $0, %ebx
        int $0x80
```

The `nanotest.s` program uses the `nanosleep` system call (system call value 162) to sleep for five seconds between displaying a text message on the standard output (using the `write` system call). The `nanosleep` system call is another system call that uses a tricky data type for the input values. The synopsis shown in the man pages is as follows:

```
SYNOPSIS
        #include <time.h>

        int  nanosleep(const struct timespec *req, struct timespec *rem);
```

The first input parameter is the time the system call will wait until it releases. The second input parameter specifies a location in which to store the time left over if the system call is interrupted before the set time expires. Both input values use the `timespec` structure to hold a time value. The nanosleep man page is nice enough to specify the format of the `timespec` structure:

```
struct timespec
{
        time_t  tv_sec;         /* seconds */
        long    tv_nsec;        /* nanoseconds */
};
```

The structure uses two values. The first specifies the seconds part of the time (using the `time_t` data type), and the second value specifies the nanoseconds part of the time (using a long integer data type). Both of these values can be represented by 32-bit integer values in the assembly language program. The `timespec` structure was created in memory using the `.int` directive, with two values:

```
timespec:
    .int 5, 0
```

The first integer value specifies the seconds the timer will wait, and the second integer value specifies the nanoseconds. This configuration sets the `nanosleep` system call to wait five seconds. The `rem` memory location is used to hold any return value from the `nanosleep` system call if it should be interrupted before it finishes.

The `LOOP` instruction is used to loop through the program ten times (with the loop value stored in the `ECX` register). Because the `write` and `nanosleep` system calls can alter the value for the `ECX` register, the value must be pushed onto the stack before the system calls, and popped from the stack when the calls are complete.

After assembling and linking the program, it is ready to be traced. If you can open two terminal sessions at the same time on your Linux system, run the `nanotest` program as normal in one of them, and run the strace program in the other. If you cannot run two terminal sessions at the same time, you can run the program in background mode using the ampersand sign, like this:

```
$ ./nanotest &
[1] 4181
$
```

The program starts, and a command prompt is immediately returned, ready for another command. The output from the nanotest program will still appear on the display, so be careful while you are typing.

When running the program in background, it conveniently gives us the PID number of the running process to trace. If you run the program in a separate terminal, you will need to manually determine the PID of the process using the grep command:

```
$ ps ax | grep nanotest
 4181 pts/0    S      0:00 ./nanotest
$
```

According to the ps command, the PID for the running process is 4181. Now that you know the PID, you can attach the strace program to the running nanotest program and watch the system calls:

```
$ strace -p 4181
write(1, "This is a test\n", 15)        = 15
nanosleep({5, 0}, {0, 140000000})       = 0
write(1, "This is a test\n", 15)        = 15
nanosleep({5, 0}, {0, 140000000})       = 0
write(1, "This is a test\n", 15)        = 15
nanosleep({5, 0}, {0, 140000000})       = 0
write(1, "This is a test\n", 15)        = 15
nanosleep({5, 0}, {0, 140000000})       = 0
write(1, "This is a test\n", 15)        = 15
nanosleep({5, 0}, {0, 140000000})       = 0
write(1, "This is a test\n", 15)        = 15
nanosleep({5, 0}, {0, 140000000})       = 0
write(1, "This is a test\n", 15)        = 15
nanosleep({5, 0}, {0, 140000000})       = 0
write(1, "This is a test\n", 15)        = 15
nanosleep({5, 0},
```

You will see the calls for the write and the nanosleep system calls, and the return values they generate.

You can only attach to running processes to which you have the privileges to attach. If a process is running as root, you must have root privileges to attach to it.

System Calls versus C Libraries

As you have seen scattered throughout the examples in this book, there is another way to tap into existing functions on the Linux system. The C libraries provide a wealth of functions that can also be utilized in assembly language programs. This section shows how to get information about the C library functions available on your system and how to use them. It then presents a short comparison with system calls.

The C libraries

As you have already seen, the C library functions provide many useful functions for programmers. The functions are contained in the libc library, which must be linked into the assembly language program (see Chapter 4, "A Sample Assembly Language Program").

The C library functions are documented in section 3 of the man pages. Just like the system calls, the C library function man pages describe the format of the function:

```
$ man 3 exit
NAME
        exit - cause normal program termination

SYNOPSIS
        #include <stdlib.h>

        void exit(int status);

DESCRIPTION
        The exit() function causes normal program termination  and  the  value
        of status & 0377 is returned to the parent (see  wait(2)).  All   func-
        tions registered with atexit() and on_exit() are called in the reverse
        order of their registration, and  all  open  streams  are  flushed and
        closed.  Files created by tmpfile() are removed.

        The C standard specifies two defines EXIT_SUCCESS and EXIT_FAILURE that
        may be passed to exit() to indicate successful or unsuccessful termina-
        tion, respectively.

RETURN VALUE
        The exit() function does not return.
```

Just as you did with the system calls, as an assembly language programmer you must interpret the C-format function definition into assembly language format. The definition for the exit function requires a single input parameter, which is the integer value that is returned.

As discussed in Chapter 11, "Using Functions," C style functions use the stack to pass input values. This also holds true for C library functions. All input parameters are placed on the stack in the opposite order from which they are listed in the synopsis for the function. The classic example that has been used throughout the book is the printf C function, which looks like this:

```
printf("The answer is %d\n", k);
```

The assembly version looks like this:

```
pushl k
pushl $output
call printf
addl $8, %esp
```

The last line is used to reset the stack pointer to clear the input values off of the stack.

Tracing C functions

The C library functions perform their magic by using the underlying system calls as well. You can still use the `strace` program to watch what the C functions are doing. As an example, the `cfunctest.s` program replicates the `nanotest.s` program, but using C function calls:

```
# cfunctest.s - An example of using C functions */
.section .data
output:
    .asciz "This is a test\n"
.section .text
.globl _start
_start:
    movl $10, %ecx
loop1:
    pushl %ecx
    pushl $output
    call printf
    addl $4, %esp
    pushl $5
    call sleep
    addl $4, %esp
    popl %ecx
    loop loop1
    pushl $0
    call exit
```

Similar to the `nanotest.s` program, the ECX register is used as the loop counter. It must be pushed onto the stack before the calls to the `printf` and `sleep` functions, as its value will be corrupted within the function calls.

Remember that in order to create the executable program, you must link the `cfunctest.s` program with the C libraries on the Linux system, and with the dynamic loader:

```
$ as -o cfunctest.o cfunctest.s
$ ld -dynamic-linker /lib/ld-linux.so.2 -lc -o cfunctest cfunctest.o
$
```

After the executable file is created, you can run it within the `strace` program. The first thing you will notice is that it contains a lot more system calls than the `nanotest.s` version. Here're just a few of the first system calls made:

```
$ strace ./cfunctest
execve("./cfunctest", ["./cfunctest"], [/* 17 vars */]) = 0
uname({sys="Linux", node="elijah", ...}) = 0
brk(0)                                  = 0x80492e4
old_mmap(NULL, 4096, PROT_READ|PROT_WRITE, MAP_PRIVATE|MAP_ANONYMOUS, -1, 0) =
0x40017000
access("/etc/ld.so.nohwcap", F_OK)      = -1 ENOENT (No such file or directory)
open("/etc/ld.so.preload", O_RDONLY)    = -1 ENOENT (No such file or directory)
open("/etc/ld.so.cache", O_RDONLY)      = 3
fstat64(3, {st_mode=S_IFREG|0644, st_size=57406, ...}) = 0
old_mmap(NULL, 57406, PROT_READ, MAP_PRIVATE, 3, 0) = 0x40018000
```

```
close(3)                               = 0
access("/etc/ld.so.nohwcap", F_OK)     = -1 ENOENT (No such file or directory)
open("/lib/libc.so.6", O_RDONLY)       = 3
read(3, "\177ELF\1\1\1\0\0\0\0\0\0\0\0\0\3\0\3\0\1\0\0\0`^\1\000"..., 512) = 512
fstat64(3, {st_mode=S_IFREG|0644, st_size=1243076, ...}) = 0
old_mmap(NULL, 1253316, PROT_READ|PROT_EXEC, MAP_PRIVATE, 3, 0) = 0x40027000
old_mmap(0x4014e000, 36864, PROT_READ|PROT_WRITE, MAP_PRIVATE|MAP_FIXED, 3,
0x126000) = 0x4014e000
old_mmap(0x40157000, 8132, PROT_READ|PROT_WRITE,
MAP_PRIVATE|MAP_FIXED|MAP_ANONYMOUS, -1, 0) = 0x40157000
close(3)                               = 0
munmap(0x40018000, 57406)              = 0
fstat64(1, {st_mode=S_IFCHR|0620, st_rdev=makedev(136, 0), ...}) = 0
old_mmap(NULL, 4096, PROT_READ|PROT_WRITE, MAP_PRIVATE|MAP_ANONYMOUS, -1, 0) =
0x40018000
write(1, "This is a test\n", 15This is a test
)            = 15
rt_sigprocmask(SIG_BLOCK, [CHLD], [], 8) = 0
rt_sigaction(SIGCHLD, NULL, {SIG_DFL}, 8) = 0
rt_sigprocmask(SIG_SETMASK, [], NULL, 8) = 0
nanosleep({5, 0},
```

As you can see, many more system calls are made using the C library functions than with directly using the system calls. These first few system calls are performed to load the system dynamic loader into memory (note the open system call to open the /lib/libc.so.6 library file). Note that the printf C function uses the same write system call to file descriptor 1 (STDOUT) as the nanotest.s program did.

You can use the -c strace parameter to see all of the system calls made by the C functions:

% time	seconds	usecs/call	calls	errors	syscall
89.67	0.001146	115	10		write
2.82	0.000036	2	20		rt_sigprocmask
1.64	0.000021	2	10		rt_sigaction
1.56	0.000020	3	6		old_mmap
1.02	0.000013	4	3	1	open
0.86	0.000011	1	10		nanosleep
0.63	0.000008	4	2	2	access
0.47	0.000006	2	3		fstat64
0.39	0.000005	5	1		munmap
0.31	0.000004	2	2		close
0.23	0.000003	3	1		read
0.23	0.000003	3	1		uname
0.16	0.000002	2	1		brk
100.00	0.001278		70	3	total

Comparing system calls and C libraries

While the C library functions required more system calls than directly using the system calls in the assembly language program, it is unlikely that you will notice all that much of a difference. In fact, if you use the -c strace option for the nanotest.s program, you should get results like the following:

```
% time     seconds  usecs/call     calls    errors syscall
------ ----------- ----------- --------- --------- ----------------
 90.71    0.000781          78        10           write
  9.29    0.000080           8        10           nanosleep
------ ----------- ----------- --------- --------- ----------------
100.00    0.000861                    20           total
$
```

Notice that the total time for the system calls in the nanotest program was 0.000861 seconds, whereas the total time for system calls in the cfunctest program was 0.001278. Obviously, the majority of the time difference was due to the C functions having to load the dynamic loader programs before executing the program. This overhead will be less obvious in larger assembly language programs.

The major reasons to use raw Linux system calls are as follows:

❑ It creates the smallest size code possible because no external libraries need to be linked into the programs.

❑ It creates the fastest possible code, again because no external libraries are linked into the programs.

❑ Linked executable files are independent of any external library code.

The major reasons for using C library functions in assembly language programs are as follows:

❑ The C libraries contain many functions that would require major assembly language code to emulate (such as the ASCII-to-integer or floating-point data type conversions).

❑ The C libraries are portable between operating systems (such as compiling programs on FreeBSD running on the Intel platform as well as Linux systems).

❑ C library functions can utilize shared libraries between programs, reducing memory requirements.

Clearly, there are reasons for using each type of function. The bottom line becomes which method is more suitable for your application, and which method you are more comfortable using. If you are writing assembly language programs that interface with C or C++ programs, you may already be comfortable using the C library functions, and you know they will be available to use.

Summary

This chapter discussed the Linux system calls that are available for assembly language programmers. The Linux kernels provide the system calls, which in turn provide access to the resources the kernel controls. The Linux kernel is responsible for managing and providing program access to memory, devices on the system, file systems on the system, and processes running on the system.

Many kernel system calls are available for use. The /usr/include/asm/unistd.h file lists all of the system calls and the numeric system call value of each one that is used in assembly language programs to access the system calls. The system call definitions are provided in the standard Linux man pages, in section 2.

When reading the system call definitions, you must determine what input values are required for the system call, and what return value (or values) must be handled. The kernel system calls use a register-based method for passing input and output values. The input values are passed to the system call in the order they are documented in the man page. The register order used is EBX, ECX, EDX, ESI, EDI, and EBP. This enables up to six input values to be used. The output value is returned in the EAX register.

Programs that use a lot of system calls can often be difficult to troubleshoot, as control is passed to the kernel to handle the system call. The strace program is one method you can use to track what system calls are used, and the results of the system call. The strace program monitors a program as it is running, and displays each of the system calls made, the input values provided to the system call, and the output value produced by the system call. Not only can the strace program start a new program to trace, but it can also attach to an existing program that is already running.

While many assembly language programmers utilize kernel system calls to provide low-level access to memory, devices, and process information, there are also other ways to obtain the information. The C library functions provide an intermediary approach to kernel features. The C library functions are standard functions that can be used on different systems to provide standard access to functions. Assembly language programs can access the C library functions by linking to the libraries on the system. Many programmers prefer using the C library functions, especially the more advanced ones that require a lot of extra assembly language coding. There is usually a small overhead associated with using the C library functions, but often the benefits outweigh the overhead penalty in applications.

The next chapter ties together the C and C++ high-level languages with assembly language. The chapter discusses inline assembly language programming, a method of creating small assembly language routines within larger C and C++ applications. Many programmers use inline assembly language programming to either increase performance of a complicated process or perform actions that the C compiler cannot perform.

13

Using Inline Assembly

Now that you know the basics of assembly language programming, it's time to start putting those concepts to practical use. One very common use of assembly language programming is to code assembly functions within higher-level languages, such as C and C++. There are a couple of different ways to do this. This chapter describes how to place assembly language functions directly within C and C++ language programs. This technique is called *inline assembly*.

The chapter begins by describing how C and C++ programs use functions, and how the functions are converted to assembly language code by the compiler. Next, the basic inline assembly format is discussed, including how to incorporate simple assembly functions. After that, the extended inline assembly format is described. This format enables you to incorporate more complex assembly language functions within the C or C++ programs. Finally, the chapter explains how to define macros using complex inline assembly language functions within C programs.

What Is Inline Assembly?

In a standard C or C++ program, code is entered in the C or C++ syntax in a text source code file. The source code file is then compiled into assembly language code using the compiler. After that step, the assembly language code is linked with any required libraries to produce an executable program (see Chapter 3, "The Tools of the Trade").

In the Linux world, the GNU compiler (gcc) is used to create the executable program from the text source code file. Normally, the step of converting the code to assembly language is hidden from the programmer. But as shown in Chapter 3, you can use the -S option of the GNU compiler to view the actual assembly language code generated from the source code.

A common programming technique in C and C++ programming is to create separate standalone functions within the source code file. These functions perform individual processes that can be called multiple times from the main program. When a C or C++ program is divided into functions, the compiler compiles each function into separate assembly functions (see Chapter 11, "Using

Functions"). The functions are still contained within the same assembly language file, but as separate functions. To see what is produced, you can still use the –S option to compile the program and view the generated assembly language code.

To demonstrate this, the cfunctest.c program uses separate functions within a simple C language program:

```
/* cfunctest.c - An example of functions in C */
#include <stdio.h>

float circumf(int a)
{
        return 2 * a * 3.14159;
}

float area(int a)
{
        return a * a * 3.14159;
}

int main()
{
        int x = 10;
        printf("Radius: %d\n", x);
        printf("Circumference: %f\n", circumf(x));
        printf("Area: %f\n",area(x));
        return 0;
}
```

The two functions are defined as having a single integer value for the input, and producing a double-precision floating-point value as the output. The mathematical calculations are performed within the individual functions, separate from the main program code. The functions can be called as many times as required within the main program without having to write additional code.

To view the assembly language code generated by the compiler, compile using the –S option:

```
$ gcc -S cfunctest.c
```

This command creates the file cfunctest.s, which looks like this:

```
.file   "cfunctest.c"
        .version        "01.01"
gcc2_compiled.:
                .section        .rodata
        .align 8
.LC0:
        .long   0xf01b866e,0x400921f9
.text
        .align 16
.globl circumf
        .type   circumf,@function
circumf:
```

```
        pushl   %ebp
        movl    %esp, %ebp
        subl    $4, %esp
        movl    8(%ebp), %eax
        addl    %eax, %eax
        pushl   %eax
        fildl   (%esp)
        popl    %eax
        fldl    .LC0
        fmulp   %st, %st(1)
        fstps   -4(%ebp)
        flds    -4(%ebp)
        movl    %ebp, %esp
        popl    %ebp
        ret
.Lfe1:
        .size   circumf,.Lfe1-circumf
                .section        .rodata
        .align 8
.LC2:
        .long   0xf01b866e,0x400921f9
.text
        .align 16
.globl area
        .type   area,@function
area:
        pushl   %ebp
        movl    %esp, %ebp
        subl    $4, %esp
        movl    8(%ebp), %eax
        imull   8(%ebp), %eax
        pushl   %eax
        fildl   (%esp)
        popl    %eax
        fldl    .LC2
        fmulp   %st, %st(1)
        fstps   -4(%ebp)
        flds    -4(%ebp)
        movl    %ebp, %esp
        popl    %ebp
        ret
.Lfe2:
        .size   area,.Lfe2-area
                .section        .rodata
.LC4:
        .string "Radius: %d\n"
.LC5:
        .string "Circumference: %f\n"
.LC6:
        .string "Area: %f\n"
.text
        .align 16
.globl main
```

```
          .type    main,@function
main:
          pushl    %ebp
          movl     %esp, %ebp
          subl     $8, %esp
          movl     $10, -4(%ebp)
          subl     $8, %esp
          pushl    -4(%ebp)
          pushl    $.LC4
          call     printf
          addl     $16, %esp
          subl     $4, %esp
          subl     $8, %esp
          pushl    -4(%ebp)
          call     circumf
          addl     $12, %esp
          leal     -8(%esp), %esp
          fstpl    (%esp)
          pushl    $.LC5
          call     printf
          addl     $16, %esp
          subl     $4, %esp
          subl     $8, %esp
          pushl    -4(%ebp)
          call     area
          addl     $12, %esp
          leal     -8(%esp), %esp
          fstpl    (%esp)
          pushl    $.LC6
          call     printf
          addl     $16, %esp
          movl     $0, %eax
          movl     %ebp, %esp
          popl     %ebp
          ret
.Lfe3:
          .size    main,.Lfe3-main
          .ident   "GCC: (GNU) 2.96 20000731 (Linux-Mandrake 8.0 2.96-0.48mdk)"
```

By now you should be able to understand the assembly language code generated by the compiler. The two C functions were created as separate assembly language functions, set apart from the main program code. The main program uses the standard C style function format to pass the input parameter to the functions (by placing the input value onto the top of the stack). The CALL instruction is used to invoke the functions from the main program.

In this simple example, the assembly code generated to implement the functions was fairly trivial. However, in a more complex application, you may not want the compiler to generate the assembly language code, or you may want to use assembly language instructions that the compiler is incapable of producing (such as the CPUID instruction).

If you want to directly control what assembly language code is generated to implement a function, you can do one of three things:

❑   Implement the function from scratch in assembly language code and call it from the C program.

❑   Create the assembly language version of the C code using the -s option, modify the assembly language code as necessary, and then link the assembly code to create the executable.

❑   Create the assembly language code for the functions within the original C code and compile it using the standard C compiler.

The first option is discussed in Chapter 14, "Calling Assembly Libraries." The second option is discussed in Chapter 15, "Optimizing Routines." The third option is exactly how inline assembly language programming works. This method enables you to create assembly language functions within the C or C++ source code itself, without having to link additional libraries or programs. It gives you greater control over how certain functions are implemented at the assembly language level of the final program.

Basic Inline Assembly Code

Creating inline assembly code is not much different from creating assembly functions, except that it is done within a C or C++ program. This section describes how to create basic inline assembly code functions that can implement simple assembly language code within C or C++ programs.

The asm format

The GNU C compiler uses the asm keyword to denote a section of source code that is written in assembly language. The basic format of the asm section is as follows:

```
asm( "assembly code" );
```

The assembly code contained within the parentheses must be in a specific format:

❑   The instructions must be enclosed in quotation marks.

❑   If more than one instruction is included, the newline character must be used to separate each line of assembly language code. Often, a tab character is also included to help indent the assembly language code to make lines more readable.

The second rule is required because the compiler takes the assembly code in the asm section verbatim and places it within the assembly code generated for the program. Each assembly language instruction must be on a separate line — thus, the requirement to include the newline character.

Some assemblers also require instructions to be indented by a tab character to distinguish them from labels. The GNU assembler does not require this, but many programmers include the tab character for consistency.

These requirements can create some confusing-looking assembly code in the source code, but it helps make things sane in the generated assembly language code.

A sample basic inline assembly section could look like this:

```
asm ("movl $1, %eax\n\tmovl $0, %ebx\n\tint $0x80");
```

This example uses three instructions: two MOVL instructions to place a one value in the EAX register and a zero value in the EBX register, and the INT instruction to perform the Linux system call.

This format can get somewhat messy when using a lot of assembly instructions. Most programmers place instructions on separate lines. When doing this, each instruction must be enclosed in quotation marks:

```
asm ( "movl $1, %eax\n\t"
      "movl $0, %ebx\n\t"
      "int $0x80");
```

This format is much easier to read when trying to debug an application. The asm section can be placed anywhere within the C or C++ source code. The following asmtest.c program demonstrates how the asm section would look in an actual program:

```
/* asmtest.c - An example of using an asm section in a program*/
#include <stdio.h>

int main()
{
    int a = 10;
    int b = 20;
    int result;
    result = a * b;
    asm ( "nop");
    printf("The result is %d\n", result);
    return 0;
}
```

The assembly language instruction used in the asm statement (the NOP instruction) does not do anything in the C program, but will appear in the assembly language code generated by the compiler. To generate the assembly language code for this program, use the -S option of the gcc command. The generated assembly code file should look like this:

```
.file   "asmtest.c"
        .section        .rodata
.LC0:
        .string "The result is %d\n"
        .text
.globl main
        .type   main, @function
main:
        pushl   %ebp
        movl    %esp, %ebp
        subl    $24, %esp
        andl    $-16, %esp
        movl    $0, %eax
        subl    %eax, %esp
        movl    $10, -4(%ebp)
        movl    $20, -8(%ebp)
```

```
        movl    -4(%ebp), %eax
        imull   -8(%ebp), %eax
        movl    %eax, -12(%ebp)
#APP
        nop

#NO_APP
        movl    -12(%ebp), %eax
            movl    %eax, 4(%esp)
        movl    $.LC0, (%esp)
        call    printf
        movl    $0, %eax
        leave
        ret
        .size   main, .-main
        .section        .note.GNU-stack,"",@progbits
        .ident  "GCC: (GNU) 3.3.2 (Debian)"
```

The generated code uses the normal C style function prologue and the LEAVE instruction to implement the standard epilogue (see Chapter 11). Within the prologue and epilogue code is the code generated by the C source code, and within that is a section identified by the #APP and #NO APP symbols. This section contains the inline assembly code specified by the asm section. Note how the code is placed using the newline and tab characters specified.

Using global C variables

Just implementing assembly language code itself won't be able to accomplish much. To do any real work, there must be a way to pass data into and out of the inline assembly language function.

The basic inline assembly code can utilize global C variables defined in the application. The word to remember here is "global." Only globally defined variables can be used within the basic inline assembly code. The variables are referenced by the same names used within the C program.

The globaltest.c program demonstrates how to do this:

```
/* globaltest.c - An example of using C variables */
#include <stdio.h>

int a = 10;
int b = 20;
int result;

int main()
{
        asm ( "pusha\n\t"
              "movl a, %eax\n\t"
              "movl b, %ebx\n\t"
              "imull %ebx, %eax\n\t"
              "movl %eax, result\n\t"
              "popa");
        printf("the answer is %d\n", result);
        return 0;
}
```

The a, b, and result variables are defined as global variables in the C program, and are used within the asm section of the code. Note that the values are used as memory locations within the assembly language code, and not as immediate data values. The variables can also be used elsewhere in the C program as normal.

*Remember that the data variables must be declared as global. You cannot use local variables within the **asm** section.*

The generated assembly code from the compiler looks like this:

```
.file   "globaltest.c"
.globl a
        .data
        .align 4
        .type   a, @object
        .size   a, 4
a:
        .long   10
.globl b
        .align 4
        .type   b, @object
        .size   b, 4
b:
        .long   20
        .section        .rodata
.LC0:
        .string "The result is %d\n"
        .text
.globl main
        .type   main, @function
main:
        pushl   %ebp
        movl    %esp, %ebp
subl    $8, %esp
        andl    $-16, %esp
        movl    $0, %eax
        subl    %eax, %esp
#APP
        pusha
        movl a, %eax
        movl b, %ebx
        imull %ebx, %eax
        movl %eax, result
        popa
#NO_APP
        movl    result, %eax
        movl    %eax, 4(%esp)
        movl    $.LC0, (%esp)
        call    printf
        movl    $0, %eax
        leave
        ret
        .size   main, .-main
        .comm   result,4,4
```

```
.section        .note.GNU-stack,"",@progbits
.ident  "GCC: (GNU) 3.3.2 (Debian)"
```

Notice how the a and b variables are declared in the .data section and assigned the proper values. The result variable, because it is not initialized in the C code, is declared as a .comm value.

One other important feature is shown in this example program. Notice the PUSHA instruction at the start of the assembly language code, and the POPA instruction at the end. It is important to remember to store the initial values of the registers before entering your code, and then restore them when you are done. It's quite possible that the compiler will use those registers for other values within the compiled C source code. If you modify them in your asm section, unpredictable things may occur.

Using the volatile modifier

When creating inline assembly code in your application, you must be aware of what the compiler may do to it during the compile operation. In a normal C or C++ application, the compiler may attempt to optimize the generated assembly code to increase performance. This is usually done by eliminating functions that are not used, sharing registers between values that are not concurrently used, and rearranging code to facilitate better flow of the program.

Sometimes optimization is not a good thing with inline assembly functions. It is possible that the compiler may look at the inline code and attempt to optimize it as well, possibly producing undesirable effects.

If you want the compiler to leave your hand-coded inline assembly function alone, you can just say so! The volatile modifier can be placed in the asm statement to indicate that no optimization is desired on that section of code. The format of the asm statement using the volatile modifier is as follows:

```
asm volatile ("assembly code");
```

The assembly code within the statement uses the standard rules it would use without the volatile modifier. Nor does the addition of the volatile modifier change the requirement to store and retrieve the register values within the inline assembly code.

Using an alternate keyword

The asm keyword used to identify the inline assembly code section may be altered if necessary. The ANSI C specifications use the asm keyword for something else, preventing you from using it for your inline assembly statements. If you are writing code using the ANSI C conventions, you must use the __asm__ keyword instead of the normal asm keyword.

The assembly code section within the statement does not change, just the asm keyword, as shown in the following example:

```
____asm__ ("pusha\n\t"
        "movl a, %eax\n\t"
        "movl b, %ebx\n\t"
        "imull %ebx, %eax\n\t"
        "movl %eax, result\n\t"
        "popa");
```

The __asm__ keyword can also be modified using the __volatile__ modifier.

Extended ASM

The basic `asm` format provides an easy way to create assembly code, but it has its limitations. For one, all input and output values have to use global variables from the C program. In addition, you have to be extremely careful not to change the values of any registers within the inline assembly code.

The GNU compiler provides an extended format for the `asm` section that helps solve these problems. The extended format provides additional options that enable you to more precisely control how the inline assembly language code is generated within the C or C++ language program. This section describes the extended `asm` format.

Extended ASM format

Because the extended `asm` format provides additional features to use, they must be included in the new format. The format of the extended version of `asm` looks like this:

```
asm ("assembly code" : output locations : input operands : changed registers);
```

This format consists of four parts, each separated by a colon:

❑ **Assembly code:** The inline assembly code using the same syntax used for the basic `asm` format

❑ **Output locations:** A list of registers and memory locations that will contain the output values from the inline assembly code

❑ **Input operands:** A list of registers and memory locations that contain input values for the inline assembly code

❑ **Changed registers:** A list of any additional registers that are changed by the inline code

Not all of the sections are required to be present in the extended `asm` format. If no output values are associated with the assembly code, the section must be blank, but two colons must still separate the assembly code from the input operands. If no registers are changed by the inline assembly code, the last colon may be omitted.

The following sections describe how to use the extended `asm` format.

Specifying input and output values

In the basic `asm` format, input and output values are incorporated using the C global variable name within the assembly code. Things are a little different when using the extended format.

In the extended format, you can assign input and output values from both registers and memory locations. The format of the input and output values list is

```
"constraint"(variable)
```

where `variable` is a C variable declared within the program. In the extended `asm` format, both local and global variables can be used. The `constraint` defines where the variable is placed (for input values) or moved from (for output values). This is what defines whether the value is placed in a register or a memory location.

The constraint is a single-character code. The constraint codes are shown in the following table.

Constraint	Description
a	Use the %eax, %ax, or %al registers.
b	Use the %ebx, %bx, or %bl registers.
c	Use the %ecx, %cx, or %cl registers.
d	Use the %edx, %dx, or $dl registers.
S	Use the %esi or %si registers.
D	Use the %edi or %di registers.
r	Use any available general-purpose register.
q	Use either the %eax, %ebx, %ecx, or %edx register.
A	Use the %eax and the %edx registers for a 64-bit value.
f	Use a floating-point register.
t	Use the first (top) floating-point register.
u	Use the second floating-point register.
m	Use the variable's memory location.
o	Use an offset memory location.
V	Use only a direct memory location.
i	Use an immediate integer value.
n	Use an immediate integer value with a known value.
g	Use any register or memory location available.

In addition to these constraints, output values include a constraint modifier, which indicates how the output value is handled by the compiler. The output modifiers that can be used are shown in the following table.

Output Modifier	Description
+	The operand can be both read from and written to.
=	The operand can only be written to.
%	The operand can be switched with the next operand if necessary.
&	The operand can be deleted and reused before the inline functions complete.

The easiest way to see how the input and output values work is to see some examples. This example:

```
asm ("assembly code" : "=a"(result) : "d"(data1), "c"(data2));
```

places the C variable data1 into the EDX register, and the variable data2 into the ECX register. The result of the inline assembly code will be placed into the EAX register, and then moved to the result variable.

Using registers

If the input and output variables are assigned to registers, the registers can be used within the inline assembly code almost as normal. I use the word "almost" because there is one oddity to deal with.

In extended asm format, to reference a register in the assembly code you must use two percent signs instead of just one (the reason for this will be discussed a little later). This makes the code a little odd looking, but not too much different.

The regtest1.c program demonstrates using registers within the extended asm format:

```
/* regtest1.c - An example of using registers */
#include <stdio.h>

int main()
{
    int data1 = 10;
    int data2 = 20;
    int result;

    asm ("imull %%edx, %%ecx\n\t"
         "movl %%ecx, %%eax"
         : "=a"(result)
         : "d"(data1), "c"(data2));

    printf("The result is %d\n", result);
    return 0;
}
```

This time, the C variables are declared as local variables, which you couldn't do with the basic asm format. Each C variable is assigned to a specific register. The output register is modified with the equal sign to indicate that it can only be written to by the assembly code (this is required for all output values in the inline code).

When the C program is compiled, the compiler automatically generates the assembly code necessary to place the C variables in the appropriate registers to implement the inline assembly code. You can see what is generated again by using the -S option. The inline code generated looks like this:

```
            movl    $10, -4(%ebp)
            movl    $20, -8(%ebp)
            movl    -4(%ebp), %edx
            movl    -8(%ebp), %ecx
#APP
            imull %edx, %ecx
```

```
        movl %ecx, %eax
#NO_APP
        movl    %eax, -12(%ebp)
```

The compiler moved the data1 and data2 values onto the stack spaces reserved for the C variables. The values were then loaded into the EDX and ECX registers required by the inline assembly code. The resulting output in the EAX register was then moved to the result variable location on the stack.

You don't always need to specify the output value in the inline assembly section. Some assembly instructions already assume that the input values contain the output values.

The MOVS instructions include the output location within the input values. The movstest.c program demonstrates this:

```
/* movstest.s - An example of instructions with only input values */
#include <stdio.h>

int main()
{
   char input[30] = {"This is a test message.\n"};
   char output[30];
   int length = 25;

   asm volatile ("cld\n\t"
       "rep movsb"
       :
       : "S"(input), "D"(output), "c"(length));

   printf("%s", output);
   return 0;
}
```

The movstest.c program specifies the required three input values for the MOVS instruction as input values. The location of the string to copy is placed in the ESI register, the location of the destination is placed in the EDI register, and the length of the string to copy is placed in the ECX register (remember to include the terminating null character in the string length).

The output value is already defined as one of the input values, so no output values are specifically defined in the extended format. Because no specific output values are defined, it is important to use the volatile keyword; otherwise, the compiler may remove the asm section as unnecessary, as it doesn't produce an output.

Using placeholders

In the regtest1.c example, the input values were placed in specific registers declared in the inline assembly section, and the registers were specifically utilized in the assembly instructions. While this worked fine for just a few input values, for functions that require a lot of input values this is a somewhat tedious way in which to use them.

To help you out, the extended `asm` format provides *placeholders* that can be used to reference input and output values within the inline assembly code. This enables you to declare input and output values in any register or memory location that is convenient for the compiler.

The placeholders are numbers, preceded by a percent sign. Each input and output value listed in the inline assembly code is assigned a number based on its location in the listing, starting with zero. The placeholders can then be used in the assembly code to represent the values.

For example, the following inline code:

```
asm ("assembly code"
       : "=r"(result)
       : "r"(data1), "r"(data2));
```

will produce the following placeholders:

❑   %0 will represent the register containing the `result` variable value.

❑   %1 will represent the register containing the `data1` variable value.

❑   %2 will represent the register containing the `data2` variable value.

Notice that the placeholders provide a method for utilizing both registers and memory locations within the inline assembly code. The placeholders are used in the assembly code just as the original data types would be:

```
imull %1, %2
movl %2, %0
```

*Remember that you must declare the input and output values as the proper storage elements (registers or memory) required by the assembly instructions in the inline code. In this example, both of the input values were required to be loaded into registers for the **IMULL** instruction.*

To demonstrate using placeholders, the `regtest2.c` program performs the same function as the `regtest1.c` program, but enables the compiler to choose which registers to use:

```
/* regtest2.c - An example of using placeholders */
#include <stdio.h>

int main()
{
   int data1 = 10;
   int data2 = 20;
   int result;

   asm ("imull %1, %2\n\t"
          "movl %2, %0"
          : "=r"(result)
          : "r"(data1), "r"(data2));

   printf("The result is %d\n", result);
   return 0;
}
```

The regtest2.c program uses the r constraint when defining the input and output values, using registers for all of the data requirements. The compiler selects the registers used when the assembly language code for the program is generated. You can see this by viewing the generated assembly code with the -S option:

```
        movl    $10, -4(%ebp)
        movl    $20, -8(%ebp)
        movl    -4(%ebp), %edx
        movl    -8(%ebp), %eax
#APP
        imull %edx, %eax
        movl %eax, %eax
#NO_APP
        movl    %eax, -12(%ebp)
```

My compiler elected to do something interesting when the assembly code was generated. It used the EDX register to hold the data1 value, and the EAX register to hold the data2 value, as we would normally expect. The interesting part is that it noticed that the result was generated after the input values were finished being used, so it assigned the result variable to the EAX register as well. My poorly constructed inline assembly code still performed the MOVL instruction, but it just moved the EAX register to itself.

You can watch the running program in the debugger to see if the MOVL instruction is really executed. To generate an executable that can be used in the debugger, you can use the -gstabs option with the gcc compiler:

```
$ gcc -gstabs -o regtest2 regtest2.c
```

When the executable is created, it can then be run in the debugger:

```
$ gdb -q regtest2
(gdb) break *main
Breakpoint 1 at 0x8048364: file regtest2.c, line 4.
(gdb) run
Starting program: /home/rich/palp/chap13/regtest2

Breakpoint 1, main () at regtest2.c:4
4       {
(gdb) s
5           int data1 = 10;
(gdb) s
6           int data2 = 20;
(gdb) s
9           asm ("imull %1, %2\n\t"
(gdb) s
14          printf("The result is %d\n", result);
(gdb) info reg
eax            0xc8      200
ecx            0x1       1
edx            0xa       10
```

To set a breakpoint in a C program, you can specify either the line number to start or a function label. This example set the breakpoint at the main() function label, or the start of the program.

One thing you may notice as you are stepping through the program is that the asm section is considered a single statement by the debugger. You can step into the asm section using the stepi debugger command and execute each instruction separately.

The registers listing shows that after the asm section, the data1 value was loaded into the EDX register, and the EAX register was used as the result variable.

Referencing placeholders

As you saw in the regtest2.c program, I needlessly used a MOVL instruction to produce the output value in the proper variable. Sometimes it is beneficial to use the same variable as both an input value and an output value. To do this, you must define the input and output values differently in the extended asm section.

If an input and output value in the inline assembly code share the same C variable from the program, you can specify that using the placeholders as the constraint value. This can create some odd-looking code, but it comes in handy to reduce the number of registers required in the code.

To fix the inline code from the regtest2.c program, you could write the following:

```
asm ("imull %1, %0"
      : "=r"(data2)
      : "r"(data1), "0"(data2));
```

The 0 tag signals the compiler to use the first named register for the output value data2. The first named register is defined in the second line, which assigns a register to the data2 input variable. This ensures that the same register will be used to hold the input and output values. Of course, the result will be placed in the data2 value when the inline code is complete.

The regtest3.c program demonstrates this:

```
/* regtest3.c - An example of using placeholders for a common value */
#include <stdio.h>

int main()
{
    int data1 = 10;
    int data2 = 20;

    asm ("imull %1, %0"
          : "=r"(data2)
          : "r"(data1), "0"(data2));

    printf("The result is %d\n", data2);
    return 0;
}
```

The regtest3.c program uses the data2 value as both an input value and the output value.

Alternative placeholders

If you are working with a lot of input and output values, the numeric placeholders can quickly become confusing. To help keep things sane, the GNU compiler (starting with version 3.1) enables you to declare alternative names as placeholders.

The alternative name is defined within the sections in which the input and output values are declared. The format is as follows:

```
%[name]"constraint"(variable)
```

The name value defined becomes the new placeholder identifier for the variable in the inline assembly code, as shown in the following example:

```
asm ("imull %[value1], %[value2]"
    : [value2] "=r"(data2)
    : [value1] "r"(data1), "0"(data2));
```

The alternative placeholder names are used in the same way as the normal placeholders were, as demonstrated in the following alttest.c program:

```
/* alttest.c - An example of using alternative placeholders */
#include <stdio.h>

int main()
{
   int data1 = 10;
   int data2 = 20;

   asm ("imull %[value1], %[value2]"
       : [value2] "=r"(data2)
       : [value1] "r"(data1), "0"(data2));

   printf("The result is %d\n", data2);
   return 0;
}
```

Changed registers list

You may have noticed in the examples presented so far that I have not used the changed registers list in the extended asm format, even though it is obvious that each of the programs contained registers that were changed.

The compiler assumes that registers used in the input and output values will change, and handles that accordingly. You do not need to include these values in the changed registers list. In fact, if you do, it will produce an error message, as demonstrated in the following badregtest.c program:

```
/* badregtest.c - An example of incorrectly using the changed registers list */
#include <stdio.h>

int main()
```

```
{
   int data1 = 10;
   int result = 20;

   asm ("addl %1, %0"
        : "=d"(result)
        : "c"(data1), "0"(result)
        : "%ecx", "%edx");

   printf("The result is %d\n", result);
   return 0;
}
```

The `badregtest.c` program specifies that the result variable should be loaded into the EDX register and the `data1` variable into the ECX register. The changed registers list incorrectly specifies that the ECX and EDX registers change within the inline code. Note that the registers are listed in the changed registers list using the full register names, not just a single letter as with the input and output register definitions. Using the percent sign with the register name is optional.

When you try to compile this program, an error will be produced:

```
$ gcc -o badregtest badregtest.c
badregtest.c: In function 'main':
badregtest.c:8: error: can't find a register in class 'DREG' while reloading 'asm'
$
```

The compiler already knew that the EDX register was used as a register, and it could not properly handle the request for the changed register list.

The proper use of the changed register list is to notify the compiler if your inline assembly code uses any additional registers that were not initially declared as input or output values. The compiler must know about these registers so it knows to avoid using them, as demonstrated in the `changedtest.c` program:

```
/* changedtest.c - An example of setting registers in the changed registers list */
#include <stdio.h>

int main()
{
   int data1 = 10;
   int result = 20;

   asm ("movl %1, %%eax\n\t"
        "addl %%eax, %0"
        : "=r"(result)
        : "r"(data1), "0"(result)
        : "%eax");

   printf("The result is %d\n", result);
   return 0;
}
```

In the `changedtest.c` program, the inline assembly code uses the EAX register as an intermediate location to store a data value. Because the register was not declared as an input or output value, it must be included in the changed registers list.

Now that the compiler knows that the EAX register is not available, it will work around that. The input and output values were declared using the r constraint, which enables the compiler to select the registers to use. Looking at the generated assembly language code, you can see which registers were selected:

```
        movl    $10, -4(%ebp)
        movl    $20, -8(%ebp)
        movl    -4(%ebp), %ecx
        movl    -8(%ebp), %edx
#APP
        movl %ecx, %eax
        addl %eax, %edx
#NO_APP
        movl    %edx, %eax
```

The code for moving the C variables into registers uses the ECX and EDX registers (remember that in the `regtest2.c` program it used the EAX and EDX registers). The compiler purposely avoided using the EAX register, as it was declared as being used in the inline assembly code.

> There is one oddity with the changed registers list: If you use any memory locations within the inline assembly code that are not defined in the input or output values, that must be tagged as being corrupted as well. The word "memory" is used in the changed registers list to flag the compiler that memory locations were altered within the inline assembly code.

Using memory locations

Although using registers in the inline assembly language code is faster, you can also directly use the memory locations of the C variables. The m constraint is used to reference memory locations in the input and output values. Remember that you still have to use registers for the assembly instructions that require them, so you may have to define intermediate registers to hold the data. The `memtest.c` program demonstrates this:

```
/* memtest.c - An example of using memory locations as values */
#include <stdio.h>

int main()
{
   int dividend = 20;
   int divisor = 5;
   int result;

   asm("divb %2\n\t"
       "movl %%eax, %0"
       : "=m"(result)
       : "a"(dividend), "m"(divisor));

   printf("The result is %d\n", result);
   return 0;
}
```

The asm section loads the dividend value into the EAX register as required by the DIV instruction. The divisor is kept in a memory location, as is the output value. The generated assembly code looks like the following:

```
        movl    $20, -4(%ebp)
        movl    $5, -8(%ebp)
        movl    -4(%ebp), %eax
#APP
        divb -8(%ebp)
        movl %eax, -12(%ebp)
#NO_APP
```

The values are loaded into memory locations (in the stack), with the dividend value also moved to the EAX register. When the result is determined, it is moved into its memory location on the stack, instead of to a register.

*Because this example uses the **DIVB** instruction, it will only work with dividend values less than 65,536 and divisor values less than 256. If you want to use larger values, you must modify the inline assembly language code to use the **DIVW** or **DIVL** instructions.*

Using floating-point values

Because of the way the FPU uses registers as a stack, things are a little different when using floating-point values in inline assembly language coding. You must be more careful about how the FPU registers are handled by the inline code.

You may have noticed that three different constraints dealt with the FPU register stack:

❑   f references any available floating-point register

❑   t references the top floating-point register

❑   u references the second floating-point register

When retrieving output values from the FPU, you cannot use the f constraint; you must declare the t or u constraints to specify the FPU register in which the output value will be, as shown in the following example:

```
asm( "fsincos"
    : "=t"(cosine), "=u"(sine)
    : "0"(radian));
```

The FSINCOS instruction places the output in the first two registers in the FPU stack. You must be sure to specify the correct register for the correct output value. Because the input value must also be in the ST(0) register, it uses the same register as the first output value, and is declared using the placeholder. The sincostest.c program demonstrates using this inline assembly code:

```
/* sincostest.c - An example of using two FPU registers */
#include <stdio.h>

int main()
{
```

```
float angle = 90;
float radian, cosine, sine;

radian = angle / 180 * 3.14159;

asm("fsincos"
    :"=t"(cosine), "=u"(sine)
    :"0"(radian));

printf("The cosine is %f, and the sine is %f\n", cosine, sine);
return 0;
}
```

The assembly language code generated by the compiler for this function looks like this:

```
        flds    -8(%ebp)
#APP
        fsincos
#NO_APP
        fstps   -24(%ebp)
        movl    -24(%ebp), %eax
        movl    %eax, -12(%ebp)
        fstps   -24(%ebp)
        movl    -24(%ebp), %eax
        movl    %eax, -16(%ebp)
```

The radian variable is loaded into the FPU stack from the program stack using the FLDS instruction. After the FSINCOS instruction, the two output values are popped from the FPU stack using the FSTPS instruction and moved to their appropriate C variable location.

In the preceding example, because the compiler knows the output values are in the first two FPU registers, it pops the values, restoring the FPU stack to its previous condition. If you perform any operations within the FPU stack that are not cleared, you must specify the appropriate FPU registers in the changed registers list. The areatest.c program demonstrates this:

```
/* areatest.c - An example of using floating point regs */
#include <stdio.h>

int main()
{
   int radius = 10;
   float area;

   asm("fild %1\n\t"
       "fimul %1\n\t"
       "fldpi\n\t"
       "fmul %%st(1), %%st(0)"
       : "=t"(area)
       :"m"(radius)
       : "%st(1)");

   printf("The result is %f\n", area);
   return 0;
}
```

The `areatest.c` program places the radius value into a memory location, and then loads that value into the top of the FPU stack with the `FILD` instruction. That value is multiplied by itself, with the result still in the `ST(0)` register. The pi value is then placed on top of the FPU stack, shifting the squared radius value down to the `ST(1)` position. The `FMUL` instruction is then used to multiply the two values within the FPU.

The output value is taken from the top of the FPU stack and assigned to the `area` C variable. Because the `ST(1)` register was used, but not assigned as an output value, it must be listed in the changed registers list so the compiler knows to clean it up afterward.

Handling jumps

The inline assembly language code can also contain labels to define locations in the inline assembly code. Normal assembly conditional and unconditional branches can be implemented to jump to the defined labels.

The `jmptest.c` program demonstrates this:

```
/* jmptest.c - An example of using jumps in inline assembly */
#include <stdio.h>

int main()
{
    int a = 10;
    int b = 20;
    int result;

    asm("cmp %1, %2\n\t"
        "jge greater\n\t"
        "movl %1, %0\n\t"
        "jmp end\n"
        "greater:\n\t"
        "movl %2, %0\n"
        "end:"
        : "=r" (result)
        : "r" (a), "r" (b));

    printf("The larger value is %d\n", result);
    return 0;
}
```

The inline assembly code defines two labels within the instructions. The `JGE` instruction is used along with the `CMP` instruction to compare the two input values loaded into registers. The `JMP` instruction is used to unconditionally jump to the end of the inline assembly code.

The assembly code generated by the compiler contains the labels as well as the instructions:

```
        movl    -4(%ebp), %edx
        movl    -8(%ebp), %eax
#APP
        cmp %edx, %eax
        jge greater
        movl %edx, %eax
        jmp end
```

```
greater:
        movl %eax, %eax
end:
#NO_APP
        movl    %eax, -12(%ebp)
```

There are two restrictions when using labels in inline assembly code. The first one is that you can only jump to a label within the same asm section. You cannot jump from one asm section to a label in another asm section.

The second restriction is somewhat more complicated. The jmptest.c program uses the labels greater and end. However, there is a potential problem with this. As you saw from the assembled code listing, the inline assembly labels are encoded into the final assembled code. This means that if you have another asm section in your C code, you cannot use the same labels again, or an error message will result due to duplicate use of labels. In addition, if you try to incorporate labels that use C keywords, such as function names or global variables, you will also generate errors.

There are two solutions to solve this. The easiest solution is to just use different labels within different asm sections. If you are hand-coding each of the asm sections, this is a viable alternative.

If you are using the same asm sections (such as if you declare macros as explained in the "Using Inline Assembly Code" section later) you cannot alter the labels within the inline assembly code. The solution is to use local labels.

Both conditional and unconditional branches allow you to specify a number as a label, along with a directional flag to indicate which way the processor should look for the numerical label. The first occurrence of the label found will be taken. To demonstrate this, the jmptest2.c program can be used:

```
/* jmptest2.c - An example of using generic jumps in inline assembly */
#include <stdio.h>

int main()
{
   int a = 10;
   int b = 20;
   int result;

   asm("cmp %1, %2\n\t"
       "jge 0f\n\t"
       "movl %1, %0\n\t"
       "jmp 1f\n "
       "0:\n\t"
       "movl %2, %0\n "
       "1:"
       :"=r"(result)
       :"r"(a), "r"(b));

   printf("The larger value is %d\n", result);
   return 0;
}
```

The labels have been replaced with 0: and 1:. The JGE and JMP instructions use the f modifier to indicate the label is forward from the jump instruction. To move backward, you must use the b modifier.

Using Inline Assembly Code

While you can place inline assembly code anywhere within the C program, most programmers utilize inline assembly code as macro functions. The C macro functions enable you to declare a single macro that contains a function. When the macro is referenced in the main program, the macro is expanded to the full function defined by the macro. This section shows how to create inline assembly macros in your C programs.

What are macros?

In C and C++ programs, macros are used to define anything from a constant value to complex functions. A macro is defined using the #define statement. The format of the #define statement is as follows:

```
#define NAME expression
```

By convention, the macro name NAME is always defined using uppercase letters (this is to ensure it will not conflict with C library functions). The expression value can be a numeric or string value that is constant.

If you have done much coding in C or C++, you are most likely familiar with defining constant macros. The constant macro assigns a specific value to a macro name. The macro name can then be used throughout the program to represent the value.

A macro can be defined as a numeric value, such as the following:

```
#define MAX_VALUE 1024
```

Whenever the macro MAX_VALUE is used in the program code, the compiler substitutes the value associated with it:

```
data = MAX_VALUE;
if (size > MAX_VALUE)
```

The macro value is not treated like a variable in that it cannot be altered. It remains a constant value throughout the program. It can, however, be used in numeric equations:

```
data = MAX_VALUE / 4;
```

Another aspect of the C macro is the macro functions. These are described in the next section.

C macro functions

While constant macros come in handy for defining values, macro functions can be utilized to save typing time throughout the program. An entire function can be assigned to a macro at the beginning of the program and used everywhere in it.

The macro function defines input and output values, and then defines the function that processes the input values and produces the output values. The format of the macro function is as follows:

```
#define NAME(input values, output value) (function)
```

The input values are a comma-separated list of variables used for input to the function. The function defines how the input values are processed to produce the output value.

Macros are defined as a single line of text. With macro functions, that can create a very long line of text. To help make the macro more readable, a line continuation character (the backslash) can be used to split the function. Here's an example of a simple C macro function:

```
#define SUM(a, b, result) \
        ((result) = (a) + (b))
```

The macro SUM is defined as requiring two input values, and producing a single output value, which is the result of the addition of the two input values. Whenever the SUM() macro function is used in a program, the compiler expands it to the full macro function definition.

It is important to note that this is the opposite of standard C functions, which are used to save coding space. The compiler expands the full macro function before the code is assembled, creating a larger code.

An example of a C macro function is shown in the mactest1.c program:

```
/* mactest1.c - An example of a C macro function */
#include <stdio.h>

#define SUM(a, b, result) \
          ((result) = (a) + (b))

int main()
{
   int data1 = 5, data2 = 10;
   int result;
   float fdata1 = 5.0, fdata2 = 10.0;
   float fresult;

   SUM(data1, data2, result);
   printf("The result is %d\n", result);
   SUM(1, 1, result);
   printf("The result is %d\n", result);
   SUM(fdata1, fdata2, fresult);
   printf("The floating result is %f\n", fresult);
   SUM(fdata1, fdata2, result);
   printf("The mixed result is %d\n", result);
   return 0;
}
```

There are a few things of interest to note in the mactest1.c example program. First, note that the variables defined in the macro function are completely independent of the result variables defined in the program. You can use any variables in the SUM() macro function.

Second, note that the same SUM() macro function worked for integer input values, numeric input values, floating-point input values, and even mixed input and output values! You can see how versatile macro functions can be. Now it's time to apply that to the inline assembly functions.

*If you want to see the code with the expanded macro lines, you can use the **-E** command-line option when compiling.*

Creating inline assembly macro functions

Just as you can with the C macro functions, you can declare macro functions that include inline assembly code. The inline assembly code must use the extended asm format, so the proper input and output values can be defined. Because the macro function can be used multiple times in a program, you should also use numeric labels for any branches required in the assembly code.

An example of defining an inline assembly macro function is as follows:

```
#define GREATER(a, b, result) ({ \
    asm("cmp %1, %2\n\t" \
        "jge 0f\n\t" \
        "movl %1, %0\n\t" \
        "jmp 1f\n " \
        "0:\n\t" \
        "movl %2, %0\n " \
        "1:" \
        :"=r"(result) \
        :"r"(a), "r"(b)); })
```

The a and b input variables are assigned to registers so they can be used in the CMP instruction. The JGE and JMP instructions use numeric labels so the macro function can be used multiple times in the program without duplicating assembly labels. The result variable is copied from the register that contains the greater of the two input values. Note that the asm statement must be in a set of curly braces to indicate the start and end of the statement. Without them, the compiler will generate an error each time the macro is used in the C code.

The mactest2.c program demonstrates using this macro function in a C program:

```
/* mactest2.c - An example of using inline assembly macros in a program */
#include <stdio.h>

#define GREATER(a, b, result) ({ \
    asm("cmp %1, %2\n\t" \
        "jge 0f\n\t" \
        "movl %1, %0\n\t" \
        "jmp 1f\n\t" \
        "0:\n\t" \
        "movl %2, %0\n\t" \
        "1:" \
        :"=r"(result) \
        :"r"(a), "r"(b)); })

int main()
{
    int data1 = 10;
    int data2 = 20;
    int result;

    GREATER(data1, data2, result);
    printf("a = %d, b = %d    result: %d\n", data1, data2, result);
```

```
        data1 = 30;
        GREATER(data1, data2, result);
        printf("a = %d, b = %d    result: %d\n", data1, data2, result);
        return 0;
    }
```

Summary

This chapter discussed how to use assembly language code inside of C and C++ programs. The technique of inline assembly code enables you to place assembly language functions inside C or C++ programs, pass program variables to the assembly language code, and place output from the assembly language code into C program variables.

The C asm statement contains assembly language code that is transferred to the compiled assembly language program from the C program code. The asm statement has two formats. The basic asm format enables you to code assembly language instructions directly, using C global variables as input and output values.

The extended asm format provides advanced techniques for passing input values to the assembly code, and moving output values to the C program code. Any type of C data, such as local variables, can be passed to either registers or memory locations using the extended asm format. The input values can be assigned to specific registers or you can allow the compiler to assign the registers as necessary. Similarly, output values can be assigned to either registers or memory locations. Numerous features can be used to control how the variables are used within the inline assembly language code.

Inline assembly language code in the asm section is often defined using C macro functions. The C macro function uses a format that defines a function name, the input values used, and the output values used, along with the asm section function. Each time the macro function is called in the main program, the compiler expands the inline assembly language code.

The next chapter digs deeper into using assembly language in mixed programming environments. Besides inline assembly language code, you can create complete assembly language libraries that can be utilized by C and C++ programs. This technique is discussed and demonstrated in the next chapter.

14

Calling Assembly Libraries

The previous chapter demonstrated how to incorporate assembly language code within C programs by using inline assembly programming. This chapter discusses another way to incorporate assembly language code into your C or C++ programs.

Both C and C++ programs can directly call assembly language functions, pass input values to the functions, and retrieve the output value from them. This chapter discusses how to do this. First, the basics of C style assembly language functions are reviewed. Following that, you will learn how to compile C programs and assembly language functions. The next section explains how to pass values between the C program and assembly language functions, both input and output values. Then you will learn how to combine your assembly language functions into common libraries that can be used with C programs. Both static and dynamic libraries are discussed, with examples of each presented. Finally, the topic of debugging assembly language functions within C programs is discussed.

Creating Assembly Functions

Chapter 11, "Using Functions," demonstrated how to create assembly language functions that can be used in any assembly language program. This same technique can be used to provide assembly language functions for high-level C and C++ programs. This section provides a brief refresher on creating assembly language functions.

If you remember from Chapter 11, there are many ways to pass input values to an assembly function, and many ways to retrieve the output results. C programs use a specific format for passing input values on the program stack, and retrieving the results from the EAX register.

If you want your assembly language functions to work with C and C++ programs, you must explicitly follow the C style function format. This means that all input variables must be read from the stack, and that most output values are returned in the EAX register. (The exception to this is discussed in more detail later in the chapter.)

Figure 14-1 shows the way input values are placed on the stack, and how they are accessed by the assembly language function.

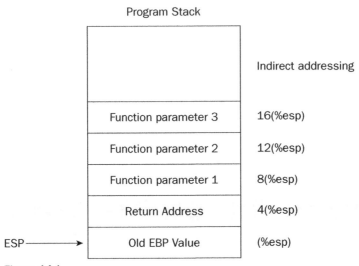

Program Stack

Figure 14-1

The EBP register is used as the base pointer to access values from the stack. The program calling the assembly language function must know the order in which the input values are placed on the stack, and the size (and data type) of each input value.

While in the assembly function code, C style functions have specific rules about which registers can be modified and which ones must be preserved by the function. If a register that must be preserved is modified within the function, its original value must be restored or unexpected things may happen when execution returns to the calling C program. The MMX and SSE registers are safe for use within the function, but care must be taken when using the general-purpose and FPU registers. The following table lists the status of the registers within functions.

Register	Status
EAX	Used to hold the output value, but may be modified until the function returns
EBX	Used to point to the global offset table; must be preserved
ECX	Available for use within the function
EDX	Available for use within the function
EBP	Used as the base stack pointer by the C program; must be preserved
ESP	Used to point to the new stack location within the function; must be preserved
EDI	Used as a local register by the C program; must be preserved
ESI	Used as a local register by the C program; must be preserved
ST(0)	Used to hold a floating-point output value, but may be modified until the function returns
ST(1) - ST(7)	Available for use within the function

As shown in the table, the EBX, EDI, ESI, EBP and ESP registers must be preserved by the called function. This requires pushing the registers onto the stack before the function code, and popping them off when the function is ready to return to the calling program. This is usually done in a standard prologue and epilogue format (similar to what was used for assembly language functions in Chapter 11).

The basic template for an assembly language function that is called by C functions should look like this:

```
.section .text
.type func, @function
func:
    pushl %ebp
    movl %esp, %ebp
    subl $12, %esp
    pushl %edi
    pushl %esi
    pushl %ebx

    <function code>

    popl %ebx
    popl %esi
    popl %edi
    movl %ebp, %esp
    popl %ebp
    ret
```

This code template can be used on all assembly language functions that are used by C or C++ functions. Of course, if a particular function does not alter the EBX, ESI, or EDI registers, you may omit the pertinent PUSH and POP instructions.

Notice the SUBL instruction included in the prologue. If you remember from Chapter 11, this is used to reserve space on the stack for local variables used within the function. This instruction reserves 12 bytes of memory space on the stack. This can be used to hold three 4-byte data values. If more space is needed for local variables, you must subtract that from the ESP value. The local variables are referenced within the function relative to the EBP register. For example, if the first local variable is used as a 4-byte value, its location would be at -4(%ebp). A second variable could be referenced at location -8(%ebp), and the third at -12(%ebp).

However, assembly language functions called by C programs may also declare their own .data and .bss sections to store data. These memory areas will be combined with the memory requirements for the C program at compile time. A pointer can be passed back to the calling program to access any data stored in these memory locations (as demonstrated later in "Using Assembly Functions in C Programs").

Compiling the C and Assembly Programs

When the main application is contained in a C or C++ program, and the functions are contained within assembly language programs, you must compile both to produce the single executable file. The GNU C compiler provides several alternatives that can be used to produce the final program file. This section describes two methods that you can use to manually create executable files from the source code files.

Compiling assembly source code files

When compiling a C program that contains assembly language functions, the compiler must know how to access the functions. If the compiler cannot resolve the functions used in the program, an error message will be generated:

```
$ gcc -o mainprog mainprog.c
/tmp/cc9hGAnP.o: In function `main':
/tmp/cc9hGAnP.o(.text+0xc): undefined reference to `asmfunc'
collect2: ld returned 1 exit status
$
```

The `mainprog.c` C program made a function call to an assembly language function called `asmfunc()`. When the program was compiled, the linker could not resolve the function name, and produced an error message.

To solve this problem, the compiler must have the assembly language function code available at compile time along with the C program code. One way to do this is to include the assembly language function source code file in the compiler command line. The compiler command line would look something like this:

```
$ gcc -o mainprog mainprog.c asmfunc1.s asmfunc2.s asmfunc3.s
```

The output from the compiler is a single executable file, `mainprog`, which contains all of the necessary program code for the main program and all of the assembly language functions. No intermediate object files are produced by this method, just the final executable file. This may or may not be a good idea, depending on how you handle the assembly language functions. The next section describes how to use individual assembly language object files to compile the program.

Using assembly object code files

Instead of assembling the assembly language functions at compile time, you can assemble them individually, and reference the object files in the C program compiler command. The GNU compiler is able to obtain the assembly language functions from the object code files, and link them with the main C program to produce the executable file.

When you create the assembly language function object file, you do not have to link the code using the `ld` command, as by itself it will do nothing, but you must assemble it using the `as` command.

> *If you try to link an assembly language function by itself, the linker will produce an error indicating that no __start__ label is defined, but will assume the start of the .__text__ section is the start of the program.*

Once the object file is created, it can be included on the compiler command line with the main C program:

```
$ as -o asmfunc.o asmfunc.s
$ gcc -o mainprog mainprog.c asmfunc.o
```

This produces the `mainprog` executable file, which contains both the code for the main C program and the assembly language function. If more than one assembly language function is used within a C program, all of the functions can be assembled separately, and added to the compiler command-line list:

```
$ gcc -o mainprog mainprog.c asmfunc1.o asmfunc2.o asmfunc3.o
```

If one of the assembly language functions is changed, it must be assembled and the main program re-compiled. While this may seem trivial for small programs, in large applications that use dozens of functions in separate files this process can become tedious. A very handy tool to have is the GNU make utility.

The GNU make utility enables you to create a definition file (called a *makefile*) that defines what code files are used to create an executable file. When the make program is run, it automatically assembles and compiles the necessary program files needed to create the executable. If any program file changes after the original make is run, only that file is assembled (or compiled) to create to new executable.

The executable file

The final product of the compile process is an executable file that can be run on the Linux system. The executable file contains the instructions from the main program plus all of the functions that were called by the main program. You can use the objdump program to view the separate parts of the executable file to see how the main program assembly language code interacts with the assembly language function code.

To demonstrate this, a sample assembly language function and C language main program can be created and compiled together. The asmfunc.s program creates a sample assembly language function that displays a message on the console screen to prove that it ran:

```
# asmfunc.s - An example of a simple assembly language function
.section .data
testdata:
    .ascii "This is a test message from the asm function\n"
datasize:
    .int 45
.section .text
.type asmfunc, @function
.globl asmfunc
asmfunc:
    pushl %ebp
    movl %esp, %ebp
    pushl %ebx

    movl $4, %eax
    movl $1, %ebx
    movl $testdata, %ecx
    movl datasize, %edx
    int $0x80

    popl %ebx
    movl %ebp, %esp
    popl %ebp
    ret
```

The asmfunc.s program uses the standard C style function prologue and epilogue code. The EDI and ESI registers are not modified, so they are not pushed, and no local variables are declared. Because the EBX register is modified within the function code, it is pushed onto the stack and retrieved at the end of the function.

The function stores an output text message in the `.data` section, and declares the message size as an integer value. The Linux `write()` system call (system call value 4) is used to display the message on `STDOUT` using file descriptor 1.

A sample C program that uses this function is shown in program `mainprog.c`:

```
/* mainprog.c - An example of calling an assembly function */
#include <stdio.h>

int main()
{
        printf("This is a test.\n");
        asmfunc();
        printf("Now for the second time.\n");
        asmfunc();
        printf("This completes the test.\n");
        return 0;
}
```

The `mainprog.c` program calls the assembly language function by name, using parentheses to indicate that the name is a function. Because the function does not require any input values, none are supplied in the function. Similarly, no return value is used by the function, so none is declared in the C program.

Use the following to create the executable and run the program:

```
$ gcc -o mainprog mainprog.c asmfunc.s
$ ./mainprog
This is a test.
This is a test message from the asm function
Now for the second time.
This is a test message from the asm function
This completes the test.
$
```

The program worked as expected. Each time the assembly language function was called, it produced the message and returned control to the main program.

Now that you have a complete executable program, you can use the `objdump` program to view the compiled code:

```
$ objdump -D mainprog > dump
```

The file `dump` contains the complete disassembled source code for the executable file. You can view it using any text editor on the system. You will notice that there are several sections in the source code. Within the sections is one called `main`. This section contains the assembly language code generated by my Mandrake Linux system implementing the C program code (your Linux system compiler may generate different code):

```
08048460 <main>:
 8048460:       55                      push   %ebp
 8048461:       89 e5                   mov    %esp,%ebp
 8048463:       83 ec 08                sub    $0x8,%esp
 8048466:       83 ec 0c                sub    $0xc,%esp
```

```
8048469:      68 34 85 04 08         push    $0x8048534
804846e:      e8 c9 fe ff ff         call    804833c <_init+0x58>
8048473:      83 c4 10               add     $0x10,%esp
8048476:      e8 31 00 00 00         call    80484ac <asmfunc>
804847b:      83 ec 0c               sub     $0xc,%esp
804847e:      68 45 85 04 08         push    $0x8048545
8048483:      e8 b4 fe ff ff         call    804833c <_init+0x58>
8048488:      83 c4 10               add     $0x10,%esp
804848b:      e8 1c 00 00 00         call    80484ac <asmfunc>
8048490:      83 ec 0c               sub     $0xc,%esp
8048493:      68 5f 85 04 08         push    $0x804855f
8048498:      e8 9f fe ff ff         call    804833c <_init+0x58>
804849d:      83 c4 10               add     $0x10,%esp
80484a0:      b8 00 00 00 00         mov     $0x0,%eax
80484a5:      89 ec                  mov     %ebp,%esp
80484a7:      5d                     pop     %ebp
80484a8:      c3                     ret
80484a9:      90                     nop
80484aa:      90                     nop
80484ab:      90                     nop
```

The objdump program produces the disassembled assembly language code from the executable file. The first column is the memory location within the program memory space. The section column shows the IA-32 instruction code generated by the assembly language code. The last column shows the disassembled assembly language code.

Notice the two places where the code uses the CALL instruction to call the asmfunc function. The assembly code for this function is in another section, called asmfunc:

```
080484ac <asmfunc>:
80484ac:      55                     push    %ebp
80484ad:      89 e5                  mov     %esp,%ebp
80484af:      53                     push    %ebx
80484b0:      b8 04 00 00 00         mov     $0x4,%eax
80484b5:      bb 01 00 00 00         mov     $0x1,%ebx
80484ba:      b9 8c 95 04 08         mov     $0x804958c,%ecx
80484bf:      8b 15 b9 95 04 08      mov     0x80495b9,%edx
80484c5:      cd 80                  int     $0x80
80484c7:      5b                     pop     %ebx
80484c8:      89 ec                  mov     %ebp,%esp
80484ca:      5d                     pop     %ebp
80484cb:      c3                     ret
80484cc:      90                     nop
80484cd:      90                     nop
80484ce:      90                     nop
80484cf:      90                     nop
```

Using Assembly Functions in C Programs

The C or C++ program that calls the assembly language functions must know the proper format to use to pass input values to the assembly function, and how to handle any return values. This section demonstrates how to access data from assembly language functions from C and C++ programs.

Using integer return values

The most basic of assembly language function calls return a 32-bit integer value in the EAX register. This value is retrieved by the calling function, which must assign the return value to a C variable defined as an integer:

```
int result = function();
```

The assembly language code generated for the C program extracts the value placed in the EAX register and moves it to the memory location (usually a local variable on the stack) assigned to the C variable name. The C variable contains the return value from the assembly language function, and can be used as normal throughout the C program.

As an example, here's an assembly language function and the C program that uses it. First, the square.s assembly language program defines a function that requires one integer input value, squares it, and returns the result in the EAX register:

```
# square.s - An example of a function that returns an integer value
.type square, @function
.globl square
square:
  pushl %ebp
  movl %esp, %ebp
  movl 8(%ebp), %eax
  imull %eax, %eax
  movl %ebp, %esp
  popl %ebp
  ret
```

The input value is read from the stack and placed in the EAX register. The IMUL instruction is used to multiply the value by itself, with the results placed in the EAX register. Because the EBX, EDI, and ESI registers are not affected by the function, they are not included in the prologue and epilogue. In addition, no local data storage is required, so the ESP register is not modified.

The corresponding C program, inttest.c, uses the square assembly language function:

```
/* inttest.c - An example of returning an integer value */
#include <stdio.h>

int main()
{
        int i = 2;
        int j = square(i);
        printf("The square of %d is %d\n", i, j);

        j = square(10);
        printf("The square of 10 is %d\n", j);
        return 0;
}
```

The inttest.c program calls the square function using two different input values. The first time it uses the i C variable, which has the value of 2. The second time it uses an immediate data value of 10. In both instances the input value is passed to the assembly language function as an integer value and processed. The return value is assigned to the j C variable. The j variable can be handled like any other C variable.

The assembly language function can be assembled separately from the C program, or along with it in the gcc compiler command line:

```
$ gcc -o inttest inttest.c square.s
$ ./inttest
The square of 2 is 4
The square of 10 is 100
$
```

*For using 64-bit long integer values, the returned value is placed in the **EDX:EAX** register pair.*

Using string return values

Working with functions that return string values can be somewhat tricky. Unlike functions that return an integer value in the EAX register, a function cannot return an entire string of data in the EAX register (unless, of course, the string is four characters long).

Instead, functions that return strings return a pointer to the location where the string is stored. The C or C++ program that calls the function must use a pointer variable to hold the return value. The string can then be referenced from the pointer value, as shown in Figure 14-2.

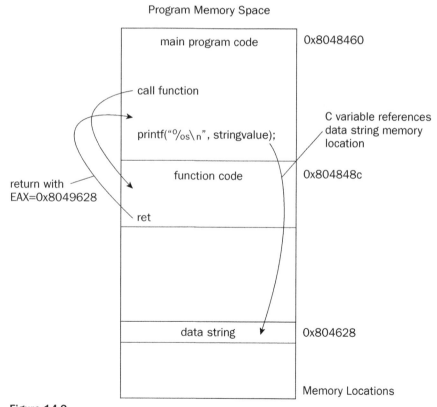

Figure 14-2

The string value is contained within the memory space of the function, but the main program can access it because the function memory space is contained within the memory space of the main program. The 32-bit pointer value returned by the function contains the memory address where the start of the string is located.

When working with string values in C and C++ programs, remember that the strings must always be terminated with a null character.

The C and C++ languages use an asterisk before a variable name to indicate that the variable contains a pointer. You can create pointers to any data type, but for strings you will want to create a pointer to a char data type. The variable declaration should look something like this:

```
char *result;
```

This creates a variable called result that can be used to contain a pointer to a character string.

Unfortunately, by default, the C program assumes that the return value from a function is an integer value. You must inform the compiler that the function will return a string pointer. Creating a *prototype* of the function call does this.

A prototype defines the function format before it is used, so the C compiler knows how to handle the function call. The prototype defines the input value data types required by the function, as well as the return value data type. Individual values are not defined, just the required data types. A sample prototype looks like the following:

```
char *function1(int, int);
```

This prototype defines a function named function1, which requires two input values, both of the integer data type. The return data type is defined as a pointer to a char data type. It is important to remember the semicolon after the function template. Without it, the compiler will assume you are defining the entire function in your code and produce an error message. If the function does not use any input values, you must still specify a void data type:

```
char *function(void);
```

The prototype must appear before the main() section in the source code, and is usually placed after any #include or #define statements.

As an example of using string return values, here's an assembly language function that uses the CPUID instruction and returns a pointer to a string that contains the CPUID string retrieved from the processor. The cpuidfunc.s program performs the assembly language function part.

```
# cpuidfunc.s - An example of returning a string value
.section .bss
   .comm output, 13
.section .text
.type cpuidfunc, @function
.globl cpuidfunc
cpuidfunc:
    pushl %ebp
    movl %esp, %ebp
    pushl %ebx
```

```
movl $0, %eax
cpuid
movl $output, %edi
movl %ebx, (%edi)
movl %edx, 4(%edi)
movl %ecx, 8(%edi)
movl $output, %eax
popl %ebx
movl %ebp, %esp
popl %ebp
ret
```

It is important that the assembly language program define a buffer area for the output string. This value will be contained within the final program, and will be accessed by the main C program. In this example, the output value is declared in the .bss memory section. It is declared with an additional byte. This byte will contain the terminating null character (a zero) so the value will be a proper C string value. The .bss memory area is initialized with zeros, so we are guaranteed that it will contain a zero value.

Because the CPUID instruction modifies the EBX register, the function code pushes the original value of the EBX register before the function code, and pops it just before the function exits.

The stringtest.c program demonstrates a C program that uses the cpuid function:

```
/* stringtest.c - An example of returning a string value */
#include <stdio.h>

char *cpuidfunc(void);

int main()
{
        char *spValue;
        spValue = cpuidfunc();
        printf("The CPUID is: '%s'\n", spValue);
        return 0;
}
```

The function prototype is defined first in the source code before the main program code. When the function is used in the main program, the return value is assigned to the character pointer variable spValue. The variable can then be used in any type of C string manipulation function.

Similar to the integer function, you can either assemble the cpuidfunc.s program separately and use the object file in the compiler command line, or you can just include the assembly language source code file in the compiler command line. Here's an example of assembling the function separately:

```
$ as -o cpuidfunc.o cpuidfunc.s
$ gcc -o stringtest stringtest.c cpuidfunc.o
$ ./stringtest
The CPUID is: 'GenuineIntel'
$
```

String values are not the only things that can have a pointer value returned. Functions can use the same technique to return pointers to integer and floating-point values.

Using floating-point return values

Floating-point return values are a special case. Both the integer and string return values use the EAX register to return values from the assembly language function to the C calling program. If you want to return a floating-point value, things are a little different.

Instead of using the EAX register, C style functions use the ST(0) FPU register to transfer floating-point values between functions. The function places the return value onto the FPU stack, and the calling program is responsible for popping it off of the stack and assigning the value to a variable.

Because floating-point values are always converted to double-extended-precision when placed in the FPU stack, it does not matter what floating-point data type the original value was, or what floating-point data type the C program uses to contain the result value. The proper conversion will be done by the FPU.

C and C++ programs use two data types to represent floating point values:

❑ **float:** Represents a single-precision floating-point value

❑ **double:** Represents a double-precision floating-point value

Either of these two data types can be used to retrieve the result value from the FPU stack. It does not matter what precision was used to place the value onto the FPU stack by the assembly language function.

When using a function that returns a floating-point value in a C program, a function prototype must be defined. The same rules apply as for the string return value prototype:

```
float function1(float, float, int);
```

This example defines a function that requires three input values (two single-precision floating-point values and an integer value), and returns a single-precision floating-point value. If the C variable must use double precision, the double return type must be used:

```
double function1(double, int);
```

As an example of using floating-point return values, the areafunc.s function is written to accommodate the C return value style:

```
# areafunc.s - An example of a floating point return value
.section .text
.type areafunc, @function
.globl areafunc
areafunc:
    pushl %ebp
    movl %esp, %ebp

    fldpi
    filds 8(%ebp)
    fmul %st(0), %st(0)
    fmul %st(1), %st(0)
    movl %ebp, %esp
    popl %ebp
    ret
```

The `areafunc.s` function loads the pi value onto the FPU stack, and then loads the integer input value (a radius value) from the stack onto the FPU stack. The first value (the integer radius value) is multiplied by itself, and then multiplied by the pi value, with the result left in the `ST(0)` FPU stack register. Again, because the `EBX`, `EDI`, and `ESI` registers are not used in the function, their values are not specifically preserved using `PUSH` and `POP` instructions.

It is important to ensure that the return value is in the `ST(0)` register at the end of the function. You may have to write the function code specifically to accommodate this, or just push the floating-point value onto the top of the FPU stack when the calculations are done.

The `floattest.c` program is a sample C program that uses the `areafunc` function:

```
/* floattest.c - An example of using floating point return values */
#include <stdio.h>

float areafunc(int);

int main()
{
        int radius = 10;
        float result;
        result = areafunc(radius);
        printf("The result is %f\n", result);

        result = areafunc(2);
        printf("The result is %f\n", result);
        return 0;
}
```

As usual, you must ensure that the `areafunc` code is available when the `floattest.c` program is compiled:

```
$ gcc -o floattest floattest.c areafunc.o
$ ./floattest
The result is 314.159271
The result is 12.566371
$
```

Using multiple input values

When working with assembly functions, you may need to pass more than one input value. There is no limit to the number of input values you can pass to the assembly language function. Each of the input values is placed on the stack before the function is called.

When using multiple input values, you must be careful with the order in which they are passed to the function. The input values are placed in order left to right as they are listed in the C function. Thus, the function

```
int i = 10;
int j = 20;
result = function1(i, j);
```

would place the input values onto the stack in the order shown in Figure 14-3.

401

Program Stack

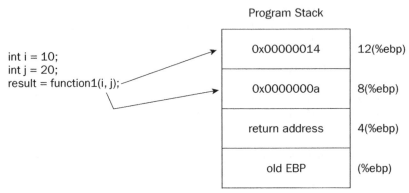

Figure 14-3

The second input value, j, is placed in the stack first, with the first input value, i, placed next. Remember that the stack grows downward. The first input value is referenced within the function using the location 8(%ebp), while the second input value is referenced using the location 12(%ebp).

This can be demonstrated in a simple assembly language function example. The greater.s function accepts two integer input values, and returns the largest value:

```
# greater.s - An example of using multiple input values
.section .text
.globl greater
greater:
    pushl %ebp
    movl %esp, %ebp
    movl 8(%ebp), %eax
    movl 12(%ebp), %ecx
    cmpl %ecx, %eax
    jge end
    movl %ecx, %eax
end:
    movl %ebp, %esp
    popl %ebp
    ret
```

The greater.s program obtains both of the input values from their location in the stack and loads them into scratch registers. The registers are compared using the CMP instruction. The JGE instruction is used to determine whether the EAX register (containing the first input value) is greater than or equal to the ECX register (containing the second input value). If the ECX register value is larger, it is copied into the EAX register, and the function returns to the calling program.

A C program that uses the greater function is demonstrated in the multtest.c program:

```
/* multtest.c - An example of using multiple input values */
#include <stdio.h>

int main()
{
```

```
        int i = 10;
        int j = 20;
        int k = greater(i, j);
        printf("The larger value is %d\n", k);
        return 0;
}
```

The multtest.c program places two integer values into the stack and assigns the return value to the k variable.

Using mixed data type input values

Things can get even more complicated when an assembly language function requires multiple input values of different data types. Two problems can occur when using mixed data type input values:

❏   The calling program can place values on the stack in the wrong order.

❏   The assembly function can read values from the stack in the wrong order.

Care must be taken to ensure that the input values are placed in the function properly by the calling program, and that the input values are read from the stack in the proper order by the assembly language function. This section provides a couple of examples of how this should be done.

Placing input values in the proper order

If you are working with data types that use different data sizes, you must ensure that the calling program places input values into the stack in the order in which the assembly language function reads them. If some input values are 4-byte integer values and others are 8-byte double-precision floating-point values, bad things will happen if the data is not read properly by the function. Figure 14-4 shows what will happen when double and integer data type input values are placed on the stack in an order other than the one the function was expecting.

To demonstrate this, let's create an assembly language function that requires a double-precision floating-point input value and an integer input value. The testfunc.s program can be used for this:

```
# testfunc.s - An example of reading input values wrong
.section .text
.type testfunc, @function
.globl testfunc
testfunc:
    pushl %ebp
    movl %esp, %ebp

    fldl 8(%ebp)
    fimul 16(%ebp)

    movl %ebp, %esp
    popl %ebp
    ret
```

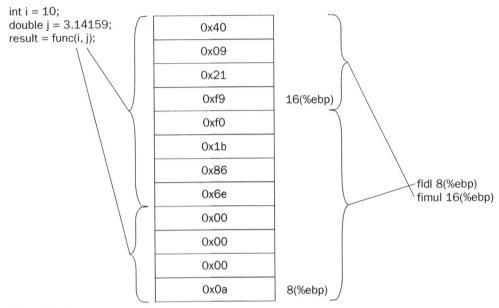

Figure 14-4

The `testfunc.s` function assumes that the first input value is an 8-byte double-precision floating-point value, and loads it into the FPU stack. It then assumes that the next input value is located 8 bytes away from the first value, and is a 4-byte integer value. That value is multiplied with the first value in the FPU stack. The result is returned in the `ST(0)` register in the FPU stack.

Now let's write a program that passes the input values in the wrong order. The `badprog.c` program does just that:

```
/* badprog.c - An example of passing input values in the wrong order */
#include <stdio.h>

double testfunc(int, double);

int main()
{
        int data1 = 10;
        double data2 = 3.14159;
        double result;

        result = testfunc(data1, data2);
        printf("The bad result is %g\n", result);
        return 0;
}
```

The function prototype incorrectly shows the order of the input values as the integer value first, then the double-precision floating-point value. The data is loaded in the wrong order, and the result is not what we would expect to happen:

```
$ ./badprog
The bad result is -
9291274822480358678995369145328760099241096905433756554130209688187885291554357289
4413772962747966214641165081767300396982323052894859942400431429279594359396233998
2113800211710644388852457538528298713650846052599048994660587547918336.000000
$
```

Wow, that's really bad. To show you how it should work, here's the goodprog.c program, which correctly uses the testfunc function:

```
/* goodprog.c - An example of passing input values in the proper order */
#include <stdio.h>

double testfunc(double, int);

int main()
{
        double data1 = 3.14159;
        int data2 = 10;
        double result;

        result = testfunc(data1, data2);
        printf("The proper result is %f\n", result);
        return 0;
}
```

This time the function prototype correctly defines the testfunc function, and the function is used properly in the program code. When the program is run, the correct result is obtained:

```
$ gcc -o goodprog goodprog.c testfunc.s
$ ./goodprog
The proper result is 31.415900
$
```

Reading input values in the proper order

Besides ensuring that the input values are placed in the correct order by the calling program, you must also ensure that the assembly function reads the input values properly. The fpmathfunc.s program demonstrates reading multiple input values from the stack. This program duplicates the fpmath.s program presented in Chapter 9, "Advanced Math Functions," to solve the mathematical expression ((43.65 / 22) + (76.34 * 3.1)) / ((12.43 * 6) – (140.2 / 94.21)):

```
# fpmathfunc.s - An example of reading multiple input values
.section .text
.type fpmathfunc, @function
.globl fpmathfunc
fpmathfunc:
    pushl %ebp
    movl %esp, %ebp
    flds 8(%ebp)
    fidiv 12(%ebp)
    flds 16(%ebp)
    flds 20(%ebp)
```

```
        fmul %st(1), %st(0)
        fadd %st(2), %st(0)
        flds 24(%ebp)
        fimul 28(%ebp)
        flds 32(%ebp)
        flds 36(%ebp)
        fdivrp
        fsubr %st(1), %st(0)
        fdivr %st(2), %st(0)
        movl %ebp, %esp
        popl %ebp
        ret
```

The function reads the input values in their indexed position relative to the EBP register value, which points to the start of the stack. Each of the input values must use the proper index value to point to the correct location on the stack or the value will be read wrong.

To test this, the mathtest.c program uses the fpmathfunc.s function to calculate the equation using the assigned data values:

```c
/* mathtest.c - An example of using multiple input values */
#include <stdio.h>

float fpmathfunc(float, int, float, float, float, int, float, float);

int main()
{
        float value1 = 43.65;
        int value2 = 22;
        float value3 = 76.34;
        float value4 = 3.1;
        float value5 = 12.43;
        int value6 = 6;
        float value7 = 140.2;
        float value8 = 94.21;
        float result;
        result = fpmathfunc(value1, value2, value3, value4,
                        value5, value6, value7, value8);
        printf("The final result is %f\n", result);
        return 0;
}
```

The function prototype for the fpmathfunc function declares the format of the function. The input value order is crucial in placing the proper values in the proper order. The function return value is declared as a single-precision floating-point value.

The programs can be compiled and run from the command line:

```
$ gcc -o mathtest mathtest.c fpmathfunc.s
$ ./mathtest
The final result is 3.264907
$
```

The result matches the result obtained from the fpmath.s program in Chapter 9.

Using Assembly Functions in C++ Programs

The rules for using assembly language functions in C++ programs are almost the same as using them in C programs. There is only one difference, but that difference is a major point.

By default, C++ programs assume that all functions used in a C++ program use the C++ style naming and calling conventions. However, the assembly language functions used in the program use the C calling convention (see the "Creating Assembly Functions" section). You must tell the compiler which functions used are C functions. This is done with the `extern` statement.

The `extern` statement is used to define the functions that use the C calling convention, using the following format:

```
extern "C"
{
    int square(int);
    float areafunc(int);
    char *cpuidfunc();
}
```

Each assembly language function prototype used must be placed within the `extern` statement. This ensures that the compiler will use the C calling convention when accessing the function, and not mangle the function name.

The `externtest.cpp` program demonstrates using the assembly language functions in a C++ program:

```
/* externtest.cpp - An example of using assembly language functions with C++ */
#include <iostream.h>

extern "C" {
   int square(int);
   float areafunc(int);
   char *cpuidfunc(void);
}


int main()
{
   int radius = 10;
   int radsquare = square(radius);
   cout << "The radius squared is " << radsquare << endl;
   float result;
   result = areafunc(radius);
   cout << "The area is " << result << endl;
   cout << "The CPUID is " << cpuidfunc() << endl;
   return 0;
}
```

The only difference between the C++ code and the C program examples is the use of the `extern` statement to declare the assembly language functions (aside from using `cout` instead of `printf` for displaying the output, of course). To compile the program, you need to include all of the appropriate assembly language object files on the command line:

```
$ g++ -o externtest externtest.cpp square.o areafunc.o cpuidfunc.o
$ ./externtest
The radius squared is 100
The area is 314.159
The CPUID is GenuineIntel
$
```

Creating Static Libraries

When working on programming projects that use C programs and assembly language functions, it is easy to get bogged down in building the executable file from the myriad of object files. If you create a separate object file for each assembly language function, there can easily be dozens of different files that need to be compiled into your C programs. Not only do the C programs call assembly functions, the assembly functions themselves can call other assembly functions.

The problem of trying to organize large quantities of assembly function object files can be simplified by using *libraries*. This section describes how libraries work, and shows how to create a library of assembly functions that can be used to compile C programs.

What is a static library?

As you saw earlier in "Compiling the C and Assembly Programs," the GNU C compiler has numerous options for how it compiles the assembly language functions with the main C program. For a C program that relies on several functions, each function object file can be included on the compiler command line for the compiler to include with the main program.

Instead of including each separate function object file separately on the command line, the GNU C compiler enables you to combine all of the object files into a single archive file. When you compile the main C program, all you need to include is the single object archive file. The compiler can pick the proper object file required out of the archive file at compile time, as shown in Figure 14-5.

The archive file can be used to compile any program that uses any of the functions contained within the archive file. This archive is referred to as a *library file*.

The library file contains object files for many functions. Functions are often grouped together by application type or function type into a library file. Multiple library files can be used within a single application project.

This type of library file is called static, because the object code contained in the library file is compiled into the main program from the compiler. Once the function object code is compiled into the executable code, the library file is not needed for the executable program to run. However, this means that every copy of the program contains the code for the functions within it. As you will see in the section "Using Shared Libraries," shared libraries can help programs share object file code among themselves to conserve memory requirements.

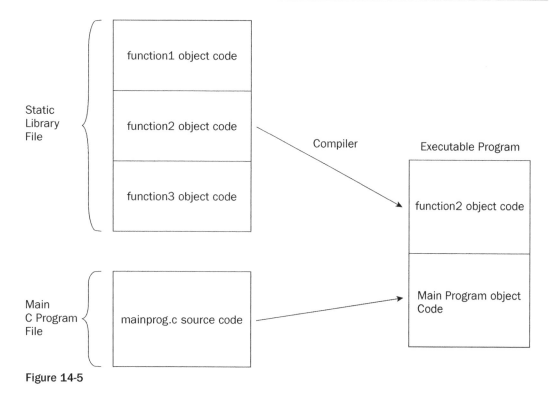

Figure 14-5

The ar command

In Linux, static library files are created using the ar command. The ar command creates an archive file of the function object files that can be read by the compiler. You can use several command-line options with the ar command, as described in the following table.

Option	Description
d	Delete files from the archive.
m	Move files in the archive.
p	Print to stdout a specified file in the archive.
q	Quickly append a file to the archive.
r	Insert files (with replacement) into the archive.
t	Display a table of files in the archive.
x	Extract files from the archive.

The basic options can be modified using one or more modifiers, shown in the next table.

Modifier	Description
a	Add new files after existing files in the archive.
b	Add new files before existing files in the archive.
c	Create a new archive.
f	Truncate names in the archive.
i	Insert new files before existing files in the archive.
P	Use the full pathname of files in the archive.
s	Write an index for the archive.
u	Update files in the archive (replace older ones with newer ones).
v	Use verbose mode.

The command-line format of the `ar` command is as follows:

```
ar [-]{dmpqrtx}[abcfilNoPsSuvV] [membername] [count] archive files...
```

The `archive` parameter defines a name for the library, and `files` is the list of object files to include in the library file, each separated by a space.

Creating a static library file

Before using the `ar` command, you must have an object file for each function you want to include in the library. This can be done using the `as` command with the `-o` option as normal.

Before creating the library file, you should decide on a naming convention for the library. Different operating systems use different conventions for identifying library files. The Linux operating system uses the convention

```
libx.a
```

where `x` is the name of the library. The `a` extension identifies the file as a static library file.

The `ar` command format for creating a new archive and adding new files is fairly straightforward. The following command creates an archive of the assembly language functions shown thus far in this chapter:

```
$ ar r libchap14.a square.o cpuidfunc.o areafunc.o greater.o fpmathfunc.o
```

No output results from the `ar` command, other than the library file that is created. You can use the `t` command-line option to display the files that are contained in the library:

```
$ ar t libchap14.a
cpuid.o
square.o
area.o
```

```
cpuidfunc.o
areafunc.o
greater.o
fpmathfunc.o
$
```

If you want a more detailed listing of the library files, you can include the v option:

```
$ ar tv libchap14.a
rw-r--r-- 501/501      592 Sep 21 19:03 2004 cpuid.o
rw-r--r-- 501/501      480 Sep 21 19:03 2004 square.o
rw-r--r-- 501/501      482 Sep 21 19:03 2004 area.o
rw-r--r-- 501/501      596 Sep 22 11:56 2004 cpuidfunc.o
rw-r--r-- 501/501      486 Sep 22 20:06 2004 areafunc.o
rw-r--r-- 501/501      940 Sep 22 18:00 2004 greater.o
rw-r--r-- 501/501     1104 Sep 21 20:55 2004 fpmathfunc.o
$
```

The timestamps on the files represent the times they were created by the assembler, not the time they were added to the archive file.

After the library file is created, it is a good idea to create an index for the library to help speed up the compilation when other programs must link with the library. The ranlib program is used to create the index for the library. The index is placed inside of the library file.

When you run the ranlib program, nothing too exciting is displayed:

```
$ ranlib libchap14.a
$
```

The archive index can be displayed using the nm program. The nm program is used to display symbols on object files:

```
$ nm -s libchap14.a | more

Archive index:
output in cpuid.o
cpuid in cpuid.o
square in square.o
area in area.o
output in cpuidfunc.o
cpuidfunc in cpuidfunc.o
areafunc in areafunc.o
greater in greater.o
fpmath in fpmathfunc.o
```

The nm command displayed each function name, and showed which object file contained the function. After displaying the function listings, a detailed listing of labels found in each object file is produced.

Compiling with static libraries

Once the static library file is created, you can use it to compile the C programs that require any of the functions contained within the library:

```
$ gcc -o intttest inttest.c libchap14.a
$ gcc -o stringtest stringtest.c libchap14.a
$ gcc -o floattest floattest.c libchap14.a
$
```

Using the library to compile the programs does not affect the size of the produced executable file. You can see this yourself by comparing the results from using just the single function object file and the static library file:

```
$ gcc -o inttest inttest.c square.o
$ ls -al inttest
-rwxr-xr-x   1 rich     rich         13838 Sep 22 16:36 inttest
$ gcc -o inttest inttest.c libchap14.a
$ ls -al inttest
-rwxr-xr-x   1 rich     rich         13838 Sep 22 16:37 inttest
$
```

The produced files are exactly the same size, and both run with the same results.

Using Shared Libraries

Thanks to Microsoft Windows, just about anyone familiar with computers knows about shared libraries. The Microsoft version of a shared library is the infamous DLL file. Nearly everyone has had the experience of an updated DLL file that has broken applications.

This section discusses what shared libraries are and how to create and use them in the Linux environment with your assembly language functions.

What are shared libraries?

The preceding section mentioned that when an application is compiled with a static library, the function code is compiled into the application. This means that all of the code the application needs is located within the executable program file.

Note the following disadvantages to this setup:

❑   If something changes in the function code, every application that uses the function must be recompiled with the new version.

❑   Multiple programs that use the same functions must all contain the same code. This can make a small application program larger than it needs to be, as it must contain all of the code from each function used.

❑   Multiple programs running on a system using the same function means that the same function is loaded into memory multiple times.

Shared libraries attempt to solve these problems. A separate file that contains the function object code is located in a common area on the operating system. When an application needs to access a function within the shared library, the operating system automatically loads the function code into memory, and allows the application to access it.

If another application also needs to use the function code, the operating system allows it to access the same function code already loaded in memory. Only one copy of the function code is needed in memory, and each of the individual programs that use the function code do not need it loaded into their memory space, or in their executable files. This is shown in Figure 14-6

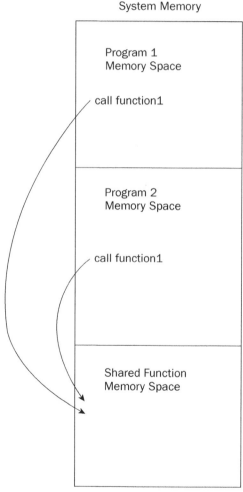

Figure 14-6

If any changes need to be made to the function, the single shared library file is the only file that needs to be updated. Each program that uses the shared library will automatically use the new version of the function. Of course, the trouble begins when a change to a function alters its previous behavior. This is what causes applications using shared libraries to break in the Windows environment. (Linux provides a method of creating a version number that can be compared by a calling program.)

Creating a shared library

The gcc compiler is used to create shared libraries from object files. You must assemble the assembly language functions using as before creating the shared library. Just as with static libraries, Linux has a naming convention that is used for shared libraries:

```
libx.so
```

where x is the name of the library, and the .so extension indicates that it is a shared library.

The gcc command-line option that creates a shared library is the -shared option:

```
$ gcc -shared -o libchap14.so square.o cpuidfunc.o areafunc.o \
greater.o fpmathfunc.o
```

The libchap14.so file contains all of the object code from the included assembly functions. To identify version information, the filename is usually appended with the version, such as libchap14.so.1. Unlike static libraries, the object code in shared libraries is not compiled into the executable programs.

Compiling with a shared library

Even though the shared library files are not compiled into the C program, the compiler must still know how to access the functions. The shared libraries are included on the compile command line using the -l option, along with the name of the shared library (minus the lib part and the .so extension). Before you can use the shared library, you must tell the compiler where to look for it, using the -L option. The parameter used with the -L option is any additional locations for the compiler to look for the shared library, besides the ones defined in the operating system (more on that in the next section). If the shared library is located in the same directory as the program file, you can use a period to indicate the same directory.

This makes the compile command line look like this:

```
$ gcc -o inttest -L. -lchap14 inttest.c
```

The compiler creates the executable file inttest without the function code included. To verify this, you can use the objdump program to disassemble the inttest executable file. The main section does not include a call to the square function. Instead, it includes the following line:

```
80484c1:       e8 ea fe ff ff          call   80483b0 <_init+0x28>
```

The call is not made to the square function. In fact, you will not find the square function code anywhere in the disassembled executable file. The call is to the Linux dynamic loader. This was discussed in Chapter 4 when the printf function was used in an assembly language program. The dynamic loader is used to automatically load the necessary shared library to provide the function requested at runtime. Now your assembly functions can be dynamically loaded as well.

To see what shared libraries an executable file relies on, you can use the `ldd` command:

```
$ ldd inttest
        libchap14.so => not found
        libc.so.6 => /lib/libc.so.6 (0x40027000)
        /lib/ld-linux.so.2 => /lib/ld-linux.so.2 (0x40000000)
$
```

The `ldd` command shows that the `inttest` executable program requires the `libchap14.so` shared library file to execute, and that it was not found on the system. This is a huge problem. If you try to run the new executable, this is what you will get:

```
$ ./inttest
./inttest: error while loading shared libraries: libchap14.so: cannot open shared
object file: No such file or directory
$
```

While you know the shared library is located in the same directory as the executable file, the Linux dynamic loader doesn't. There is one more piece of business you must take care of before you can use the shared library.

Running programs that use shared libraries

The dynamic loader must know how to access the `libchap14.so` shared library. There are two ways to inform it where the file is located:

❑   The `LD_LIBRARY_PATH` environment variable

❑   The `/etc/ld.so.conf` file

The following sections describe these two methods.

The LD_LIBRARY_PATH environment variable

The `LD_LIBRARY_PATH` environment variable is an easy way for any user on the system to add a path for the dynamic loader for the current process. It contains a list of paths (separated by colons) where the dynamic loader should look for library files apart from the ones listed in the `ld.so.conf` file. You do not need any special privileges to use the `LD_LIBRARY_PATH` environment variable; just set it:

```
$ export LD_LIBRARY_PATH="$LD_LIBRARY_PATH:."
$ ldd inttest
        libchap14.so => libchap14.so (0x40017000)
        libc.so.6 => /lib/libc.so.6 (0x40028000)
        /lib/ld-linux.so.2 => /lib/ld-linux.so.2 (0x40000000)
$ ./inttest
The square of 2 is 4
The square of 10 is 100
$
```

415

This example appends a period to the end of the existing LD_LIBRARY_PATH value. The period represents the current directory in Linux. This means that the dynamic loader will look for the libchap14.so library file in the current working directory. Now when the ldd command is used, it can properly find the libchap14.so library file, and the program runs the way it should.

The /etc/ld.so.conf file

The ld.so.conf file located in the /etc directory keeps a list of the directories in which the dynamic loader will look for libraries. On my Debian system it looks like this:

```
$ cat /etc/ld.so.conf
/lib
/usr/lib
/usr/X11R6/lib
/usr/i486-linuxlibc1/lib

/usr/lib/libc5-compat
/lib/libc5-compat
$
```

These are the directories where the system shared library files should be located for the dynamic loader to find them. You can place the libchap14.so library file in any of these directories and the dynamic loader will find it just fine. However, it is not a good idea to mix system libraries with application libraries.

It is best to create a separate directory for your application libraries, and add it to the ld.so.conf file. Most Linux distributions include a /usr/local/lib directory in which application shared libraries can be stored. To avoid having a mess of library files in this directory, you can create a separate subdirectory in here for your applications, and store the application library files required.

After the new directory is added to the ld.so.conf file, you must run the ldconfig command (as the root user) to update the ld.so.cache file, which is what is used by the dynamic loader:

```
$ ldconfig
$ ldd inttest
        libchap14.so => /usr/local/lib/apps/libchap14.so (0x40026000)
        libc.so.6 => /lib/libc.so.6 (0x40028000)
        /lib/ld-linux.so.2 => /lib/ld-linux.so.2 (0x40000000)
$ ./inttest
The square of 2 is 4
The square of 10 is 100
$
```

*The **ldconfig** program inventories the library files in the directories to add to the **ld.so.cache** file. If your library file is not located in one of the directories when the **ldconfig** program is run, it will not work if added later. Each time you add a new library file, you must run **ldconfig**.*

Now the ldd command indicates that it found the shared library in the /usr/local/lib/apps directory.

Once the shared library is in place, any application that requires it will work:

```
$ gcc -o stringtest -L/usr/local/lib/apps -lchap14 stringtest.c
$ ./stringtest
The CPUID is: 'GenuineIntel'
$
```

Debugging Assembly Functions

If you have been following along in the book, by now you should be proficient at using the GNU debugger (gdb) to troubleshoot your assembly language applications. However, there are still a couple of tricks to learn when trying to debug assembly language functions that operate within C or C++ programs. This section covers a couple of things that you need to know to debug assembly language functions.

Debugging C programs

Using the gdb debugger to debug C programs is very similar to using it to debug assembly language programs. You must use the -g option when the C program is compiled. For more information specific to the Linux environment, you can use the -gstabs option:

```
$ gcc -gstabs -o inttest inttest.c square.s
```

This command produces an executable file that includes debugging information for the C program code. You can then start the program in the debugger and use the 1 command to list the source code lines:

```
$ gdb -q inttest
(gdb) 1
1       /* inttest.c - An example of returning an integer value */
2       #include <stdio.h>
3
4       int main()
5       {
6               int i = 2;
7               int j = square(i);
8               printf("The square of %d is %d\n", i, j);
9
10              j = square(10);
(gdb) 1
11              printf("The square of 10 is %d\n", j);
12              return 0;
13      }
(gdb)
```

When debugging C programs, you can set breakpoints using either labels or line numbers. To set a breakpoint at the start of the program, you would use the following:

```
(gdb) break *main
Breakpoint 1 at 0x8048460: file inttest.c, line 5.
(gdb)
```

417

Now the program can be started, and you can single-step though the C statements. If any C variables are present they can be displayed using the `print` command:

```
(gdb) run
Starting program: /home/rich/palp/chap14/inttest

Breakpoint 1, main () at inttest.c:5
5       {
(gdb) s
main () at inttest.c:6
6               int i = 2;
(gdb) s
7               int j = square(i);
(gdb) s
8               printf("The square of %d is %d\n", i, j);
(gdb) print i
$1 = 2
(gdb) print j
$2 = 4
(gdb)
```

Notice that when the assembly function was encountered in the C statements, the debugger treated it as a single statement. When the debugger stepped into the function, it finished within the single step. This may or may not be the result you intended.

Even though the assembly language function source code was included in the compile, the debugging information was not added to the executable program. The next section shows how you can alter this.

Debugging assembly functions

If you want the debugger to step into an assembly language function within a C program, you must assemble the function separately, and include the debugging information within the object code file generated by the assembler. The resulting object file can then be compiled with the C program:

```
$ as -gstabs -o square.o square.s
$ gcc -gstabs -o inttest inttest.c square.o
```

Now when the executable file is run in the debugger, you will see a different result when stepping into the assembly language function:

```
$ gdb -q inttest
(gdb) break *main
Breakpoint 1 at 0x8048460: file inttest.c, line 5.
(gdb) run
Starting program: /home/rich/palp/chap14/inttest

Breakpoint 1, main () at inttest.c:5
5       {
(gdb) s
main () at inttest.c:6
```

```
6                    int i = 2;
(gdb) s
7                    int j = square(i);
(gdb) s
square () at square.s:5
5           pushl %ebp
Current language:  auto; currently asm
(gdb)
```

Now when the assembly language function is reached, taking another step enters the source code of the function. Notice that the debugger indicates that it is switching over to assembly language format. When the end of the assembly language function is reached, the next step returns to the C program:

```
(gdb) s
10          popl %ebp
(gdb) s
square () at square.s:11
11          ret
(gdb) s
main () at inttest.c:8
8                    printf("The square of %d is %d\n", i, j);
Current language:  auto; currently c
(gdb)
```

If you have a lot of assembly language functions in an application but only want to step through a particular one, you can use the next command to skip over stepping into the function:

```
(gdb) run
Starting program: /home/rich/palp/chap14/inttest

Breakpoint 1, main () at inttest.c:5
5       {
Current language:  auto; currently c
(gdb) s
main () at inttest.c:6
6                    int i = 2;
(gdb) s
7                    int j = square(i);
(gdb) n
8                    printf("The square of %d is %d\n", i, j);
(gdb)
```

When the next command is issued, the debugger processes the function without stepping into it.

Because the assembly language functions must be assembled with the debugging information in them, it is often beneficial to create two libraries: one containing the assembly language function object files without the debugging information and one containing object files with debugging information. This enables you to choose which versions are compiled into the program to create both development and production versions of the program.

Summary

This chapter described how to use assembly language functions with C and C++ programs. Assembly functions that are called by C or C++ programs must be in a specific format. The C style function format requires that any input values for the function be placed on the stack. The function must preserve the registers that are used by the calling program, such as the EBX, EBP, ESP, EDI, and ESI registers. This is done by pushing the register values onto the stack at the start of the function and popping them off of the stack before the function returns to the calling program.

The function reads any input values from the stack, and places integer and string pointer results in the EAX register to be read by the calling function. If a floating-point value is returned, it is placed in the FPU ST(0) register, which is read and cleared by the calling program. If the C calling program expects a pointer or floating-point return value, the assembly function must be prototyped in the source code, defining the expected return value for the compiler.

When building applications that use both C programs and assembly language functions, you must ensure that all of the functions are available to the compiler when the C program is compiled. This can be accomplished by either including the assembly language function source code files in the compiler command line or by assembling the assembly language functions separately, and including the object code files on the compiler command line.

When an application uses a lot of assembly language functions, it can become tiresome to include all of the required files in the compiler command line. Instead, you can create a library file that contains all of the assembly function object files in a single location. Two types of library files can be used on Linux systems.

A static library file contains the object code for all of the assembly language functions in one file that is compiled into the main C program executable file. Each program that is created using the static library file contains the full object code for the assembly language functions it uses. The executable file can be run by itself and does not require any additional files from the operating system.

Shared library files also combine multiple assembly language function object files into a single library file. The difference with shared libraries is that the object code is not compiled into the main C executable file. Instead, the Linux system's dynamic loader program is used by the C executable file to call the object code from the shared library file when it is required. Because the function object code is loaded separately into system memory, the dynamic loader can reuse the same code for other programs that are running.

Now that you know how to use assembly language functions within C programs, it's time to start experimenting with them. The next chapter shows you how to take a C program and determine how assembly language functions can be used to help increase performance in specific areas of the application.

15

Optimizing Routines

If you have been programming professionally using C or C++, you probably picked up this book to learn assembly language to help optimize your applications. Now that you are familiar with assembly language, you are ready to start analyzing your applications and putting your assembly language knowledge to use.

However, just writing functions in assembly language code instead of C or C++ does not necessarily make them perform better. Remember, the GNU compiler already converts all of your high-level language code to assembly language, so writing a function in assembly language just means that you did it instead of the compiler.

To truly optimize high-level language functions, you need to write better assembly language code than the compiler does. This can be quite a challenge. There are several optimization tricks the compiler can be instructed to perform on the generated assembly language code. Before you begin diving into writing your own assembly language functions, it's a good idea to see what techniques the experts use to optimize assembly language code, and then duplicate and possibly even improve on them.

To view optimized assembly language code, you need to know how to generate it from the compiler. This chapter first discusses how to use the various optimization levels when compiling C or C++ programs, and what optimization techniques are utilized within each optimization level. After that, a sample optimization session is shown to acquaint you with the techniques to use to view, modify, and recompile the optimized code. After that, five of the more common optimization techniques used by the compiler are dissected, enabling you to learn how the optimization techniques work, and how to duplicate them in your own assembly language coding.

Optimized Compiler Code

In the old days of C programming, it was commonplace for programmers who wanted to optimize an application to pore over lines and lines of assembly language code, looking for instruction code to improve. Now, thanks to optimizing compilers, most of that work is already done for us. The GNU compiler is no different. It includes options that enable you to specify optimizations geared specifically to the program type and the processor for which the code is compiled.

The -O family of compiler options provides steps of optimization for the GNU compiler. Each step provides a higher level of optimization. There are currently three steps available for optimizing:

- ❑   **-O:** Provides a basic level of optimization
- ❑   **-O2:** Provides more advanced code optimization
- ❑   **-O3:** Provides the highest level of optimization

The optimization techniques incorporated in the different optimization levels can also be individually applied to the code. Each individual optimization technique can be referenced using the -f command-line option. The -O options bundle various -f options together in a single option.

This section describes the different -O optimization levels, and shows what -f options are included in each level.

Compiler optimization level 1

At the first level of optimization, basic code optimization is performed. Nine separate optimization functions are attempted at this level. I used the word "attempted" because there is no guarantee that any of them will be implemented, only that the compiler attempts to perform them. The -f optimization functions included at this level are described in the following list:

- ❑   **-fdefer-pop:** This optimization technique is related to how the assembly language code acts when a function is finished. Normally, input values for functions are placed on the stack and accessed by the function. When the function returns, the input values are still on the stack. Normally, the input values are popped from the stack immediately following the function return.

   This option permits the compiler to allow input values to accumulate on the stack across function calls. The accumulated input values are then removed all at once with a single instruction (usually by changing the stack pointer to the proper value). For most operations this is perfectly legal, as input values for new functions are placed on top of the old input values. However, this does make things somewhat messy on the stack.

- ❑   **-fmerge-constants:** With this optimization technique, the compiler attempts to merge identical constants. This feature can sometimes result in long compile times, as the compiler must analyze every constant used in the C or C++ program, comparing them with one another.

- ❑   **-fthread-jumps:** This optimization technique relates to how the compiler handles both conditional and unconditional branches in the assembly code. In some cases, one jump instruction may lead to another conditional branch statement. By threading jumps, the compiler determines the final destination between multiple jumps and redirects the first jump to the final destination.

- ❑   **-floop-optimize:** By optimizing how loops are generated in the assembly language, the compiler can greatly increase the performance of the application. Often, programs consist of many loops that are large and complex. By removing variable assignments that do not change value within the loops, the number of instructions performed within the loop can be reduced, greatly improving performance. In addition, any conditional branches made to determine when to leave the loop are optimized to reduce the effects of the branching.

❑ **-fif-conversion:** Next to loops, `if-then` statements are the second most time-consuming part of an application. A simple `if-then` statement can generate numerous conditional branches in the final assembly language code. By reducing or eliminating conditional branches and replacing them with conditional moves, setting flags, and performing arithmetic tricks, the compiler can reduce the amount of time spent in the `if-then` statements.

❑ **-fif-conversion2:** This technique incorporates more advanced mathematical features that reduce the conditional branching required to implement the `if-then` statements.

❑ **-fdelayed-branch:** This technique attempts to reorder instructions based on instruction cycle times. It also attempts to move as many instructions before conditional branches as possible to maximize the use of the processor instruction cache.

❑ **-fguess-branch-probability:** As its name suggests, this technique attempts to determine the most likely outcome of conditional branches, and moves instructions accordingly, similar to the delayed-branch technique. Because the code placement is predicted at compile time, it is quite possible that compiling the same C or C++ code twice using this option can produce different assembly language source code, depending on what branches the compiler thought would be used at compile time.

Because of this, many programmers prefer not to incorporate this feature, and specifically include the `-fno-guess-branch-probability` option to turn it off.

❑ **-fcprop-registers:** As registers are allocated to variables within functions, the compiler performs a second pass to reduce scheduling dependencies (two sections requiring the same register) and eliminate needlessly copying registers.

Compiler optimization level 2

The second level of code optimization (`-O2`) incorporates all of the optimization techniques of the first level, plus a lot of additional techniques. These techniques are related to more specific types of code, such as loops and conditional branches. If the basic assembly language code generated by the compiler does not utilize the type of code analyzed in this level, no additional optimization will be performed. The following list describes the additional `-f` optimization options that are attempted at this level.

❑ **-fforce-mem:** This optimization forces all variables stored in memory locations to be copied to registers before using them in any instructions. For variables that are only involved in a single instruction, this may not be much of an optimization. However, for variables that are involved in a lot of instructions (such as mathematical operations), this can be a huge optimization, as the processor can access the value in a register much quicker than in memory.

❑ **-foptimize-sibling-calls:** This technique deals with function calls that are related and/or recursive. Often, recursive function calls can be unrolled into a common string of instructions, rather than using branching. This enables the processor instruction cache to load the unrolled instructions and process them faster than if they remain as separate function calls requiring branching.

❑ **-fstrength-reduce:** This optimization technique performs loop optimization and eliminates iteration variables. Iteration variables are variables that are tied to loop counters, such as for-next loops that use a variable and then perform mathematical operations using the loop counter variable.

❏ **-fgcse:** This performs Global Common Subexpression Elimination (gcse) routines on all of the generated assembly language code. These optimizations attempt to analyze the generated assembly language code and combine common pieces, eliminating redundant code segments.

It should be noted that the gcc instructions recommend using -fno-gcse if the code uses computed gotos.

❏ **-fcse-follow-jumps:** This particular Common Subexpression Elimination (cse) technique scans through a jump instruction looking for destination code that is not reached via any other means within the program. The most common example of this is the else part of if-then-else statements.

❏ **-frerun-cse-after-loop:** This technique reruns the Common Subexpression Elimination routines after any loops have been optimized. This enables loop code to be further optimized after it has been unrolled.

❏ **-fdelete-null-pointer-checks:** This optimization technique scans the generated assembly language code for code that checks for null pointers. The compiler assumes that dereferencing a null pointer would halt the program. If a pointer is checked after it has been dereferenced, it cannot be null.

❏ **-fexpensive-optimizations:** This performs various optimization techniques that are expensive from a compile-time point of view, but it can have a negative effect on runtime performance.

❏ **-fregmove:** The compiler will attempt to reassign registers used in MOV instructions and as operands of other instructions in order to maximize the amount of register tying.

❏ **-fschedule-insns:** The compiler will attempt to reorder instructions in order to eliminate processor waits for data. For processors that have delays associated with floating-point arithmetic, this enables the processor to load other instructions while it waits for the floating-point results.

❏ **-fsched-interblock:** This technique enables the compiler to schedule instructions across blocks of instructions. This provides greater flexibility in moving instructions around to maximize work done during wait times.

❏ **-fcaller-saves:** This option instructs the compiler to save and restore registers around function calls to enable the functions to clobber register values without having to save and restore them. This can be a time-saver if multiple functions are called because the registers are saved and restored only once, instead of within each function call.

❏ **-fpeephole2:** This option enables any machine-specific peephole optimizations.

❏ **-freorder-blocks:** This optimization technique enables blocks of instructions to be reordered to improve branching and code locality.

❏ **-fstrict-aliasing:** This technique enforces strict variable rules for the higher-level language. For C and C++ programs, it ensures that variables are not shared between data types. For example, an integer variable cannot use the same memory location as a single-precision floating-point variable.

❏ **-funit-at-a-time:** This optimization technique instructs the compiler to read the entire assembly language code before running the optimization routines. This enables the compiler to reorder non-time-sensitive code to optimize the instruction cache. However, it takes considerably more memory during compile time, which may be a problem for smaller machines.

❏ **-falign-functions:** This option is used to align functions at the start of a specific boundary in memory. Most processors read memory in pages, and enabling an entire function code to reside in a single page can improve performance. If a function crosses pages, another page of memory must be processed to complete the function.

❑ **-falign-loops:** Similar to aligning functions, loops that contain code that is processed multiple times can benefit from being aligned within a page boundary in memory. When the loop is processed, if it is contained within a single memory page, no swapping of pages is required for the code.

❑ **-fcrossjumping:** The process of cross-jumping transforms code to combine equivalent code scattered throughout the program. This saves code size, but it may not have a direct impact on program performance.

Compiler optimization level 3

The highest level of optimization provided by the compiler is accessed using the -O3 option. It incorporates all of the optimization techniques listed in levels one and two, along with some very specific additional optimizations. Again, there is no guarantee that this level of optimization will improve performance of the final code. The following -f optimization options are included at this level:

❑ **-finline-functions:** Instead of creating separate assembly language code for functions, this optimization technique includes the function code within the code from the calling program. For functions that are called multiple times, the function code is duplicated for each function call. While this may not be good for code size, it can increase performance by maximizing the instruction cache code usage, instead of branching on each function call.

❑ **-fweb:** This constructs a web of pseudo-registers to hold variables. The pseudo-registers contain data as if they were registers, but can be optimized by the various other optimization techniques, such as cse and loop optimizing.

❑ **-fgcse-after-reload:** This technique performs a second gcse optimization after completely reloading the generated and optimized assembly language code. This helps eliminate any redundant sections created by the different optimization passes.

Creating Optimized Code

The gcc compiler can be used to create optimized assembly language code for you from C and C++ programs. By default, the optimized code is compiled into object code files and linked into executable files. If you want to analyze the optimized code and either learn from it or even improve on it, you must intercept the generated assembly language code before it is compiled.

This section describes the steps to take to create and view the optimized assembly language code generated from the compiled C or C++ source code, and how to assemble it back into the normal executable application.

Generating the assembly language code

The first step to optimizing assembly language code is to view the non-optimized version so you can get an idea of what the compiler is doing with your C or C++ source code. This involves using the -S option of the GNU compiler.

The -S option creates a file that contains the generated assembly language code from the higher-level language source code. To demonstrate this, the tempconv.c program is a simple C program that uses a single function to convert temperatures in Fahrenheit to Celsius:

```c
/* tempconv.c - An example for viewing assembly source code */
#include <stdio.h>

float convert(int deg)
{
        float result;
        result = (deg - 32.) / 1.8;
        return result;
}

int main()
{
        int i = 0;
        float result;
        printf("    Temperature Conversion Chart\n");
        printf("Fahrenheit        Celsius\n");
        for(i = 0; i < 230; i = i + 10)
        {
                result = convert(i);
                printf("  %d                %5.2f\n", i, result);
        }
        return 0;
}
```

There is nothing special about the tempconv.c program. It uses a single function to calculate the temperature conversion. The main part of the program uses a simple loop to loop through a set of input values to use for the calculations.

To generate the basic assembly language code for the application, you would use the following command:

```
$ gcc -S tempconv.c
```

This creates the file tempconv.s, which contains the assembly language code generated by the compiler:

```
.file   "tempconv.c"
        .version        "01.01"
gcc2_compiled.:
                .section        .rodata
        .align 8
.LC0:
        .long   0x0,0x40400000
        .align 8
.LC1:
        .long   0xcccccccd,0x3ffccccc
.text
        .align 16
.globl convert
        .type   convert,@function
convert:
```

```
        pushl    %ebp
        movl     %esp, %ebp
        subl     $8, %esp
        fildl    8(%ebp)
        fldl     .LC0
        fsubrp   %st, %st(1)
        fldl     .LC1
        fdivrp   %st, %st(1)
        fstps    -4(%ebp)
        flds     -4(%ebp)
        movl     %ebp, %esp
        popl     %ebp
        ret
.Lfe1:
        .size    convert,.Lfe1-convert
                 .section        .rodata
        .align 32
.LC3:
        .string "      Temperature Conversion Chart\n"
.LC4:
        .string "Fahrenheit        Celsius\n"
.LC5:
        .string "  %d              %5.2f\n"
.text
        .align 16
.globl main
        .type    main,@function
main:
        pushl    %ebp
        movl     %esp, %ebp
        subl     $8, %esp
        movl     $0, -4(%ebp)
        subl     $12, %esp
        pushl    $.LC3
        call     printf
        addl     $16, %esp
        subl     $12, %esp
        pushl    $.LC4
        call     printf
        addl     $16, %esp
        movl     $0, -4(%ebp)
        .p2align 4,,7
.L4:
        cmpl     $229, -4(%ebp)
        jle      .L7
        jmp      .L5
        .p2align 4,,7
.L7:
        subl     $12, %esp
        pushl    -4(%ebp)
        call     convert
        addl     $16, %esp
        fstps    -8(%ebp)
        flds     -8(%ebp)
```

```
        leal    -8(%esp), %esp
        fstpl   (%esp)
        pushl   -4(%ebp)
        pushl   $.LC5
        call    printf
        addl    $16, %esp
        leal    -4(%ebp), %eax
        addl    $10, (%eax)
        jmp     .L4
        .p2align 4,,7
.L5:
        movl    $0, %eax
        movl    %ebp, %esp
        popl    %ebp
        ret
.Lfe2:
        .size   main,.Lfe2-main
        .ident  "GCC: (GNU) 2.96 20000731 (Linux-Mandrake 8.0 2.96-0.48mdk)"
```

By now you should be comfortable with analyzing the generated assembly language code for the application. The code generated for the convert() function should be easy to follow. First, the normal C style function prologue is used to set the base stack pointer, and to reserve space for two local variables:

```
convert:
        pushl   %ebp
        movl    %esp, %ebp
        subl    $8, %esp
```

Next, the input value is read from the stack and loaded into the FPU stack, and the first numeric constant (32) is loaded into the FPU stack:

```
        fildl   8(%ebp)
        fldl    .LC0
```

Next, the subtraction is performed, with the result stored in the ST(0) FPU register:

```
        fsubrp  %st, %st(1)
```

After that, the divisor value is loaded into the FPU stack, and the division step is performed:

```
        fldl    .LC1
        fdivrp  %st, %st(1)
```

Now the result is located in the ST(0) register, which will be read by the main program when the function returns. However, the compiler performs something odd. First, it pops the value off of the FPU stack and loads it into the local variable, and then it loads that value from the local variable back into the FPU stack:

```
        fstps   -4(%ebp)
        flds    -4(%ebp)
```

This is definitely something that can be eliminated in the optimization process.

Viewing optimized code

Now that you have seen the basic assembly language code generated by the compiler, it's time to see what the optimized code looks like. Again, to view the assembly language code you must use the -S compiler option, along with the -O3 option to perform all of the optimizations. By default, the generated assembly language file will be placed in the tempconv.s file. To be able to compare it to the original generated code, you can use the -o option to declare a different file name:

```
$ gcc -O3 -S -o tempconv2.s tempconv.c
```

This command generates the tempcon2.s assembly language file, which contains the optimized code. The convert() function code in the optimized file looks like this:

```
convert:
        pushl   %ebp
        movl    %esp, %ebp
        pushl   %eax
        fildl   8(%ebp)
        fsubl   .LC0
        fdivl   .LC1
        fstps   -4(%ebp)
        flds    -4(%ebp)
        movl    %ebp, %esp
        popl    %ebp
        ret
```

Note some subtle differences that have been made. The constant values were not loaded separately using FLD instructions. Instead, they were used directly in the mathematical instructions. However, the optimization did not remove the unnecessary popping of the result from the FPU stack, and pushing it back on. To further optimize this function, you can remove the final FSTPS and FLDS instructions.

Recompiling the optimized code

After you have made any optimization changes to the assembly language code generated by the compiler, you must use it to create the optimized executable file. This can be done using one of two methods. The first method is by assembling and linking the optimized assembly language code file using the normal as and ld commands (remember to link with the C libraries to support any C functions in the code):

```
$ as -o tempconv.o tempconv2.s
$ ld -dynamic-linker /lib/ld-linux.so.2 -lc -o tempconv tempconv.s
```

The second method is to use the gcc compiler with the assembly language source code file:

```
$ gcc -o tempconv tempconv2.s
```

The new executable file contains the fully optimized code you created using the compiler and your own optimizations.

Optimization Tricks

Many optimizations used by the compiler come in handy not only with assembly language functions, but in assembly language programs in general. If you plan on doing serious assembly language programming, it is a good idea to become familiar with some of the more common tricks used to optimize assembly language code.

This section demonstrates five of the most common optimizations used in assembly language:

❑ Optimizing calculations

❑ Optimizing variables

❑ Optimizing loops

❑ Optimizing conditional branches

❑ Optimizing common subexpressions

The following sections demonstrate these optimization techniques by providing a sample C program that presents C code that can be optimized, generating the non-optimized assembly language code, and showing how the generated assembly language code can be optimized by the compiler.

Optimizing calculations

When working with equations, there are almost always some calculations that can be simplified. Sometimes these calculations are entered into the C or C++ source code in an unsimplified form on purpose to show the flow of the equation while using the variables involved. Other times the source code is just a jumbled mess entered by an inexperienced programmer.

In either case, the compiler can optimize the assembly language code generated by the calculations. This section demonstrates how calculations can be optimized in your assembly language code to help increase the performance of your programs.

Calculations without optimization

To demonstrate how the compiler optimizes calculations, the `calctest.c` program will be used:

```
/* calctest.c - An example of pre-calculating values */
#include <stdio.h>

int main()
{
        int a = 10;
        int b, c;
        a = a + 15;
        b = a + 200;
        c = a + b;
        printf("The result is %d\n", c);
        return 0;
}
```

This sample program demonstrates using variables along with constant values to perform a simple calculation. Each of the values is calculated using a variable value that was defined previously in the code. The default assembly language source code generated for this using the -S compiler option looks like the following:

```
.file   "calctest.c"
        .version        "01.01"
gcc2_compiled.:
                .section        .rodata
.LC0:
        .string "The result is %d\n"
.text
        .align 16
.globl main
        .type   main,@function
main:
        pushl   %ebp
        movl    %esp, %ebp
        subl    $24, %esp
        movl    $10, -4(%ebp)
        leal    -4(%ebp), %eax
        addl    $15, (%eax)
        movl    -4(%ebp), %eax
        addl    $200, %eax
        movl    %eax, -8(%ebp)
        movl    -8(%ebp), %eax
        addl    -4(%ebp), %eax
        movl    %eax, -12(%ebp)
        subl    $8, %esp
        pushl   -12(%ebp)
        pushl   $.LC0
        call    printf
        addl    $16, %esp
        movl    $0, %eax
        movl    %ebp, %esp
        popl    %ebp
        ret
.Lfe1:
        .size   main,.Lfe1-main
        .ident  "GCC: (GNU) 2.96 20000731 (Linux-Mandrake 8.0 2.96-0.48mdk)"
```

The assembly language code generated by the compiler creates the program using the standard C style function format (see Chapter 14, "Calling Assembly Libraries"). The compiler reserves 24 bytes to use for local variable storage and uses that location to reference the following three program variables:

Program Variable	Stack Storage Location
a	-4(%ebp)
b	-8(%ebp)
c	-12(%ebp)

The compiler then generates the appropriate assembly language code to carry out the defined calculations on all of the local variables:

```
movl    $10, -4(%ebp)
leal    -4(%ebp), %eax
addl    $15, (%eax)
movl    -4(%ebp), %eax
addl    $200, %eax
movl    %eax, -8(%ebp)
movl    -8(%ebp), %eax
addl    -4(%ebp), %eax
movl    %eax, -12(%ebp)
```

The value of 10 is moved to the a local variable location. Indirect addressing is then used in the ADD instruction to add the 15 value to the memory location for the a variable. The result is placed in the EAX register, 200 is added to it, and that result is placed in the b variable stack location. Finally, the b variable value is loaded into the EAX register and added to the a variable value. That result is placed in the c variable stack location. The result is pushed onto the stack in the normal manner, along with the text used for the printf C function (notice that the compiler used the .string directive, which is the same as the .asciz directive).

All of the calculations are performed just as expected from the C code. However, this is a slow and monotonous way to come up with the result each time the program is run. The next section shows what happens when the compiler is allowed to optimize the code.

Viewing the optimized calculations

Instead of working through the assembly language code to implement the calculations each time, the compiler can be set to optimize the calculations. The compiler determines the values present in each of the calculations, recognizing which values won't change through the course of the program.

To generate optimized assembly language code, you can use the following command:

```
$ gcc -O3 -S -o calctest2.s calctest.c
```

This creates the file calctest2.s, which contains the optimized assembly language source code:

```
.file   "calctest.c"
        .version        "01.01"
gcc2_compiled.:
                .section        .rodata
.LC0:
        .string "The result is %d\n"
.text
        .align 16
.globl main
        .type   main,@function
main:
        pushl   %ebp
        movl    %esp, %ebp
        subl    $16, %esp
        pushl   $250
```

```
        pushl    $.LC0
        call     printf
        addl     $16, %esp
        movl     %ebp, %esp
        xorl     %eax, %eax
        popl     %ebp
        ret
.Lfe1:
.size    main,.Lfe1-main
        .ident  "GCC: (GNU) 2.96 20000731 (Linux-Mandrake 8.0 2.96-0.48mdk)"
```

That's all there is. That was quite a difference in code size! The first thing you might notice is that there are no local variables used in the code. All of the code generated to perform the calculations to determine the values of a, b, and c were eliminated. Because none of the individual variable values were used elsewhere in the program, the only value calculated was the final result. The compiler calculated the final value and used that directly in the assembly language code for the printf function. There is no need for the program to compute the values each time it is run.

Optimizing variables

One of the most obvious ways to optimize applications is to manipulate how the assembly language program handles variables. There are three ways to handle variables:

❏   Define variables in memory using the .data or .bss sections.

❏   Define local variables on the stack using the EBP base pointer.

❏   Use available registers to hold variable values.

This section shows the different techniques used for handling variables within programs, and how they can be optimized in assembly language code.

Using global and local variables without optimizing

Many C and C++ programmers don't understand the implications of using global and local variables within their programs. For many programmers, it's just a matter of where the variables are declared in the program. However, when the assembly language code is generated, there is a huge difference in how the variables are handled.

The vartest.c program demonstrates how the variables are created when the C program is converted to assembly language code:

```
/* vartest.c - An example of defining global and local C variables */
#include <stdio.h>

int global1 = 10;
float global2 = 20.25;

int main()
{
        int local1 = 100;
        float local2 = 200.25;
```

```
        int result1 = global1 + local1;
        float result2 = global2 + local2;
        printf("The results are %d and %f\n", result1, result2);
        return 0;
}
```

The vartest.c program defines two global variables (an integer and a floating-point value), along with two local variables (again both an integer and a floating-point value). To create the basic assembly language code from this C code, you use the compiler's -S option, which creates the file vartest.s.

```
.file   "vartest.c"
        .version        "01.01"
gcc2_compiled.:
.globl global1
.data
        .align 4
        .type   global1,@object
        .size   global1,4
global1:
        .long   10
.globl global2
        .align 4
        .type   global2,@object
        .size   global2,4
global2:
        .long   0x41a20000
                .section        .rodata
.LC1:
        .string "The results are %d and %f\n"
        .align 8
.LC0:
        .long   0xf01b866e,0x400921f9
.text
.align 16
.globl main
        .type   main,@function
main:
        pushl   %ebp
        movl    %esp, %ebp
        subl    $24, %esp
        movl    $100, -4(%ebp)
        movl    $0x43484000, -8(%ebp)
        movl    -4(%ebp), %eax
        addl    global1, %eax
        movl    %eax, -12(%ebp)
        flds    global2
        fadds   -8(%ebp)
        fstps   -16(%ebp)
        flds    -16(%ebp)
        leal    -8(%esp), %esp
        fstpl   (%esp)
        pushl   -12(%ebp)
        pushl   $.LC0
        call    printf
```

```
        addl    $16, %esp
        movl    $0, %eax
        movl    %ebp, %esp
        popl    %ebp
        ret
.Lfe1:
        .size   main,.Lfe1-main
        .ident  "GCC: (GNU) 2.96 20000731 (Linux-Mandrake 8.0 2.96-0.48mdk)"
```

You should be able to follow along with the assembly code to pick out what is happening. The two global variables were defined in the .data section as long type values (which creates a 4-byte value):

```
global1:
        .long   10
global2:
        .long   0x41a20000
```

The compiler converted the 20.25 floating-point value into the hexadecimal equivalent of the single-precision floating-point data type and stored that directly using the .long directive.

It's a little harder to pick out where the local variables are stored. Just as in a C style function code (see Chapter 14), space is reserved in the stack for the local variables by subtracting the total amount of space from the stack pointer, ESP. The two local variables are then stored in the first two locations reserved for local variables:

```
pushl   %ebp
movl    %esp, %ebp
subl    $24, %esp
movl    $100, -4(%ebp)
movl    $0x43484000, -8(%ebp)
```

Space is reserved for 24 bytes on the stack. The first two locations are used to hold the local variables. The first local variable is stored in the -4(%ebp) location. The second local variable is stored in the -8(%ebp) location.

Once the local variables are stored in the stack, the values are referenced from those locations for the integer calculation:

```
movl    -4(%ebp), %eax
addl    global1, %eax
movl    %eax, -12(%ebp)
```

The local variable is moved to the EAX register, and the global variable is added to it in the ADD instruction. The result is stored in the third reserved local variable location on the stack.

The floating-point calculation utilizes the FPU register stack:

```
flds    global2
fadds   -8(%ebp)
fstps   -16(%ebp)
flds    -16(%ebp)
```

First the global value is loaded into the ST(0) register, and then the local variable is used for the FADD instruction to add the values. As you saw before in the tempconv.s program, the compiler again pops the result from the FPU stack into a local variable, and then loads it back into the FPU stack to be retrieved by the main program:

```
leal    -8(%esp), %esp
fstpl   (%esp)
pushl   -12(%ebp)
pushl   $.LC0
call    printf
```

The LEA instruction is used to clear the local variables from the stack, and the floating-point result is retrieved from the FPU stack and placed on the program stack, along with the display string for the printf() function.

Global and local variables with optimization

Using the same vartest.c program, you can see how the GNU compiler optimizes the global and local variables with the following command-line options:

```
$ gcc -O3 -S -o vartest2.s vartest.c
```

This produces the assembly language file vartest2.s, which contains the optimized code for the program:

```
.file   "vartest.c"
        .version        "01.01"
gcc2_compiled.:
.globl global1
.data
        .align 4
        .type   global1,@object
        .size   global1,4
global1:
        .long   10
.globl global2
        .align 4
        .type   global2,@object
        .size   global2,4
global2:
        .long   0x41a20000
                .section        .rodata
.LC1:
        .string "The results are %d and %f\n"
        .align 4
.LC0:
        .long   0x43484000
.text
.align 16
.globl main
        .type   main,@function
main:
        flds    global2
```

```
        pushl   %ebp
        movl    global1, %eax
        fadds   .LC0
        movl    %esp, %ebp
        addl    $100, %eax
        subl    $16, %esp
        fstpl   (%esp)
        pushl   %eax
        pushl   $.LC1
        call    printf
        addl    $16, %esp
        movl    %ebp, %esp
        xorl    %eax, %eax
        popl    %ebp
        ret
.Lfe1:
        .size   main,.Lfe1-main
        .ident  "GCC: (GNU) 2.96 20000731 (Linux-Mandrake 8.0 2.96-0.48mdk)"
```

The first thing you should notice is that instead of the clean C style function prologue we are used to seeing, the compiler mixed other instructions within the prologue instructions:

```
flds    global2
pushl   %ebp
movl    global1, %eax
fadds   .LC0
movl    %esp, %ebp
addl    $100, %eax
```

The very first instruction in the main section is the FLD instruction to load the global value into the FPU. The compiler knows that there is an inherent delay in storing the value in the FPU register and that the processor can continue executing other instructions while the FPU instruction is processing. While the global value is stored in the FPU stack, the EBP register value is stored on the program stack. After the EBP value is stored, the integer global value is stored in an available register, to help increase access speed to the value.

The next thing you may notice is that the local variables are not defined on the stack. Instead of creating local variables on the stack, the values of the local variables are moved directly into the mathematical instructions (FADD and ADD). This is a big processor time savings over using the global variables in memory. Variables stored in global memory locations would require additional time to be loaded into the FPU. Note also that this time the optimizer determined that the floating-point result could be removed from the FPU stack and used directly, instead of popping it and pushing it again.

Optimizing loops

Program loops can be one of the most time-consuming parts of an application. The assembly language code generated to simulate a do-while or for-next loop can often be optimized for speed. Several optimizations are attempted by the compiler to decrease the amount of code required for loops.

This section shows how a normal for-next loop in a program can be optimized to minimize the time spent in the loop.

Normal for-next loop code

Chapter 6, "Controlling Execution Flow," demonstrated the basics of how to implement a for-next loop in assembly language code. The pseudocode to implement a for-next loop in assembly looks something like the following:

```
for:
   <condition to evaluate for loop counter value>
   jxx forcode    ; jump to the code of the condition is true
   jmp end        ; jump to the end if the condition is false
forcode:
   < for loop code to execute>
   <increment for loop counter>
   jmp for         ; go back to the start of the For statement
end:
```

This code requires three branch statements to implement the for-next loop. Branching in assembly language code can be catastrophic for performance, as it makes any instructions preloaded into the instruction cache useless.

The best way to optimize loops is to either eliminate them or at least try to simplify them, using loop unrolling. Unrolling a loop requires a lot of extra code (instead of branching to repeat code, the code is written out as many times as the loop would process). While this does not save on program size, it does enable the instruction prefetch cache to do its job and load instructions ahead of time. The performance savings may or may not outweigh the cost of the larger program.

Viewing loop code

To demonstrate how to optimize simple loops, the sums.c program is converted to assembly code. First, here's the C program code:

```
/* sums.c - An example of optimizing for-next loops */
#include <stdio.h>

int sums(int i)
{
        int j, sum = 0;
        for(j = 1; j <= i; j++)
                sum = sum + j;
        return sum;
}

int main()
{
        int i = 10;
        printf("Value: %d    Sum: %d\n", i, sums(i));
        return 0;
}
```

The sums.c program contains a single function that determines the sum of the consecutive integers, starting at 1 to the input value. To determine the sums, a for-next loop is used. The non-optimized assembly language code generated by the compiler to implement this program looks like the following:

```
        .file   "sums.c"
        .version        "01.01"
gcc2_compiled.:
.text
        .align 16
.globl sums
        .type   sums,@function
sums:
        pushl   %ebp
        movl    %esp, %ebp
        subl    $8, %esp
        movl    $0, -8(%ebp)
        movl    $1, -4(%ebp)
        .p2align 4,,7
.L3:
        movl    -4(%ebp), %eax
        cmpl    8(%ebp), %eax
        jle     .L6
        jmp     .L4
        .p2align 4,,7
.L6:
        movl    -4(%ebp), %eax
        leal    -8(%ebp), %edx
        addl    %eax, (%edx)
        leal    -4(%ebp), %eax
        incl    (%eax)
        jmp     .L3
        .p2align 4,,7
.L4:
        movl    -8(%ebp), %eax
        movl    %eax, %eax
        movl    %ebp, %esp
        popl    %ebp
        ret
.Lfe1:
        .size   sums,.Lfe1-sums
                .section        .rodata
.LC0:
        .string "Value: %d   Sum: %d\n"
.text
        .align 16
.globl main
        .type   main,@function
main:
        pushl   %ebp
        movl    %esp, %ebp
        subl    $8, %esp
        movl    $10, -4(%ebp)
        subl    $4, %esp
        subl    $8, %esp
        pushl   -4(%ebp)
        call    sums
        addl    $12, %esp
        movl    %eax, %eax
```

```
          pushl    %eax
          pushl    -4(%ebp)
          pushl    $.LC0
          call     printf
          addl     $16, %esp
          movl     $0, %eax
          movl     %ebp, %esp
          popl     %ebp
          ret
.Lfe2:
          .size    main,.Lfe2-main
          .ident   "GCC: (GNU) 2.96 20000731 (Linux-Mandrake 8.0 2.96-0.48mdk)"
```

The for-next loop is implemented in the sums assembly language function. It contains a complex mix of conditional branch and compare instructions.

First, two local variables are created to hold the loop count (stored at -4(%ebp), and set to 1) and the running sum value (stored at -8(%ebp) and set to 0). The code to implement the loop looks like the following:

```
.p2align 4,,7
.L3:
          movl     -4(%ebp), %eax
          cmpl     8(%ebp), %eax
          jle      .L6
          jmp      .L4
          .p2align 4,,7
.L6:
          movl     -4(%ebp), %eax
          leal     -8(%ebp), %edx
          addl     %eax, (%edx)
          leal     -4(%ebp), %eax
          incl     (%eax)
          jmp      .L3
```

The loop count is loaded into the EAX register and compared to the function input value (stored at the normal 8(%ebp) location). If the loop count is less than or equal to the input value, the code jumps to the section that adds the loop count to the sum value. When the addition is completed, the loop count is incremented by one, and the code jumps back to load the loop count value again. Note that the loop count value is already loaded into the EAX register, so reloading it for every loop iteration is wasted time within the loop.

Optimizing the for-next loop

Now we can look at how the compiler optimizes the code, but using the -O3 command-line option on the compiler:

```
$ gcc -O3 -S -o sums2.s sums.c
```

This creates the following assembly language code:

```
.file    "sums.c"
          .version          "01.01"
```

```
gcc2_compiled.:
                .section        .rodata
.LC0:
        .string "Value: %d    Sum: %d\n"
.text
        .align 16
.globl sums
        .type   sums,@function
sums:
        pushl   %ebp
        movl    $1, %edx
        movl    %esp, %ebp
        xorl    %eax, %eax
        movl    8(%ebp), %ecx
        cmpl    %ecx, %edx
        jg      .L30
        .p2align 4,,7
.L21:
        addl    %edx, %eax
        incl    %edx
        cmpl    %ecx, %edx
        jle     .L21
.L30:
        popl    %ebp
        ret
.Lfe1:
        .size   sums,.Lfe1-sums
        .align 16
.globl main
        .type   main,@function
main:
        pushl   %ebp
        xorl    %edx, %edx
        movl    %esp, %ebp
        movl    $1, %eax
        subl    $12, %esp
        .p2align 4,,7
.L26:
        addl    %eax, %edx
        incl    %eax
        cmpl    $10, %eax
        jle     .L26
        pushl   %edx
        pushl   $10
        pushl   $.LC0
        call    printf
        addl    $16, %esp
        movl    %ebp, %esp
        xorl    %eax, %eax
        popl    %ebp
        ret
.Lfe2:
        .size   main,.Lfe2-main
        .ident  "GCC: (GNU) 2.96 20000731 (Linux-Mandrake 8.0 2.96-0.48mdk)"
```

441

Notice the optimization that has occurred within the `sums` function code. Instead of using local variables for the loop count and the sum values, register values are used (EDX for the loop count and EAX for the running sum value). The input value is also immediately loaded into the ECX register, so all mathematical instructions are now done completely with values stored in registers.

Once the values are loaded into registers, the first compare instruction ensures that the loop count is not already larger than the final value. If so, no loop iterations are required, and the code skips over the loop:

```
cmpl    %ecx, %edx
jg      .L30
```

Next, an extremely tight loop is created to perform the sums:

```
.L21:
        addl    %edx, %eax
        incl    %edx
        cmpl    %ecx, %edx
        jle     .L21
```

Again, all of the values are contained within registers, so no memory access is required within the loop. Also note that when the loop completes, the result is already contained in the EAX register to be returned to the calling program without having to move it from memory.

Optimizing conditional branches

Another issue in optimizing assembly language programs is conditional branches. Similar to loops, conditional branches can upset the instructions preloaded into the instruction cache, causing additional work for the processor if unpredicted branches are taken.

One of the main uses of conditional branches is in `if-then` type statements. It is not uncommon for C and C++ programs to contain numerous `if-then` statements to evaluate conditions within the program code, and process data dependent on those conditions.

This section demonstrates how the GNU compiler converts `if-then` statements into assembly language code, and how the compiler optimizes `if-then` type statements. Knowing how the compiler optimizes conditional branches within assembly language programs can greatly benefit your own assembly language coding skills.

Generic if-then code

Chapter 6 also presented a generic formula for implementing `if-then` logic within assembly language code:

```
if:
   <condition to evaluate>
   jxx  else        ; jump to the else part if the condition is false
<code to implement the "then" statements>
jmp end             ;jump to the end
else:
   < code to implement the "else" statements>
end:
```

The standard if-then template utilizes one conditional jump and one unconditional jump to implement the coding logic. The next section shows how this is implemented by the compiler from if-then code in an actual C program.

Viewing if-then code

To view the assembly language code generated by the compiler, we first need an application that uses an if-then statement. The condtest.c program provides a simple example of the if-then-else statement used in a function to return a specific value based on two input values:

```c
/* condtest.c - An example of optimizing if-then code */
#include <stdio.h>

int conditiontest(int test1, int test2)
{
        int result;
        if (test1 > test2)
        {
                result = test1;
        } else if (test1 < test2)
        {
                result = test2;
        }else
        {
                result = 0;
        }
        return result;
}

int main()
{
        int data1 = 10;
        int data2 = 30;
        printf("The result is %d\n", conditiontest(data1, data2));
        return 0;
}
```

This example performs a simple if-then-else condition to return the larger value of the two input values. If the two input values are equal, a zero is returned. The non-optimized assembly language code generated for this program is shown in the condtest.s file:

```asm
.file   "condtest.c"
        .version        "01.01"
gcc2_compiled.:
.text
        .align 16
.globl conditiontest
        .type   conditiontest,@function
conditiontest:
        pushl   %ebp
        movl    %esp, %ebp
        subl    $4, %esp
        movl    8(%ebp), %eax
```

```
        cmpl    12(%ebp), %eax
        jle     .L3
        movl    8(%ebp), %eax
        movl    %eax, -4(%ebp)
        jmp     .L4
        .p2align 4,,7
.L3:
        movl    8(%ebp), %eax
        cmpl    12(%ebp), %eax
        jge     .L5
        movl    12(%ebp), %eax
        movl    %eax, -4(%ebp)
        jmp     .L4
        .p2align 4,,7
.L5:
        movl    $0, -4(%ebp)
.L4:
        movl    -4(%ebp), %eax
        movl    %eax, %eax
        movl    %ebp, %esp
        popl    %ebp
        ret
.Lfe1:
        .size   conditiontest,.Lfe1-conditiontest
                .section        .rodata
.LC0:
        .string "The result is %d\n"
.text
        .align 16
.globl main
        .type   main,@function
main:
        pushl   %ebp
        movl    %esp, %ebp
        subl    $8, %esp
        movl    $10, -4(%ebp)
        movl    $30, -8(%ebp)
        subl    $8, %esp
        pushl   -8(%ebp)
        pushl   -4(%ebp)
        call    conditiontest
        addl    $8, %esp
        movl    %eax, %eax
        pushl   %eax
        pushl   $.LC0
        call    printf
        addl    $16, %esp
        movl    $0, %eax
        movl    %ebp, %esp
        popl    %ebp
        ret
.Lfe2:
        .size   main,.Lfe2-main
        .ident  "GCC: (GNU) 2.96 20000731 (Linux-Mandrake 8.0 2.96-0.48mdk)"
```

Notice the classic `if-then-else` code implementation within the `conditiontest()` function:

```
        movl    8(%ebp), %eax
        cmpl    12(%ebp), %eax
        jle     .L3
        movl    8(%ebp), %eax
        movl    %eax, -4(%ebp)
        jmp     .L4
        .p2align 4,,7
.L3:
        movl    8(%ebp), %eax
        cmpl    12(%ebp), %eax
        jge     .L5
        movl    12(%ebp), %eax
        movl    %eax, -4(%ebp)
        jmp     .L4
        .p2align 4,,7
.L5:
        movl    $0, -4(%ebp)
.L4:
        movl    -4(%ebp), %eax
```

The first input value is loaded from the stack into the EAX register and compared to the second input value directly accessed from the stack in the CMP instruction. If the first value is less than or equal to the second value, the program jumps to the first `else` part of the logic. If not, the original condition of the `if-then` statement is true and the `then` part is performed. This incorporates loading the first input value into the first local variable value and jumping to the end code.

The `else` part of the `if-then-else` logic starts at the `.L3` label. Note that before the label, a new directive is used, the `.p21align` directive.

You have already seen the `.align` directive in Chapter 5, "Moving Data." It is used to ensure that data elements are aligned on proper memory boundaries to help speed up loading the values into registers (especially FPU registers). The `.p2align` directive is similar, but provides more control over how the elements are aligned.

The format of the `.p2align` directive is as follows:

```
.p2align number, value, max
```

The `number` parameter defines the number of low-order zero bits that must be zero in the address. For this example, the value of 4 indicates that the memory must be a multiple of 16 (the low four bits must be zero).

The `value` parameter defines the value that will be used in the padded bytes. If this value is skipped (as in this example) zeroes are used in the padded bytes.

The `max` parameter defines the maximum number of bytes that should be skipped by the alignment directive. In this example, the value is 7, which indicates that no more than 7 bytes should be skipped to align the next section, or the `.p2align` directive will be ignored.

The code after the .L3 label implements the second if-then-else statement by comparing the first and second input values from the stack. If the if-then condition is false, the code jumps to the second else part, at label .L5. If the condition is true, it loads the second input value into the first local variable value, and jumps to the end code.

The second else part directly loads a zero value into the first local variable value. The end code moves the first local variable value into the EAX register so it can be returned to the calling program.

Optimized If-Then Code

Again, the optimized version of the program can be obtained using the -03 compiler option. The condtest2.s file shows the optimized code:

```
.file    "condtest.c"
        .version        "01.01"
gcc2_compiled.:
                .section        .rodata
.LC0:
        .string "The result is %d\n"
.text
        .align 16
.globl conditiontest
        .type   conditiontest,@function
conditiontest:
        pushl   %ebp
        movl    %esp, %ebp
        movl    8(%ebp), %edx
        movl    12(%ebp), %ecx
        movl    %edx, %eax
        cmpl    %ecx, %edx
        jg      .L19
        xorl    %eax, %eax
        cmpl    %ecx, %edx
        setge   %al
        decl    %eax
        andl    %ecx, %eax
.L19:
        popl    %ebp
        ret
.Lfe1:
        .size   conditiontest,.Lfe1-conditiontest
        .align 16
.globl main
        .type   main,@function
main:
        pushl   %ebp
        movl    %esp, %ebp
        subl    $16, %esp
        pushl   $30
        pushl   $.LC0
        call    printf
        addl    $16, %esp
        movl    %ebp, %esp
```

```
        xorl    %eax, %eax
        popl    %ebp
        ret
.Lfe2:
        .size   main,.Lfe2-main
        .ident  "GCC: (GNU) 2.96 20000731 (Linux-Mandrake 8.0 2.96-0.48mdk)"
```

The optimized code greatly reduces the amount of code required to implement the dual if-then-else statements:

```
        movl    8(%ebp), %edx
        movl    12(%ebp), %ecx
        movl    %edx, %eax
        cmpl    %ecx, %edx
        jg      .L19
        xorl    %eax, %eax
        cmpl    %ecx, %edx
        setge   %al
        decl    %eax
        andl    %ecx, %eax
.L19:
```

The first optimization move is to load the two input values into registers. If the first input value (contained in the EAX register) is the greater value, it is immediately known that it is the return value, and the function can return to the calling program.

If the value in EAX is not larger than the second input value (contained in the ECX register), some mathematical trickery is used to determine the final return value. In this case, the compiler knows that the second input value must be either equal to or greater than the first input value. The two values are compared again using the CMP instruction. This time the conditional instruction is the SETGE instruction, which sets the value of the AL register to 1 if the first value is greater than or equal to the second value. Because we know the first value cannot be greater than the second at this part (if it were it would have satisfied the first conditional branch), we know the value must be equal, and the AL register value is set to 1. If the first value is less than the second value, the AL register is set to zero.

The next part is the tricky part. The EAX register is decremented by one, so if the first value was equal to the second, the EAX value is now zero; if it was less than the second, the EAX value is now -1, or all ones. The next instruction uses the AND operation with the second input value. Because EAX is either zero or all ones, the final value will be either zero if the values were equal, or the value of the second input value if it was larger. This kind of "thinking outside the box" is crucial when trying to optimize complicated assembly language code.

Common subexpression elimination

One of the more advanced optimization techniques performed by the compiler is the common subexpression elimination (cse). The compiler must scan the entire assembly language code looking for common expressions. When commonly used expressions are found, the expression only needs to be calculated once; after that, the value can be used in all of the other places where the expression is used.

This section shows a simple example of how cse works in assembly language code.

A program example

The `csetest.c` program demonstrates a simple situation in which a common expression is coded into a C program:

```
/* csetest.c - An example of implementing cse optimization */
#include <stdio.h>

void funct1(int a, int b)
{
   int c = a * b;
   int d = (a * b) / 5;
   int e = 500 / (a * b);
   printf("The results are c=%d  d=%d  e=%d\n", c, d, e);
}

int main()
{
   int a = 10;
   int b = 25;
   funct1(a, b);
   funct1(20, 10);
   return 0;
}
```

The `funct1()` function contains three equations, each of which incorporates the same expression, a * b. The non-optimized version of the function code performs the multiplication each of the three times for the three equations:

```
funct1:
        pushl   %ebp
        movl    %esp, %ebp
        subl    $40, %esp
        movl    8(%ebp), %eax
        imull   12(%ebp), %eax
        movl    %eax, -4(%ebp)
        movl    8(%ebp), %eax
        movl    %eax, %ecx
        imull   12(%ebp), %ecx
        movl    $1717986919, %eax
        imull   %ecx
        sarl    %edx
        movl    %ecx, %eax
        sarl    $31, %eax
        subl    %eax, %edx
        movl    %edx, %eax
        movl    %eax, -8(%ebp)
        movl    8(%ebp), %eax
        movl    %eax, %edx
        imull   12(%ebp), %edx
        movl    $500, %eax
        movl    %edx, %ecx
        cltd
        idivl   %ecx
```

```
        movl    %eax, -12(%ebp)
        movl    -12(%ebp), %eax
        movl    %eax, 12(%esp)
        movl    -8(%ebp), %eax
        movl    %eax, 8(%esp)
        movl    -4(%ebp), %eax
        movl    %eax, 4(%esp)
        movl    $.LC0, (%esp)
        call    printf
        leave
        ret
```

Notice that in three instances, the IMUL instruction is used to multiply the second input with the first input value, which has been loaded into a register. Even though the compiler did not optimize the common expressions in this round, you may notice an interesting mathematical optimization that was performed by the compiler. To obtain the result for the d variable, the compiler must divide the multiplication result by five. Instead of using the DIV instruction to perform a division, the SAR instruction is used to shift the register values right to perform the division.

Because the SAR instruction can only divide by a power of two, an additional subtraction is required to make the division by five possible. Even though more instructions are used, this method is still quicker than using the single DIV instruction.

Optimizing with cse

After compiling the same program with optimizations, you can see what has happened to the funct1() function assembly language code:

```
funct1:
        pushl   %ebp
        movl    %esp, %ebp
        subl    $24, %esp
        movl    %ebx, -8(%ebp)
        movl    12(%ebp), %ecx
        movl    8(%ebp), %ebx
        movl    %esi, -4(%ebp)
        movl    $1717986919, %esi
        imull   %ebx, %ecx
        movl    $.LC0, (%esp)
        movl    %ecx, %eax
        imull   %esi
        movl    $500, %eax
        movl    %ecx, 4(%esp)
        movl    %edx, %ebx
        movl    %ecx, %edx
        sarl    $31, %edx
        sarl    %ebx
        subl    %edx, %ebx
        movl    %ebx, 8(%esp)
        cltd
        idivl   %ecx
        movl    %eax, 12(%esp)
        call    printf
```

```
movl    -8(%ebp), %ebx
movl    -4(%ebp), %esi
movl    %ebp, %esp
popl    %ebp
ret
```

With the optimized code, the multiplication is performed once by loading the first input value into the EBX register, loading the second input value into the ECX register, and using the IMUL instruction to multiply the two values. The result is kept in the ECX register and used in the other two equations to represent the a * b expression without having to recalculate the value.

Summary

Just replacing C or C++ functions with hand-coded assembly language code does not necessarily increase program performance. You must be able to improve the assembly language code the compiler generates to recognize any performance increase. With today's optimizing compilers, this is not an easy task, but it is doable.

The first step to optimizing assembly language routines is to see how the compiler creates them. This chapter showed how to use the -O family of GNU compiler options to create optimized assembly language code from C programs. The -S option is also used to create the assembly language source code file to analyze. By viewing how the GNU compiler optimizes specific functions within assembly language, you can learn how to duplicate the code in your own assembly language applications.

The chapter described five common optimization methods used for optimizing assembly language functions. The first method is optimizing calculations. Most high-level language programs utilize mathematical equations to process data. Often the data involves calculations using known values within the program. Instead of blindly moving constants into memory locations or registers for the calculations, the compiler analyzes the final results from the calculations and attempts to create shortcuts. Constant values can often be directly used in mathematical instructions instead of using memory locations. This saves processing time loading and unloading values in memory.

The second method discussed is optimizing how variables are handled. In C and C++ programs, variables can be declared as local or global. Global variables are defined in the .data section of the assembly language code, stored in memory locations. By default, local variables are defined on the stack in the assembly language code. When the compiler attempts to optimize the code, local variables are moved to registers when possible. This can greatly increase the performance of an application, as access to the registers is significantly faster than accessing values in memory. Of course, for larger applications with numerous variables, there are not enough registers to go around. To maximize performance, the compiler will swap variables between registers and the stack as necessary to increase performance.

The third optimization method discussed involves loops. Loops can be one of the trickiest things to optimize in the program, but they can also have a huge effect on performance if optimized correctly. One of the main features of Pentium computers is their ability to prefetch instructions and load them into the instruction cache before the processor needs to execute them. Unfortunately, branches disrupt this process and cause the instruction cache to be flushed and start over from scratch. The goal is to eliminate loops as much as possible. For short iteration loops, this can be accomplished by unrolling the code, duplicating the code within the loop for each iteration instead of looping. While this increases the program's size, the time saved by allowing the processor to continue through the code without looping often outweighs the larger size.

The fourth optimization method discussed is similar to the loop problem, but with conditional branches. Just like loops, conditional branches cause the processor to reload the instruction cache if a different path is taken. The way to solve this problem is to allow the most frequently used path to directly follow the jump instructions (jump on the lesser used condition). In addition, when setting variables to different values based on another value, mathematical tricks can often be used to eliminate the extra jump instruction.

The fifth optimization method is often the most confusing. It deals with eliminating common expressions used throughout the assembly language program. Programs that work with mathematical equations often contain expressions that are used throughout the equations, such as the multiplication of two variables. The compiler can detect when a previously calculated value is used multiple times in the assembly language code and store the results from the calculation in a location (usually a register) where it can be easily accessed later. At runtime, this enables the program to just perform the calculation once, instead of each time the expression is used.

While many programmers think of assembly language code from the perspective of increasing performance, there is a lot more to assembly language than just that. The next chapter discusses how to perform high-level file access using assembly language programs. When programmers think of file access, they usually think they must resort to higher-level language functions, but assembly language programs can access files just as easily as C and C++ programs.

16

Using Files

There are many occasions when an application must store data for later use, or read configuration information from a configuration file. To handle these functions, the assembly language program must be able to interact with files on the UNIX system.

This chapter describes how to handle files within assembly language programs, both writing data out to them and reading data in from them. Two basic methods are used to access files from assembly language programs. One method is to use the standard C functions. If you already program in C or C++, you should be familiar with these — `fopen()`, `read()`, and `write()`. The C file I/O functions in turn use the Linux system calls (described in Chapter 12, "Using Linux System Calls") to access files. In assembly language programming, you can bypass the C function calls and directly access the Linux file I/O system calls provided by the kernel. This is the method described in this chapter.

The chapter starts out with a brief explanation of how the UNIX system handles files. Next it shows how to write data to files, specifying the proper permissions and access types. After that, how to read data from files is shown, along with how to process the data and write to another file. Finally, the topic of using memory-mapped files is presented. This feature enables you to read a complete file into memory, process and modify the data within the memory-mapped file, and write the data back to the original file.

The File-Handling Sequence

Just as in C and C++ programming, a specific sequence must be used when working with data files in assembly language programs. Figure 16-1 shows the sequence of events that must be taken.

Each of these actions — open, read, write, and close — is performed by a Linux system call. As shown in Chapter 12, "Using Linux System Calls," the system call value representing the system call is loaded into the EAX register, and any parameter values are loaded into other general-purpose registers.

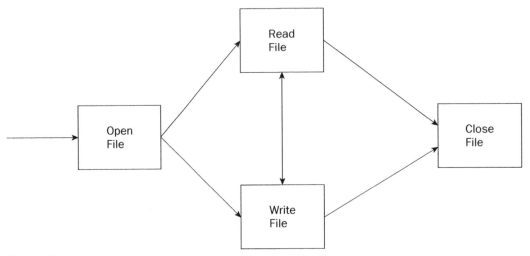

Figure 16-1

The following table shows the Linux system call values for the file-handling system calls.

System Call	Value	Description
Open	5	Open a file for access and create a file handle pointing to the file.
Read	3	Read from an open file using the file handle.
Write	4	Write to the file using the file handle.
Close	6	Close the file and remove the file handle.

Each file system call has its own set of input values that must be configured before the system call is made. The following sections describe each of these system calls in detail and show examples of how to use them in assembly language programs.

Opening and Closing Files

If you are familiar with opening and closing files in the C or C++ languages, opening and closing them in assembly language using the Linux system calls is exactly the same. The open() C function uses the open system call, passing the necessary parameters to the system call. The open system call returns a file handle, which is used to identify the open file to other file-handling system calls. When you are finished using the file, the close system call is used to close the file.

The format of the open system call is as follows:

```
int open(const char *pathname, int flags, mode_t mode);
```

The `pathname` is the full null-terminated file path including any subdirectories. If only a filename is specified, it is assumed to be in the same directory from which the application program was run. The `flags` input value determines the file access allowed for the file, and the `mode` input value determines the UNIX permissions set if the file is created.

The `open` assembly language system call reads its necessary parameters from the following registers:

- ❏   **EAX:** Contains the system call value 5
- ❏   **EBX:** Contains the memory address of the start of the null-terminated filename string
- ❏   **ECX:** Contains an integer value representing the flags requesting the type of access to the file
- ❏   **EDX:** Contains an integer value representing the UNIX permissions used if a new file is created

The access type and UNIX permissions defined for the file are crucial. The following sections describe the possible settings for these two values.

Access types

The type of access used to open the file must be declared for all file `open` requests. If you have opened files using the `open()` C function, you are probably familiar with using predefined constants such as `O_RDONLY` or `O_RDWR`. Unfortunately, these constants are not defined for you within your assembly language program. You must use the numeric values they represent or define the constants yourself. The numeric values for these constants are usually represented as octal values. The numeric values of the constants are shown in the following table.

C Constant	Numeric Value	Description
O_RDONLY	00	Open the file for read-only access.
O_WRONLY	01	Open the file for write-only access.
O_RDWR	02	Open the file for both read and write access.
O_CREAT	0100	Create the file if it does not exist.
O_EXCL	0200	When used with O_CREAT, if the file exists, do not open it.
O_TRUNC	01000	If the file exists and is open in write mode, truncate it to a length of zero.
O_APPEND	02000	Append data to the end of the file.
O_NONBLOCK	04000	Open the file in nonblocking mode.
O_SYNC	010000	Open the file in synchronous mode (allow only one write at a time).
O_ASYNC	020000	Open the file in asynchronous mode (allow multiple writes at a time).

The file access types can be combined to enable multiple access features. For example, if you want to create a file and open it for both read and write access, you would use the following instruction:

```
movl $0102, %ecx
```

This combines the O_CREATE value of 0100 with the O_RDWR value of 02. The leading zero in the constant value is important. This signifies that the value is in octal format. If you used the constant $102, you would get the wrong results, as the assembler would use the decimal value of 102.

If you want to append new data to an existing file, you would use this instruction:

```
movl $02002, %ecx
```

This combines the O_APPEND value of 02000 with the O_RDWR value of 02, and does not set the O_CREAT value. If the file does not exist, it will not be created.

UNIX permissions

Setting the UNIX permissions can often lead to complicated situations. Care must be taken to ensure that the proper permissions are set for the file access. The standard UNIX permissions are set for three categories of users:

❑   The owner of the file

❑   The default group for the file

❑   Everyone else on the system

Each of the three categories is assigned specific permissions for the file. Three bits are used to indicate the access for each category:

❑   The read bit

❑   The write bit

❑   The execute bit

The three bits are aligned to form a three-bit value for each category, as shown in Figure 16-2.

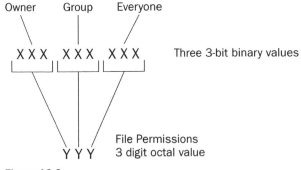

Figure 16-2

As shown in Figure 16-2, the three bits can also be represented by an octal value, indicating which bits are set. The values can be combined to produce various access levels, shown in the following table.

Permission Bits	Value	Access
001	1	Execute privileges
010	2	Write privileges
011	3	Execute and write privileges
100	4	Read privileges
101	5	Execute and read privileges
110	6	Execute and write privileges
111	7	Execute, write, and read privileges

The file mode properties are combined to form a single three-digit octal number, representing the owner, group, and everyone privileges. This three-digit octal number is what is defined in the open system call, along with a leading zero to make it an octal value.

The instruction

```
movl $0644, %edx
```

assigns the octal value 644 to the EDX register. The 6 digit indicates that the file will have read/write privileges for the owner. The middle 4 digit indicates that the file will have read-only privileges for the file's assigned group, and the second 4 digit indicates that the file will have read-only privileges for everyone else on the system.

Note one caveat to this: The Linux system assigns an umask value for every user that logs into the system. The umask value masks the default privileges assigned to files created by that user. The final privileges for the created file would be as follows:

```
file privs = privs & ~umask
```

The umask is inverted, and AND'd with the requested privileges in the open system call. You can see the umask value assigned to your user account by using the umask command:

```
$ umask
022
$
```

The umask assigned to this account is the octal value 022. If an open system call is performed requesting the creation of a file with 0666 privileges (read/write for everyone), the final privileges assigned to the created file will be as follows:

```
final privileges = privs & ~umask
                 = 666 & ~022
                 = 666 & 755
                 = 644
```

The requested privileges for the owner are not modified, but the requested write privileges for the group and for everyone else are denied by the umask value. This is a commonly used umask value for systems. It prevents unintentionally granting write privileges to files.

If you really intended to grant write privileges to everyone for the file, you must either change your umask value, or use the chmod command to manually change the privileges of the file.

Open file code

The last piece of the system call is to declare the filename to open. If no path is used, the filename is assumed to be located in the same directory from which the executable program was run.

The filename must be declared as a null-terminated string. This can be done using the .asciz declaration:

```
.section .data
filename:
    .asciz "output.txt"
.
.
.section .text
.
.
    movl $filename, %ebx
```

Because the EBX register contains the memory address for the location of the string, you must use the dollar sign with the variable name to get the memory address location of the string.

Another method that is commonly used is to allow the filename to be declared as a command-line parameter for the program. Chapter 11, "Using Functions," showed how to access command-line parameters from the program stack. The location 8(%ebp) contains a pointer to the memory location containing the first command-line parameter. This is exactly what we need for the filename; thus, you can use the instructions

```
movl %esp, %ebp
.
.
movl 8(%ebp), %ebx
```

to move the filename listed as the first command-line parameter into the open system call function call. This is shown in more detail in the examples later in this chapter.

Putting all of the pieces together, you can open a file with a simple code snippet such as this:

```
movl $5, %eax
movl $filename, %ebx
movl $0102, %ecx
movl $0644, %edx
int $0x80
test %eax, %eax
js badfile
```

This code snippet opens a file (declared by the filename data variable) with O_CREAT and O_WRONLY access, using UNIX permissions 0644 (read/write access for the owner, and read access for anyone else).

When the system call returns, the EAX register contains a signed integer value. This value will be either non-negative, which is the file handle for the open file, or negative, which is an error code indicating why the file could not be opened. Because the error code is a negative value, you can test for it by checking the sign bit using the JS conditional branch instruction.

Usually, you will want to store the file handle to the open file somewhere for use later in the program. Because the file handle is a simple 32-bit signed integer value, it can be kept anywhere you would store any other integer value:

❑ A memory location defined in the .data section

❑ A memory location defined in the .bss section

❑ The stack, in the local variables section

❑ A register

*The file handle value will remain valid during the entire time the file is considered open by the operating system. When the file is closed using the **close** system call, the file handle becomes invalid, and cannot be used to access the file.*

Open error return codes

If the open system call does return an error code, you can compare it to the errno values defined in the errno.h header file on the system (the assembly language errorno.h file is usually located in the /usr/include/asm directory on the system). The following table describes some of the more common error codes that may be returned.

Error Name	Error Value	Description
EPERM	1	Operation not permitted
ENOENT	2	No such file
EBADF	9	Bad file handle number
EACCES	13	Permission denied
EFAULT	14	Bad file address
EBUSY	16	Device or resource busy
EEXIST	17	File exists
EISDIR	21	Is a directory
EMFILE	24	Too many open files
EFBIG	27	File too large
EROFS	30	Read-only file system
ENAMERTOOLONG	36	File name is too long

*Remember that the error code is returned as a negative number, so the value will be the negative of the value shown in the **errno** table.*

Closing files

When you are finished using a file, the proper thing to do is to close it; otherwise, file corruption is possible. The `close` system call uses a single input parameter, the file handle of the opened file to close. The parameter is placed in the `EBX` register:

```
movl filehandle, %ebx
movl $6, %eax
int $0x80
```

The close system call returns an error code in the `EAX` register, using the `errno.h` error codes. If the file was successfully closed, the `EAX` register will contain a zero.

Writing to Files

Once the file is open, you can use the `write` system call to write to it. You have already seen examples of using the `write` system call in this book when we wrote data to the console display (such as in Chapter 4, "A Sample Assembly Language Program"). The console `STDOUT` file handle always defaults to the value 1. In this special case, you do not need to open the file handle, you just write to it. For writing to files, instead of writing to the console `STDOUT` file handle, the file handle returned from the file's `open` system call is used. The default `STDERR` file handle behaves similarly (it uses a file handle of 2).

A simple write example

A simple assembly language program that writes to a file is demonstrated in the following `cpuidfile.s` program:

```
# cpuidfile.s - An example of writing data to a file
.section .data

filename:
    .asciz "cpuid.txt"
output:
    .asciz "The processor Vendor ID is 'xxxxxxxxxxxx'\n"
.section .bss
    .lcomm filehandle, 4
.section .text
.globl _start
_start:
    movl $0, %eax
    cpuid
    movl $output, %edi
    movl %ebx, 28(%edi)
    movl %edx, 32(%edi)
    movl %ecx, 36(%edi)

    movl $5, %eax
    movl $filename, %ebx
    movl $01101, %ecx
    movl $0644, %edx
    int $0x80
```

```
    test %eax, %eax
    js badfile
    movl %eax, filehandle

    movl $4, %eax
    movl filehandle, %ebx
    movl $output, %ecx
    movl $42, %edx
    int $0x80
    test %eax, %eax
    js badfile

    movl $6, %eax
    movl filehandle, %ebx
    int $0x80

badfile:
    movl %eax, %ebx
    movl $1, %eax
    int $0x80
```

The cpuidfile.s program takes the original cpuid.s program from Chapter 4, "A Sample Assembly Language Program," and modifies it to place the output in a text file. It uses the O_TRUNC, O_CREAT, and O_WRONLY file access modes to open (or create) the cpuid.txt file for writing. If the file already exists, it is truncated (erased), as the O_APPEND access mode was not included. The UNIX permissions were set to 0644 to allow the user to read and write to the file, but only allow read access for others on the system. After the open system call is made, the return value is checked to ensure that it does not contain an error code. If it is a valid file handle, it is stored in the memory location labeled filehandle.

The file handle is then loaded into the EBX register and used with the write system call to write the output value stored from the CPUID instruction to the file.

You can test this program by simply assembling, linking, and running the program:

```
$ as -o cpuidfile.o cpuidfile.s
$ ld -o cpuidfile cpuidfile.o
$ ./cpuidfile
$ ls -al cpuid.txt
-rw-r--r--    1 rich     rich              42 Oct  6 09:18 cpuid.txt
[rich@test2 chap16]$ cat cpuid.txt
The processor Vendor ID is 'GenuineIntel'
$
```

The program successfully created the file and placed the output string into it as expected. You can test the file access settings by rerunning the program again and examining the output file:

```
$ ./cpuidfile
$ ls -al cpuid.txt
-rw-r--r--    1 rich     rich              42 Oct  6 09:20 cpuid.txt
$ cat cpuid.txt
The processor Vendor ID is 'GenuineIntel'
$
```

The output from the second run erased the original data, writing the new data into the existing file starting at the beginning of the file. This caused the new data to replace the data contained in the existing file (of course, you can't see that because it used the same data). You can test this by using an editor to add other lines to the cpuid.txt output file, and then rerun the cpuidfile program.

Changing file access modes

The new file generated by the program replaced the data in the existing file. If you want to append the new data to the existing data in the file, you can change the file access mode values. Just replace the open system call lines with the following:

```
movl $5, %eax
movl $filename, %ebx
movl $02101, %ecx
movl $0644, %edx
int $0x80
test %eax, %eax
js badfile
movl %eax, filehandle
```

Note that the only change was to the value set in the ECX register, which now adds the O_APPEND access mode value, along with the O_CREAT and O_WRONLY values. After reassembling and linking the new code, you can test it out:

```
$ ./cpuidfile2
$ ls -al cpuid.txt
-rw-r--r--    1 rich      rich              84 Oct   6 09:26 cpuid.txt
$ cat cpuid.txt
The processor Vendor ID is 'GenuineIntel'
The processor Vendor ID is 'GenuineIntel'
$
```

As expected, the new version of the program appended the output test string to the existing contents of the cpuid.txt file.

Handling file errors

In Linux, there are many reasons why a file access attempt can fail. Other processes can lock files, users can accidentally delete files, or even novice system administrators can assign the wrong permissions to the file. You must ensure that your assembly language code is prepared to deal with failure.

As shown in the cpuidfile.s example, it is best to test the return code from the file access system calls. This example doesn't do anything other than use it as the return code for the exit system call, but in a production program you would want to display some type of error message related to the specific error code encountered.

A simple way to test the error code handling is to force an error condition. For this example, I will change the output file to a read-only file and run the program again:

```
$ chmod 444 cpuid.txt
$ ls -al cpuid.txt
-r--r--r--    1 rich     rich              84 Oct  6 09:46 cpuid.txt
$ ./cpuidfile
$ echo $?
243
$
```

The UNIX file mode of the cpuid.txt output file was set to 444, indicating read-only access for the owner of the file, as well as everyone else on the system. When the cpuidfile program was run and the return code checked, an error code was returned.

Because UNIX program return codes are unsigned integers, the return code value is interpreted as a positive value. You can determine the true error code value by subtracting this value from 256, which results in 13. From the errno.h file, you can determine that error code 13 is the EACCES error, which indicates that you do not have permission to write to the file.

Reading Files

The next step is to work on reading data contained in files. This function uses the read system call. The UNIX man page for the read system call is as follows:

```
ssize_t read(int fd, void *buf, size_t count);
```

The read system call uses three input values and produces a single output value. The three input values are as follows:

❑   The file handle of the file from which to read the data

❑   A buffer location to place the read data

❑   The number of bytes to attempt to read from the file

The return value represents the number of bytes actually read from the file by the system call. The data type ssize_t is similar to the size_t data type, but is a signed integer value. This is because the read function can return a negative value if an error occurs. If the read system call returns a zero, the end of the file has been reached.

It is possible that fewer bytes can be read than the number specified in the input value. This can be caused by reaching the end of the file, or by the data not being available at the time the read call was made.

Of course, the input values are placed in registers before the read system call is made. The registers used for the read system call are as follows:

❑   **EAX:** The read system call value (3)

❑   **EBX:** The file handle of the open file

❑   **ECX:** The memory location of a data buffer

❑   **EDX:** An integer value of the number of bytes to read

As you can see, the read system call requires the file handle of an open file, so before you can use the read system call you must use the open system call to open a file. It is important to ensure that the file was opened with the read access mode set (using the O_RDONLY or O_RDWR mode values). There is one exception to this: Similar to the STDOUT situation, the STDIN file handle (value 0) can be used to read data from the standard input device (usually the keyboard) without having to open it.

A simple read example

The readtest1.s program demonstrates reading data from the cpuid.txt file created by the cpuidfile.s program shown earlier:

```
# readtest1.s - An example of reading data from a file
.section .bss
    .lcomm buffer, 42
    .lcomm filehandle, 4
.section .text
.globl _start
_start:
    nop
    movl %esp, %ebp
    movl $5, %eax
    movl 8(%ebp), %ebx
    movl $00, %ecx
    movl $0444, %edx
    int $0x80
    test %eax, %eax
    js badfile
    movl %eax, filehandle

    movl $3, %eax
    movl filehandle, %ebx
    movl $buffer, %ecx
    movl $42, %edx
    int $0x80
    test %eax, %eax
    js badfile

    movl $4, %eax
    movl $1, %ebx
    movl $buffer, %ecx
    movl $42, %edx
    int $0x80
    test %eax, %eax
    js badfile

    movl $6, %eax
    movl filehandle, %ebx
    int $0x80

badfile:
    movl %eax, %ebx
    movl $1, %eax
    int $0x80
```

The `readtest1.s` program opens the filename specified in the first command-line parameter from the program (located at `8(%ebp)`). Because the program just reads the data, the file is opened in `O_RDONLY` mode. Next, the `read` system call is performed, pointing to the buffer area specified by the `buffer` label in the `.bss` section. The `read` system call is instructed to read 42 bytes of data (the output from the `cpuidfile.s` program, including the newline character).

The next section uses the `write` system call and the `STDOUT` file handle to display the data stored in the buffer area (again, specifying 42 bytes of data). Finally, the file handle pointing to the `cpuid.txt` file is closed using the `close` system call, and the `exit` system call is used to exit the program.

When you run the program, remember to include the `cpuid.txt` file name on the command line, as that is where the program will get the filename to open:

```
$ ./readtest1 cpuid.txt
The processor Vendor ID is 'GenuineIntel'
$
```

The program behaved as expected. If you forget to include the filename on the command line, nothing is displayed, and error code will result. You can view the error code using the `$?` shell value:

```
$ ./readtest1
$ echo $?
242
$
```

This equates to error code 256 − 242 = 14, or the EFAULT error, showing that no filename address is specified at the `8(%ebp)` location.

Of course, in a real program it is far better to first check the number of parameters to ensure there is something on the command line to read, rather than let the **open** *function error out.*

A more complicated read example

The `readtest1.s` program was somewhat of an unrealistic example. It specified exactly the amount of data that needed to be read from the file. More often, you will not know exactly how much data you need to read. Instead, you must loop through the entire file until you reach the end.

This method can be used because of the way the `read` system call works. Each time the `read` system call is used, a file pointer is used within the open file to indicate the last byte of data read from the file. If another `read` system call is used, it starts at the byte immediately following the file pointer location. When it is done reading, it moves the file pointer to the last byte read. This continues until the end of the file is reached.

The way you know the `read` system call is at the end of the file is that it returns a zero value from the read. You must check the return value at each iteration for either an error or a zero value. If the value is zero, you know that the end of the file has been reached.

The `readtest2.s` program demonstrates this technique:

```
# readtest2.s - A more complicated example of reading data from a file
.section .bss
    .lcomm buffer, 10
    .lcomm filehandle, 4

.section .text
.globl _start
_start:
    nop
    movl %esp, %ebp
    movl $5, %eax
    movl 8(%ebp), %ebx
    movl $00, %ecx
    movl $0444, %edx
    int $0x80
    test %eax, %eax
    js badfile
    movl %eax, filehandle

read_loop:
    movl $3, %eax
    movl filehandle, %ebx
    movl $buffer, %ecx
    movl $10, %edx
    int $0x80
    test %eax, %eax
    jz done
    js done
    movl %eax, %edx
    movl $4, %eax
    movl $1, %ebx
    movl $buffer, %ecx
    int $0x80
    test %eax, %eax
    js badfile
    jmp read_loop

done:
    movl $6, %eax
    movl filehandle, %ebx
    int $0x80

badfile:
    movl %eax, %ebx
    movl $1, %eax
    int $0x80
```

The `readtest2.s` program again gets the filename to open from the first command-line parameter. The file is opened, and a loop is started to read 10-byte blocks of data from the file, placing them into the buffer location. The buffer location is then written to the display using the `write` system call. When the `read` system call returns a zero value, we know we have reached the end of the file, and the file handle can be closed.

Now the `readtest2.s` program can be used to display a file of any size:

```
$ ./readtest2 cpuid.txt
The processor Vendor ID is 'GenuineIntel'
The processor Vendor ID is 'GenuineIntel'
$
```

The `readtest2` program displayed the entire `cpuid.txt` file. You can test it out on any text file, including its own source code file:

```
$ ./readtest2 readtest2.s
# readtest2.s - A more complicated example of reading data from a file
.section .bss
    .lcomm buffer, 10
    .lcomm filehandle, 4
    .lcomm size, 4
.section .text
    .
    .
    .
badfile:
    movl %eax, %ebx
    movl $1, %eax
    int $0x80
$
```

The entire source code file was displayed, and the `readtest2` program properly stopped when it reached the end of the file.

*The 10-byte block size was used to show the looping effect. In a production application, you would want to use a larger block size to perform fewer **read** system calls, improving the application's performance.*

Reading, Processing, and Writing Data

Often when processing data that is read from a file, you want to write it back out to a file. In the `readtest` and `readtest2` examples, the output file was the STDOUT console display. It could just as easily have been a file handle to another file.

Just as the `read` system call uses a file pointer to keep track of what data has been read from a file, the `write` system call keeps a file pointer pointing to the last data that has been written to a file. You can write a block of data to an output file and then use another `write` system call to write more data after the original block of data.

The `readtest3.s` program demonstrates reading data in from a file, processing the data, and writing it out to another file:

```
# readtest3.s - An example of modifying data read from a file and outputting it
.section .bss
    .lcomm buffer, 10
    .lcomm infilehandle, 4
```

```
        .lcomm outfilehandle, 4
        .lcomm size, 4
.section .text
.globl _start
_start:
        # open input file, specified by the first command line param
        movl %esp, %ebp
        movl $5, %eax
        movl 8(%ebp), %ebx
        movl $00, %ecx
        movl $0444, %edx
        int $0x80
        test %eax, %eax
        js badfile
        movl %eax, infilehandle

        # open an output file, specified by the second command line param
        movl $5, %eax
        movl 12(%ebp), %ebx
        movl $01101, %ecx
        movl $0644, %edx
        int $0x80
        test %eax, %eax
        js badfile
        movl %eax, outfilehandle

        # read one buffer's worth of data from input file
read_loop:
        movl $3, %eax
        movl infilehandle, %ebx
        movl $buffer, %ecx
        movl $10, %edx
        int $0x80
        test %eax, %eax
        jz done
        js badfile
        movl %eax, size

        # send the buffer data to the conversion function
        pushl $buffer
        pushl size
        call convert
        addl $8, %esp

        # write the converted data buffer to the output file
        movl $4, %eax
        movl outfilehandle, %ebx
        movl $buffer, %ecx
        movl size, %edx
        int $0x80
        test %eax, %eax
        js badfile
        jmp read_loop
```

```
done:
    # close the output file
    movl $6, %eax
    movl outfilehandle, %ebx
    int $0x80

    # close the input file
    movl $6, %eax
    movl infilehandle, %ebx
    int $0x80
badfile:
    movl %eax, %ebx
    movl $1, %eax
    int $0x80

# convert lower case letters to upper case
.type convert, @function
convert:
    pushl %ebp
    movl %esp, %ebp
    movl 12(%ebp), %esi
    movl %esi, %edi
    movl 8(%ebp), %ecx
convert_loop:
    lodsb
    cmpb $0x61, %al
    jl skip
    cmpb $0x7a, %al
    jg skip
    subb $0x20, %al
skip:
    stosb
    loop convert_loop
    movl %ebp, %esp
    popl %ebp
    ret
```

If you have been following along in the book, you probably recognize the assembly language function convert used in the readtest3.s program. It is basically the convert.s program used in Chapter 10, "Working with Strings." It uses the LODS instruction to load a string of bytes into the EAX register one at a time. The ESI register points to the memory location of the source string, and the EDI register points to the memory location of the destination string (they are both set to point to the same buffer area).

The convert function checks each byte to see if it is a lowercase ASCII character. If so, 32 is subtracted from the value to convert it to an uppercase ASCII character. The STOS instruction is used to store the string back in the destination memory location.

The function was rewritten as an assembly language function, taking the buffer and buffer size variables from the stack. These values are pushed onto the stack by the main program before calling the function. When the function returns, the converted bytes are located in the same buffer area, which is then written to the output file.

The `readtest3.s` program uses two command-line parameters. The first is the filename of the input file to convert. The second parameter is the filename of the output file. Here's an example of using the assembled program:

```
$ ./readtest3 cpuid.txt test.txt
$ cat test.txt
THE PROCESSOR VENDOR ID IS 'GENUINEINTEL'
THE PROCESSOR VENDOR ID IS 'GENUINEINTEL'
$ cat cpuid.txt
The processor Vendor ID is 'GenuineIntel'
The processor Vendor ID is 'GenuineIntel'
$
```

The output file contains the converted data from the input file. Because the `readfile3` program uses the same block reading method as the `readfile2` program, you can use this program to convert any size of text file you want.

Memory-Mapped Files

You may have been unfortunate enough to notice a problem with the `readtest3` program. If you made the mistake of trying to use the same filename as the input and output filename, here's what happened:

```
$ ./readtest3 cpuid.txt cpuid.txt
$ echo $?
0
$ cat cpuid.txt
$ ls -l cpuid.txt
-rw-r--r--    1 rich      rich               0 Oct  6 15:00 cpuid.txt
$
```

The program ran and did not produce an error code, but the output file was empty. It exists, but has no output data in it.

The problem is that the system cannot simultaneously write the data to the same file it is reading. There are many applications for which it is necessary to update a file. If you need to use this function within your application, there are a few different ways to get around it. One method is called *memory-mapped files*.

What are memory-mapped files?

Memory-mapped files use the `mmap` system call to map parts of a file into memory on the system. Once the file (or part of the file) is placed in memory, programs can access the memory locations using standard memory-access instructions, and modify them if necessary. The memory locations can be shared by multiple processes, enabling multiple programs to update the same file simultaneously. This is shown in Figure 16-3.

After the file is loaded into memory, the operating system controls who has what type of access to the memory area. The contents of the memory-mapped file can be written back to the original file, replacing the contents of the file with the contents from the memory-mapped file. This is a quick and easy way to update files of almost any size (up to the virtual memory limits of the system).

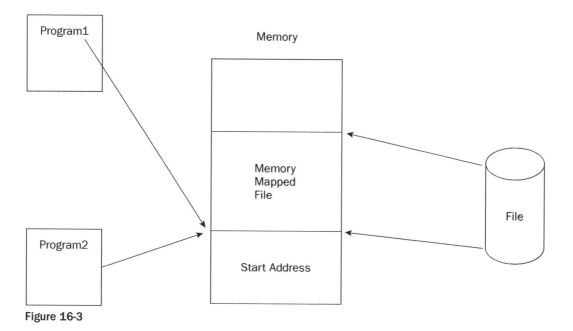

Figure 16-3

The mmap system call

The mmap system call is provided to create memory-mapped files. The format of the mmap system call is as follows:

```
void *mmap(void *start, size_t length, int prot, int flags, int fd, off_t offset);
```

Here are the input values:

- ❑ **start:** Where in memory to map the file
- ❑ **length:** The number of bytes to load into memory
- ❑ **prot:** The memory protection settings
- ❑ **flags:** The type of mapped object to create
- ❑ **fd:** The file handle of the file to map to memory
- ❑ **offset:** The starting point in the file to copy to memory

The start value can be set to 0 to enable the system to choose where to place the memory-mapped file in memory. If the offset value is set to 0 and the length value is set to the size of the file, the entire file is mapped to memory. The mmap function is heavily dependent on the system memory page size. If the length value does not fill an entire page (or fills multiple pages with a non-full page left over) the remainder of the page is zero-filled. If an offset value is used, it must be a multiple of the system page size.

The `prot` value contains settings to determine the access privileges allowed to the memory-mapped file (similar to the access privileges used in the `open` system call). The available values to use are shown in the following table.

Protection Name	Value	Description
PROT_NONE	0	No data access is allowed.
PROT_READ	1	Read access is allowed.
PROT_WRITE	2	Write access is allowed.
PROT_EXEC	4	Execute access is allowed.

The flag's value defines how the operating system controls the memory-mapped file. Many different flags can be used, but the two most common are shown in the following table.

Protection Name	Value	Description
MAP_SHARE	1	Share changes to the memory-mapped file with other processes.
MAP_PRIVATE	2	Keep all changes private to this process.

There is also one other huge difference between these two modes. The MAP_SHARE flag instructs the operating system to write any changes made to the memory-mapped file to the original file. The MAP_PRIVATE flag disregards any changes made to the memory-mapped file when it is closed. While this may seem odd, it actually comes in handy if you need to create a temporary file that requires quick access.

The changes are not written to the original file at the time they are made to the memory-mapped file. This is an important point to remember. Two system calls are used to ensure that the data in the memory-mapped file is written to the original file:

❑ **msync:** Synchronizes the original file to the memory-mapped file

❑ **munmap:** Removes the memory-mapped file from memory and writes any changes to the original file

If you are planning to keep the memory-mapped file in memory for a long period of time after any changes are made, it is a good idea to use the `msync` system call to ensure that the changes have been written to the file. If the program or operating system should crash before either the `msync` or `munmap` system calls are made, any changes made to the memory-mapped file will not be made to the original file.

The `msync` and `munmap` system calls have similar formats:

```
int msync(const void *start, size_t length, int flags);
int munmap(void *start, size_t length);
```

The `start` input value is the starting point in memory where the memory-mapped file is located. This value is returned by the `mmap` system call. The `length` input value is the number of bytes to write to the original file. The `msync flags` input value enables you to define how the updates are made to the original file:

- ❑   **MS_ASYNC:** Updates are scheduled for the next time the file is available for writing, and the system call returns.

- ❑   **MS_SYNC:** The system call waits until the updates are made before returning to the calling program.

An important point to remember is that the memory-mapped file cannot change size from the original file.

mmap assembly language format

Using the `mmap` system call in assembly language requires that you use the format shown in Chapter 12, "Using Linux System Calls." You must know the system call values found in the `unistd.h` file to place in the EAX register before performing the Linux system call. The system call values for the `mmap` system calls are shown in the following table.

System Call	Value
mmap	90
munmap	91
msync	144

However, there is one problem with using the standard Linux system call format as shown in Chapter 12 and the `mmap` system call. While most system calls use the general-purpose registers for input values, system calls that have more than five input values cannot (there are not enough registers to use).

Instead, system calls that have more than five input values (such as `mmap`) read input values from a structure defined in memory. Each of the input values is placed in memory in order, starting at a specific memory location. The starting point of the memory structure is placed in the EBX register before the system call is made. This is shown in Figure 16-4.

The input values can either be placed in a separately defined memory location or pushed onto the normal program stack before the function call. If the values are pushed onto the stack, remember to place them in opposite order (from right to left) on the stack. You must also remember to remove them from the stack (move the ESP pointer back) when the system call returns.

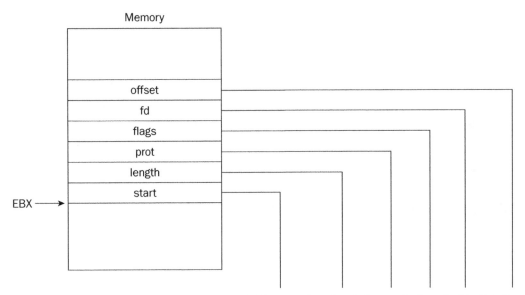

Memory

offset
fd
flags
prot
length
start

EBX ⟶

mmap(void *start, size_t length, int prot, int flags, int fd, off_t offset)

Figure 16-4

The template to use for the `mmap` system call looks something like this:

```
pushl $0     # offset of 0
pushl filehandle   # the file handle of the open file
pushl $1     # MAP_SHARED flag set to write changed data back to file
pushl $3     # PROT_READ and PROT_WRITE permissions
pushl size   # the size of the entire file
pushl $0     # Allow the system to select the location in memory to start
movl %esp, %ebx   # copy the parameters location to EBX
movl $90, %eax    # set the system call value
int $0x80
addl $24, %esp
movl %eax, mappedfile   # store the memory location of the memory mapped file
```

This example creates the memory-mapped file containing the entire file, enabling the process to both read and write data to it, and enabling all updates to be stored in the original file. The return value from the system call is in the EAX register and points to the memory location for the start of the memory-mapped file. This value can be stored and then used as any other memory location, such as the buffer location used in the `readtest` programs.

To unmap the file from memory, the format for the `unmap` system call is as follows:

```
movl $91, %eax
movl mappedfile, %ebx
movl size, %ecx
int $0x80
```

Because the munmap system call only uses two input values, they can be placed in the EBX and ECX registers before the system call is made. The munmap system call will return a value of zero if it successfully writes the data back to the file. If not, it will return a value of -1.

An mmap example

This section demonstrates how to use the mmap system call to map an entire file into memory, modify the data in the memory-mapped file, and write the data back to the original file.

Parts of the program

Before building the main mmap program, a couple of other pieces need to be built. First, to use the mmap system call, you must know the size of the file to place in memory. You can use several different methods to determine the size of a file. One of the simplest is to use the llseek Linux system call (this is an extension of the lseek POSIX system call). A function will be created using the llseek Linux system call to calculate the file size, given a file handle of an open file.

Second, there must be a function to modify the memory-mapped file data so we know it was properly placed back into the file when we are done. The convert function from the readtest3.s program should do nicely, with a few modifications to make it a proper C-style assembly language function.

The llseek system call attempts to advance the file pointer to a specific place in the file. You can instruct the llseek system call to advance the pointer to the end of the file, and see how many bytes that point is from the start of the file.

The llseek system call has the following format:

```
int_llseek(unsigned int fd, unsigned long offset_high, unsigned long offset_low,
            loff_t *result, unsigned int whence);
```

The fd input value is the file handle of the file. The offset_high and offset_low values define the high and low longs of an offset value from the start of the file. Because we are using the system call to determine the entire size of the file, we will use zeros for these values. The result input value is somewhat misleading. It is the address of a memory location where the result of the system call will be stored.

The whence input value is what determines where in the file the llseek system call will go. The value we are interested in is SEEK_END, which has a value of 2.

The sizefunc.c function uses the llseek system call to determine the size of a file:

```
# sizefunc.s - Find the size of a file
.section .text
.globl sizefunc
.type sizefunc, @function
sizefunc:
    pushl %ebp
    movl %esp, %ebp
    subl $8, %esp
    pushl %edi
    pushl %esi
    pushl %ebx
```

```
    movl $140, %eax
    movl 8(%ebp), %ebx
    movl $0, %ecx
    movl $0, %edx
    leal -8(%ebp), %esi
    movl $2, %edi
    int $0x80
    movl -8(%ebp), %eax

    popl %ebx
    popl %esi
    popl %edi
    movl %ebp, %esp
    popl %ebp
    ret
```

The first set of instructions performs the normal C-style function prologue functions, including reserving four bytes of space on the stack for a local variable (see Chapter 14, "Calling Assembly Libraries"). The local variable is used as the result value from the llseek system call.

The sizefunc function assumes the file handle of the file to check is passed as the first input value when it is called (location 8(%ebp)). The location of the local variable (-8(%ebp)) is placed in the %esi register using the LEA instruction (the local variable must be 8 bytes long because the llseek function returns the file size as a long value). When the system call completes, the size of the file will be in the local variable, which is then moved to the EAX register. This is the value that is returned to the calling program.

The convert function was modified to be a proper C-style function, and is shown in the convertit.s program:

```
# convert.s - A function to convert lower case letters to upper case
.section .text
.type convert, @function
.globl convert
convert:
    pushl %ebp
    movl %esp, %ebp
    pushl %esi
    pushl %edi

    movl 12(%ebp), %esi
    movl %esi, %edi
    movl 8(%ebp), %ecx

convert_loop:
    lodsb
    cmpb $0x61, %al
    jl skip
    cmpb $0x7a, %al
    jg skip
    subb $0x20, %al
skip:
    stosb
    loop convert_loop
```

```
pop %edi
pop %esi
movl %ebp, %esp
popl %ebp
ret
```

After the standard C-style function prologue stuff, the input values are read from the stack. First the location of the buffer is read and stored in the ESI register, and then the size of the file is read and stored in the ECX register. The next section performs the conversion function, walking through the buffer changing lowercase ASCII letters into uppercase ASCII letters. When the end of the buffer has been reached, the standard C-style function epilogue instructions are performed, and the function returns to the calling program.

The main program

Now that you have all of the required pieces, it's time to write the complete application. The file convert.s program converts the text in a file from lowercase to uppercase:

```
# fileconvert.s - Memory map a file and convert it
.section .bss
    .lcomm filehandle, 4
    .lcomm size, 4
    .lcomm mappedfile, 4
.section .text
.globl _start
_start:
    # get the file name and open it in read/write mode
    movl %esp, %ebp
    movl $5, %eax
    movl 8(%ebp), %ebx
    movl $0102, %ecx
    movl $0644, %edx
    int $0x80
    test %eax, %eax
    js badfile
    movl %eax, filehandle

    # find the size of the file
    pushl filehandle
    call sizefunc
    movl %eax, size
    addl $4, %esp

    # map file to memory
    pushl $0
    pushl filehandle
    pushl $1      # MAP_SHARED
    pushl $3      # PROT_READ | PROT_WRITE
    pushl size    # file size
    pushl $0      # NULL
    movl %esp, %ebx
    movl $90, %eax
    int $0x80    test %eax, %eax
    js badfile
    movl %eax, mappedfile
    addl $24, %esp
```

477

```
        # convert the memory mapped file to all uppers
        pushl mappedfile
        pushl size
        call convert
        addl $8, %esp

        # use munmap to send the changes to the file
        movl $91, %eax
        movl mappedfile, %ebx
        movl size, %ecx
        int $0x80
        test %eax, %eax
        jnz badfile

    # close the open file handle
        movl $6, %eax
        movl filehandle, %ebx
        int $0x80

badfile:
        movl %eax, %ebx
        movl $1, %eax
        int $0x80
```

The complete program uses the two helper functions, plus the mmap and munmap system calls. Each instruction section in the code performs a single function in the application. The steps are as follows:

1. Open the file with read/write access.

2. Determine the size of the file using the sizefunc function.

3. Map the file to memory using the mmap system call code.

4. Convert the memory-mapped file to all uppercase letters.

5. Write the memory-mapped file to the original file using munmap.

6. Close the original file and exit.

Watching the program

Because the programs do not use any C functions, you can just assemble them and link them:

```
$ as -o sizefunc.o sizefunc.s
$ as -o convert.o convert.s
$ as -o fileconvert.o fileconvert.s
$ ld -o fileconvert fileconvert.o sizefunc.o convert.o
$ cat cpuid.txt
The processor Vendor ID is 'GenuineIntel'
The processor Vendor ID is 'GenuineIntel'
$ ./fileconvert cpuid.txt
$ cat cpuid.txt
THE PROCESSOR VENDOR ID IS 'GENUINEINTEL'
THE PROCESSOR VENDOR ID IS 'GENUINEINTEL'
$
```

You can test the `fileconvert` program on any text file you like. Just remember that the original file will be converted to uppercase, so you may want to copy it before playing around.

Because the `fileconvert` program uses system calls, you can use the `strace` program (described in Chapter 12) to watch the system calls made while it is running:

```
$ strace ./fileconvert test.txt
execve("./fileconvert", ["./fileconvert", "test.txt"], [/* 38 vars */]) = 0
open("test.txt", O_RDWR|O_CREAT, 0644)    = 3
_llseek(3, 0, [1419], SEEK_END)           = 0
old_mmap(NULL, 1419, PROT_READ|PROT_WRITE, MAP_SHARED, 3, 0) = 0x40000000
munmap(0x40000000, 1419)                  = 0
close(3)                                  = 0
_exit(0)                                  = ?
$
```

Notice that the `strace` program shows the C-style version of the system calls, complete with the input values the program passed to them, and the return values generated. This is an excellent troubleshooting tool to use if you have problems with your system calls.

Summary

This chapter discussed using Linux system calls to handle file input and output in an assembly language program. Linux provides many different system calls that can be used to manipulate files. Before using a file, you must use the `open` system call. The `open` system call attempts to open a file on the system with defined permissions and an access type. You must remember to check the return value from the system call to ensure that there were no problems with opening the file.

Once the file is open, you can use the `write` system call to write data to the file. How the data is written to the file depends on the access type used in the `open` system call. You can either append new data to the end of an existing file or you can overwrite the existing file with the new data. Again, attention must be paid to the system call return value to ensure that the `write` instruction performed properly.

The `read` system call enables you to read data from a file and place the data in a memory buffer. You must specify how many bytes of the file to read from a single `read` system call. If the value is less than the number of bytes in the file, a file pointer is used to keep track of where the `read` system call left off, and another `read` system call will start reading data from that point in the file. If the value is more than the number of bytes in the file, the remaining bytes will be copied into the memory buffer, and the `read` system call return value will indicate how many bytes were read. If the return value is zero, you have reached the end of the file.

Many assembly language programs perform a complicated sequence of reading data from a file into a memory buffer, processing the data (by either modifying it or scanning it), and then writing data back out to either another file or the `STDOUT` console display. This sequence of events can be incorporated into a loop, reading blocks of data from the file, processing them, and writing them back out to another file. Each block of data is processed individually from the other blocks, performing the necessary processes on the block of data contained within the memory buffer.

Rather than manually reading blocks of data into a memory buffer and processing the data, UNIX systems provide a system call that enables you to read the contents of an entire file into memory at once (assuming the file size is less than the virtual memory size). This technique is called *memory mapping*. Once the file is mapped to memory, any number of different programs can scan and modify the data contained within the memory-map block. When the processing is done, you can choose to replace the original file with the modified memory-mapped file. This is an excellent technique to use to quickly modify large files.

The final chapter in this book dives into the advanced world of IA-32 MMX and SSE programming. The Intel MMX, SSE, SSE2, and SSE3 technologies provide programmers with advanced methods for processing large amounts of data quickly. Chapter 17 describes these technologies and demonstrates how they can be used in assembly language programs.

17

Using Advanced
IA-32 Features

The Intel Pentium family of processors provides advanced mathematical processing capabilities to the IA-32 instruction set. If you are working with applications that require a lot of mathematical processing, such as audio and video processing, utilizing the advanced mathematical features can greatly increase the performance of your application.

This chapter describes the Single Instruction Multiple Data (SIMD) family of instructions used on Pentium processors. First, a review of the main features of SIMD is presented. Following that, how to use the MMX architecture instructions is shown. Next, the SSE features are discussed, along with a demonstration of how to use SSE to process multiple data elements in a single instruction. Finally, the SSE2 features are shown, along with an example of using them in an assembly language program.

A Brief Review of SIMD

Chapters 2, "The IA-32 Platform," and 7, "Using Numbers," described the various features and data types found in the IA-32 SIMD architecture. To recap, the IA-32 SIMD architecture currently consists of four technologies:

❑   Multimedia Extensions (MMX)

❑   Streaming SIMD Extensions (SSE)

❑   Streaming SIMD Extensions Second Implementation (SSE2)

❑   Streaming SIMD Extension Third Implementation (SSE3)

As discussed in Chapter 2, different Intel Pentium processors support different versions of the SIMD architecture. The Pentium MMX and Pentium II processors support MMX. The Pentium III processor supports both MMX and SSE technology. The Pentium 4 processor supports MMX, SSE, and SSE2 technology. The Pentium 4HT (hyperthreading) and Xeon processors support MMX, SSE, SSE2, and SSE3 technologies.

The main benefit that SIMD technology provides to the programmer is the capability to perform parallel mathematical operations with a single instruction. The MMX and SSE architectures provide additional registers that can hold packed data (multiple data values in a single register). The MMX and SSE instructions have the capability to perform a single mathematical operation on all of the packed data elements in the registers at once.

This section provides a brief overview of the features each of these technologies provides to the IA-32 instruction set.

MMX

The main purpose of MMX technology is to perform SIMD operations on integer data types. The MMX SIMD architecture provides three additional types of integer values:

- ❏ 64-bit packed byte integers (contains eight single-byte integer values)
- ❏ 64-bit packed word integers (contains four word integer values)
- ❏ 64-bit packed doubleword integers (contains two doubleword integer values)

Because the MMX integer data types use 64 bits, they cannot be held by the normal general-purpose registers. Instead, the MMX technology utilizes the 80-bit FPU registers to perform all of its mathematical operations. The MMX registers are called MMX0 through MMX7. They are directly mapped to FPU registers R0 through R7. Unlike the FPU registers, however, the MMX registers are static, they cannot be used as a stack. The MMX0 register always references FPU register R0. Placing a data value in the MMX0 register does not shift the previous value down to the MMX1 register. The FPU top of stack register value does not have any effect on MMX instructions.

While the FPU registers are used to hold MMX data, they can also be used to hold FPU data. This can become extremely confusing. The registers are placed in MMX mode to handle MMX data (the exponent value of the register is set to all ones), and put in FPU mode to handle normal FPU double-extended floating-point data.

Unfortunately, when using the FPU registers in MMX mode, the FPU Tag register becomes corrupt. To solve this, it is best to separate instructions that use FPU registers from instructions that use MMX registers. The solution is to save the FPU registers in memory using the FSAVE or FXSAVE instructions, and restore them using the FRSTOR or FXRSTOR instructions when the MMX instructions are complete. The FSAVE and FRSTOR instructions save just the FPU state (this is discussed and demonstrated in Chapter 9, "Advanced Math Functions"). The FXSAVE and FXRSTOR instructions save the FPU, MMX, and SSE states.

When the MMX processing is complete, the EMMS instruction should be used to clear the FPU Tag register value, to enable any FPU instructions to perform properly.

As you can see, the 64-bit packed integer values hold multiple integer values. The MMX architecture includes additional instructions to enable processing the multiple integer values in a single instruction (thus the single instruction, multiple data nomenclature).

SSE

The main purpose of the SSE technology is to perform SIMD operations on floating-point data. The SSE architecture provides another new data type: the 128-bit, packed, single-precision floating-point data type. This data type is used to contain four single-precision floating-point values (as described in Chapter 7, a single-precision floating-point value requires 32 bits).

Because the new data type requires 128 bits, a new register set was created just for SSE processing. These new registers include eight 128-bit registers (XMM0 through XMM7) that are used to hold the 128-bit, packed, single-precision floating-point data values. SSE floating-point mathematical operations use the XMM registers.

The SSE architecture also included new instructions for performing SIMD mathematical operations on the packed, single-precision floating-point values. This enables up to four floating-point calculations in a single operation.

SSE2

The SSE2 architecture expands on the core SSE architecture by adding five new data types:

- ❑ 128-bit packed double-precision floating-point value (contains two double-precision values)
- ❑ 128-bit packed byte integer value (contains 16 single-byte integer values)
- ❑ 128-bit packed word integer value (contains eight word integer values)
- ❑ 128-bit packed doubleword integer value (contains four doubleword integer values)
- ❑ 128-bit packed quadword integer value (contains two quadword integer values)

Each of these new data types utilizes the 128-bit XMM registers to hold data for processing. The SSE2 technology provides for additional floating-point and integer SIMD operations. It includes additional instructions for performing mathematical calculations on the packed data (again using a single operation).

The SSE3 architecture does not add any additional data types to the SSE2 architecture. It does provide new instructions for advanced processing of SSE2 data types.

Detecting Supported SIMD Operations

Before diving into MMX and SSE instructions, it's best to know whether the processor your application will run on can support them. Remember that not only do you have to consider whether or not the processor is in the Pentium family, you must also consider whether it is even an Intel processor (such as the AMD processors). As discussed in Chapter 2, most of the AMD family of processors support the MMX instruction sets but do not support the SSE technologies. This section shows the logic that you can use in your assembly language programs to detect whether a processor supports MMX, SSE, SSE2, or SSE3 instructions.

Detecting support

The CPUID instruction provides a method for identifying processors that support the various SIMD technologies. If you have been following along in this book, you saw the CPUID instruction in action in Chapter 4, "A Sample Assembly Language Program."

In that example, the CPUID instruction was used to generate the vendor ID of the processor. The CPUID instruction can also be used to generate other processor information. The type of information generated by the instruction is controlled by the value of the EAX register when the CPUID instruction is executed.

When the value of EAX is 1, the CPUID instruction returns the processor signature information. The processor signature information includes two registers that contain processor feature flags. The ECX and EDX registers contain bits set to represent different features available on the processor. The bits used to represent SIMD features are shown in the following table.

REGISTER	Bit	Feature
EDX	23	Supports MMX instructions
EDX	25	Supports SSE instructions
EDX	26	Supports SSE2 instructions
ECX	0	Supports SSE3 instructions

Once you know what bits in what registers to look for, you can use the TEST instruction to compare the values in the ECX and EDX registers returned by the CPUID instruction with set values representing the feature flags. If the TEST instruction sets the zero flag, you know that the feature is not present. If the zero flag is not set, the feature bit must be enabled, and the feature must be present.

To determine the value to place in the TEST instruction, you must know the hexadecimal value of the desired feature's bit positions. Figure 17-1 demonstrates how to find these values.

Register Bits

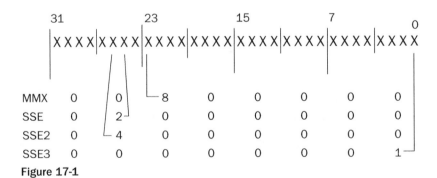

Figure 17-1

As shown in Figure 17-1, the TEST instruction to detect the MMX feature is as follows:

```
test $0x00800000, %edx
jz notfound
```

If the zero flag is set, the MMX feature is not available on the processor. Similarly, here is the TEST instruction to detect the SSE feature:

```
test $0x02000000, %edx
jz notfound
```

For the SSE2 feature:

```
test $0x04000000, %edx
jz notfound
```

Finally, for the SSE3 feature:

```
test $0x00000001, %ecx
jz notfound
```

You can now use these tests in your assembly language program to test for the SIMD features on the processor.

SIMD feature program

The features.s program uses the SIMD tests to list the SIMD features found on the processor:

```
# features.s - Determine MMX, SSE, SSE2, and SSE3 capabilities
.section .data
gotmmx:
    .asciz "Supports MMX"
gotsse:
    .asciz "Supports SSE"
gotsse2:
    .asciz "Supports SSE2"
gotsse3:
    .asciz "Supports SSE3"
output:
    .asciz "%s\n"
.section .bss
    .lcomm ecxdata, 4
    .lcomm edxdata, 4
.section .text
.globl _start
_start:
    nop
    movl $1, %eax
    cpuid
```

```
        movl %ecx, ecxdata
        movl %edx, edxdata

        test $0x00800000, %edx
        jz done
        pushl $gotmmx
        pushl $output
        call printf
        addl $8, %esp

        movl edxdata, %edx
        test $0x02000000, %edx
        jz done
        pushl $gotsse
        pushl $output
        call printf
        addl $8, %esp

        movl edxdata, %edx
        test $0x04000000, %edx
        jz done
        pushl $gotsse2
        pushl $output
        call printf
        addl $8, %esp

        movl ecxdata, %ecx
        test $0x00000001, %ecx
        jz done
        pushl $gotsse3
        pushl $output
        call printf
        addl $8, %esp

done:
    pushl $0
    call exit
```

The features.s program displays a text line for each of the SIMD features it detects on the processor. First, the EAX register is set to 1 to enable the CPUID processor signature mode. After the CPUID instruction is executed, the processor feature flags are loaded in the ECX and EDX registers. So as not to lose that information, these values are stored in memory locations defined in the .bss section.

Because the features are cumulative in successive processors, it is safe to assume that as soon as one feature is not found, the more advanced ones would also not be found. With this in mind, the features.s program exits as soon as a feature is not found. If a feature is found, the printf C function is used to display a short message.

Because the features.s program uses the printf and exit C functions, it must be linked with the C library files and the dynamic linker on the system before it will run:

```
$ as -o features.o features.s
$ ld -dynamic-linker /lib/ld-linux.so.2 -lc -o feature features.o
$ ./features
Supports MMX
Supports SSE
Supports SSE2
$
```

This particular processor supports only MMX, SSE, and SSE2 instructions. At the time of this writing, only Pentium 4 processors with hyperthreading support SSE3 instructions.

Using MMX Instructions

To utilize the MMX architecture in your assembly language programs you must perform the following steps:

1. Create packed integer values from integer values.

2. Load the packed integer values into an MMX register.

3. Perform an MMX mathematical operation on the packed integer values.

4. Retrieve the result from the MMX register to a memory location.

The following sections describe these steps in detail.

Loading and retrieving packed integer values

The first two steps and the last step, loading integer values into the MMX register in the packed integer format, and retrieving the packed integer results from the MMX register, have already been discussed in Chapter 7. The MOVQ instruction is used to move integer values into and out of an MMX register.

The integer values must be placed in the MMX register in a packed integer format. The MMX packed integer data types provide for 8-byte integer values, four word integer values, or two doubleword integer values. You can place these values in memory locations to load into the MMX register like this:

```
.section .data
packedvalue1:
    .byte 10, 20, -30, 40, 50, 60, -70, 80
packedvalue2:
    .short 10, 20, 30, 40
packedvalue3:
    .int 10, 20
.section .text
.globl _start
_start:
    movq packedvalue1, %mm0
    movq packedvalue2, %mm1
    movq packedvalue3, %mm2
```

Of course, you can also reserve 8 bytes of memory in the .bss section for each value and place the values into the memory locations programmatically as well. Similarly, the MOVQ instruction can be used to move data from an MMX register to a 64-bit memory location (as described in Chapter 5, "Moving Data").

Performing MMX operations

Once the data is loaded into the MMX register, parallel operations can be performed on the packed data using a single instruction. The operations are performed on each packed integer value in the register, utilizing the same placed packed integer values. This is shown in Figure 17-2.

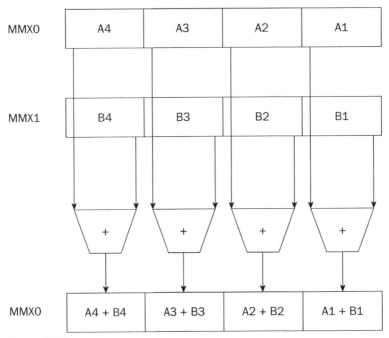

Figure 17-2

The following section describes some of the operations that can be performed on the MMX packed integer data values.

MMX addition and subtraction instructions

Normal integer addition and subtraction using the general-purpose registers is mostly a straightforward process. However, there is one problem when using packed integer mathematical operations.

With normal addition and subtraction with general-purpose registers, if an overflow condition exists from the operation, the EFLAGS register is set to indicate the overflow condition. With packed integer values, multiple result values are computed simultaneously. This means that a single set of flags cannot indicate the result of the operation, as in normal integer math.

Instead, when using MMX addition or subtraction, you must decide ahead of time what the processor should do in case of overflow conditions within the operation. You can choose from three overflow methods for performing the mathematical operations:

❑   Wraparound arithmetic

❑   Signed saturation arithmetic

❑   Unsigned saturation arithmetic

The wraparound arithmetic method performs the mathematical operation and allows the overflow to wrap around the data size. This method assumes that you will check the operands before performing the operation to ensure that an overflow condition will not be present. If it is, the resulting value will be truncated, removing any carry values.

The signed and unsigned saturation arithmetic methods set the result of an overflow condition to a pre-set value, which depends on the size of the packed integer values used, and the sign of the overflow. The following table describes these overflow values.

Data Type	Positive Overflow Value	Negative Overflow Value
Signed byte	127	-128
Signed word	32,767	-32,768
Unsigned byte	255	0
Unsigned word	65,535	0

If a positive overflow condition exists, the result is set to the highest value for the data type. If a negative overflow condition exists, the result is set to the lowest value for the data type. While the saturation arithmetic overflow values may not make sense from a mathematical point of view, there is a reason why they are set the way they are. One of the biggest uses for MMX technology is in performing graphical calculations for displaying pictures. When calculating the red, blue, and green values for pixels, a positive overflow should set the pixels to the maximum value, which is a white color. For a negative overflow condition, the pixels are set to the minimum value, which is a black color.

After deciding which arithmetic method you need for your calculations, you can choose which instruction to use based on the mathematical operation you need to perform. The following table lists some of the available MMX math operations you can use.

MMX Instruction	Description
PADDB	Add packed byte integers with wraparound
PADDW	Add packed word integers with wraparound
PADDD	Add packed doubleword integers with wraparound
PADDSB	Add packed byte integers with signed saturation
PADDSW	Add packed word integers with signed saturation
PADDUSB	Add packed byte integers with unsigned saturation
PADDUSW	Add packed word integers with unsigned saturation
PSUBB	Subtract packed byte integers with wraparound
PSUBW	Subtract packed word integers with wraparound
PSUBD	Subtract packed doubleword integers with wraparound
PSUBSB	Subtract packed byte integers with signed saturation
PSUBSW	Subtract packed word integers with signed saturation
PSUBUSB	Subtract packed byte integers with unsigned saturation
PSUBUSW	Subtract packed word integers with unsigned saturation

Each of the MMX mathematical operations has the same format:

```
PADDSB source, destination
```

where source can be either an MMX register or a 64-bit memory location, and destination is an MMX register. For example, the instruction

```
PADDSB %mm1, %mm0
```

adds the contents of register MM0 with the contents of register MM1, and places the result in register MM0.

The mmxadd.s program demonstrates a simple MMX addition:

```
# mmxadd.s - An example of performing MMX addition
.section .data
value1:
    .int 10, 20
value2:
    .int 30, 40
.section .bss
    .lcomm result, 8
.section .text
.globl _start
```

```
_start:
    nop
    movq value1, %mm0
    movq value2, %mm1
    paddd %mm1, %mm0
    movq %mm0, result

    movl $1, %eax
    movl $0, %ebx
    int $0x80
```

The mmxadd.s program creates two packed doubleword integer values by storing two long integer values in a single memory location. Both the value1 and value2 labels point to packed doubleword integer values. The MOVQ instruction is used to load the values into the MMX registers, and the PADDD instruction is used to add the two doublewords. The result is placed in the MMX0 register and copied to the result memory location.

You must run the program in the debugger to be able to see what is happening. After the two values are loaded into the MMX registers, you can view them using either their FPU register names or their MMX register names:

```
(gdb) info all
.
.
.
st0             nan        (raw 0xffff000000140000000a)
st1             nan        (raw 0xffff00000028000001e)
```

The ST0 register shows the packed doubleword integer value. The low doubleword contains the first value in the value1 memory location, and the high doubleword contains the second value. After stepping through the program, you can examine the memory locations:

```
(gdb) x/2d &value1
0x804909c <value1>:     10      20
(gdb) x/2d &value2
0x80490a4 <value2>:     30      40
(gdb) x/2d &result
0x80490b0 <result>:     40      60
(gdb)
```

Indeed, the PADDD instruction added the packed doubleword values as expected.

MMX multiplication instructions

Multiplying MMX integers is somewhat trickier. Because integer multiplication can produce a much larger value than the input operands, MMX multiplication enables two instructions to complete the multiplication process. The first instruction, PMULL, multiplies each of the packed word integer values and places the low 16 bits of the result in the destination register. This is demonstrated in Figure 17-3.

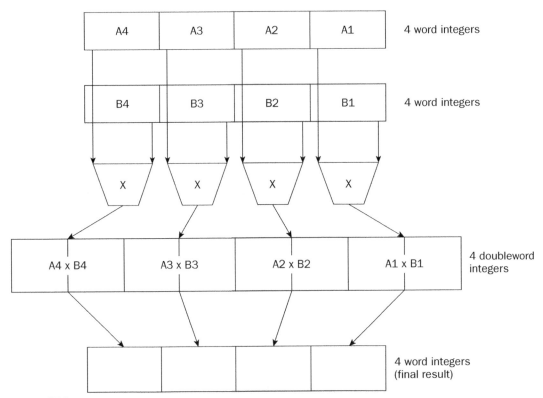

Figure 17-3

The low 16 bits of the results can then be moved to an appropriate memory location, and the two input registers reloaded with the original operands. Next, the PMULH instruction is used, which multiplies the packed word integer values and places the high 16 bits of the result in the destination register. Now you have both the low- and high-order bits for the complete result of the multiplication.

The PMULL and PMULH instructions have versions for both signed (PMULLW and PMULHW) and unsigned (PMULLUW and PMULHUW) integer values.

One additional instruction in the MMX multiplication family is the PMADDWD instruction. The PMADDWD instruction is a special-purpose instruction. It performs a multiplication of four signed word integer values in the source operand with the four signed word integer values in the destination operand. This produces four signed doubleword integer values. The adjacent doubleword integer values are then added together to produce two doubleword integer result values, as demonstrated in Figure 17-4.

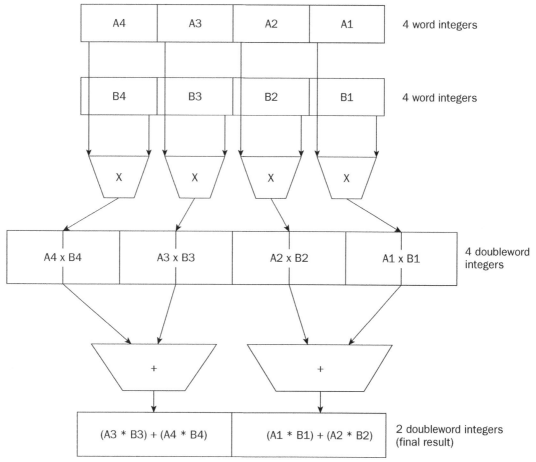

Figure 17-4

MMX logical and shift instructions

The MMX architecture also provides instructions for performing normal Boolean logic operations and bit-shifting instructions on quadword values. The following table outlines the Boolean logic instructions available in MMX.

Instruction	Description
PAND	Performs a bitwise logic AND of the source and destination operands
PANDN	Performs a bitwise logical NOT of the destination operand, and then an AND of the source and destination operands
POR	Performs a bitwise logical OR of the source and destination operands
PXOR	Performs a bitwise logical exclusive-OR of the source and destination operands
PSLL	Performs a logical left shift of the operand, filling empty bits with zeroes
PSRA	Performs a logical right shift of the operand, filling empty bits with zeroes

The format of the logic instructions is

```
PAND source, destination
```

where source can be an MMX register or a 64-bit memory location, and destination must be an MMX register. The left shift instructions can use a word, doubleword, or quadword operand, and the number of places to shift, while the right shift instructions can use a word or doubleword operand, along with the number of places to shift.

MMX comparison instructions

The MMX architecture also includes comparison instructions for comparing two values. These are described in the following table.

Instruction	Description
PCMPEQB	Compares packed byte integer values for equality
PCMPEQW	Compares packed word integer values for equality
PCMPEQD	Compares packed doubleword integer values for equality
PCMPGTB	Determines whether the packed byte integer values are greater than another
PCMPGTW	Determines whether the packed word integer values are greater than another
PCMPGTD	Determines whether the packed doubleword integer values are greater than another

The MMX comparison instructions are somewhat different than the normal CMP instruction. Because the MMX data types hold multiple values, no flags are set for equality or greater-than or less-than.

Instead, the source and destination packed integer values are compared, and the result is placed in the destination packed integer value. If a packed integer value pair meets the comparison (either equal or the destination value is greater than the source value), the result packed integer value is set to all ones. If the condition is not met, the result value is set to all zeroes, as demonstrated in Figure 17-5.

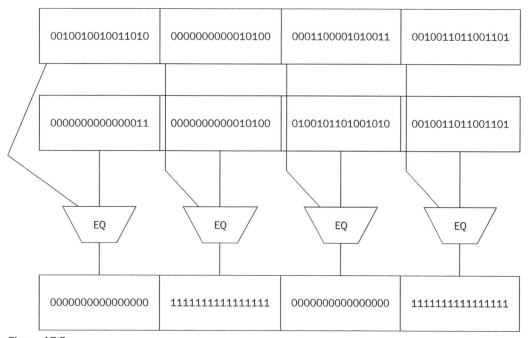

Figure 17-5

Because the second and third packed word integer values are equal, those values in the result are set to ones. The other two packed word integer values are set to zeroes.

The mmxcomp.s program demonstrates how this works:

```
# mmxcomp.s - An example of performing MMX comparison
.section .data
value1:
    .short 10, 20, -30, 40
value2:
    .short 10, 40, -30, 45
.section .bss
    .lcomm result, 8
```

```
.section .text
.globl _start
_start:
    nop
    movq value1, %mm0
    movq value2, %mm1
    pcmpeqw %mm1, %mm0
    movq %mm0, result

    movl $1, %eax
    movl $0, %ebx
    int $0x80
```

The value1 and value2 memory locations are set to hold four short integer values (word integers). They are both loaded into the MMX registers, and the PCMPEQW instruction is used to compare the four word values within the packed integer values. The result is in the MM0 register, which is moved to the result memory location.

You must use the debugger to see what happens when the program runs:

```
$ gdb -q mmxcomp
(gdb) break *_start+1
Breakpoint 1 at 0x8048075: file mmxcomp.s, line 13.
(gdb) run
Starting program: /home/rich/palp/chap17/mmxcomp

Breakpoint 1, _start () at mmxcomp.s:13
13          movq value1, %mm0
Current language:  auto; currently asm
(gdb) s
14          movq value2, %mm1
(gdb) s
15          pcmpeqw %mm1, %mm0
(gdb) s
16          movq %mm0, result
(gdb) s
18          movl $1, %eax
(gdb) x/x &value1
0x804909c <value1>:       0x0014000a
(gdb) x/x &value2
0x80490a4 <value2>:       0x0028000a
(gdb) x/x &result
0x80490b0 <result>:       0x0000ffff
(gdb)
```

The two packed doubleword integer values are loaded into two separate MMX registers, and the PCMPEQW instruction is performed. The result is placed in the result memory location. By looking at the hexadecimal values of the memory locations, you can see that for the packed integer values that were equal, the result contained FFFF, whereas for the packed integer values that were not equal, the result contained the value 0000.

Using SSE Instructions

The SSE architecture provides SIMD support for packed single-precision floating-point values. As with the MMX architecture, SSE provides new instructions for moving data into XMM registers, processing mathematical operations on the SSE data, and retrieving data from the XMM registers.

One difference with MMX is that each SSE instruction has two versions. The first version uses a PS suffix. These instructions perform the arithmetic operation on the packed single-precision floating-point value similarly to how MMX operates — each value within the packed data value is run through the operation, and the resulting packed value contains the results from each of the packed value operations (as shown earlier in Figure 17-2).

The second version of the arithmetic instruction uses an SS suffix. These instructions perform the arithmetic operation on a scalar single-precision floating-point value. Instead of performing the operation on all of the floating-point values in the packed value, it is performed on only the low doubleword in the packed value. The remaining three values from the source operand are carried through to the result, as demonstrated in Figure 17-6.

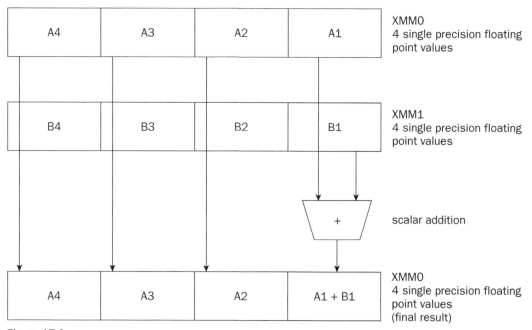

Figure 17-6

The scalar operations enable normal FPU-type arithmetic operations to be performed on one single-precision floating-point value in the XMM registers.

This section describes how to use SSE instructions to help increase performance in your assembly language programs.

Moving data

Chapter 7 explained how to move packed single-precision floating-point data into the XMM registers. To recap, the following table describes these instructions.

Instruction	Description
MOVAPS	Move four aligned, single-precision values to XMM registers or memory.
MOVUPS	Move four unaligned, single-precision values to XMM registers or memory.
MOVSS	Move a single-precision value to memory or the low doubleword of a register.
MOVLPS	Move two single-precision values to memory or the low quad-word of a register.
MOVHPS	Move two single-precision values to memory or the high quad-word of a register.
MOVLHPS	Move two single-precision values from the low quadword to the high quadword.
MOVHLPS	Move two single-precision values from the high quadword to the low quadword.

As you can see from the table, moving single-precision floating-point values is highly dependent on whether or not the values are aligned in memory. The MOVAPS instruction requires that the data be aligned on a 16-byte boundary in memory. This makes it easier for the processor to read the data in a single operation.

The ssefloat.s program in Chapter 7 used the MOVUPS instruction to move unaligned data into the XMM register. If you tried using the MOVAPS instruction in its place, you would get a segmentation fault when you ran the program. You can, however, force the assembler to align the data stored in memory.

The .align directive instructs the gas assembler to align the data on a specific memory boundary. It takes a single operand, the size of the memory boundary on which to align the data. The SSE MOVAPS instruction expects the data to be located on a 16-byte memory boundary, so the instruction should look like the following:

```
.section .data
.align 16
value1:
    .float 12.34, 2345.543, -3493.2, 0.4491
.section .text
.globl _start
_start:
    movaps value1, %xmm0
```

Now that the data is aligned on a 16-byte boundary, the MOVAPS instruction will properly load the memory value into the XMM0 register without throwing a segmentation fault.

Processing data

The SSE architecture provides many additional instructions for processing packed single-precision floating-point data. This section describes some of these instructions and how they are used.

Arithmetic instructions

Numerous arithmetic operations are available for use with data in the XMM registers. The following table lists the arithmetic instructions available (using the packed single-precision floating-point value nomenclature).

Instruction	Description
ADDPS	Add two packed values.
SUBPS	Subtract two packed values.
MULPS	Multiply two packed values.
DIVPS	Divide two packed values.
RCPPS	Compute the reciprocal of a packed value.
SQRTPS	Compute the square root of a packed value.
RSQRTPS	Compute the reciprocal square root of a packed value.
MAXPS	Compute the maximum values in two packed values.
MINPS	Compute the minimum values in two packed values.
ANDPS	Compute the bitwise logical AND of two packed values.
ANDNPS	Compute the bitwise logical AND NOT of two packed values.
ORPS	Compute the bitwise logical OR of two packed values.
XORPS	Compute the bitwise logical exclusive-OR of two packed values.

Each of these instructions uses two operands: a source operand that can be a 128-bit memory location or an XMM register, and a destination operand that must be an XMM register.

The ssemath.s program demonstrates using some of these instructions:

```
# ssemath.s - An example of using SSE arithmetic instructions
.section .data
.align 16
value1:
    .float 12.34, 2345., -93.2, 10.44
```

```
value2:
    .float 39.234, 21.4, 100.94, 10.56
.section .bss
    .lcomm result, 16
.section .text
.globl _start
_start:
    nop
    movaps value1, %xmm0
    movaps value2, %xmm1

    addps %xmm1, %xmm0
    sqrtps %xmm0, %xmm0
    maxps %xmm1, %xmm0
    movaps %xmm0, result

    movl $1, %eax
    movl $0, %ebx
    int $0x80
```

The ssemath.s program loads the sets of packed single-precision floating-point values into XMM registers and performs some basic arithmetic operations. The result from register XMM0 is moved back into memory at the location tagged with the result label. After assembling and linking the program, you can run it in the debugger and watch the results:

```
$ gdb -q ssemath
(gdb) break *_start+1
Breakpoint 1 at 0x8048075: file ssemath.s, line 14.
(gdb) run
Starting program: /home/rich/palp/chap17/ssemath

Breakpoint 1, _start () at ssemath.s:14
14          movaps value1, %xmm0
Current language:  auto; currently asm
(gdb) s
15          movaps value2, %xmm1
(gdb) s
17          addps %xmm1, %xmm0
(gdb) print $xmm0
$1 = {f = {12.3400002, 2345, -93.1999969, 10.4399996}}
(gdb) print $xmm1
$2 = {f = {39.2340012, 21.3999996, 100.940002, 10.5600004}}
```

After the MOVAPS instructions, the two XMM registers contain the packed single-precision floating-point values. Next, the ADDPS instruction is run, and the XMM0 register displayed:

```
(gdb) s
18          sqrtps %xmm0, %xmm0
(gdb) print $xmm0
$3 = {f = {51.5740013, 2366.3999, 7.74000549, 21}}
```

The two packed values were added, and the results were placed in the XMM0 register. Next, the SQRTPS instruction is performed:

```
(gdb) s
19          maxps %xmm1, %xmm0
(gdb) print $xmm0
$4 = {f = {7.18150425, 48.6456566, 2.78208661, 4.5825758}}
```

The square root of all four values was performed with the single instruction. Next, the maximum values between the two packed values are determined, and moved to the result memory location:

```
(gdb) s
20          movaps %xmm0, result
(gdb) print $xmm0
$5 = {f = {39.2340012, 48.6456566, 100.940002, 10.5600004}}
(gdb) s
22          movl $1, %eax
(gdb) x/4f &result
0x80490c0 <result>:       39.2340012      48.6456566      100.940002      10.5600004
(gdb)
```

The single-precision floating-point values in the result memory location correspond to the maximum values between the two packed single-precision floating-point values. Notice that each maximum value was determined with its corresponding packed value.

Comparison instructions

Similar to the MMX comparison instructions, the SSE comparison instructions compare each element of the 128-bit packed single-precision floating-point value separately. The result is a mask of all ones for values that satisfy the comparison, or all zeroes for values that do not meet the comparison (remember that the scalar version of these instructions only perform on the lowest doubleword value).

The following table lists the comparison instructions available.

Instruction	Description
CMPPS	Compare packed values.
CMPSS	Compare scalar values.
COMISS	Compare scalar values and set the EFLAGS register.
UCOMISS	Compare scalar values (including invalid values) and set the EFLAGS register.

The UCOMISS instruction enables you to compare single-precision floating-point values that also include special values, such as not-a-number (NaN) values.

The CMPPS instruction is somewhat different. It can be used to compare the two packed values for all types of comparisons (equality, greater than, less than, and so on). The basic CMPPS instruction has three operands:

```
CMPPS imp, source, destination
```

The source and destination operands are as expected (the destination must be an XMM register, but the source can be a 128-bit memory location or an XMM register). The oddity is the imp operand. This operand (called the *implementation operand*) determines what type of comparison will be performed by the instruction. This is an unsigned integer value, which can be coded as an immediate value or a variable. The value of the operand determines the comparison type, as shown in the following table.

Implementation Value	Comparison
0	Equal
1	Less than
2	Less than or equal
3	Unordered
4	Not equal
5	Not less than
6	Not less than or equal
7	Ordered

Therefore, to determine whether two XMM registers are equal, you would use the following instruction:

```
CMPPS $0, %xmm1, %xmm0
```

The result will be the bit mask (all ones for values that are equal, and all zeroes for values that are not), placed in the XMM0 register.

You may not be familiar with the ordered and unordered comparisons. These are used for finding data values that are not valid floating-point number representations (described in Chapter 7, "Using Numbers"). The unordered comparison is true when at least one of the values is not a valid floating-point number. The ordered comparison is true only when both operands are valid floating-point numbers.

The gas assembler also provides pseudo-instructions in place of the implementation operand. Instead of using the CMPPS instruction with the implementation operand, you can use the pseudo-instruction with just the source and destination operands. The pseudo-instructions are shown in the following table.

Pseudo Instruction	Description
CMPEQPS	Equal
CMPLTPS	Less than
CMPLEPS	Less than or equal
CMPUORDPS	Unordered
CMPNEQPS	Not equal
CMPNLTPS	Not less than
CMPNLEPS	Not less than or equal
CMPORDPS	Ordered

The ssecomp.s program demonstrates how to use the CMPEQPS instruction:

```
# ssecomp.s - An example of using SSE comparison instructions
.section .data
.align 16
value1:
    .float 12.34, 2345., -93.2, 10.44
value2:
    .float 12.34, 21.4, -93.2, 10.45
.section .bss
    .lcomm result, 16
.section .text
.globl _start
_start:
    nop
    movaps value1, %xmm0
    movaps value2, %xmm1

    cmpeqps %xmm1, %xmm0
    movaps %xmm0, result

    movl $1, %eax
    movl $0, %ebx
    int $0x80
```

The ssecomp.s program loads the two packed single-precision floating-point values into the XMM registers, and uses the CMPEQPS instruction to compare them. The result is moved to the result memory location.

After assembling and linking the program, run it in the debugger to see what happens:

```
(gdb) x/4x &result
0x80490c0 <result>:  0xffffffff   0x00000000   0xffffffff   0x00000000
(gdb) print $xmm0
$1 = {f = {-NaN(0x7fffff), 0, -NaN(0x7fffff), 0}}
(gdb)
```

The results show that the first and third values in the packed value were equal.

SSE integer instructions

The SSE architecture also provides some expanded features for handling 64-bit packed integer values in addition to what MMX provides. These instructions, described in the following table, perform operations on data located in the MMX registers.

Instruction	Description
PAVGB	Computes the average of packed unsigned byte integers
PAVGW	Computes the average of packed unsigned word integers
PEXTRW	Copies a word from an MMX register to a general-purpose register
PINSRW	Copies a word from a general-purpose register to an MMX register
PMAXUB	Computes the maximum value of packed unsigned byte integers
PMAXSW	Computes the maximum value of packed signed word integers
PMINUB	Computes the minimum value of packed unsigned byte integers
PMINSW	Computes the minimum value of packed signed word integers
PMULHUW	Multiplies packed unsigned word integers and stores the high result
PSADBW	Computes the sum of the absolute differences of unsigned byte integers

Using SSE2 Instructions

The SSE2 architecture expands on the SSE instructions by providing instructions for performing mathematical operations on packed double-precision floating-point values, and 128-bit packed integer values.

The SSE2 instructions use the 128-bit XMM registers to hold two double-precision floating-point values, four doubleword integer values, or two quadword integer values. The SSE2 instructions provided can perform mathematical operations on each of these data types. The double-precision floating-point value operations can be either packed or scalar (similar to the SSE instructions).

The following sections describe how to use SSE2 instructions in your assembly language programs.

Moving data

As shown in Chapter 7, five instructions are provided by the SSE2 architecture to move 128-bit double-precision floating-point values between memory and XMM registers. The following table describes these instructions.

Instruction	Description
MOVAPD	Moves two aligned, double-precision values to XMM registers or memory
MOVUPD	Moves two unaligned, double-precision values to XMM registers or memory
MOVDQA	Moves two aligned, quadword integer values to XMM registers or memory
MOVDQU	Moves two unaligned, quadword integer values to XMM registers to memory
MOVSD	Moves one double-precision value to memory or the low quadword of a register
MOVHPD	Moves one double-precision value to memory or the high quadword of a register
MOVLPD	Moves one double-precision value to memory or the low quadword of a register

Similar to the SSE data moving instructions, the SSE2 instructions provide for moving both aligned and unaligned data. To use the MOVAPD and MOVDQA instructions, the data in memory must be located on a 16-byte boundary.

To define aligned data, you must use the .align directive:

```
.section .data
.align 16
packedvalue1:
    .double 10.235, 289.1
packedvalue2:
    .int 10, 20, 30, 40
.section .text
.globl _start
_start:
    movapd packedvalue1, %xmm0
    movdqa packedvalue2, %xmm1
```

Processing data

The SSE2 instruction set provides mathematical instructions for processing packed double-precision floating-point values, packed word integer values, packed doubleword integer values, and packed quadword integer values. Each data type has its own instruction code for each mathematical operation instruction, as demonstrated in the following table of SSE2 addition instructions.

Instruction	Description
ADDPD	Adds packed double-precision floating-point values
ADDSD	Adds scalar double-precision floating-point values
PADDSB	Adds packed signed byte integer values
PADDSW	Adds packed signed word integer values
PADDD	Adds packed doubleword integer values
PADDQ	Adds packed quadword integer values

As you can see, the list gets very long for each mathematical operation. These options also exist for the multiplication and division operations as well (MULPD, MULSD, DIVPD, DIVSD, and so on).

Just as in the SSE instruction set, the SSE2 instruction set provides specialty mathematical operations: SQRT, MAX, and MIN.

The sse2math.s program demonstrates how to use these functions:

```
# sse2math.s - An example of using SSE2 arithmetic instructions
.section .data
.align 16
value1:
    .double 10.42, -5.330
value2:
    .double 4.25, 2.10
value3:
    .int 10, 20, 30, 40
value4:
    .int 5, 15, 25, 35
.section .bss
    .lcomm result1, 16
    .lcomm result2, 16
.section .text
.globl _start
_start:
    nop
    movapd value1, %xmm0
    movapd value2, %xmm1
    movdqa value3, %xmm2
    movdqa value4, %xmm3

    mulpd %xmm1, %xmm0
    paddd %xmm3, %xmm2

    movapd %xmm0, result1
    movdqa %xmm2, result2

    movl $1, %eax
    movl $0, %ebx
    int $0x80
```

Because the sse2math.s program uses the MOVAPD and MOVDQA instructions to load the XMM registers, the .data section must be aligned on a 16-byte boundary. This requires the .align directive. After the data is loaded into the XMM registers, the SSE2 MULPD instruction is used to perform the multiplication of the two double-precision floating-point values, and the PADDD instruction is used to perform the addition of the four doubleword integer values.

After assembling and linking the program, you can watch it in the debugger to ensure that it works properly. First, stop the program after the four XMM registers have been loaded and examine them:

```
(gdb) print $xmm0
$1 = {v4_float = {0.0587499999, 2.57562494, -7.46297859e-36, -2.33312488},
   v2_double = {10.42, -5.3300000000000001},
   v16_int8 = "xxp=\nx$@R,\036\205ëQ\025x", v8_int16 = {-23593, 15728, -10486,
     16420, -18350, -31458, 20971, -16363}, v4_int32 = {1030792151, 1076156170,
     -2061584302, -1072344597}, v2_int64 = {4622055556569408471,
     -4605684971923916718}, uint128 = 0xc01551eb851eb8524024d70a3d70a3d7}
(gdb) print $xmm1
$2 = {v4_float = {0, 2.265625, -107374184, 2.01249981}, v2_double = {4.25,
   2.1000000000000001},
   v16_int8 = "\000\000\000\000\000\000\021@xxxxxx\000@", v8_int16 = {0, 0, 0,
     16401, -13107, -13108, -13108, 16384}, v4_int32 = {0, 1074855936,
     -858993459, 1073794252}, v2_int64 = {4616471093031469056,
     4611911198408756429}, uint128 = 0x4000cccccccccccd4011000000000000}
(gdb) print $xmm2
$3 = {v4_float = {1.40129846e-44, 2.80259693e-44, 4.20389539e-44,
     5.60519386e-44}, v2_double = {4.2439915824246103e-313,
     8.4879831653432862e-313},
   v16_int8 = "\n\000\000\000\024\000\000\000\036\000\000\000(\000\000",
   v8_int16 = {10, 0, 20, 0, 30, 0, 40, 0}, v4_int32 = {10, 20, 30, 40},
   v2_int64 = {85899345930, 171798691870},
   uint128 = 0x000000280000001e000000140000000a}
(gdb) print $xmm3
$4 = {v4_float = {7.00649232e-45, 2.1019477e-44, 3.50324616e-44,
     4.90454463e-44}, v2_double = {3.1829936866949413e-313,
     7.4269852696136172e-313},
   v16_int8 = "\005\000\000\000\017\000\000\000\031\000\000\000#\000\000",
   v8_int16 = {5, 0, 15, 0, 25, 0, 35, 0}, v4_int32 = {5, 15, 25, 35},
   v2_int64 = {64424509445, 150323855385},
   uint128 = 0x000000230000001900000000f00000005}
(gdb)
```

Notice that when you print the XMM register values out in the debugger, it does not know what data types have been loaded into the registers, so it provides the output in all possible formats. The XMM0 and XMM1 register data uses the v2_double format, and the XMM2 and XMM3 register data is in the v4_int32 format.

After stepping through the SSE2 math instructions and the MOV instructions, you can display the results stored in the memory locations using the proper data formats:

```
(gdb) x/2gf &result1
0x8049100 <result1>:     44.284999999999997      -11.193000000000001
(gdb) x/4wd &result2
0x8049110 <result2>:     15        35        55        75
(gdb)
```

This output shows that indeed the proper results were calculated for all of the values and stored in the memory locations.

SSE3 Instructions

The SSE3 architecture does not provide for any new data types, just a few new instructions to either help perform standard functions quicker, or to provide new fancier instructions.

The following SSE3 instructions are provided:

❏ **FISTTP:** Converts the first FPU register value to an integer (with rounding) and pops it from the FPU stack

❏ **LDDQU:** Loads a 128-bit unaligned data value from memory quickly

❏ **MOVSHDUP:** Moves a 128-bit value, duplicating the second and fourth 32-bit data elements

❏ **MOVSLDUP:** Moves a 128-bit value, duplicating the first and third 32-bit data elements

❏ **MOVDDUP:** Moves a 64-bit value, duplicating the value to make a 128-bit value

❏ **ADDSUBPS:** With packed single-precision floating-point values, performs an addition on the second and fourth 32-bit values, and a subtraction on the first and third 32-bit values

❏ **ADDSUBPD:** With packed double-precision floating-point values, performs an addition on the second pair of 64-bit values, and a subtraction on the first pair

❏ **HADDPS:** Performs a single-precision floating-point addition on contiguous data elements of the operands

❏ **HADDPD:** Performs a double-precision floating-point addition on contiguous data elements of the operands

❏ **HSUBPS:** Performs a single-precision floating-point subtraction on contiguous data elements of the operands

❏ **HSUBPD:** Performs a double-precision floating-point subtraction on contiguous data elements of the operands

Summary

For programs that do a lot of mathematical processing of numerical arrays, trying to loop through the arrays using the standard processor math functions can be time-consuming. Recent chips in the IA-32 platform provide an alternative to programmers to help speed things up.

The IA-32 Single Instruction Multiple Data (SIMD) technology provides both instructions and new registers to handle data arrays in parallel with a single instruction. Multimedia Extensions (MMX) provide for processing packed integer values with single instructions. The MMX architecture uses the FPU registers to provide eight 64-bit MMX registers for holding packed byte, word, and doubleword integer values. Data values can be loaded into the MMX registers from memory locations, processed in the MMX registers, and stored back into memory locations. The MMX instruction set provides instructions for performing normal arithmetic, Boolean, and comparison operations on packed integer values. This enables programmers to process two doubleword integer, four word integer, or 8 byte integer values simultaneously.

The Streaming SIMD Extension (SSE) provides an entirely new set of registers to process 128-bit packed data. Eight 128-bit XMM registers are used to process SSE data types. The SSE data types provide for packed single-precision floating-point values. This enables four single-precision floating-point data values to be processed with a single mathematical instruction.

Similar to the MMX instructions, SSE instructions provide methods for performing arithmetic, Boolean, and comparison instructions. The SSE comparison instructions are somewhat odd in that only one true instruction is provided. The CMPPS instruction uses an implementation operand to determine what comparison is made between the two input operand values. Most assemblers (including gas) use pseudo-instructions to replace the CMPPS instruction and the implementation operand.

Besides operating on packed single-precision floating-point values, the SSE architecture also provides instructions for processing scalar arithmetic operations. Scalar arithmetic performs arithmetic functions on only the low doubleword value in the register. The other values duplicate the entries in the source operand.

The SSE2 architecture provides additional instructions for performing mathematical operations on additional packed data types. SSE2 includes instructions for processing packed double-precision floating-point values (two values per data element), and packed byte, packed word, packed doubleword, and packed quadword integer values. This provides a vast array of processing capabilities for the programmer to utilize. Each packed data type includes mathematical instructions for processing the packed data types in parallel using a single instruction.

The SSE3 architecture does not provide any new data types but does provide several additional instructions for handling data in the XMM registers. There are several instructions for performing hybrid arithmetic operations, such as combined addition and subtraction on elements within the register. These instructions are used to perform specific functions often used in digital and audio data processing.

This concludes the chapters in this book, but it should not conclude your assembly language learning. It is hoped that this book has helped you get started in using assembly language programs along with your high-level language programs to help optimize your applications, but there is always more to learn. As new processors appear on the market, new optimization features are added. I strongly recommend that you frequent the various Web sites of chip vendors. They provide excellent documentation describing new instructions and data types available in new processors. I hope that you have enjoyed your journey through this book and are able to put your new knowledge to use in your professional programming career.

Index

B

G

O

Printed and bound by CPI Group (UK) Ltd, Croydon, CR0 4YY

27/10/2024

14580183-0005